CW01603774

THIS BOOK BELONGS TO | QUESTO LIBRO APPARTIENE A | ESTE LIBRO PERTENCE A | DIT BOEK IS VAN | CE LIVRE APPARTIENT À | DIESES BUCH GEHÖRT |

Michael Marten
London September 2006

Britain and the Middle East

An Economic History 1945–87

Middle East Studies

General Editor

Sir James Craig GCMG

Director General: The Middle East Association

Britain and the Middle East

An Economic History 1945 – 87

by

Frank Brenchley

Lester Crook Academic Publishing
London House, 271 – 273 King Street, Hammersmith, London W6 9LZ

First published 1989

British Library Cataloguing in Publication Data
Brenchley, Frank
Britain and the Middle East : an economic history 1945 – 87.
1. Middle East. Economic relations, 1945 – 1987 with Great Britain.
2. Great Britain. Economic relations, 1945 – 1987 with Middle East
I. Title
337.56041

ISBN 1 – 870915 – 07 – 0

Set in 12/13pt Bembo by Action Typesetting Limited, Gloucester
Printed by Dotesios Printers Ltd., Trowbridge

This book is dedicated
to the memory of
IDRIS DEANE JONES
Fellow of Merton College, Oxford
1921–1947

Contents

Abbreviations

ADMA	Abu Dhabi Marine Areas
ADPC	Abu Dhabi Petroleum Company
AIOC	Anglo-Iranian Oil Company
APOC	Anglo-Persian Oil Company
ARAMCO	Arabian-American Oil Company
BBME	British Bank of the Middle East
b/d	barrels a day
BOTB	British Overseas Trade Board
BP	British Petroleum
CENTO	Central Treaty Organization
CFP	Compagnie Française des Pétroles
COMET	Council for Middle East Trade
ECGD	Export Credits Guarantee Department
EEC	European Economic Communities
EFTA	European Free Trade Area
Esso	Standard Oil of New Jersey
FCO	Foreign and Commonwealth Office
GATT	General Agreement on Tariffs and Trade
GCC	Gulf Cooperation Council
GIC	Gulf Investment Corporation
GOIC	Gulf Organization for Industrial Consulting
IBRD	International Bank for Reconstruction and Development
ICAO	International Civil Aviation Organization
IEA	International Energy Agency
IMF	International Monetary Fund
INOC	Iraq National Oil Company
IPC	Iraq Petroleum Company
KOC	Kuwait Oil Company
LNG	Liquified Natural Gas
MEA	Middle East Airlines
NATO	North Atlantic Treaty Organization
NIOC	National Iranian Oil Company

NLF	National Liberation Front
NOCs	National Oil Companies
OAPEC	Organization of Arab Petroleum Exporting Countries
OEEC	Organization for European Economic Cooperation
OPEC	Organization of Petroleum Exporting Countries
PDRY	People's Democratic Republic of Yemen
PLO	Palestine Liberation Organization
PRO	Public Record Office
PSBR	Public Sector Borrowing Requirement
QPC	Qatar Petroleum Company
R/P	Reserves to Production Ratio
SABIC	Saudi Arabian Basic Industries Corporation
SEATO	South-East Asia Treaty Organization
SoCal	Standard Oil of California
Texaco	Texas Company
UAE	United Arab Emirates
UNEF	United Nations Emergency Force
UNIFIL	United Nations Force in Lebanon
UNRWA	United Nations Relief and Works Agency
UNTSO	United Nations Truce Supervisory Organization
YAR	Yemen Arab Republic

Foreword and Acknowledgements

The 'Middle East' for the purposes of this book comprises Iran, Israel and all the members of the League of Arab States except Jibouti, Mauritania and Somalia. I have to apologise to the Province of Northern Ireland for using the terms Britain and United Kingdom as though they were coextensive. It has been done for no political reason, but merely because saying UK all the time produced an unreadably turgid result. Fortunately, in this particular context the effects of this 'deliberate error' are never seriously misleading.

Most of the period 1945 to 1987 is too recent for the primary sources to be available. That is, I assume, why I, as a practitioner of international relations for almost the whole of the period, was invited to write it, rather than a professional historian. Even so, I have had to draw heavily on the help of others to supplement my own knowledge. For giving me encouragement and advice at an early stage in the planning of the book, I am indebted to Dr Roger Highfield of Merton College, Oxford, to Professor Philip Khoury of the Massachusetts Institute of Technology and to Dr Roger Owen of St. Antony's College, Oxford. At various later stages, I have had the advantage of discussions with Sir James Craig and Mr Ernest Noble of the Middle East Association (both ex-diplomats); Dr Ferrier of British Petroleum; Sir John Wilton, Mr St. John Armitage, Mr Donal McCarthy and others of my former diplomatic colleagues; and Mr Sinclair Road of the Committee of Middle East Trade. Naturally, none of these bears any responsibility for errors which I may have perpetrated despite their help.

In planning the chapters which follow, I had to recognise that in a book of this length I could not give a comprehensive account of economic developments in all the countries concerned. This was the more so as it was necessary to trace, however briefly, those political events (for example Buraimi, Suez, Arab-Israeli Wars, the Gulf War) which led to economic changes in the Middle East or in the United Kingdom's relations with the Middle East. I have therefore adopted what might be termed a 'spotlight' approach, turning the beam on different countries or groups of countries in different chapters (and having to refuse a separate chapter to some important countries such as Jordan and Syria).

For the same reason, I could not follow a strictly chronological sequence, though the layout of the book is generally chronological. When, usually because some political event changed its economic course, I was dealing with a particular country, I sometimes had to follow its development over an extended period of time because I knew that there would be no opportunity to return to it in any detail.

I hope that it will be found that I have in these ways given some account of all the principal factors which were important during the period to economic relations between Britain and the Middle East.

The two supreme influences on those relations have of course been trade and the oil industry, so these subjects have been treated at regularly recurring intervals. Fortunately, there is ample published material on both of them. On some other subjects I have found the sources patchy or almost non-existent. Two particularly difficult matters to present have been invisible trade and arms sales, but I have given what account I could of them since both are of considerable financial importance, even if precise figures are maddeningly elusive. Investment in both directions is another area of difficulty.

Since it was as a practitioner in the field of international relations that I have been writing this book, I have made occasional mention in the Chapter Notes of some points at which my career brought me into direct contact with the matters under discussion. This will, I hope, make clear the subjects on which I have spoken from direct knowledge, as distinct from the many on which I have had to seek information from the memories or writings of others. In the latter connection, I must express my gratitude to the librarians of many libraries, but particularly the London Library and the Library of the Royal Institute of International Affairs, both of which allow members to borrow their books for use at home. I am also grateful to Mrs Lloyd Phillips, who allowed me to draw on the extensive collection of her late husband, Dr Ivan Lloyd Phillips. Their help made my task a great deal easier than I had at first expected.

Any writer on the Middle East is faced with the problem of transliterating proper names from languages written in other alphabets, in this case Arabic, Farsi and Hebrew. I have chosen to adopt spellings familiar in English rather than be pedantic. It seemed to me ridiculous to spell Nasser, or for that matter Cairo, in any other way. And when an Egyptian himself chooses to spell his name Mohamed in English, by what right should I 'correct' him to Muhammad? However, where variant spellings of a particular name are in vogue, I have tended to prefer the more accurate, Qaddafi for instance rather than Gaddafi, but not a less recognisable Qadhdhafi.

It would have been easier to write a longer book, but a publisher's wishes on length (and time limit) act as the literary equivalent of the prospect of hanging, to concentrate the mind. I hope that the reader will be the beneficiary.

Frank Brenchley
31 March 1988

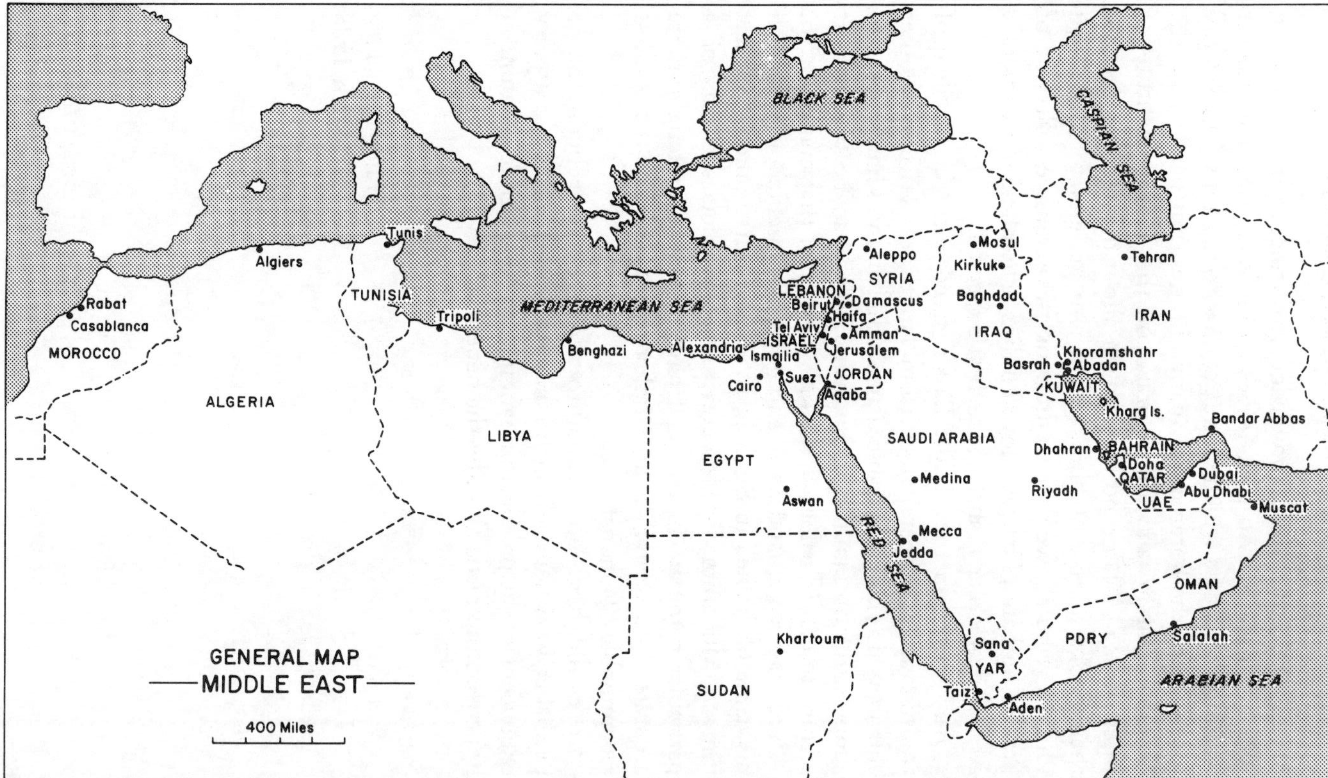
GENERAL MAP
MIDDLE EAST
400 Miles
BLACK SEA
CASPIAN SEA
MEDITERRANEAN SEA
RED SEA
ARABIAN SEA
MOROCCO
Rabat
Casablanca
ALGERIA
Algiers
TUNISIA
Tunis
Tripoli
LIBYA
Benghazi
EGYPT
Alexandria
Cairo
Ismailia
Suez
Aswan
SUDAN
Khartoum
LEBANON
Beirut
Damascus
SYRIA
Aleppo
Haifa
Tel Aviv
ISRAEL
Amman
Jerusalem
JORDAN
Aqaba
IRAQ
Mosul
Kirkuk
Baghdad
Basrah
Khoramshahr
Abadan
KUWAIT
Kharg Is.
IRAN
Tehran
Bandar Abbas
SAUDI ARABIA
Medina
Mecca
Jedda
Riyadh
Dhahran
BAHRAIN
Doha
QATAR
Dubai
Abu Dhabi
UAE
Muscat
OMAN
Salalah
PDRY
Sana
YAR
Taiz
Aden

1 The UK Economy after World War II

The sudden ending of the war with Japan in August 1945 came as a surprise to almost everyone in Britain, even those in Government. The 'need to know' secret of the atom bomb had been jealously guarded and there would have been horror at any suggestion that the 'indoctrination' list should include economists. Yet the rapid Japanese surrender had immediate economic repercussions. Large-scale demobilisation from the armed forces would need to begin at once. So would the transition from wartime to peacetime industrial production. And Lend-Lease, the provision of war materials (broadly defined, including notably food supplies) from the USA might end all too soon,[1] before the scheduled Anglo-American talks on its passing had even begun. For a Britain which had had no choice but to sell off the greater part of its overseas assets and accumulate huge foreign debts to finance the war effort,[2] this threatened a financial calamity.

Ernest Bevin, as Minister of Labour and National Service from 1940 to 1945 in the wartime Coalition Government, had presided over the plans for demobilisation.[3] Apart from those offered places in the regular forces, the wartime intakes of national servicemen, whether volunteers or conscripts, were to be discharged under the provisions of two release schemes, Class A and Class B. Class A would apply to the vast majority, with priorities for release fixed by such criteria as age and length of service. Class B provided accelerated release for those needed back urgently in their previous civilian occupations: they ranged from such obvious candidates as bricklayers and coalminers to more imaginative categories such as university students who had been close to graduating when they joined the services.[4] Those released under Class B would supplement the civilians in 'reserved occupations' who had been exempted throughout the war from service in the forces because their skills were vital on the home front.

The release schemes were complicated by the need to find shipping to bring servicemen home from distant war-theatres, but they worked much more smoothly than after World War I. Those demobilised were given an outfit of civilian clothes and a small leaving gratuity to help them to reestablish themselves in civilian life. They were also issued with ration books, since rationing, both of food and clothing, was to continue (and even, it turned out, to intensify).

Conversion of industry from wartime to peacetime production also proceeded smoothly. There had been some planning for this during the war, most of it under the auspices of Hugh Dalton.[5] As President of the Board of Trade in the Coalition Government, he had chaired the Industry Sub-Committee of the Cabinet Committee on Reconstruction Policies and had gathered around him a group of young men, whom he called his 'post-warriors',[6] to work out a detailed programme aimed at post-war full employment.

A key factor in this programme was government control over location of industry to assist the former Distressed Areas, which Dalton had had rechristened Development Areas, and to which he had already directed important factory construction during the war through his control of the issuing of building licences.[7] On 19 May 1944, the War Cabinet had adopted a White Paper on Employment Policy, including a Dalton-inspired chapter on 'The Balanced Distribution of Industry and Labour'. With this authority he had had it agreed, for instance, that Ordnance Factories located in Development Areas should after the war either be kept open for arms production or converted to civilian requirements. As early as 9 June 1945, thirty-five such factories were reported[8] to have been reassigned to civilian use. Another policy which he had sponsored was the building of 'advance' factories on new industrial estates set up during the war.[9]

On 13 December 1944, the War Cabinet had approved the inclusion of sixteen Reconstruction Bills as priority measures for the new legislative programme. Among them was a Distribution of Industry Bill, which received its Second Reading on 21 March 1945. This Bill was still in Standing Committee when it ceased to be Dalton's responsibility on the breakup of the wartime Coalition Government on 23 May 1945, but his Conservative successor at the Board of Trade, Oliver Lyttleton, supported it and it received the Royal Assent on 15 June 1945, the day on which Parliament was dissolved preparatory to the General Election. Thus when the Attlee Government took office after that election, the framework for post-war industrial planning and for a full employment policy was already largely in place.

There had been considerable fears during the war that its ending might bring a return to the depression and mass unemployment of the 1930s. In the event, these fears proved unfounded. Beveridge in 1945 had defined 'full employment' as meaning 3 per cent unemployed,[10] but it remained well below this level (with temporary exceptions such as during the fuel crisis of 1947) until the 1970s.[11] In Britain, wartime planning for the future, followed by the Attlee Government's determination to place full employment among its first priorities, contributed to this result. But it was in fact a widespread post-war phenomenon in the industrialised countries of the world, so more basic causes must have been at work.

Chief among these was the pull of demand, both in Britain and elsewhere. Investment had been low during the depression years. War damage had exacerbated the problem and arrears of construction had accumulated throughout the war. There was a huge demand for housing and consumer goods, especially when rationing was relaxed and ultimately abolished. The resulting high level of employment, together with an upward trend in real wages, financed further spending, which provided a renewed stimulus to investment. At the same time, interest rates were kept low.[12] It seemed a 'virtuous circle' – what later would have been termed an 'economic miracle'. But the circle was not wholly self-perpetuating; the fuel which kept it moving was American financing, first the Loan Agreement and then Marshall Aid.

Following the termination of Lend-Lease, negotiations for financial assistance to Britain from the United States opened in Washington in September 1945. Dalton was Chancellor of the Exchequer in Attlee's Government and, in view of their crucial importance, he might have been expected to conduct the negotiations himself. But neither he nor any other British Minister went to Washington; the task was devolved upon John Maynard Keynes, Economic Adviser to the Chancellor of the Exchequer, together with the British Ambassador, Lord Halifax. This was a tribute to Keynes's enormously high reputation as an economist and no doubt seemed logical since in March 1945 it was he who had written a paper on 'Overseas Financial Policy in Stage III', i.e. after the defeat of Japan.

Keynes set out with high hopes. Theory convinced him that it was in United States' interest to be generous to Britain; he therefore expected aid in the form of a gift or, at the very worst, an interest-free loan. Those expectations he conveyed to the Cabinet before departing, with $6000 million as the target for which he was aiming. That was a tactical error; when Keynes finally realised that no such terms were available, he had difficulty in convincing London that Britain's bargaining position was weak in the extreme and that less generous terms must be accepted. It was not until 6 December 1945 that he persuaded the British Government to authorise the signature of an Agreement for an interest-bearing loan on distinctly unwelcome conditions.

The loan itself was generous enough – $3750 million plus the conversion to credit of $650 million as a final Lend-Lease settlement.[13] Repayment and interest terms were also favourable, 50 years for repayment and interest at only 2 per cent, with a grace period for both until the end of 1951 and a special provision that interest could be cancelled whenever British exports were too small to pay for her prewar volume of imports. But there were two conditions. The first was not too onerous, that the UK should immediately accept the Bretton Woods proposals for the setting up of the International Monetary Fund (IMF) and the International Bank for Reconstruction and Development (IBRD): this would surely have happened before long in any event. The second condition was the real nightmare, that sterling must be made convertible for current transactions after only one year.[14]

It was realised in London, though evidently not in the US Government, that this provision for such early convertibility was nothing less than a time-bomb on a short setting. But Britain's need for dollars was so desperate that there seemed to be no other choice. Two relative juniors, Bevan and Shinwell, opposed the Loan Agreement, but it was accepted by all other Cabinet Ministers. In the Commons, after Dalton had told the House that there was no alternative,[15] the majority in favour was 347 to 100, with most Conservatives abstaining. The final US legislation bringing the Agreement into force was not in fact enacted until 15 July 1946, so that convertibility did not become due until 15 July 1947, but that was long before the five years foreseen at Bretton Woods. The time-bomb began to tick.

Alongside the American Loan, Britain negotiated a loan on similar terms from Canada, important as a major source of wheat. It was for $1250 million, bringing the total North American borrowing to the round figure of $5000 million (plus the $650 million Lend-Lease settlement).

On the domestic front, the Attlee Government had promised the electorate sweeping measures of nationalisation. In charge of this programme was Herbert Morrison, who, with the title of Lord President of the Council, was given extensive powers over the domestic economy. Priority was given to a mainly symbolic measure, the nationalisation of the Bank of England. The Bank of England Act was passed early in 1946. It was rapidly followed by the Borrowing (Control and Guarantee) Act in July 1946 and the Exchange Control Act in March 1947, giving statutory form to wartime powers over new capital issues and foreign exchange transactions respectively. Among industries, coal and civil aviation were nationalised in 1946; they were followed by the main inland transport systems (railways, canals, long-distance road haulage, and certain docks and harbours) plus Cable and Wireless Ltd. in 1947.

Important social measures were also enacted; the National Insurance Act, the Industrial Injuries Act, the National Health Act, children's allowances and the beginning of the abolition of the old Poor Law provisions. By the autumn of 1947 the Government could pride itself on having carried out the great majority of its electoral pledges and on having effected a considerable socio-economic revolution. It had also run into a first-rate economic crisis.

1947 began badly for Britain with terrible weather, said to be the worst winter of the century. Freezing temperatures silenced Big Ben and iced over the Thames at Windsor. Fuel reserves had been known to be low and a Cabinet Coal Committee under Dalton's chairmanship had been set up late in 1946, but it had proved ineffective, largely because its crucial member, Emmanuel Shinwell, Minister of Fuel and Power, was no administrator and had a profound distrust of statistics. Coal distribution was totally disrupted by 5 February, with coalmines blocked by snow and coal-freighters unable to leave harbour. Two days later, Shinwell had to announce the suspension of all electricity supplies to industry in London, the South-East, the Midlands and the North-West, and for five hours a day to domestic consumers everywhere. Unemployment rose temporarily to 2.25 million, with a big loss of the export production so vital to the balance of payments. The bitter weather persisted well into March.[16]

When the American and Canadian Loans were agreed, most experts on both sides of the Atlantic expected them to meet Britain's needs at least until the end of 1949. But there were many factors which the experts failed to foresee, chief among them a sharp rise in dollar prices. By the beginning of 1947, even before the fuel crisis, the rate of drawings on them was worrying the British Treasury. Dalton gave warnings to the Cabinet in January and March, but failed to carry much conviction, except with Cripps, who made speeches calling for cooperation between labour and management, for increased productivity and for concentration on export markets.[17] The trouble was that there was still a seller's market for almost everything at home, and that those who did aim at exports found the sterling area an easier market than the dollar area. And Britain no longer had the surplus on invisible income which had offset a deficit on visible trade before the war.[18]

Dalton had some success in persuading the Cabinet to reduce

military expenditure overseas by £40 million (half what he had asked for) and to hand over to the US Government responsibility for aiding Greece and Turkey to resist Communist subversion. He also used his April 1947 Budget to increase tobacco duty by 50 per cent for dollar-saving purposes. But on 5 June he had to warn Cabinet that half the American credit had already been drawn and that the drain was continuing at over $300 million a month. The date for convertibility, 15 July, was rapidly approaching.

There was one hopeful development. On 5 June 1947, General George C. Marshall, the US Secretary of State, made a speech in Harvard hinting at the possibility of American financial aid if a self-help plan were devised for the economic recovery of Europe. On the European side the first person to grasp the significance of this hint was the British Foreign Secretary, Ernest Bevin, who hailed it as an offer of major importance and set to work to put momentum behind it by organising a European team to pursue it as a matter of urgency. That, however, would still take time, and convertibility was imminent. On 7 July Dalton informed the Commons that immediate cuts must be made in dollar imports.

When, on 15 July, the time-bomb of convertibility finally exploded, there were soon heavy conversions of sterling. In theory, convertibility was only available for current transactions, but it was all too easy to dress up capital transfers as current obligations and the residents of many Transferable Account countries[19] and some Sterling Area countries feared that convertibility would be short-lived, giving them an incentive to get hold of dollars quickly. Such prophecies tend to be self-fulfilling. On 18 August, after an emergency Sunday Cabinet meeting, a British delegation flew to Washington to give warning that convertibility would have to be suspended. In the week ending 16 August, the loss of dollars had been $183 million, with only $850 million of the American credit still undrawn. On 20 August Dalton announced that convertibility would cease at midnight. As this was a breach of the American Loan Agreement, the remainder of that Loan was automatically frozen.

For a time, despite a period of harsh austerity with imports of many North American products severely cut, some upturn in the economy resulted. Times were bad, but there was still full employment and nobody starved. Cripps, whose star was rising, produced in September an export programme fixing targets for 153 items or groups of items. This was not by any means a programme plucked from the air: Cripps had used his position as President of the Board of Trade to set up 'Working Parties' for seventeen key industries, and these were followed by Development Councils established under the Industrial Organisation and Development Act of 1947. This machinery, although less successful than Cripps had hoped in fostering cooperation between labour, management and Government, at least meant that he could fairly claim to have based his export programme upon 'an extensive and careful inquiry into all the main industries of the country'.[20]

To give impetus to export planning, Attlee reorganised ministerial responsibilities. Morrison had hitherto been the overlord of home economic affairs, presiding over a Cabinet Committee charged with coordinating the activities of the Board of Trade and the Ministries of Supply, Labour, Transport, and Fuel and Power, while Attlee himself chaired a Committee on overseas economic affairs. Morrison had not been an effective overlord and Attlee now united the two Committees under his own chairmanship, with Cripps as Deputy Chairman. On 29 September, it was announced that Cripps would become Minister for Economic Affairs, taking over from Morrison the Economic Planning Staff and the Cabinet Office economic secretariat. Harold Wilson succeeded Cripps as a very young President of the Board of Trade.

Whether this reorganisation would have been effective is a moot point. It left Cripps junior to Dalton, the Chancellor of the Exchequer, and provided no machinery, other than Cabinet, for the coordination of economic and financial policy. That was a serious weakness as there was a growing realisation that one of the factors contributing to Britain's recent economic decline in the world had been Dalton's 'cheap money' policy, which, however vital to finance the nationalisation programme and Labour's social policies, had led to inflation and the uncompetitiveness of many British exports. However, before the point could be put to the test, Dalton's resignation had been brought about by the bizarre incident of his outlining to a journalist the contents of the disinflationary November Budget which he was on his way to deliver to the House of Commons. Attlee seized the opportunity to make Cripps Chancellor of the Exchequer, taking with him to the Treasury his functions as economic coordinator.

In December 1947, Bevin's hard work with the Western Europeans over the 'Marshall Plan' began to bear fruit. The US Congress, on the basis of a 16-country unified plan for economic reconstruction in Europe,[21] authorised the establishment of the European Recovery Programme and voted interim aid. On the American side, administration of the programme was vested in the Economic Cooperation Administration, and on the European side in the Organization for European Economic Cooperation with its seat in Paris.

On 3 April 1948, Truman signed the Economic Cooperation Act into law. $5600 million were appropriated for the period up to 30 June 1949 and $17000 million were voted in all for a four-year period, subject to annual appropriations.[22] This, together with the military and economic assistance already being provided for Greece and Turkey under what had been christened the Truman Doctrine, and a liberalisation of the lending policy of the American-dominated IMF, hitherto conservative in the extreme, proved that the United States had now fully accepted the argument which Keynes had earlier advanced in vain, that such generosity, as well as vying with Lend-Lease for the accolade of being 'the most unsordid act in history', was the course required by the USA's own interests. As a logical extension of this new attitude, the US Treasury Secretary authorised Britain to resume drawings on the remaining portion of the 1945 American Loan. In the same month, it was agreed that the USA would relieve Britain, for the last two months of 1947 and the whole of 1948, of its dollar costs in the American/British Bi-zone of Germany.

Another economic subject which engaged much British and American attention in 1947–8, and caused no little argument between them, was the drafting of the General Agreement on Tariffs and Trade (GATT). The Americans had set themselves the objective of dismantling Britain's system of Imperial Preference, which they regarded as discriminatory against American trade.

Indeed, an undertaking directed to this end had been included in the terms of the Anglo-American Loan Agreement of 1945. But both Cripps and Bevin held out against pressure on this point, and the Americans reluctantly gave way on the main issue, contenting themselves with minor concessions. The GATT, which was signed in the Spring of 1948, has proved of lasting importance in shaping international trade. In particular, it has largely restrained protectionist tendencies which have several times threatened to revive in the postwar period.

The Attlee Government continued in 1948 its nationalisation programme. Electricity generation and distribution were brought into public ownership and gas soon followed. Left over into 1949 were iron and steel, which excited a good deal of controversy; their nationalisation proved the final step in the programme.[23]

To counter the inflationary effects of this policy, Cripps continued the disinflationary budgets which Dalton had begun. Both in 1948 and 1949, he provided for a large budget surplus, raising indirect taxation. In 1948, he increased revenue further by a modest capital levy, described as a 'Special Contribution', which he promised would not be repeated in later years. He also made a move in 1949 towards the restraint of food subsidies. Not surprisingly, such 'austerity' measures were not universally popular, especially with the trade union leaders. There was considerable criticism of them at the Labour Party's Annual Conference in June 1949, not uninfluenced by the fact that the time for a General Election was approaching, but Cripps, with firm support from Attlee and other party leaders including Bevin, was able to carry the day.

Cripps's austerity measures were imposed for domestic reasons but they could have external repercussions. The 1948 package included a freeze on dividends paid by British companies. One such company was the Anglo-Iranian Oil Company (AIOC, now British Petroleum). Its earnings were rising and it could have afforded to pay a higher dividend; it asked for an exemption but was refused. This had two undesirable consequences. First, the British Government was itself a major shareholder in AIOC, so was holding down its own income. Secondly and more important, part of AIOC's payments to Iran was related to its dividend level, so the Shah, much to his fury, found himself deprived, at the British Government's behest, of income on which he had been counting. The part this played in the Iranian oil crisis of 1951–3 will be examined in Chapter 5.

Despite all that the Government could do to stimulate dollar exports, and despite drawings on the American and Canadian loans and receipts under Marshall Aid, Britain began again to feel the constraints of dollar shortages. As this was seen abroad, pressure on sterling built up, with rumours of devaluation which Cripps perforce denied. But, as so often, rumours before long proved self-fulfilling. On 31 August 1949, Cripps and Bevin left for Washington to thrash out with the American and Canadian authorities the many technical problems involved in an imminent devaluation.

No sooner had he returned than Cripps was obliged to announce, in a broadcast on 18 September, that the dollar-sterling exchange rate would move from $4.03 to $2.80 to the pound. He put the best possible face on it, claiming that the new exchange rate would bring stability to Britain's external economic relations and forecasting that, apart from a small increase in the price of bread (due to purchases of Canadian wheat), there would be no appreciable rise in the cost of living for the ordinary consumer. Nevertheless, the announcement marked a defeat for the Government's economic policies and when the devaluation was debated in the Commons there were slighting references to Cripps's personal denials before the event that devaluation was under consideration. These he felt bitterly.[24]

A General Election held on 23 February 1950 produced a narrow Labour victory, with a majority reduced from 136 before the dissolution to a mere 8. Attlee's new Cabinet contained one change of significance on the economic front – Hugh Gaitskell was made Minister of State for Economic Affairs with a seat in the Cabinet. This looked like a return to the dubious Dalton-Cripps economic dyarchy, but the purpose was different. The intention was not to change economic policy but to relieve the work load on Cripps, whose health was showing clear signs of over-strain. Cripps himself welcomed Gaitskell's appointment.

The 1949 devaluation was by now producing beneficial effects.

Confidence in the pound had strengthened, especially as the amount of the adjustment in the exchange rate had been greater than most experts had been expecting. Moreover, with the exception of countries whose currencies were closely linked with the USA, virtually the whole world had followed Britain's example, changing their own rates against the dollar, many though not all of them to the same extent.[25] The net effect was thus for the most part an upward movement of the dollar rather than a downward movement of sterling, so that the cost to Britain of imports from the non-dollar area was not greatly changed. Before the Commons rose for the Easter 1950 recess, Cripps was able to tell them that Britain's dollar balance of payments was in surplus on current account, even before crediting the dollars being received in grants and loans from the USA and Canada.

On returning from the recess, he could with a clear conscience introduce a more or less 'standstill' budget, the only notable new piece of 'austerity' being an increase in the tax on petrol and commercial vehicles. This in fact paved the way for the derationing of petrol in May 1950, which would certainly not have been possible without devaluation.[26] With Britain's exchange rate at a more realistic level and exports to the dollar area so increased in volume that they were earning more in sterling terms than they had done before devaluation, it had at last become possible to move towards the dismantling of the remaining wartime physical controls which had already disappeared in almost all other European countries.[27]

This chapter has sketched some crucial economic developments in Britain in the 1945–50 period with little specific reference to the Middle East, an omission which will be rectified in succeeding chapters. It serves as a background against which to view the development of the British economy for the next thirty years. For whatever the failures of the economic policies of the Attlee Government, with the debacle of sterling convertibility in 1947 and the humiliating devaluation of 1949, the Labour Party had shaped a new Britain, whose features – full employment, the welfare state, public ownership of the major industries, high direct taxation and recurrent balance of payments crises – were to persist relatively unchanged until Mrs Thatcher's reversal of economic policy from 1979 onwards.

No mention has been made of many events of major importance to Britain in non-economic fields, especially in defence (Western European Union, NATO, the Berlin crisis, the Korean War), though they had of course their economic repercussions. Even in the economic field itself, relations with European countries have had to be left largely unrecorded (for example the European Payments Union). But one aspect of them must be mentioned briefly, Britain's decision in May 1950 not to attend the discussions on the Schuman Plan for collaboration at a supra-national level on coal and steel production in Western Europe. This was anathema to Britain for a host of powerful reasons, ranging from imperial sentiment to the chauvinism of British miners and steel workers. This decision was fraught with consequences for the future, since it marked a turning away by Britain from the path that was to lead the EEC's founder members, without Britain, to the Treaty of Rome.

2 The Middle East Economies after World War II

Unlike Europe, the countries of the Middle East had suffered little war damage. There had been extensive fighting in North Africa, but more in the desert areas than in the towns, and there had been time, since the war shifted elsewhere in 1943, to repair such damage as had occurred. Egypt, the headquarters of British Middle East Command, had been free of hostilities since 1942 and had suffered little before that. Sudan had seen no operations since being used early in 1941 as the forming-up area for the capture of Ethiopia from the Italians. The 1941 campaign to drive the Vichy French out of Lebanon and Syria had been relatively undestructive. Iraq and Iran had been occupied without protracted fighting.

Indeed, most of these countries were net beneficiaries from the not inconsiderable improvements to infrastructure, especially communications, made by the British and (mainly in Iran) the Americans for their own military reasons. As just one example, the Egypt-Palestine railway network had been extended northwards from Haifa to Tripoli (Lebanon).[1] Purchases by the armed forces and construction contracts placed by them with local firms had considerably improved the economies of Middle Eastern countries. The closure for a time of the Mediterranean and the acute shortage of shipping at all times had forced Middle East Command to seek regional sources of supply for a wide range of manufactures. Where these did not exist, encouragement had been given to bring them into being. The main instrument of this policy had been the Middle East Supply Centre, set up by the British Government in Cairo.[2]

One important consequence of all this activity was that many Middle East countries, whether or not members of the Sterling Area,[3] found themselves in 1945 in possession of sizeable sterling balances. As these holdings were a major factor in their ability to finance their overseas trade, especially with Britain, it would be most desirable to list them here. This, unfortunately, is no easy undertaking. There are two main reasons. First, the sterling balance of any country was a composite figure, made up of both public and private holdings, and comprising Government and other securities, sterling accounts with banks, and such miscellaneous items as insurance policies. Secondly, banks, including most importantly in this context the Bank of England, regard their dealings with their depositors as confidential, so were not prepared to publish details of sterling balances, even in a consolidated form.

Nevertheless, some information did become known, usually as a result of statements by Treasury Ministers to Parliament or the publication as White Papers of inter-governmental financial agreements. Table 1 lists the Middle East countries and shows for which of them estimates of their sterling balances at the end of the war are possible. It can be said with a high degree of confidence that the largest sterling holders were Egypt, Palestine and Iraq, in that (descending) order.

Table 1: Sterling holdings in June 1945 (£ million: estimates)

Aden	*	10	Oman		–
Algeria		–	Palestine	*	120
Bahrain	*	–	Qatar	*	–
Egypt	*	390	Saudi Arabia		–
Iran		20	Sudan	*	10
Iraq	*	70	Syria		–
Kuwait	*	–	Transjordan	*	10
Lebanon		–	Trucial States	*	–
Libya	*	–	Tunisia		–
Morocco		–	Yemen		–

*Member of the Sterling Area in June 1945

Those countries listed which were members of the Sterling Area kept their reserves in London and their currencies were aligned with the pound sterling. (Several of the remainder were members of the French franc area, having similar links with Paris.) Sterling holdings could be spent anywhere within the Sterling Area, but not elsewhere without the sanction of the exchange control authorities in London. There was thus scope for negotiations between the Middle East Governments and the UK Government on what sums could be made freely convertible and on what timescale.

An outline of the long negotiations which took place in the case of Egypt, the largest holder, is given as an Annex to this Chapter. It will be seen that Egypt's sterling holdings rose from £195 million in December 1943 to about £390 million at the end of the war and went on rising to a peak of about £470 million in December 1946. In July 1947, when Egypt left the Sterling Area, they stood at £430 million, of which £400 million were then blocked. These blocked balances had fallen to £230 million by March 1951, when a long-term agreement was reached to reduce them to £80 million by the end of 1960 (or at the very latest July 1963).

It is noteworthy that the negotiations were both hard-fought (the agreements being often reached several months late) and complicated, with provision being made not only for monetary matters (gold, dollars and transferable sterling) but also for 'essential' goods such as cotton and especially petroleum products otherwise likely to cost dollars. Similar negotiations were conducted with other major sterling holders.

The ending of the war faced Middle East countries, as it did Britain, with the need to realign their industries from wartime to peacetime production. But the scale of their problem was smaller. Manufacturing to meet the needs of the occupying armed forces was virtually all light industry, which could usually be switched without too much difficulty to production of civilian consumer goods for which there was a demand.

Nor did all foreign forces leave rapidly after the end of the war. Sizeable British forces remained in Egypt (by treaty[4]) and in Palestine (mandated to Britain after World War I by the League of Nations). Smaller British contingents stayed on in Libya, Iraq and Aden (a Crown Colony). France likewise kept substantial forces in the Maghreb countries, Morocco, Algeria and Tunisia (of which Algeria was technically part of France and the other two were protectorates), although no longer in the now independent Levant States of Syria and Lebanon.[5] Whether or not all these forces were welcome politically, their local expenditure was economically beneficial to the host countries. Indeed, one of the overseas savings which Dalton, as Chancellor of the Exchequer, more than once (unsuccessfully) urged on his Cabinet colleagues was a thinning of the garrison in Egypt.

One major Middle East industry which had no problem of conversion to peacetime requirements, and which was clearly destined to go from strength to strength, was oil. In 1945, this was the only industry in the region (with the possible exceptions of cotton and gum arabic) which could be said to be of world importance. Nevertheless, it was then much smaller and much less widespread geographically than it is today. It was also, and this was only just beginning to be a source of unrest, virtually entirely in foreign ownership.

A British company (Anglo-Iranian Oil Company or AIOC, now British Petroleum) had a concession covering all but the five northern provinces of Iran; an American consortium (ARAMCO) had the concession for Saudi Arabia; and a British-Dutch-American-French consortium (Iraq Petroleum Company, usually known as IPC) had that for Iraq. These were the only countries in the region with large-scale oil production in 1945. Oil had been discovered in Kuwait in 1938 by a British-American consortium (Kuwait Oil Company or KOC), but because of the war it had not yet been brought on stream. A field in Bahrain, American-owned, had come into production in 1934, but it was small. IPC through subsidiaries held concessions in Qatar, Abu Dhabi (one of the Trucial States) and Oman, and had found oil in Qatar in 1939, not developed because of the war; it had not yet explored seriously elsewhere in these territories. Concessions had been let in Egypt (to Shell-controlled Anglo-Egyptian Oilfields) but they seemed unpromising. Algeria and Libya had scarcely come into real consideration yet as potential oil producers.

It also needs to be remembered that at this time all oil production was on-shore; off-shore operations in the Middle East were entirely postwar developments. Moreover, natural gas was not yet an export product in the Middle East; no important gasfields had yet been discovered there and it was normal practice for 'associated' gas to be separated from the oil it accompanied and flared at the well-head. The situation was therefore very different in many respects from that found in the Middle East today.

The share-holdings in the various oil consortia mentioned above were important in the subsequent history of the industry, so it will be as well to clarify them at this point. In 1945, ownership was as follows:

IRAN: AIOC (British)

SAUDI ARABIA: SoCal (Standard Oil of California) 50 per cent; Texaco (Texas Company) 50 per cent (both American)

IRAQ: AIOC 23.75 per cent; Shell 23.75 per cent (Dutch/British); CFP (Compagnie Francaise des Pétroles) 23.75 per cent (French); Esso (Standard Oil of New Jersey) 11.875 per cent (American); Socony Vacuum (later Mobil) 11.875 per cent (American); and Gulbenkian 5 per cent.

KUWAIT: AIOC 50 per cent; Gulf Oil 50 per cent (American)

BAHRAIN: as SAUDI ARABIA

QATAR)
ABU DHABI) as IRAQ
OMAN)

It will be seen that British and US ownership pre-dominated. Indeed, the French were resentful that they had not been accorded a larger share; CFP was regularly crude-short. There were also smaller American oil companies which were eyeing the Middle East holdings of their larger compatriots with envy and were looking for ways of moving in. Two other points need to be mentioned. For historical reasons, the British Government owned 51 per cent of AIOC's shares,[6] but (even under the Attlee Government with its nationalisation programme) took care to observe its undertaking not to interfere in the company's commercial decisions (a fact which many in the Middle East, and especially in Iran, naturally found hard to credit). And both IPC and KOC were British-registered companies: indeed, London already was, and increasingly became,[7] the world's Middle East oil capital.

Soon after the end of the war, a change took place in ARAMCO's ownership. SoCal and Texaco reduced their holdings to 30 per cent each, with Esso taking 30 per cent and Mobil 10 per cent. This created an overlap between the share-holdings in ARAMCO and IPC. Shell also obtained an interest in Kuwait by entering into a long-term contract with Gulf Oil for the purchase of substantial quantities of its Kuwaiti crude. The interlocking of interests between the oil majors was thus very extensive, a factor which complicated their negotiations with the host Government concerned on changes in the terms of any particular concession.

One distinguishing feature of the structure of these major oil companies was that they were all 'vertically integrated', i.e. in addition to producing crude they owned refineries, tanker fleets, port facilities, road haulage fleets and retail outlets. These structures were usually not in perfect balance, so there was trading between the companies, particularly between those that were 'crude-short' and 'crude-long'. Further inter-company trading took the form of 'swaps', designed to cut down tanker movements by supplying from nearer sources; but crude oil is far from being a homogeneous substance, its chemical composition varying considerably from field to field, so swaps were limited by the types of crude which any particular refinery could accept. Before the war it was thought most profitable to site refineries at ports close to producing fields; thus the Abadan Refinery, the largest in the world in 1945, was in Khuzistan, the province in which lay AIOC's major Iranian oil-fields. But after the war, Western Governments put pressure on oil companies to build refineries close to markets, so saving foreign exchange and maximising domestic employment.

It should be appreciated that for vertically integrated oil companies the main source of revenues was the sale of oil products to the ultimate consumers and that the companies were competitors at this stage even though they might be co-owners at the oil production stage. This had considerable effects on the liftings of crude oil by members of consortia and on their willingness or otherwise to sell crude to third parties. Members of production consortia normally (Kuwait was a partial exception) had the right to lift oil in proportion to their shareholdings, but this might not suit their downstream needs. Complicated arrangements consequently had to be made for 'under-liftings' and 'over-liftings' and for the price at which these transactions should take place.

It is not necessary to go into these here in any detail, but two points arising from them are relevant to later developments in relations between Middle East Governments and their concessionaires. The first is that they could lead to conflicts of interest between members of consortia over expansion of production in any particular concession: this tended for instance to speed expansion in Kuwait, which had an unusually flexible offtake arrangement between the two shareholders, and to retard it in Iraq, where the arrangements between the many shareholders were distictly inflexible. The second effect was upon the system of 'posted' prices (which will be discussed in later Chapters), particularly when posted prices diverged from the prices at which oil was actually traded in the markets.[8]

In terms of population employed and proportions of gross national products, agriculture was by far the Middle East's most important occupation in 1945. Much of this agriculture was of a subsistence nature, or at least directed towards the domestic market. But there were important export products, some marketed only within the region,[9] others supplying more distant markets, particularly in Europe, including Britain.

The crop with the strongest links with Britain was cotton; high-quality long-staple cotton from Egypt and Sudan and shorter-staple cotton from Syria had for many years been sold through the Cotton Exchange in Liverpool. Indeed, it was British money which had developed this production in Sudan, through the Gezira cotton scheme.[10] Other crops which found markets in Britain were citrus fruits, mainly from Palestine and Lebanon, and vegetables from Egypt (especially onions). Dates and figs were exported from several countries, but chiefly from Iraq. There were some cereal exports to Britain, especially of barley, the chief supplier being Iraq. Tobacco exports came from the Lataqia area of Syria; they were used mainly for blending in so-called Turkish cigarettes. The Maghreb countries had substantial agricultural exports, mainly to France, but in smaller quantities to Britain; Algerian wine for instance filled a gap in the British market soon after the war.

Despite the euphoria created in the immediate postwar period by the setting up of the United Nations Organization, political problems in the region, which had often been latent during the war years, soon began to trouble a number of countries in the Middle East, and these were bound to have their economic repercussions. For Britain, the obvious problem areas were Palestine and Egypt; these will be covered in Chapters 3 and 7. Not so clearly a problem area,[11] but soon to become one, was Iran, which will be the subject of Chapter 5. France, with the loss of her position in the Levant States, had no immediate problems to face, but these were to come not many years later in the Maghreb, especially in Algeria. French interests can for the most part receive no more than glancing references in this book, though they of course contributed to the general climate of thought and attitudes in the Arab countries as a whole. They will be relevant to Chapter 10.

Annex to Chapter 2

Negotiations between Britain and Egypt on Egypt's Sterling Balances accumulated during World War II

11 August 1944. Total Egyptian sterling balances were officially estimated by the British Government at £250 million, as against £195 million at the end of 1943.

11 January 1945. White Paper on the Anglo-Egyptian Financial and Commercial Agreement for 1945:

(a) It was agreed that Egyptian exchange controls would be aligned with Sterling Area controls.

(b) £E10 million (the £E was worth £1.025) was agreed as the maximum (gross) target figure for Egyptian hard currency requirements outside the Sterling Area; this was made up of £E7.5 for visible imports, £E1.5 for invisibles and £E1 for specified contingencies including hard currency price rises of up to 10 per cent.

(c) Up to a further £E4 million was provided to cover 'special supplies' to Egypt, for example wheat and fertilisers.

(d) If US prices rose by more than 10 per cent, Britain would supply the extra dollars required against £E or sterling.

4 January 1946. UK White Paper:

(a) The January 1945 Agreement was extended to 31 March 1946.

(b) For the 15 months to 31 March 1946, £14,350,500 of 'scarce currencies' would be provided to Egypt.

(c) The Egyptian Government undertook to list all Egyptian public and private sterling holdings.

6 April 1946. UK Government Statement:
Up to £E12 million of hard currency would be made available for the year to 31 March 1947.

1 February 1947. The *Economist* published its estimates of net sterling balances. For Egypt and Sudan together it estimated £400 million at 30 June 1945 and £470 million at December 1946.

26 February – 3 March 1947. Talks aimed at scaling down sterling balances by agreement were held in Cairo. No agreement emerged. (These talks were part of a series of such discussions held around this time.)

9 April 1947. The Egyptian Finance Minister informed the Senate that the Government had refused to scale down the 'old' sterling balances on the ground i.a. that they were the backing for the

Egyptian banknote issue. He said that in renewed negotiations Egypt would suggest the reduction of the sterling balances as counterpart for the transfer to Egypt of the British Government's holding of shares in the Suez Canal Company and of other British-owned shares such as those in Anglo-Egyptian Oilfields. (If such proposals were put forward, they were clearly not accepted by Britain. Nevertheless, the statement is interesting in the light of later events.)

2 July 1947. White Paper of a UK-Egyptian Agreement signed in London on 30 June:

(a) Egypt was to leave the Sterling Area.
(b) The hard currency equivalent of £30 million was to be made available to Egypt for the remainder of 1947.
(c) The remaining Egyptian sterling holdings, estimated at under £400 million, were to be transferred to blocked 'No.2' Accounts.
(d) From these blocked accounts, releases would be made to the Egyptian Government of £8 million, plus another £12 million as a 'working balance', and to Egyptian private holders of £8 to 12 million.
(e) 'Several' £ million would be released as cover for 'confirmed credits' relating to current transactions and for any sterling received by Egyptian banks after 14 July in respect of current transactions (which were defined as payments due to Egypt for visible and invisible exports, together with interest payments to Egyptian holders of British securities).
(f) Releases would be made in respect of any unspent balances from the wartime Hard Currency Agreement, plus the proceeds from the sales in Egypt of British military supplies or surplus stores.

5 January 1948. Publication of a new Anglo-Egyptian Agreement signed in Cairo following negotiations held there between 8 and 29 December 1947:

(a) Gold to the value of $4 million would be sold to Egypt against sterling for payment of her IMF quota and IBRD subscription, so enabling Egypt to draw up to $15 million from the IMF for 1948.

(b) £32 million would be released from blocked balances for 1948, of which £21 million would cover Egypt's 'irreducible' adverse balance of payments for the year and the other £11 million would increase her working balance from £12 million to £23 million.

(c) Egypt guaranteed substantial cotton deliveries to Britain and promised to issue open import licences for many British goods whilst the UK promised 'best endeavours' to provide Egypt with essential supplies including water-pipes for rural water distribution. (Bilateral trade commitments of this kind were becoming increasingly common as a result of dollar shortages, with each country striving to secure supplies from non-dollar sources of goods and materials otherwise available only against dollar payment.)

27 April 1948. Statement to UK Parliament:

(a) £80 million had been released to Egypt between 14 July 1947 and 1 February 1948, this total including both releases from blocked balances and new sterling accruing to Egypt's free No.1 Account.

(b) Dollar facilities equivalent to £7.75 million had been made available to Egypt between 20 August 1947 and 1 February 1948 against payment in transferable account sterling (i.e. sterling earned by Egypt from transferable account countries).

24 December 1948. The Egyptian Prime Minister announced that in the period 31 December 1947 to 27 November 1948 Egypt's blocked balances had fallen from £310 million to £272 million, whilst her free sterling had increased from £34 million to £71 million (due chiefly to large British purchases of Egyptian cotton at a time of high cotton prices).

31 March 1949. UK- Egyptian Agreement signed covering 1949, after negotiations which had been in progress since 29 December 1948:

(a) Immediate release of £12 million, plus up to another £18 million (as needed) to prevent the Egyptian No.1 (free) Account from falling below £45 million.

(b) $US in equal instalments on 31 March and 30 June to be sold to Egypt against payment of £5 million sterling, to enable Egypt to make hard currency payments for current transactions.
(c) UK to facilitate supply to Egypt during 1949 of petroleum products to the value of £5 million against sterling payment.
(d) UK to facilitate importation into Egypt by Anglo-Egyptian Oilfields and Shell of essential dollar equipment against payment in sterling. (Anglo-Egyptian Oilfields and Socony Vacuum had made a commercial oil strike in Sinai, announced on 13 January 1949.)
(e) The two Governments agreed that they would use their best endeavours to enable UK exports to Egypt to be worth £47 million or more (such indicative figures rarely proved to be realistic; exports in fact amounted to only £36.5 million in 1949 – see Chapter 4 below).

10 September 1950. It was announced in London that the British and Egyptian Governments would begin negotiations in November 1950 for a 'long-term or permanent settlement' of Egypt's sterling balances. Meanwhile the agreement for 1949 would remain in force for 1950, with the following amendments:
(a) The UK would facilitate supply to Egypt in 1950 against sterling payment of petroleum products worth £7.5 million.
(b) UK exports to Egypt during 1950 'might' reach a c.i.f. value of £52 million, of which £43 million would be 'essential goods' (£43 million was in fact the value of total exports - see Chapter 4 below).

15 March 1951. The Financial Secretary to the Treasury (Douglas Jay) informed the House of Commons that an Anglo-Egyptian Agreement on Egypt's blocked sterling balances had been concluded as follows:
(a) Out of a total of about £230 million blocked sterling, £150 million would be released over a period of 10 to 13.5 years.
(b) The remaining £80 million, considered to be the amount that Egypt would normally hold in London, would be discussed before the end of that period.

(c) In each of the years 1951 to 1960, there would be a release of £10 million, plus a further £5 million p.a. in any year in which the level of the Egyptian No.1 Account fell below £45 million.
(d) In 1951 only, there would be an additional special release of £15 million, of which £14 million would be in $US
(e) Should £35 million or any less sum remain undrawn at the end of the 10th year, it would be released at a rate of £10 million p.a. for 3 years plus £5 million on 1 July 1963.
(f) UK would facilitate the supply against sterling payment of petroleum products to the value of £11 million p.a. in each of the 10 years.

This Agreement was debated in the Commons, where it was strongly criticised by several members including Churchill and Eden (Conservative, Opposition) and Crossman (Labour, pro-Israel) as being over-generous. Gaitskell replied that the proposed releases were less than the average releases in the preceding three years. The Government's majority for the Agreement was only 3 votes (294 to 291), the 4 Liberals present voting with the Conservatives. The Agreement was signed on 1 July 1951.

3 The Emergence of Israel

In Palestine, trouble between Arabs and Jews had flared long before 1945. Its origins stemmed from incompatible promises made by Britain to the two peoples during World War I, when Palestine was part of the Ottoman Empire. The Arabs of the whole region had been led to believe they would achieve independence, which most of them expected to take the form of a Hashemite Greater Syria ruled from Damascus. Instead Britain and France had sought and obtained Mandates from the League of Nations: the French for Syria and Lebanon; and the British for Palestine, initially including Transjordan. Hashemite rulers had been installed by Britain in Iraq (which was given independence in 1932) and in Transjordan (later to be renamed the Hashemite Kingdom of Jordan, but at that stage only an Emirate). Palestine (west of the Jordan) remained under a British High Commissioner. The Jews, for their part, had been promised a 'national home' in Palestine under the terms of the Balfour Declaration of 2 November 1917.

At the time of the granting of the Mandate in 1920, the population of Palestine was predominantly Arab, as it had been for well over a thousand years. There had all along been a small Jewish minority living in the land of their ancestors; they had coexisted peacefully with the Arabs there, as in other Arab countries, many of which had considerably larger Jewish communities than the one in Palestine. On the strength of the 'national home' promise, some Jews, mainly from Europe (especially Poland) began to move to Palestine, but the numbers were at first small, a few thousands a year.

In the 1930s, with the coming to power in Germany of the Nazis with their terrifying doctrine of racial purity, Jewish emigration to Palestine greatly increased, to an extent which alarmed the Arab population. They rebelled unsuccessfully in 1936, by which time the Jewish community had grown to some 375,000, with Tel Aviv a Jewish city of well over 100,000 people. During World War II the German seizure of nearly the whole of continental Europe virtually stopped Jewish emigration to Palestine and led to the horror of the Holocaust, in which millions of European Jews were massacred.

By 1945, the proportion of Jews to Arabs in Palestine was approaching 1 to 2, some 600,000 to 1,300,000. With the end of the war in Europe, those Central European Jews who had survived the Holocaust began to move, in an unorganised but single-minded way, into the American, British and French occupation sectors of Germany, and to a lesser extent into Austria and Italy. Under the general description of 'displaced persons' they were accommodated in refugee camps until new homes could be found for them; in Germany, they eventually numbered some 250,000. The great majority (encouraged to do so by the Jewish Agency) clamoured to go to Palestine and this, despite doubts in the State Department, was President Truman's policy. He wrote to Attlee on 31 August 1945, urging that 100,000 of them should be allowed to go there forthwith. The Jewish community in Palestine, by this time highly organised politically and some of them with military training,[1] naturally campaigned for the Jewish refugees to be allowed to join them, but with no limitation to Truman's proposed 100,000.

This pressure for large-scale Jewish immigration led to very severe unrest in Palestine, the course of which is outside the scope of this book.[2] It resulted in Britain, in April 1947, referring the whole problem to the United Nations General Assembly. That body, on 29 November 1947, approved by the required two-thirds majority a plan for the partition of Palestine into an Arab state and a Jewish state, with the Jerusalem-Bethlehem area constituting an international zone, and all three parts forming an economic union.[3] This plan was at once rejected by the Arab Higher Committee representing the Palestinian Arabs, and by the

Arab countries, who had voted solidly against it in the UN, as had other countries with sizeable Muslim populations.

The British Government was not prepared to use its own forces to put a disagreed partition plan into effect. After considerable heart-searching,[4] it fixed 15 May 1948 as the date for termination of the Mandate and began evacuation of its personnel[5]; the High Commissioner departed on 14 May. Ben Gurion at once proclaimed the independence of the State of Israel, open to all Jews who wished to enter,[6] and only sixteen minutes later Truman gave it American recognition.[7]

There had been widespread fighting within Palestine between improvised Jewish and Arab forces in the weeks preceding 14 May, with the Jewish forces gaining the upper hand and the first Arab refugees fleeing their homes. On termination of the Mandate, the armed forces of Egypt, Transjordan and Iraq and (to a minor extent) Syria and Lebanon joined in the struggle. They at first achieved some penetration, but were soon driven back by the surprisingly effective Israeli forces.

On 18 July 1948, when a (second) United Nations truce took effect, the Israelis held much more of Palestine than had been allotted to them in the UN partition plan. They won further territory, particularly the Negev Desert (except for the coastal 'Gaza strip' held by Egyptian forces), before armistice agreements were signed in 1949. The State of Israel was recognised by the UK Government on 30 January 1949 and was admitted to United Nations membership on 11 May 1949.

One result of the fighting, with very serious economic as well as political consequences, was that some 650,000 Palestinian Arabs had fled their homes, over 50 per cent of the Arab population.[8] Not all had crossed the borders of Palestine; about 240,000 had stayed their flight on the West bank of the Jordan River and another 180,000 had moved into the Gaza area. But some 230,000 had left the country. Of these nearly 100,000, mainly from the Haifa area, had taken refuge in Lebanon; about 70,000 in Syria; and up to 60,000 had crossed the Jordan river into Transjordan. Small numbers went to Egypt and Iraq.

It became Israeli policy that these population movements should in practice be irreversible.[9] Filling the gaps, about 300,000

European Jews moved to Israel, mainly from the refugee camps. In addition, between 1948 and 1957, some 467,000 Jews from the ancient communities in the Arab countries fled their ancestral homes, the vast majority of them to Israel.[10] By doing so, they added a large admixture of 'Oriental' Jews to the mainly 'European' Jews already living there. Less than 300,000 Arabs (Muslims, Christians and Druze) remained in Israel.

The influx of the Palestinian refugees put considerable strain on the economies of Lebanon, Syria and Transjordan. However, perhaps as many as 60 per cent of them were soon absorbed into local economic life, joining relatives or using their skills and such capital as they had been able to get out of Palestine to set themselves up in middle-class occupations. The other 40 per cent were mainly agricultural workers, for whom no employment was available since cultivable land was scarce and already exploited.

These penniless and workless refugees were housed in makeshift camps and faced a dismal future. The burden of providing for their minimum needs was taken over to a considerable (but never fully adequate) extent by the United Nations Organization, somewhat reluctantly facing up to the practical consequences of its own partition plan. On 1 May 1950, a new body, the United Nations Relief and Works Agency (UNRWA), which had been set up by a General Assembly Resolution of 8 December 1949, began its task of looking after the physical needs of the refugees, providing food, accommodation (initially mainly tented), medical services, and later, when it became clear that the problem was an enduring one, school education and vocational training.[11] The Palestinians, an intelligent people and relatively well-educated before 1948, made good use of the training facilities provided, and it was not long before some of the children from the refugee camps began to move out into skilled employment in the Arab countries, including particularly Kuwait and other states of the Arabian Peninsula. But the camps themselves remained, and a high birthrate among their inhabitants caused their numbers to grow. They were a breeding-ground also for hatred of Israel, giving rise to militant groups dedicated to the recovery of their homeland from those whom they inevitably saw as usurpers.

Another economic consequence of the rise of Israel was the

decision of the Arab countries which had failed to defeat it by military means to use the weapon of economic boycott against it. Not only did they all refuse to trade with Israel themselves but they set out to hamper Israel's economic and commercial relations with the rest of the world.

The League of Arab States, established in 1945 with its headquarters in Cairo, a consultative rather than a supranational institution, set up a Boycott Committee to organise this activity. It proved an effective body, which has had a perhaps surprising degree of success over a long period of time (it still continues) in persuading virtually all Arab Governments to refuse to trade with what soon became a long list of 'black-listed' firms in the non-Arab world. The criteria used in drawing up the list have never been published officially, but word soon spread that a firm wishing to trade in the Arab markets must not supply defence equipment to Israel nor strengthen the Israeli economy by investing there or licensing manufacture of its products there. Firms with directors prominent in Zionist activities, such as fund-raising for Israel, were also likely to be 'listed'.

The black-list is treated as secret, though it has been leaked on a few occasions; it is a variable document, with additions and deletions being made quite frequently as commercial circumstances change. The fact that it is secret creates problems for firms which are not themselves black-listed but may buy materials or sub-assemblies to incorporate in their products from firms which, unknown to the purchasers, have been so listed. To alleviate this problem, Arab embassies around the world are willing to legalise Certificates of Origin for goods being exported to their countries; indeed, this legalisation is compulsory for most Arab countries. Some firms have also run into trouble through setting up jointly-owned subsidiaries with companies which are on the fateful list; in such a case there is a danger that not only the subsidiary but also the parent which has established it may find itself black-listed.

One notable application of the boycott was that the Egyptian Government refused transit through the Suez Canal to Israeli shipping and to other ships with cargoes bound to or from Israel. This caused some international unease as it appeared to be a breach of the Convention of 1888 under which the Canal was operated by the Suez Canal Company, a French company in which the British Government had the largest single share-holding.[12] However, certain international lawyers considered that the Egyptians could rely on the fact that they had signed only an armistice and not a peace treaty with Israel to argue that they had valid defence grounds for banning Israeli shipping (and perhaps cargoes) from use of the Canal. No legal case was ever brought to put the issue to the test.

Another consequence of the Arab refusal to trade with Israel was the closure of the Iraq Petroleum Company's pipeline to Haifa, leaving the pipeline to Tripoli in Lebanon as, for the time being, the only Mediterranean outlet for Iraqi oil. The Israeli Government seized the Haifa Refinery but had to find crude oil from elsewhere to process there. IPC soon completed a second pipeline to Tripoli, which had been already under construction, and later built another to Banias in Syria.

In general, it can be said that Lebanon benefited from the isolation of Israel not only from receipt of increased transit dues for Iraqi oil but more widely. With the competition of Haifa and Jaffa removed, Beirut was left as the principal Arab port on the Eastern Mediterranean coast and Lebanon was able to boost its transit trade, especially to Jordan which had hitherto used the Palestinian ports. Syria also received increased transit dues for oil and was for a long time in the position of having a strangle-hold over Iraqi oil exports, an important factor when relations between Syria and Iraq later became strained. Jordan, on the other hand, lost its IPC transit dues, as well as having to bear increased freight costs on its imports via Beirut.

The Israeli economy, despite the Arab boycott, and despite the even more debilitating factor of needing to spend a huge proportion of its national product on defence requirements, proved viable. It was helped by a very great influx of funds from Jewish communities abroad, especially in the USA.[13] One contributory cause of this generosity was said (perhaps unkindly) to be that many Jews, well established in countries in which they judged themselves to be safe, had no wish to emigrate to Israel, but felt guilty at not doing so in view of their centuries-old pledge 'next year in Jerusalem'; they quieted their consciences by paying for the absorption into Israel of other emigrants. There were naturally other and nobler motives also at work. In addition, official aid was provided by the US Government. In January 1949, the Export-Import Bank gave Israel a line of credit of $100 million, of which $35 million could be drawn immediately. And of course Arab property abandoned by the refugees had provided Israel with an initial accession of wealth, particularly in the agricultural sector.[14]

From the early days of the Zionist movement, it had been planned that many Jews settling in Palestine should become farmers, even if they had had no previous experience of that calling.[15] This determination had led to the establishment of 'kibbutzim' and 'moshavim', communal and cooperative settlements aiming at a high degree of self-sufficiency, combined where possible with cash crops for sale. A number of these had come into existence before 1948, and they proved an excellent pattern for the speedy settlement of some of the new immigrants into independent Israel. The living conditions they provided were often harsh, especially where, sometimes for defence reasons, they were set up on arid soil, but a highly motivating idealism inspired their inhabitants to great efforts to overcome such natural difficulties. Israeli scientists, of whom there were many among the ex-European Jews, turned their considerable talents to solving the problems of arid land cultivation, with the result that Israel has become a world leader in this branch of agriculture.

The wide coastal plain of Palestine is far from arid; indeed, it is some of the best agricultural land in the Middle East. Palestine had been a considerable exporter of citrus fruits before 1939, when Jaffa oranges were already famous, especially in Britain. The citrus groves had been largely Arab- owned and Arab-cultivated, so that there was inevitably some loss of production when the Israelis first took them over, but this was rapidly overcome, and irrigation soon considerably extended the cultivable area.

In addition, the Jews brought with them to Israel skills which could be put to good use in the establishment of industries new to the area. One which deserves special mention, since it has had close links with London, is diamond-cutting and polishing (established in Palestine in 1941, when Amsterdam and Antwerp were in German hands). Ups and downs in the trade statistics between the UK and Israel often derive from movements of rough diamonds to Israel and their reimportation as gems for the British and other markets.[16] Manufactures introduced or developed by Israel included electrical goods, chemicals (where Dead Sea potash, magnesium and bromine salts provided opportunities), tyres, paper and textiles. Nevertheless the Israeli balance of visible trade was initially highly adverse, imports being by value in a ratio of 5:1 to exports in 1949.

The termination of the Mandate left a number of financial problems to be sorted out between the ex-Mandatory and the new state of Israel. There were sterling balances belonging to Palestine, not all of which necessarily now belonged to Israel, since it was only a partial successor state.[17] And even those sterling funds which were judged to belong to Israel were blocked by exchange control regulations, giving rise to negotiations about the pace at which they might be unblocked.

One point to which great importance was attached on the British side was the Israeli obligation, as the Colonial Office in London saw it, to pay the pensions of British officials who had served in the Palestine administration. Negotiations on this dragged on for a long time since the Colonial Office was extremely reluctant to set a 'bad' precedent for future settlements with other newly independent countries as the British Empire entered its foreseeable phase of dismantlement. In the end London made some concessions and an acceptable compromise was reached.[18]

In May 1949, Israel was made a 'transferable account' country and nearly £7 million of her £35 million blocked sterling balances were released to cover the six months to 31 October 1949. The remaining £28 millions were released at fairly regular intervals over the next few years.

Britain's relations with Israel were complicated not only by past antagonisms still fresh in the memories of both sides, and by irritants such as the pensions issue, but by the 1946 treaty link between the UK and Transjordan. Transjordanian forces had taken part in the 1948 war against Israel and had been able to hold only part of the area assigned to the Arabs; but the British-trained

Arab Legion had performed more creditably than most other Arab armies. The Israelis were sure to keep a close eye on British arms supplies to this, in their view, enemy force. The Israelis also wished to buy some arms from Britain themselves, and any such sales by the UK were bound to be resented in Jordan, and indeed in other Arab states. This question of arms supplies to the Middle East area will be examined in more detail in Chapter 6.

A careful reader may notice that in the last paragraph the name Transjordan has been modified to Jordan. This represents a political change with considerable economic and social consequences. As long ago as April 1946, the Emir Abdullah of Transjordan had awarded himself the title of King. In December 1948, he unilaterally annexed those areas of Palestine of which his forces were still in occupation, some 2000 square miles of the Judea-Samaria plateau, now commonly known as 'the West Bank'. There were protests both from the Palestinians and from other Arab states, but he ignored them. In April 1949, the month in which the Armistice Agreement with Israel was signed, he took the final step of renaming Transjordan plus the West Bank as the Hashemite Kingdom of Jordan.

In an effort to obtain access to the Mediterranean, Abdullah then entered into secret talks with Israel for the cession to him of a corridor to Haifa in return for his signing a peace treaty, but these talks failed and leaks about them led to his assassination on 20 July 1951.[19] However, the kingdom which he had created survived him and until 1967 it included the West Bank (indeed, in certain respects it went on doing so after 1967; the 'West Bankers' continued to hold Jordanian passports and seats were allocated to them in the Jordanian Parliament).

The absorption into the population of Jordan of the Palestinian refugees who had fled across the river plus the West Bankers created a state with a Palestinian majority. The economic resources of this state were meagre, as Jordan has wide desert areas and few mineral resources. Its only port was Aqaba at the head of the Gulf of Aqaba, approachable only from the Red Sea. Jordan, through no economic fault of its own, thus found itself cast in the role of a partial dependant on international aid. It says much for the diplomatic skills of King Hussein that his kingdom has nevertheless achieved a very reasonable standard of living and has at the same time maintained its dignity.

To complete the story of the Arab remnants of Palestine, the Gaza strip was administered from Egypt, but Egypt was more sensitive to Palestinian feelings than King Abdullah had been and refrained from annexing it. The strip was fertile, but the large influx of refugees from elsewhere in Palestine caused it to be grossly overpopulated and made it an economic liability. Here too UNRWA played an important part in alleviating the worst distress, but as elsewhere refugee camps, with all their misery and their dangerous frustrations, became a permanent feature of the landscape. Egypt had its own population problems and little in the way of employment opportunities for Palestinians, so the Gaza Strip became the worst black-spot of all for the refugees.

4 Trade Between Britain and the Middle East 1946–50

Visible Trade

The statistics used in this section are derived from the *Accounts Relating to Trade and Navigation of the United Kingdom*, presented to Parliament at quarterly intervals by the Chancellor of the Exchequer. This means that the figures are presented from the viewpoint of the UK. 'Imports', for instance, mean imports into the UK and their valuation is given cif (charges in full, i.e. including the cost of shipping and marine insurance). 'Exports' correspondingly mean exports from the UK and are valued fob (free on board, i.e. including the cost of freight to the port but not of shipping etc.). Britain of course often provided the shipping and even more often the insurance: earnings under these heads are shown as part of the country's 'invisible' income.

For the purpose of illustrating visible trade earnings of Britain and the Middle East countries, few of which in this period had much in the way of shipping and insurance resources to offer, it would be nearer the truth (though still not entirely accurate) if one could value UK imports fob and exports cif, but the data for this are not available (at least not completely and not on a unified basis). The reader must therefore bear this minor complication in mind; it presents a picture slightly disadvantageous to the UK. However, with rounded figures, as used here, the effect is small.

Table 2 shows the value of visible trade in the two directions, with the favourable or unfavourable balance in respect of individual ME countries (+ meaning favourable to the UK), and sets the whole in perspective by giving the value of the UK's trade world-wide. As further perspective, it includes the figures for 1938. Exports include re-exports.

Table 2: Visible Trade (£ millions) with:

	1938	1946	1947	1948	1949	1950
ADEN (Colony and Protectorates)						
Exports to	0.5	2.2	2.0	2.5	2.8	3.5
Imports from	0.1	1.5	0.6	0.9	0.9	1.0
Balance	+0.4	+0.7	+1.4	+1.6	+1.9	+2.5
ALGERIA						
Exports to	1.0	2.0	2.3	1.6	1.9	2.3
Imports from	2.9	4.9	5.3	9.1	10.9	10.4
Balance	-1.9	-2.9	-3.0	-7.5	-9.0	-8.1
EGYPT						
Exports to	8.9	23.7	22.2	34.6	36.5	43.0
Imports from	11.6	15.3	14.8	47.6	29.0	40.2
Balance	-2.7	+8.4	+7.4	-13.0	+7.5	+2.8
IRAN						
Exports to	5.5	12.0	15.9	24.6	31.0	30.3
Imports from	9.1	21.0	16.1	36.1	34.5	47.7
Balance	-3.6	-9.0	-0.2	-11.5	-3.5	-17.4
IRAQ						
Exports to	2.5	10.7	14.5	17.6	14.4	14.6
Imports from	2.7	2.0	3.3	7.2	6.6	8.7
Balance	-0.2	+8.7	+11.2	+10.4	+7.8	+5.9
ISRAEL						
Exports to					6.6	10.0
Imports from					5.6	5.2
Balance					+1.0	+4.8
KUWAIT (incl. Bahrain, Qatar and Trucial States)						
Exports to			3.3	8.6	8.3	7.0
Imports from			3.1	6.2	17.8	34.8
Balance			+0.2	+2.4	-9.5	-27.8
LEBANON (figures combined with Syria before 1947)						
Exports to			3.9	5.6	8.6	8.1
Imports from			—	—	0.1	0.3
Balance			+3.9	+5.6	+8.5	+7.8

LIBYA						
Exports to		0.3	0.4	1.3	2.7	3.0
Imports from		0.1	0.2	0.5	0.5	1.1
Balance		+0.2	+0.2	+0.8	+2.2	+1.9
MOROCCO (incl. Spanish Ports in North Africa)						
Exports to	0.4	1.5	1.6	3.1	2.8	3.5
Imports from	1.0	5.8	5.6	6.0	10.6	13.6
Balance	-0.6	-4.3	-4.0	-2.9	-7.8	−10.1
OMAN						
Exports to		0.7	—	0.1	0.1	0.1
Imports from		0.6	—	—	—	
Balance		+0.1	—	+0.1	+0.1	+0.1
PALESTINE (incl. Transjordan before 1947)						
Exports to	1.6	17.1	17.6	10.2		
Imports from	3.1	5.7	13.0	12.9		
Balance	-1.5	+11.4	+4.6	-2.7		
SAUDI ARABIA (incl. Yemen and before 1947 Kuwait etc.)						
Exports to	0.1	0.5	0.8	1.6	3.5	2.9
Imports from	—	—	1.5	5.3	6.8	8.2
Balance	+0.1	+0.5	-0.7	-3.7	-3.3	-5.3
SUDAN						
Exports to	1.2	3.0	4.1	5.4	7.8	9.3
Imports from	3.4	5.0	6.7	15.7	22.2	21.8
Balance	-2.2	-2.0	-2.6	-10.3	-14.4	-12.5
SYRIA (incl. Lebanon before 1947)						
Exports to	0.7	4.8	2.0	1.9	2.4	3.0
Imports from	0.3	0.4	0.3	0.3	0.9	2.0
Balance	+0.4	+4.4	+1.7	+1.6	+1.5	+1.0
TRANSJORDAN (figures combined with Palestine before 1947)						
Exports to	— -		0.8	2.3	2.1	3.1
Imports from			—	—	—	—
Balance			+0.8	+2.3	+2.1	+3.1
TUNISIA						
Exports to	0.3	1.0	0.5	0.5	0.5	1.0
Imports from	1.7	2.0	4.1	5.0	5.9	6.0
Balance	-1.4	-1.0	-3.6	-4.5	-5.4	-5.0

TOTAL – MIDDLE EAST COUNTRIES						
Exports to	22.7	79.5	91.9	121.5	132.0	144.7
Imports from	35.9	64.3	74.6	152.8	152.3	201.0
Balance	-13.2	+15.2	+17.3	-31.3	-20.3	-56.3
TOTAL – ALL COUNTRIES						
Exports to	532.3	964.9	1196.3	1646.5	1844.4	2455.0
Imports from	919.5	1301.0	1787.5	2078.0	2274.1	2602.9
Balance	-387.2	-336.1	-591.2	-431.5	-429.7	-147.9
M.E. TRADE AS per cent OF TOTAL TRADE						
Exports to	4.26	8.24	7.68	7.38	7.16	5.89
Imports from	3.90	4.94	4.17	7.35	6.70	7.72

(Note: Apparent minor arithmetical errors result from rounding)

These figures show that, over this period in Britain's history, trade with the Middle East formed a small but by no means insignificant part of her trade world-wide. A favourable balance was achieved in 1946 and 1947 but thereafter the balance became unfavourable to the UK, as it had been in 1938. Both exports and imports rose in value over the period, although some allowance must be made for decline in the international value of the £ sterling due to inflation and to the devaluation of 1949 (the latter had less effect on the figures than might be supposed as most trade between Britain and the Middle East was conducted in sterling). The doubling of imports in 1948 as compared with 1947 was due to increased imports of oil from the Middle East, and it was this which swung the balance of visible trade back to being unfavourable to Britain.

Turning to individual countries, the figures show that Egypt, Iran, Iraq and Palestine were Britain's chief Middle Eastern trading partners in the early postwar years. Imports from Egypt consisted mainly of cotton and cotton-seeds, with minor contributions from fruit and vegetables, especially onions. Iraq supplied dates and a relatively small amount of crude petroleum. Iran was the principal oil supplier, mainly in the form of products (motor spirit, fuel oil, kerosene and gas oil, in decreasing order of importance) since Iranian crude oil was refined by AIOC at Abadan in Iran. From Palestine, Britain took mainly citrus fruits, some chemicals (potash) and some oil products (crude was sent by pipeline from Iraq to Haifa and processed in the small refinery there; this stopped when Haifa fell into Israeli hands and the pipeline was closed as part of the Arab boycott of Israel - see Chapter 3).

It will be seen that imports from Kuwait rose sharply in 1949 and again in 1950. This was entirely accounted for by crude oil; as already mentioned in Chapter 2, the development of Kuwait's oilfields had been held over until after the war. There were also increases in imports from Morocco in 1949 and 1950; in this case phosphates were responsible. By contrast, when Israel displaced Palestine in the Trade and Navigation Accounts, imports fell off in 1949 and 1950; as was noted in Chapter 3, the replacement of Arab by Israeli cultivators caused a temporary decline in citrus fruit production. Imports from Saudi Arabia began to grow steadily from 1947 onwards, again due to oil; the American oil majors participating in ARAMCO were keen to build up their outlets in Britain, and the UK import licensing system was not used to frustrate this process, as it could have been.

British exports to the Middle East countries covered a wide range of products, especially manufactured goods. The major destinations were Egypt, Palestine, Iran and Iraq, the same countries which were the major suppliers to Britain. This was not due to any conscious plan to balance imports and exports bilaterally, but was a natural result of their population size and purchasing power. The latter depended not only on current earnings but on the gradual release of the sterling balances built up during the war.

Special factors also played their part. Exports to Egypt and Palestine were directed to the British forces stationed there as well as to the indigenous population, while in Iran and Iraq the London-based oil companies were purchasers from Britain. Before the 1950s there was little attempt by the oil companies to source purchases locally or even to import through local traders.[1] Exports to Palestine fell in 1948, when the mandate was terminated; exports to Israel were lower still in 1949 but began to grow in 1950. Exports to Kuwait were also affected by purchases by the oil company; it will be seen that their build-up paved the way for the sharp growth in oil imports from Kuwait a year later. There was some gradual increase in exports to Saudi Arabia, but on a small scale, less than the rise in imports from that country. The same is true of Sudan; exports grew only steadily, while imports from Sudan rose sharply in value over the 1948–50 period, resulting mainly from a rise in cotton prices.

For the Middle East as a whole, the value of British exports grew year by year, but by less than to the rest of the world. The percentage figures bring this out; the Middle East markets accounted for over 8 per cent of UK exports in 1946, but for a smaller percentage each year until the figure dipped below 6 per cent in 1950 (though this was still above the percentage of 4.26 per cent in 1938).

Invisible Trade

Figures for invisible trade are much more difficult to collect than those for visible trade. For that reason there are no country-by-country statistics available and it is only possible to discuss the issue in unsatisfactorily general terms.

Before 1939, shipping had been one of the UK's leading invisible earners, but heavy shipping losses during the war had seriously reduced this source of income. Nevertheless, it was still a significant factor in Britain's postwar Middle East trade with a tendency to grow as newly built ships replenished the merchant fleet. Insurance was a major UK earner both before and after the war. Middle Eastern insurance companies were still at an early stage in their development where they existed at all, and such as did exist were virtually certain to reinsure at Lloyds of London. Banking in the Middle East was another field in which Britain was prominent (see below); it became increasingly lucrative as oil earnings grew.

The oil industry itself provided the British Treasury with sizeable revenues, both from taxes on profits and from the dividends on the British Government's shareholding in AIOC. Indeed, Middle East host Governments regularly used the argument against their concession-holders that the British Government's 'take' was greater than their own.[2] Tourism to Britain was of small dimensions after the devastations of the war and amid the continuation of rationing, but students from Middle East countries began to come there again in growing numbers. Remittances to Britain from expatriates working in the region added a little to the positive side of the UK account. So did the fees earned by British experts providing advice to Middle East Governments and enterprises; among these, special mention should be made of consultant engineers, who had a high reputation for designing major civil engineering projects, such as port installations, airports, industrial complexes and dams.

On the other side of the account, far the most easily identifiable item was payment of tolls by British shipping for passage through the Suez Canal, but there were other shipping outgoings for harbour dues, agents' charges etc. Tourism from Britain to the Middle East was too expensive for all but the rich and even for them took some time to revive after the war, but there was some local tourism by members of the British forces stationed in the area. As civil aviation began to grow, charges for the use of airports produced revenues for geographically well-placed countries, especially Egypt and later Lebanon. It is not easy to extend this rather short list, so there can be no doubt that the net balance on the Middle East invisible account was very much in Britain's favour.[3]

Arms sales

This was very much a one-way traffic, from Britain to the Middle East countries. More will be said about it in Chapter 6.

Overall Assessment

In 1946 and 1947, when the balance even of visible trade was positive for the UK, it is clear that Britain was running a very favourable balance of payments with the Middle East as a whole. From 1948 to 1950, the UK's negative balance of visible trade was offset, to an extent which unfortunately cannot be calculated precisely, by a positive balance of invisible trade and by earnings from arms sales. The importance of invisibles is such that the overall balance of payments may well have been favourable throughout; it seems safe to estimate that it was so for the five year period taken as a whole.

Some of the wartime debt owing to Middle East countries was repaid during this period, but at the same time a number of these countries were building up new holdings of sterling in accounts which were not blocked. Part of these were converted into dollars during the brief period of British convertibility in 1947, but this would have been only a small percentage of the accumulations over the whole five years. Another factor to be considered is overseas investment, which was of course one-way at this time. British investment in the Middle East was mainly in the oil industry and this was considerable: output in both Iran and Iraq was expanded and there was a massive investment in Kuwait, as well as exploration expenditure in other countries. There was also British investment in a few other industries, such as Sudanese cotton.

The total picture of British economic relations with the Middle East during the first five years after the war is thus a bright one. Imports from the region, especially of oil and cotton, were of great value to the UK and would otherwise have had to have been bought from dollar sources. Earnings from the region, visible plus invisible, seem to have more than paid for these imports. And at the same time Britain had the opportunity to build up valuable investments in the region's oil which would be highly profitable for many years to come.

Technical Assistance

The Middle East Supply Centre (see Chapter 2) came to an end when the wartime conditions which had justified its existence ceased to apply. But there was a strong feeling in well-informed circles in Britain that the good work it had done, for the Middle East countries as well as for the war effort, should be continued in some other form. The Foreign Office thought along these lines, and had ministerial support for its view since Bevin was keen to shift the focus of British aid 'from Pashas to peasants', for political as well as economic reasons.

The outcome was the formation as a British regional organisation of the Middle East Development Division, familiarly known as 'DevDiv'. Based initially in Cairo but later moving to

Beirut, it was staffed with practical men, experienced in such matters as soil improvement, management of water resources, crop selection and vocational training. It performed for decades a low-profile advisory role, at UK expense, for those Middle East countries which chose to ask for its help. Jordan, Iraq, Sudan and Oman were among its principal beneficiaries.

Export Credits Guarantee Department (ECGD)[4]

This Department has played a crucial role in furthering Britain's exports to the Middle East, as to other regions of the world. It was set up as long ago as 1919, as at first a tiny sub-Department of the Department of Overseas Trade. Between the wars it grew in importance, especially after becoming a separate Department in 1930 with its own vote, though still answerable to Parliament through the President of the Board of Trade. It is significant that from the beginning its offices were in the 'Square Mile' of the City of London rather than in Whitehall. From 1928, it gradually opened branch offices around the UK, of which there were six by 1939.

After a false start in export banking, its function was to provide insurance to exporters against losses due to non-payment by overseas customers, usually because of insolvency. It was required by Parliament to operate on a 'commercial' basis, i.e. to charge fees for its services on a scale sufficient to cover its costs and to build up prudent reserves. From 1933, it also offered insurance against 'transfer risk', i.e. the danger that buyers, although solvent and wishing to pay, might be prevented from doing so by exchange controls blocking the transfer of their local currency into sterling. This was a valuable service to exporters, not available from the commercial market, and business grew in consequence. In 1934, ECGD played a leading part in setting up the Berne Union of Credit Insurers as a forum in which it could discuss matters of mutual interest with its equivalents in other countries.

In 1937, Parliament passed an Export Guarantees Act, the first time that the Department's affairs had been the subject of separate legislation. Over the years, a series of such Acts followed, most of them raising the maximum liability up to which ECGD could provide cover. During the war, ECGD accepted that its transfer risk cover should be regarded as covering 'war risk', a considerable benefit to exporters as Germany conquered and occupied more and more countries on the Continent of Europe. This led to its paying out over £4.5 million in claims, with the result that by 31 March 1945 its reserves had slumped to £1.5 million, but they quickly recovered in the early postwar years. ECGD thus emerged from the war with its balance sheet still in the black and its reputation among exporters standing high. It had by now great experience in credit insurance activities, with a range of policies suitable for short-term and medium-term cover.

In 1945, ECGD's maximum liability was raised by Parliament from £75 million to £200 million. It was also authorised to cover trading operations conducted by British residents entirely outside the UK, for example, raw materials bought overseas and sold to a third country without entering Britain. A further Act in 1949 separated its activities into Section 1 and Section 2 business: Section 1 was ordinary business such as it had been conducting hitherto and Section 2 was business 'in the national interest', on which ECGD was advised by a committee of officials from the relevant Whitehall Departments. This flexible provision was of great benefit in allowing ECGD to embark on experimental cover of new kinds; if the experiment succeeded, it could of course then be transferred to Section 1.

The 1949 date is significant; the devaluation of sterling had launched British exporters on a 'dollar drive', and ECGD's first experiment under Section 2 was to give cover for the costs involved to exporters in entering new markets in North America. By 1950, ECGD was insuring over 12 per cent of all UK export business. Separate figures for the Middle East are not available, but there is no reason to suppose that ECGD's activity there was not of this order of magnitude.

Overseas Banking

There were several British Banks operating in the Middle East, only one of them closely linked with a clearing bank. This was Barclays (Dominion Colonial and Overseas), which was strongly based in Palestine and Egypt, with a spillover from the latter into

Sudan and Libya. The heavy expenditure by British forces in the Barclays (DCO) area made it very profitable during the war, but this profitability was likely to decline in peacetime. The Ottoman Bank, despite its name, was a British Bank (though it had some Turkish and French shareholders): it was strong in Iraq and in Transjordan and had branches elsewhere in the former Ottoman territories. The Eastern Bank (which later became a subsidiary of the Chartered Bank) was also strong in Iraq and had a banking monopoly in Bahrain: it was keen to expand in Arab countries.

Most expansionist of all, however, was the Imperial Bank of Iran. This British bank operated, as its name implied, chiefly in Iran, where it was founded as long ago as 1889, but it also had branches in Iraq, both in Baghdad and Basra.[5] Well before the Second World War, its position in Iran was weakened by the foundation of an indigenous bank, the Bank Melli Iran, set up in 1928, and during the war it began to diversify its operations into neighbouring territories. A branch was opened in Kuwait in 1942 (where the Imperial Bank negotiated a 15-year monopoly) and in Bahrain (breaking the Eastern Bank's monopoly there) in 1944. Soon after the war a branch was opened in 1946 in Dubai (with a 20-year monopoly). The Kuwait branch quickly proved to be very profitable because of oil's rapid development in the country after the war; by 1950 it had become the Imperial Bank's main source of profit.[6]

Encouraged by this experience, the Imperial Bank decided to open in Lebanon and Syria, where it was thought that the French banks already operating there might have been weakened by the removal of French political influence. A branch was opened in Beirut in 1946 and in Damascus in 1947; further branches in the two countries were opened in Tripoli (Lebanon) in 1949 and in Aleppo in 1951. The Beirut branch prospered, but the branches in Syria were a disappointment. So was a branch opened in 1949 in Amman, largely because of the competition of the very successful Palestinian-owned Arab Bank, which after 1948 had its headquarters in Jordan. The Kuwait success encouraged the Imperial Bank to expand further in the Arabian Peninsula. A branch was opened in Muscat in 1948 (with a 20-year monopoly) and two branches were opened in Saudi Arabia in 1950, at Al-Khobar and Jedda.

Thus by 1950 the Imperial Bank's centre of activities had shifted decisively from Iran (where branches were by now being closed) to the Arab countries. Inexperience in these countries, and the sheer speed of the expansion, caused the results to be somewhat patchy. Successes in Kuwait, Beirut and ultimately in Muscat were matched by failures, particularly in Syria, but unprofitable branches were kept open because of a policy of a wide presence in the area, with the profits of the successful branches covering the relatively minor losses elsewhere.

5 The Iranian Oil Crisis[1]

The history of the Anglo-Iranian Oil Company (AIOC) dates back to 1901 when William Knox D'Arcy (an Englishman who as a boy had emigrated to Australia with his father, made a fortune there and returned to England) was invited to put money into oil-mining and formed a small syndicate to prospect for oil in Persia, where oil-seepages were known to occur. After protracted negotiations, a 60-year concession was obtained from the Shah, signed on 26 May 1901; royalties were fixed at 16 per cent of profits. With financial support from the much older Burmah Oil Company (encouraged to help by the British Admiralty), D'Arcy's syndicate struck oil on 26 May 1908 in the southern province of Khuzistan and the Anglo-Persian Oil Company (APOC) was incorporated on 14 April 1909. The field, Masjid-i-Sulaiman, proved among the richest then known in the world. A 140-mile pipeline was laid to Abadan, an uninhabited shoal island in the estuary of the Shatt-al-Arab, where a refinery and loading terminal were constructed. The refinery came on stream in 1913, in time for the First World War; a contract for the supply of fuel oil to the Royal Navy was signed in 1914.

This whole enterprise had been an expensive undertaking and it proved necessary to seek the help of another investor, the British Government itself, where the First Lord of the Admiralty, Winston Churchill, had been persuaded of the need to conclude a long-term contract for oil supplies to the Navy. As the counterpart to a favourably priced contract, the Government invested £2,001,000 in Anglo-Persian in return for a 51 per cent shareholding in the company. In 1919, by which time wartime experience had amply justified the involvement, the Government put in another £3 million. (As the sales of this shareholding to the public in recent years have demonstrated, the British Treasury can never have made a more profitable investment.)

For a variety of reasons,[2] relations between Anglo-Persian and the Shah proved distinctly uneasy. Riza Shah was ambitious to modernise his country and to arm it with warships and other expensive weapons systems; he looked to the oil royalties for the means to do so quickly. But 1931 was disastrous for the company's profits as a result of the Depression, so that royalties fell to just over £300,000, not much more than a fifth of their level two years earlier. The Shah, disappointed with the company and angry with his ministers for not having negotiated better terms, decided to put on pressure. He cancelled the concession on 27 November 1932. This was an act of clear illegality and led to a formal complaint by the British Government against Persia in the Council of the League of Nations.

Under the auspices of the League, negotiations were reopened with the Company in Tehran and the outcome was a revised agreement, the 1933 Concession. This had a number of new features. The 16 per cent royalty on profits was replaced by a payment of 4 shillings (£0.20) gold per ton of crude oil, calculated at the official price of gold (a provision which was to lead to later trouble). The Persian Government was also to receive a payment of 20 per cent of the dividends on ordinary shares declared by the company on its worldwide operations, with a guaranteed total annual payment of not less than £1,050,000. In return for an extension of the duration of the concession, the area it covered was reduced to 100,000 square miles. A refinery was to be built by APOC at Kirmanshah. Persian students were to be sent to Britain for technical education at the company's expense. The number of non-Persian employees working for the company in Persia was to be reduced. And to 'sweeten' the whole, a cash payment of £1 million was made to wipe out any other outstanding claims. The chairman of APOC called this 'the fairest concession in the world'[3] and it did in fact endure for eighteen years (as against its theoretical life of sixty years to 1993). The fact remained that a notable precedent had been set; the Shah had unilaterally cancelled a concession and by doing so had won better terms.

Following a change in the official name of the country from Persia to Iran in June 1935, the company's name was changed to Anglo-Iranian Oil Company (AIOC) at the wish of the Shah. By that time it was not entirely appropriate as a title, since the company had important holdings outside Iran, but it was still true that the Khuzistan fields and the Abadan Refinery remained its chief assets. With the Depression easing, oil production in Iran followed an upward course. From 5.75 million tons in 1931 it rose to nearly 10.2 million tons in 1938, outstripping the rate of increase in oil production in the rest of the world. Refinery throughput increased proportionately. What mattered most from the point of view of the Shah was that his revenues from oil rose from just over £1.5 million in 1932 to nearly £4.3 million in 1939. They provided the bulk of the finance for his programme to modernise Iran.

All this changed with the outbreak of the Second World War, which had at first a very different effect from its predecessor. Instead of production being stimulated, it had to be cut back, since the British Government, because of the U-boat menace, decided to concentrate its scarce shipping resources in the Atlantic, drawing oil products from the USA and the Caribbean instead of from more distant Iran. This reduced the Shah's royalties with the result that in July 1940 he again threatened to cancel the concession, but he was persuaded to acquiesce in a fixed royalty of £4 million p.a. until oil exports revived.

The British Government was unhappy about the political situation in Iran. The Germans, who had won the Shah's favour by giving him an important commercial credit before the war, had considerable influence there, and although the Shah had accepted AIOC's £4 million p.a. royalty he had done so reluctantly; it was a great deal less than the unrealistic £14 million p.a. he had demanded, and was less than the royalties he could reasonably have expected had production continued to grow on its prewar trend.

When Hitler invaded Russia in 1941, Churchill of all people

was not likely to overlook the importance of safeguarding Iranian oil from the chronically oil-short Nazis. He joined with Stalin in demanding the expulsion of all Germans from Iran. When the Shah refused, British forces on 25 August 1941 occupied South Iran and Soviet forces moved into North Iran. The Iranians put up some resistance but were hopelessly outmatched and soon had to surrender. On 27 September 1941 Riza Shah abdicated in favour of his 22-year-old eldest son Muhammad Riza; he went into exile in Mauritius and from there to South Africa, where he died in 1944.

Meanwhile AIOC's role in the war effort grew in importance. Not only was Iran now a crucial route for supplies to the Soviet Union, but after Japan attacked the USA on 7 December 1941 and went on to overrun most of South-East Asia, Abadan became the major source of petroleum products to sustain the Allied war effort in India and the Pacific. AIOC's labour force in Khuzistan more than doubled, from 32000 to 68000, with the company (helped by the Middle East Supply Centre in Cairo) having to meet their needs for housing, food and all requirements. Abadan was developed into a ship-repair centre. A major plant for the production of 100-octane aviation spirit was built; this proved invaluable for wartime supplies to all the Allies, including the Soviet Union. In 1945, oil production in Iran was 19.2 million tons, well above the prewar peak of 10.2 million tons.

One other wartime development deserves mention. AIOC's concession area had never included the five northern provinces of Iran and the company had relinquished a large part of its holdings in the rest of the country under the 1933 Agreement. There was therefore room available for other companies to seek concessions. In 1943 there were tentative approaches from Shell and from two American companies, although these came to nothing. More seriously, strong pressure for a concession in the north was mounted by the Soviet Union in the second half of 1944. When the issue went to the Majlis (the Iranian Parliament) in December 1944, nationalist sentiment led to the passage of a Bill prohibiting negotiations for the letting of any oil concession to foreigners. The mover of the Bill was a Dr Muhammad Musaddiq.

This brief account of prewar and wartime developments has

been provided to give some understanding of the background to the 1951 crisis which confronted AIOC. The British Government had incurred odium for its invasion of Iran, with the Company, however unfairly, being seen as its agent. And independently of that, among the not very numerous but nevertheless influential nationalist groups in Tehran, there was resentment against it as a foreign presence.

Iran's first postwar oil crisis was not with AIOC but with the continuing Soviet demand for a concession in the northern provinces. Soviet troops had not left the country within 6 months of the end of the war as had been promised (parallel to a British and American evacuation of the south). Under their protection, an autonomous regime had been established in the Iranian province of Azerbaijan, virtually a Communist Republic. The Iranian Government's first priority was to get rid of Soviet troops and to achieve that it was prepared to compromise over an oil concession. On 4 April 1946, an agreement was signed in Tehran granting a concession to a company 51 per cent-owned by the Soviet Government. However, the concession was subject to ratification by the Majlis under the law passed in 1944 on the instance of Dr Musaddiq. By the time it came to the Majlis on 22 October 1946 the situation in Azerbaijan had changed. Soviet troops had at last gone and the Iranian Government had taken vigorous action to suppress the autonomous regime and restore central authority. The concession was rejected in the Majlis by 102 votes to 2.

At the same time a law was passed laying down a national oil policy. It provided that:

(a) The negotiations with the Soviet Union regarding an oil concession were null and void.

(b) Henceforth, no concessions were to be granted to foreign countries nor would foreign partners be used in exploration for oil.

(c) Iran would alone finance and carry out its own exploration programme; if this resulted in commercial finds within five years, the Government might negotiate an agreement for the sale of oil to the Soviet Union.

(d) The Government was to negotiate with existing concessionaires'to protect the national rights'. (This was perhaps a trade-off for the move against the Soviet Union rather than a threat to the 1933 Agreement; certainly the Iranian Prime Minister denied to the British Ambassador[4] that there was any intention to revoke the concession. Nevertheless, it was a phrase with an ominous ring to it.)

Soundings for a revision of the 1933 Agreement did in fact open, rather tentatively, in 1947. Postwar oil production in Iran had been moving up, from 19.2 million tons in 1945 to nearly 20.2 million in 1946 and on its way towards 24.9 million in 1947, but there was as yet no certainty that this trend would continue. (What ensured that it did so was the Marshall Plan for the rebuilding of the economies of Europe: financially, that plan was fuelled by US dollars, but physically by Iranian and Saudi oil.) Meanwhile, AIOC was hesitant about how far it could safely go to improve the level of payments to Iran.

Real negotiations did not get under way until the autumn of 1948. They were then wide-ranging, with complaints on the Iranian side against almost every aspect of the company's commercial and employment policies. One point of particular bitterness was in fact beyond AIOC's control. As part of the austerity programme of Britain's 1948 Budget, a freeze on dividend payments had been declared, and although the company had asked for an exemption because of its 20 per cent dividend obligation to the Shah, this had been refused. The payment to Iran from the dividend declared on the profits for 1947 was therefore pegged to that for the much less productive year 1946. It is true that the unpaid dividend went to general reserve, in which the Iranian Government had in effect a 20 per cent interest. But that was a rather sophisticated point and to the Iranian negotiators the delay in payment seemed unreasonable.

The Iranian economy was as usual under considerable pressure. An ambitious Seven-Year Plan had been drawn up for the period 1949–56 and oil royalties were the only conceivable way to finance it. The advisers to the Plan were American and they were not slow to criticise AIOC. The Plan was essentially a long-term programme, providing for heavy expenditure on infrastructure and on social improvements, for example, in education. It was therefore not likely to produce short-term economic gains, but these were just what the Iranian people, and probably the Majlis, expected from it.

Two new complaints had emerged on the Iranian side. The first was that Venezuela had negotiated an oil concession agreement giving it a 50/50 share in profits, and the Iranians saw no reason why they should not have the same. This was an idea which Bevin had much earlier put privately to AIOC,[5] but the company had not felt able to go along with it. One difficulty about it, which AIOC now explained to the Iranians, was that the Venezuelan concessionaire was a subsidiary company set up to work that particular concession, whereas AIOC was a world-wide company with no separate subsidiary for its Iranian operations. It was, the negotiators pointed out, illogical that the company should pay to Iran 50 per cent of its profits earned, for instance, from Kuwaiti oil, and certain that the Ruler of Kuwait would have the gravest objection to such an arrangement.

The other complaint was over the gold price used to calculate AIOC's tonnage royalties. This was stipulated in the 1933 Agreement to be the official price of gold, which postwar meant the price used by the IMF, but the market value of gold was much higher in the bazaars of Tehran than in New York or London. Altogether, the Iranians felt they were being cheated, both over their royalty income and over their dividend-related receipts.

Despite all these problems, AIOC did eventually succeed in negotiating a package of offers, which on legal advice was presented as a Supplemental Agreement so as not to call in question the validity of the existing 1933 Agreement. The company's representative and the Iranian Minister of Finance signed the Supplemental Agreement on 17 July 1949. It provided for very substantially increased royalty payments, backdated to 1947, and for a guaranteed minimum of £2.5 million p.a. in respect of dividends and allocations to the company's general reserve.

The Supplemental Agreement was submitted for ratification by the Majlis. This had not been achieved by 30 July 1949 when the Majlis session ended, and the devaluation of sterling in September of that year did nothing for the standing of Britain. In Iran there was political controversy over the Shah's role in the reform programme, which was disliked both by influential landowners and by the very conservative religious leaders, always fearful that modernisation would lead to impiety. Two Iranian Prime Ministers hesitated to commend the Supplemental Agreement to the Majlis.[6] The arrival in Tehran of a new American Ambassador with a dislike for Britain complicated matters further. An Oil Committee of the Majlis was chaired by Dr Musaddiq and his nationalism led him to find fault with the Supplemental Agreement, ignoring the fact that its ratification would bring Iran a massive payment of £50 million; in December the Oil Committee rejected it. The final blow to its chances came when ARAMCO reached a 50/50 profit-sharing agreement with the Saudi Government, announced at the end of December. On 20 March 1951 the Majlis approved a recommendation from the Oil Committee for nationalisation of AIOC; on 28 April it passed a Bill to implement this nationalisation and on the same day Musaddiq was appointed Prime Minister.

It is worth interrupting the flow of events in Iran here to look briefly at ARAMCO's 50/50 agreement. Although following the Venezuelan precedent, it was of historic importance as being the first such agreement in the Middle East, and it at once set a benchmark for all future concession agreements there. The paradoxical feature of it is that it cost ARAMCO, or rather its American owners, precisely nothing. There were two reasons for this surprising situation. The first, which has already been mentioned, was that ARAMCO was a one-country subsidiary, all of whose profits came from operations in Saudi Arabia. The second and crucial point was that its parent companies benefited from American tax law, under which taxes paid to a foreign country could be deducted from US tax liabilities. The result was that ARAMCO in effect paid the Saudi Government out of the pockets of the American tax-payer, with no reduction in profits to its owners.

Neither of these advantages applied to AIOC. It could, and probably should, have reorganised its company structure to bring into being an Iranian subsidiary, although that would have involved replacing, and not merely supplementing, its 1933 Concession Agreement. But it did not have the power to change the British tax system to its own advantage. A 50/50 agreement in Iran would therefore have been expensive to it in a way which it was not to ARAMCO in Saudi Arabia.[7]

The nationalisation of AIOC posed grave problems for the British Government. It had, after all, itself been carrying out a long series of nationalisations in Britain, so it could hardly object to the principle. On the other hand, Morrison, who had moved from Home Secretary to Foreign Secretary to replace Bevin, knew that the British public would be outraged by any display of apparent weakness in the face of Iranian high-handedness, and that this would adversely affect the Labour Party's election prospects. He was in regular touch with the US Government, whose thinking was dominated by a fear of driving Iran into the arms of the Soviet Union and who, having no American interests directly at stake, tended to counsel surrender. Several American mediators went out to Tehran, urging a variety of compromises, but made no progress with Musaddiq, who had no conception of the practical problems he faced in running an oil industry on which he had never even set eyes.

Morrison had the Navy send a cruiser, HMS *Mauritius*, to lie off Abadan, but it had orders merely to stand by in case British lives became at risk. Its inactivity (however high-principled) lowered British prestige even further in the eyes of the Iranians (and of other spectators of the crisis). On 25 September 1951, Musaddiq ordered all British staff of AIOC out of the country by 4 October and they were evacuated peacefully by that deadline.[8]

Legal steps taken by the British Government to resolve the dispute got nowhere. On 22 June 1951, it had applied to the International Court of Justice for an interim injunction to protect British rights in Iran, which it obtained on 9 July 1951, but the Iranian Government refused to accept the Court's jurisdiction in the matter. At the end of September HMG took the issue to the UN Security Council. Musaddiq declared that body also to be disqualified from dealing with what for Iran was a matter of national sovereignty, but said that he would go to New York to set out the Iranian position. The US Government seized on his presence in the USA as an opportunity to negotiate a settlement and intensive talks were held with him in October and November, parallel with Anglo-American talks in Paris.[9] But all the talking led to no solution. Musaddiq returned to Tehran on 25 November 1951, as inflexible as ever.

As many intermediaries had fruitlessly warned Musaddiq, the economic consequences of his nationalisation measure were very serious. Iran had a few oil technicians (trained by the now denigrated AIOC) but nothing like enough in numbers or experience to operate the oilfields and particularly the Abadan Refinery at normal levels. Nor was the production, nor even the refining, of crude oil sufficient; the products had to be got to market, requiring a tanker fleet and a distribution network which Iran wholly lacked. AIOC's major competitors were not prepared to buy oil from a nationaliser, for fear of the precedent set for their own concessions, and such independents as might have been ready to consider doing so were threatened by AIOC with legal action against them anywhere in the world for dealing in stolen oil. For the most part the threat was sufficient, and during the whole of the conflict the company had to bring only two suits to impound cargoes of Iranian oil.[10] Musaddiq lost revenues of perhaps £60 million p.a. and brought his country into a serious foreign exchange crisis.

For its part, AIOC seemed hardly to suffer at all financially from the denial to it of its largest oilfields and its principal refinery (though there was certainly great disruption in its trading patterns and enormous efforts had to be made to rectify matters). By now AIOC's name was certainly a misnomer, since it had plenty of other available sources of crude.[11] Additional liftings were made from Iraq and production in both Kuwait and Qatar was stepped up rapidly; Kuwaiti oil proved to be particularly plentiful and even cheaper to produce than Iranian oil, being so located and under such natural pressure as to flow through quite short pipelines to waiting tankers without need for pumping. The company's profits remained very sound and higher dividends were paid once the Government freeze on them was lifted.

Musaddiq, though still a popular hero, became increasingly discredited in Iran among politicians, merchants and with the army. The Seven-Year Plan was in ruins. In August 1953, fifty members of the Majlis resigned, and the Shah issued a *firman* (decree) replacing Musaddiq as Prime Minister. But when he refused to leave office, an order for his arrest could not be implemented. Instead, it was the Shah who had to flee abroad in his private plane, perhaps as a calculated tactical ploy though it was clearly a humiliating one. Musaddiq had quarrelled with the religious leaders and under their influence the popular mood in Tehran suddenly changed. Loyalty to the Shah reasserted itself and the army acted decisively, taking control of Government buildings and arresting Musaddiq, this time without difficulty.[12] After a two-day absence the Shah returned, to popular acclaim.

These dramatic events have not lacked highly-coloured explanations. There have been sufficient well-informed leaks to make it clear that the American Central Intelligence Agency, with cooperation from the British Intelligence Service, was by this time working for Musaddiq's downfall, fearing that by ruining the economy of Iran he would open the way for a coup by the (Communist) Tudeh Party, with Soviet backing.[13] The Cold War was after all at about its coldest. There is no doubt that CIA machinations played their part in Musaddiq's downfall. But short of assassination, it is unlikely that the CIA could have rid themselves of him if he had not played into their hands by losing the support of his associates and by his ignorance of, and indeed contempt for, the hard facts of economic realities.

With Musaddiq gone from office and the Shah restored, it was time to pick up the pieces and get the Iranian oil industry back to work. There were severe problems to be overcome. Other countries had profited from Iranian absence from the market and would look askance at any attempt now to cut back their production for Iran's benefit. Some way had to be found to spread exports of Iranian oil over the world market without any too obvious loser in the process. This could not be done in an acceptable space of time by AIOC alone, and in any case the company could see that the restoration of its pre-crisis position was now politically inconceivable. The only answer was a Consortium, made up of major companies with the ability to adjust production in both the Western and the Eastern Hemispheres.[14]

AIOC at first aimed for a 50 per cent share in ownership, but had to lower its sights to 40 per cent. The shareholdings eventually agreed were:

AIOC (soon renamed British Petroleum)	40%
Royal Dutch Shell Group	14%
Standard Oil (New Jersey)	7%
Standard Oil of California	7%
Mobil Oil Company	7%
Texas Oil Company	7%
Gulf Oil Corporation	7%
Compagnie Française des Pétroles	6%
Iricon Group (7 US companies)	5%

As Dr Penrose has pointed out,[15] AIOC's 40 per cent, although a minority holding, gave the company a decisive voice in negotiations within the Consortium on the annual liftings programme. AIOC was also to be paid £25 million in compensation for its losses (phased over 10 years from 1957). Under a new Concession Agreement concluded on 19 September 1954, valid for 25 years, Iran was to receive 50 per cent of the Consortium's profits on exports of Iranian oil. The National Iranian Oil Company (set up on 24 May 1951 to take over the assets and installations of AIOC) would exploit all oil production outside the Consortium's 'Agreement Area'. It would also run for the Consortium all the ancillary services formerly provided for its employees by AIOC – housing, hospitals, training centres etc. This new Agreement came into operation on 29 October 1954, and AIOC changed its name in December 1954 to The British Petroleum Company. It was very much the end of a chapter and the beginning of a new one, both for the company and for Iran.[16]

6 Arms Exports Policy 1945–55

Prior to the Second World War, it was taken for granted that Britain, the 'Workshop of the World' as it had been called nearly a century before, would meet all its weapons requirements from domestic production. Even when, during the war, British forces were equipped with American destroyers and tanks and aircraft to supplement British products, that was regarded as a temporary aberration. With the return of peace (and the ending of Lend-Lease), industry in the UK faced the welcome task of reequipping the Royal Navy, the Army and the Royal Air Force with their smaller but still sizeable peacetime needs.

There was however a problem of costs. Technology had made considerable strides as the war progressed and weapons systems had become more sophisticated. Inevitably that meant that they were more expensive. The costs of research and development, and of tooling up for production, were high relative to the size of the production runs required for purely British needs. That problem could be solved by export orders to extend production runs and so reduce unit costs.

Another relevant factor was the second-hand market. When equipment in the British forces was replaced by more modern systems, the obsolete items could often be sold to states arming themselves against local enemies who were not major powers. This applied particularly to large items such as warships and tanks, where the most up-to-date equipment was likely to be prohibitively expensive for all but rich countries. The prices obtainable were often very far above scrap value, so offsetting a useful part of Britain's rearmament costs. Moreover, particularly in the case of warships, the new owner was likely to place with British shipyards orders for their refitting, which could provide months of lucrative work for the yards in question.

The UK had traditionally supplied many of the weapons needs of the British Commonwealth (producing the useful spin-off of compatibility of systems when Commonwealth countries rallied to Britain's help in time of war). It was reasonable to assume that for the most part this would continue to be true. Certainly American arms had been supplied under Lend-Lease arrangements to Commonwealth forces, and they may have liked what they got, but with a few exceptions such as Canada their Governments were short of dollars. German and Japanese armament factories were being dismantled under the peace settlements. French industry had been damaged by the war and would take a little time to recover. There was therefore a promising market worldwide for British arms manufacturers.

This most certainly included the Middle East. Britain had been the leading Allied power in the Middle East Command area during the war and ended it with great military prestige. Such local forces as existed were in many countries British-trained and British-armed. (The main exceptions were the French territories of North Africa and to a lesser extent the ex-French Levant States. But even there Syria and Lebanon had witnessed the expulsion of French forces from Syria by the British in 1945 and had drawn the lesson that French arms had been distinctly inferior to British, notably in respect of tanks, armoured cars and aircraft. As newly independent countries, they felt the need to build up new forces, both for defence and for ceremonial purposes.) All these countries were short of dollars, and it soon became clear that it would not be easy to persuade Britain to release to them as many dollars as they would like in exchange for the sterling balances that some of them had built up during the war. They therefore had every incentive to look to British firms for their arms requirements.

The Palestine War of 1948 brought new urgencies. The Arab armies were humiliated, with the partial exception of the Arab Legion of Transjordan which, more than any of the others, was British-trained and British-armed. In defeat, they clamoured for better weapons with which to obtain their revenge when, as all expected, the war was resumed. Israel, for its part, had mounted a clandestine arms purchase operation to supply its nascent forces, which were equipped with weapons, new and second-hand, from wherever they could be bought (including, interestingly in the light of later events in Egypt, from Czechoslovakia). They knew that they must give their defence forces an absolute priority and, unlike most of the Arabs, they had dollars (donated by American Jewry or given as aid by the US Government) to purchase arms. They were therefore likely to seek US weapons, and indeed to use the powerful lobby they possessed in the USA to get them free or on easy credit terms. But they were, as a matter of life or death for their new State, determined to have the best weapons systems available, and where they judged that British were best they would buy British. They had sterling balances, inherited from the Palestine settlement, which they could use for the purpose. And there were sterling donations from British Jewry, averaging over £2 million a year.

The Middle East, and especially the States bordering Israel, thus provided a most promising market for British arms salesmen. But there were political constraints. The United Nations, having played a major part in the armistice negotiations which ended the 1948 fighting, and having set up UNRWA to care for the Palestinian refugees, had hopes of peace settlements to resolve the problem and looked with disfavour on any arms sales likely to lead to a new Arab-Israel war. The UK and US Governments shared these sentiments and were permanent members of the UN Security Council charged with the preservation of peace. So was France, whose armament factories were eager to get back into full production. At a Security Council meeting on 4 August 1949, when it was proposed that the arms embargo on sales to the Middle East should be lifted in view of the conclusion of armistice agreements between Israel and her neighbours, the delegates of the UK and USA coupled support for this recommendation with pleas for the avoidance of an arms race in the area.

These pleas turned out to be more than the pious aspirations regularly mouthed at UN meetings. Following a meeting of Foreign Ministers in London, the Governments of the UK, USA and France on 25 May 1950 made a joint declaration on the subject of peace and stability in the Middle East, in which they bound themselves to conditions for the supply of arms to the area. In the statement, they recognised that the Arab States and Israel all needed to maintain a certain level of armed forces for self-defence and internal security, and to play their part in the defence of the area as a whole. They would consider all applications for arms or war material for these countries in the light of these principles. Moreover, they declared their unalterable opposition to the use of force or threat of force between the States in the area. Should they find that any of these States was preparing to violate frontiers or armistice lines, the three Governments would immediately take action, both within and outside the UN, to prevent such violation.

This was strong language, by any standards. Indeed, it would return to haunt some of the parties to the statement. But meanwhile it provided a real contribution to the avoidance of conflict in the area and at the same time alleviated some tension that had been growing up between Britain and the United States about their respective arms supplies to the Middle East. The UK had treaty obligations to Jordan and Iraq, under which those countries had a right to look to Britain not only for ultimate protection should they be attacked but also for help in training and equipping their armed forces. The USA for its part had become Israel's guarantor and its principal arms supplier. The Tripartite Declaration, as it came to be known, meant that the two countries henceforth would consult together about the scale of such supplies and would have a right to object to excessive supplies which might upset the military balance in the area.

On the whole, this system worked as a market-sharing agreement. Under it, Britain supplied Egypt, Jordan and Iraq, with some sales to Israel; the USA supplied Israel and to a lesser extent Egypt; France was largely left to supply Syria and Lebanon, but also began to build up Israeli interest in French weapons systems. All three countries profited pretty well from the arrangements, Britain perhaps most of all. But there was some constraint on arms purchases by the Middle East states resulting from the operation of the Tripartite Declaration.

Britain also had outlets for arms sales in Sudan and Libya, and to a small extent in the mini-states fringing the Arabian Peninsula such as Kuwait and Oman. Iran was a major market, open to all sellers, with the UK winning a reasonable share once relations were rebuilt after the Musaddiq episode.

Statistics for arms sales are virtually impossible to come by,[1] but there is no doubt that arms sales to the Middle East were (as they still are) of considerable economic importance to Britain. Arms sales are lucrative affairs, with political side-benefits. However, in 1955 the cosy system set up by the Tripartite Declaration began to crumble,[2] when Egyptian discontent with the scale of British supplies opened the market to a new supplier, the Soviet Union. From that time on, an arms race in the Middle East really got under way and cooperation between the Western producers in limiting the scale of their supplies was virtually extinguished. The nature of British sales will be indicated, to the extent possible, in subsequent chapters dealing with trade statistics.

7 The Egyptian Revolution

On the night of 22/23 July 1952, a group of middle-ranking army officers, led by Lieutenant-Colonel Gamal Abdul Nasser Hussein, seized Cairo and overthrew the Egyptian monarchy in an all but bloodless coup.[1] At a late stage before making their move they had secured the support of a popular senior officer, Major-General Mohammed Neguib, to head their rebellion, but he had played little real part in the plotting that preceded it.[2] King Farouk, summering in Alexandria, was persuaded to abdicate on 26 July, in theory in favour of his infant son, but this was no more than a polite fiction[3] and power resided with the 'Free Officers', who formed themselves into a Revolutionary Command Council (RCC).

On 10 December 1952 the Egyptian Constitution was abrogated and in January 1953 political parties were dissolved. On 10 February 1953 General Neguib assumed supreme power as 'Leader of the Revolution' and on 18 June 1953 Egypt was declared a Republic, with Neguib as its President and Prime Minister. Abdul Nasser was appointed Vice Prime Minister and Minister of the Interior.[4]

Perhaps to the surprise of the other members of the RCC, Neguib was not content to be a figurehead and a struggle for power developed between him and Nasser. After some seesawing between them from February 1954 onwards, Neguib was finally ousted on 14 November 1954 and placed under house arrest for the remainder of his life. From then until 28 September 1970, Nasser was the undisputed ruler of Egypt.

The Free Officers had some clear political aims, to sweep away the monarchy and the political parties, and to rid Egypt of British troops, but they came into power with no thought-through programme for economic reform. They intended to eliminate corruption, which they associated with the system of political parties, and they had a general aspiration towards greater social and economic equality. But Egypt suffers from chronic over-population, with a perpetual need to alleviate the poverty this entails and to provide employment for an ever-growing labour force. Economic measures were therefore soon found to be an urgent need. The obvious starting-point was land reform and the RCC acted quickly to decree their first law on this subject in September 1952, only six weeks after seizing power.

As Robert Mabro has pointed out,[5] the real agricultural revolution in Egypt had come in the nineteenth century. It was in the 1820s that the introduction of long-staple cotton as a cash crop turned Egypt into an export-based economy. It necessitated extensive irrigation works, both to extend the land under cultivation and to permit perennial irrigation of as large an area as possible, to obtain more than one crop a year. This favoured large land-holdings owned by those wealthy enough to pay for efficient irrigation and drainage works and for the chemical fertilisers needed to maximise yields. Prior to the 1952 land reform law, some 2000 owners held nearly 20 per cent of the total cultivable area while at the other end of the scale there were estimated to be 1,300,000 families of landless peasants.

The new law fixed 200 feddans (1 feddan = 1.038 acres = 4200.8 m^2) as the maximum permitted holding for an individual, although landowners could transfer another 100 feddans to their children. Owners could choose which part of their estates to retain within these limits and could sell small-holdings of not more than five feddans each to their tenants (much of the land in question had been leased out). Land in excess of the maximum holdings would be requisitioned within five years for redistribution in small lots of two to five feddans. Compensation would be paid at a multiple of seventy times the land tax, in non-negotiable bonds bearing 3 per cent interest and redeemable in 30 years time. Priorities were fixed for selection of the redistribution beneficiaries and obligations were imposed upon them to join a cooperative and to pay annual charges to the Agrarian Reform Authority. The cooperatives would discharge some of the functions previously assumed by the landlords, such as provision of credits, maintenance of pumps and other fixed equipment, and marketing of the crops. (In 1953 the estates of the Royal Family were, exceptionally, confiscated without compensation.)

This law was not a savage measure. Given the profitability of prime land under perennial irrigation, a family holding of 300 feddans in all, with two crops a year, represented a very comfortable income. Nor was it economically disastrous, as land reforms have been in some other countries. The compulsory membership of cooperatives ensured finance and a degree of efficient management for the new smallholders. There was at first some loss of output, mainly because of persistent time lags between expropriation and redistribution, but it was less than might have been expected. When the new system settled down, production actually increased, though not enormously.

The RCC also aimed at land reclamation. The Tahrir Province project (Tahrir means Liberation) was started in 1953, to irrigate a desert area along the western fringe of the Nile Delta, using sprinkler systems to conserve water, with model housing units for the peasants moved there. Although it became a show area,[6] it was not very popular with its inhabitants, who chafed at the Government-imposed restraints under which they had to live, and it was never able to earn a favourable return on the capital invested in it.

A much larger project, which had been studied even before the Revolution, was for the building of a new High Dam at Aswan near the Sudanese border to replace the British-engineered dam already in use there. This would be a multi-purpose undertaking, designed not only to supply water for agriculture but also huge amounts of cheap electricity to stimulate the rather meagre industrial sector. It would at the same time greatly simplify flood control, improve navigation on the river and provide new fishing grounds in the large lake which would fill up behind it.

Against these considerable benefits had to be set environmental problems, the need to rehouse Nubian inhabitants of the area to be flooded both in Egypt and the Sudan, and the difficulties of financing a project with enormous immediate costs (for irrigation works, land reclamation and industry, as well as for the dam itself) and a rather slow pay-back. It would also require Sudanese agreement and that in itself ruled it out as an immediate prospect, since the future of the Sudan was one of the two major problems outstanding between Egypt and Britain (the other, already mentioned, being the presence of British troops in Egypt).

Meanwhile, there were possibilities of expansion of industry even without the High Dam. The RCC was from its early days eager to diversify the Egyptian economy. In 1952, by Decree No.213, it established a Permanent Council for the Development of National Production, which later became a Planning Commission. The Council selected two areas for new industries, Helwan in Lower Egypt for the construction of a steel mill and of a factory for the building of railway wagons, and Aswan in Upper Egypt for a fertiliser plant and the completion of a hydro-electric power station already started there. In 1953, private firms were encouraged to set up factories for the manufacture of electric cables and of tyres and tubes, the inducement being a promise of contracts to supply all the requirements of the public services. A Mining Law was passed to stimulate oil exploration by foreign companies and aroused some interest among them; in 1954 Coronada Oil took a concession in the Western Desert. In that year too, work started on the enlargement of an existing oil refinery at Suez and on the building of two new refineries.

In March 1955, a National Planning Committee at Ministerial level was charged with the task of 'drafting a national comprehensive plan for social and economic development'. This was the first time that a comprehensive plan had been talked of, and it marked a significant step from a mixed towards a centrally planned economy in Egypt. However, the Committee was soon distracted from its task by major political developments and it was not until 1960 that the first Five-Year Plan came into being. Before then those developments had greatly affected the economic climate.

Egypt's international political relations at the time of the Revolution revolved around the Arab League, of which it was the leading member, and its two disputes with Britain, on Sudan and the Canal Zone Base.[7] The Sudan issue was the first to be resolved. Theoretically an Anglo-Egyptian Condominium, the country was in practice under British administration. The removal of the Egyptian monarchy by the Revolution simplified the issue by setting aside Farouk's claim to be King of Sudan as well as of Egypt. On 12 February 1953, after an understanding had been reached between Egypt and the Sudanese political parties, the British and Egyptian Governments agreed that British control of Sudan would end, with the Sudanese having the choice between independence and union with Egypt. The prospect of their making the latter choice diminished in 1954 with Nasser's ousting of Neguib, himself half-Sudanese and popular in Sudan. Although one of the two main political parties there was pro-Egyptian, it was not really surprising that the final decision went against union. After a transition period, Sudan was proclaimed an independent Republic on 1 January 1956.

The Canal Zone Base was a more difficult problem. Britain under Attlee's Labour Government had not been averse to withdrawing its troops from Egypt (both Dalton and Cripps as Chancellors of the Exchequer saw this as a desirable way of reducing foreign expenditure), but the Cold War bedevilled the issue. Bevin was determined not to leave a military vacuum in the Middle East into which the Soviet Union, neighbouring the area, might expand. At first, Palestine seemed a possible alternative site for a base, but the termination of the Mandate ended dreams of that kind. Bevin negotiated from time to time with Egyptian representatives for cancellation of the 1936 Treaty which allowed Britain to station troops in Egypt, but he always insisted upon a replacement treaty which would give British troops the right to return to Egypt in the event of a Soviet threat, not only to Egypt itself but to any part of the Middle East. That demand, and under the Egyptian monarchy the Sudan issue, made Bevin's negotiations fruitless.

With Egypt a Republic, and agreement reached between Egypt and Britain on a Sudan settlement, the way was open for a serious renewal of negotiations on the Canal Base. The RCC put pressure on the Base by keeping it virtually under seige, with the local authorities denying it facilities and the perimeters of the Base installations under constant threat of infiltration by marauders. As a result, guard duties increased and the number of troops there went on rising. Eventually there were nearly 80,000 men merely ensuring their own survival, with no opportunities for operational training or recreation outside the camp limits. It is hardly surprising that service in the Canal Zone was extremely unpopular. A few servicemen who strayed outside the military zones were kidnapped by Egyptian intelligence officers, though they came eventually to no harm.[8] What made the situation especially intolerable to the British Army chiefs in Whitehall was that plans were being mooted for the ending of conscription in Britain and the reorganisation of the Armed Services on a professional basis. For this, termination of the swollen military commitment to the guarding of the Canal Zone Base was an absolute prerequisite.[9]

The RCC, and most of all Nasser personally, were dedicated to the objective of removing British troops from Egypt. They felt the presence of a foreign army as a deep national humiliation. Negotiations had their ups and downs,[10] but finally an ingenious plan found favour with Nasser and hence with his loyal supporters. This was that a slimmed-down Base should be run by British (or Egyptian) civilian firms under contract to HMG, installations not required being handed over to the Egyptian forces free of charge. There would be provision for the return of British troops to the Base in the event of an attack on an Arab country or Turkey by an outside power and for consultations in the event of a threat of such an attack. Heads of Agreement to this effect were initialled in Cairo on 27 July 1954.

The process of converting the Heads of Agreement into a full-scale Treaty went fairly smoothly, and signature took place on 19 October 1954. Anthony Nutting, newly promoted Minister of State at the Foreign Office, went to Cairo to sign for the UK. The 20-month period of implementation of the Treaty's provisions also proceeded well.[11] The GHQ buildings of the British Middle East Command were handed over to the Egyptians on 20 November 1955 following the transfer of GHQ to Cyprus. The last British troops sailed from Egypt on 31 March 1956 and the last RAF personnel flew out on 14 April 1956. The Base installations were left in the hands of some 800 British civilian technicians.[12] Had this experiment proved successful, who knows what it might have led to in the civilianisation of military bases elsewhere? Unfortunately, that possibility was very rapidly to be overtaken by the onrush of events unforeseen at the time, which will be the subject of Chapter 10 below.

8 The Buraimi Dispute

When King Abdul Aziz (popularly known as Ibn Saud) died on 9 November 1953 after a long and successful reign, he left his family rich in sons and his country rich in oil. He also left his Kingdom in dispute over possession of a strategic oasis named Buraimi.[1]

There is no rule of primogeniture among Muslim Arabs. When the head of a shaikhly family dies, the family chooses his successor from within its ranks. Similarly, if a family does not like the way its head is conducting its affairs, it can by family consensus depose him and replace him by another member of the family. This sensible procedure derives from the days of tribal warfare (which in 1953 was not long in the past in the Arabian Peninsula), when an effective leader was vital to the tribe's survival. Respect is always due to the oldest male family member even if he does not wish to take the responsibility of becoming its head or if it is decided to pass him over for a younger and abler man, a decision which brings him no disgrace (although it may incur his displeasure).

However, in this case Abdul Aziz was in fact succeeded as King by his eldest surviving son, Saud. It was a mistake. The second oldest surviving son, Faisal, had proved his ability both in war (with Yemen) and in peacetime occupations, including the conduct of international relations, and would have been a worthier monarch. He was given the consolation prize of being named as heir apparent or Crown Prince, not a traditional Arab practice but one that was beginning to be regarded as sensible in the case of a ruling house.

Mention has already been made in earlier chapters of ARAMCO, a consortium of leading United States oil companies, as the holder of the oil concession for Saudi Arabia. The concession agreement was signed on 29 May 1933[2] and oil was struck in commercial quantities at Dammam on 5 March 1938. A beginning was made of oil shipments by barge to the refinery on Bahrain (under the same ultimate American ownership) in the autumn of that year, but export really got under way in May 1939 when the first tanker was loaded at an oil terminal built at Ras Tanura, to which a pipeline had been constructed. Additional fields of great potential were soon discovered, all in the Kingdom's eastern province of Hasa, but their development was delayed by World War II. However, despite the war, a refinery was built at Ras Tanura and came on stream in September 1945. After the war, output began to grow rapidly, reaching over 0.5 million barrels a day by 1950 and nearly 1.25 million barrels a day a decade later.

As already recounted in Chapter 2, the multinational but London-based consortium IPC held concessions in Qatar, Abu Dhabi and Oman and had struck oil in Qatar before the war. By the early 1950s, exploration by an IPC subidiary was under way in Abu Dhabi and was planned for Oman. These two countries bordered Saudi Arabia and the precise frontiers, a concept alien to the thinking of nomadic tribesmen, had never been clearly demarcated. Neither Abdul Aziz nor ARAMCO was slow to realise that it could be to their advantage for them to be fixed as far east and south as possible. Moreover, there was a fluid political situation inside Oman, where the Imam of Oman was claiming secular as well as religious authority over the interior of what was then known as the Sultanate of Muscat and Oman, and had won the support of Cairo Radio for his claims. If the Imam could turn the interior of the Sultanate into an independent state, and if this came under Saudi influence, then ARAMCO might secure a concession for part of what was now an IPC area.

The key to these hopes was the Oasis of Buraimi, not so much because there might be oil in the area of the Oasis itself (though that would be a bonus) but because it was the only watering place in the region and hence controlled important caravan routes, including a crucial supply route from the Saudis to the Imam's domain. With all these factors in mind, King Abdul Aziz, to the delight of ARAMCO, sent a former governor of Ras Tanura, Turki bin Utaishan, with forty armed retainers to occupy Buraimi[3] in 1952.

This brought British authority into question. In the nineteenth century the (British) Government of Bombay had set about the suppression of piracy in the Persian Gulf (as it was then called by all geographers). Thanks to the ingenuity of a brilliant British Resident in the Gulf, Samuel Hennel, combined with his possession of a cruiser squadron to reinforce his persuasion, the Arab Shaikhs of what was then rightly known as the Pirate Coast (the chief pirates being the Qawasim of Ras al Khaimah and Sharjah and the Bani Yas of Abu Dhabi) had been induced to enter into a series of maritime truces, which had eventually become perpetual, after which the south coast of the Gulf had been renamed the Trucial Coast.[4] In the course of time this had developed into a system under which the Shaikhs were autonomous in internal affairs, but their defence and foreign policy were conducted for them by the British Government. The Shaikhdoms thus ranked in international law as 'protected states'.

The Buraimi Oasis consisted of nine villages, six of which in the British view belonged to Abu Dhabi and the other three (including the village of Buraimi itself) to Oman. Shaikh Shakhbut of Abu Dhabi could therefore demand help from Britain in defending his villages, one of which was his own dearly loved birthplace, Al Ain. Oman was outside the Trucial Coast and was in law totally independent of the UK, but British Indian support had been given to the Sultanate in the nineteenth century to maintain its stability and there was a current Treaty of Friendship and Commerce between the two Governments. It was therefore not surprising when Sultan Said bin Taimur also asked for British help against the Saudis.

Britain at first restrained the Sultan from taking forceful action of his own to expel Turki, who had based himself in one of the Sultan's villages. With hindsight, this was probably a mistake. Quick action could have carried the day and would have saved a great deal of trouble. But there was a danger that the Saudis might have felt bound to send a more serious force to reoccupy Buraimi, and London wanted if possible to avoid a war in Arabia, which would be certain to displease the USA. Diplomacy was Britain's preferred course, but it failed and Turki was reinforced by the Saudis.

This put the British Government under a responsibility to do what they had restrained the Sultan from doing. In 1950, they had raised in the Trucial Coast a locally recruited but British-officered force known as the Trucial Oman Levies. This was ordered to occupy the Oasis and did so in January 1953. Turki's force was blockaded in the village it was occupying, Hamasa. King Abdul Aziz of course protested bitterly and claimed sovereignty over the whole Oasis, the Omani villages in which had indeed been occupied by Saudi raiding parties for lengthy periods in the nineteenth century, though always in the British view as interlopers and never since 1869.[5] It was finally agreed that the question of ownership of the villages should be submitted to international arbitration, with the main military forces withdrawn from the Oasis and order maintained there by fifteen Saudi policemen under an officer matched by an officer and fifteen men from the Trucial Oman Levies.

It is outside the scope of this book to trace the course of the arbitration in detail; like most such processes it took up considerable time. The papers on it are available in the PRO and there is an admirably thorough book on the subject by the expert on the area, Dr J.B. Kelly.[6] Suffice it to say that in September 1955 the Saudis, who had been using their oil wealth in attempts to procure supporting testimony from inhabitants of the Oasis, with no great success,[7] sought to improve their chances by offering inducements also to two of the five arbitrators. But they had misjudged their men and a scandal ensued. The Saudi-nominated arbitrator, Shaikh Yusuf Yasin, was driven to admit that, so far from acting independently of the Saudi Government, he was in fact its Minister for Buraimi and personally responsible for any Saudi irregularities there. Sir Reader Bullard, the British-nominated arbitrator, resigned in protest, followed by the Belgian President of the Tribunal and the Cuban arbitrator, and a British Government statement pinned the blame for the breakdown of the arbitration proceedings on the Saudi Arabian Government. The Saudi Ambassador in London complained that the statement sounded like a Cairo Radio broadcast, but attempted to explain away the bribery rather than to deny it.[8]

On 26 October 1955, two sqadrons of the Trucial Oman Levies, supported by a contingent from the Omani Army, occupied the Buraimi Oasis and expelled all Saudis from it. The Saudi Government protested vehemently. The US Government, with ARAMCO's interests as well as their own good relations with the Saudis in mind, sought to influence Eden, now Prime Minister, to resume arbitration, but the British Government stood firm.[9]

Buraimi faded from the headlines and now seems to have been something of a storm in a teacup, but it had its effects, both political and economic. In the nature of things, some of them were good for Britain and others bad.

On the plus side there was renewed faith among those rulers who were under the protection of the British Government in its resolve to carry out its obligations to them, on which there had been doubts since the withdrawal from Palestine and the decision not to use force at Abadan. This feeling strengthened when in January 1959 British forces helped the Sultan of Muscat and Oman to suppress the remnants of the revolt of the Imam of Oman.[10]

The way was clear for IPC to explore in the interior of Oman but they failed to find oil there. However, Shell (together with Total and Gulbenkian) took over the concession and in 1964 were successful, in the very area (Fahud) which might have gone to ARAMCO. In 1959/60, oil was found in important quantities in Abu Dhabi, though, fortunately perhaps, not in the Buraimi Oasis itself. The rulers of Abu Dhabi and Oman, when they had oil money to spend, showed their gratitude to Britain by turning to its exporters and to its providers of services, with beneficial effects on the UK's balance of both visible and invisible trade. As the trade statistics will show, these benefits proved long-lasting.

On the other hand, relations with Saudi Arabia, potentially a very rich market for British exports, were naturally soured. When diplomatic relations with the UK were broken off by Saudi

Arabia a year later, officially over the Suez affair, they remained broken until January 1963, long after they had been restored with Egypt itself; this was because of the still unresolved dispute over Buraimi. Commercial relations with Britain were not severed and trade continued to flow (see Chapter 12), but at a lower level than might otherwise have been expected in an expanding market. At the time of restoration of diplomatic relations[11] there were only six British businessmen resident in Jedda and none elsewhere in the Kingdom. In economic terms the Buraimi dispute thus brought losses for Britain to offset the gains, but the losses were limited in time and the gains almost certainly predominated. In political terms they did so overwhelmingly.

9 The Economy of Independent Sudan

When Sudan became independent on 1 January 1956, it could with very little oversimplification be regarded as a totally agricultural country. The share of manufacturing industry in its GDP was probably no more than 1 per cent.[1] Known mineral resources were negligible, mainly a tiny remnant of the gold that had once been extracted in great quantities from Sudan when it was part of the Kingdom of the Pharaohs. Agriculture, on the other hand, was prosperous and possessed enormous potential, though only if some considerable problems could be surmounted.

Sudan is the largest country in the Middle East and the largest in Africa, extending over nearly a million square miles. The southern part of it is within the tropical rain-belt, and the arid north is, like Egypt, able by irrigation to support highly productive agriculture in the valley of the Nile.

That river flows through Sudan in two great branches, the White Nile flowing from Lake Victoria in Uganda and the Blue Nile from Lake Tana in Ethiopia. They join at Khartoum to form the main Nile. The White Nile provides about 16 per cent of the Nile's water with comparatively little variation during the year, whereas the Blue Nile brings down a heavy flood stream from Ethiopia when the snows melt, plus a great deal of fertile silt, but shrinks to very low levels in its dry season.[2] At its height, the Blue Nile is flowing so fast that it forms virtually a wall of water at the Khartoum junction-point through which the more gently-flowing White Nile cannot penetrate, so that its waters back up into enormously wide swamp areas in South Sudan, fed also by the area's heavy rains in the wet season. The corollary is that when the flow of the Blue Nile is low, stored-up waters of the White Nile can discharge, keeping up a substantial flow in the main Nile. The southern marshes thus act as a natural, though highly inefficient, regulator.

Nile waters and their management are hence of very great importance to the Sudan and at the same time are absolutely vital to its downstream neighbour Egypt, which in Herodotus's famous phrase is 'the gift of the Nile', wholly dependent on its waters for agriculture. Before Sudanese independence, relations between the two countries in this crucial area were regulated by an Agreement of 7 May 1929 between the UK and Egypt. Within the Sudan a storage dam had been built at Sennar on the Blue Nile in 1925, its cost covered by a debt of £E13,613,340[3] guaranteed by the British Treasury, to provide irrigation for the highly successful Gezira Cotton Scheme. (The Gezira, meaning Island, area is so called because it lies between the Blue and White Niles, not far south of Khartoum.) Following the 1929 Agreement, another dam at Jebel Awlia was completed in 1937.

At the time of independence, the chief crop of the Sudan was millet in two varieties, durra (or sorghum) and dukhn, grown almost entirely for local consumption. But by far the main cash crop was cotton, especially the long-staple Sakellarides varieties, for which Britain was the main market. Sudan also supplied most of the world's needs of gum arabic from trees growing wild in Kordofan and neighbouring provinces. There were exports of groundnuts ('Sudan nuts' in local Arabic), some wheat and sesame, and also livestock, but on a fairly small scale. Potentially, Sudan was capable of much greater outputs of these and other commodities, especially by development of its southern provinces, but there were considerable obstacles in the way.

Some of these were political. The division of Sudan into north and south was not only a matter of climate and geography, but had deep ethnic roots. The northerners are basically Arabs and Muslims, while the southerners are Hamitic tribes, animists with a minority of Christians. Under British administration these two groups of people had (rightly or more probably wrongly) been kept totally apart, for reasons which seemed good at the time.

The integration of the two into a single national entity was the most intractable problem facing the newly independent Government of Sudan. Not surprisingly, it made grave mistakes in attempting to tackle it, which had adverse consequences for the economic development of the south.

There were other problems. Infrastructure was (and still is) a major impediment to development. The country's only seaport was Port Sudan on the Red Sea, which had taken over from the old pilgrimage port of Suakin. It was linked to Khartoum, the capital and main population centre (more strictly the 'Three Towns', a conurbation of Omdurman, Khartoum proper and Khartoum North, joined by bridges over the branches of the Nile), by a long single-track railway line which constituted a considerable bottleneck feeding back into perpetual congestion at Port Sudan. From Khartoum southwards there was a stretch of railway to Al Obeid, but communications were otherwise limited to river-steamers on the navigable stretches of the White Nile and its tributaries, and to unmetalled roads which in Upper Nile Province became impassable in the rainy season. Following independence, IBRD loans financed the extension of the railway system to Nyala in the south-west in 1958 and to Wau in the south in 1961.

A third problem lay in the cultures of the southerners. The Nilotic tribes (Dinka, Nuer and Shilluk) were proud and inflexible people, despising the way of life of the Arabs. They had their own languages and no wish to learn Arabic. They were great cattle-herders, living mainly on the milk of their cows with an admixture of blood, but generally unwilling to slaughter these animals, which were their main measure of wealth and also had religious significance as their link with the ghosts of their ancestors. Any idea of establishing trade in cattle or meat with neighbouring countries such as Saudi Arabia ran counter to their liveliest prejudices, with the result that a corned-beef factory established at Kosti in 1950 had failed. Even plans to install irrigation from the White Nile, along with measures of flood control, raised their suspicions, for fear that northerners, or even Egyptians, might be settled in their homelands to exploit the irrigation-fed agriculture so opened up.

Wishing to integrate south with north after independence, the Sudan Government not unnaturally saw the teaching of Arabic to the southerners as a priority requirement. Unfortunately, their method of achieving this involved the replacement of Christian missionary schools in the south by state schools teaching Arabic by the age-old Muslim system based on the memorisation and copying of Quranic texts. Missionaries were expelled in the process. The more educated southerners, who were Christians, were outraged by this treatment and unrest spread rapidly, turning before long into civil war.

This had disastrous economic consequences. Not only were plans for the economic development of the south frustrated but the north also suffered through heavy expenditure on military operations to suppress the rebels. Until a temporary settlement was reached in the 1972 Addis Ababa Agreement, granting a measure of autonomy to the south, almost 25 per cent of Government revenue was regularly spent on an army of about 20,000 troops deployed in the south. In a poor country this was a crippling commitment.

Some development did take place in the north, much of it with the help of foreign aid funds. In November 1959, a new Nile Waters Agreement was reached between Sudan and Egypt. On the Egyptian side this paved the way for the Aswan High Dam project, which is discussed elsewhere (Chapters 7 and 10). For Sudan, its effect was to raise the permitted extraction level for Nile water to 18.5 million cubic metres,[4] well in excess of the country's immediate requirements. Major irrigation works thus became possible at Khashm al-Qirba, where the Nubians were resettled who were displaced from the Wadi Halfa area near the Egyptian frontier (flooded by the lake created by the Aswan High Dam), and at Rusayris where a major new dam was built. Compensation of £E15 million was paid by Egypt for the resettlement of the Sudanese Nubians, although the cost in fact proved to be a good deal higher. (A British contractor who undertook a major part of this project came out of it a considerable loser.)

One drawback of this development in the north was that it tended to reinforce Sudan's status as a cotton producer, dependent for export earnings on a single crop. Cotton was exposed to competition from other cotton-producing countries and from man-made fibres, which tended to reduce demand for long-staple cotton even more than for medium and short-staple varieties. It is also liable to disease, so that supply, and therefore prices, can fluctuate unpredictably from year to year. As an example, the selling price per 100 lb. of cotton lint (grade XG_3 VS) varied from £S18.1 in 1971 to £S10.43 in 1972, up to £S20.49 in 1973 and to £S27.9 in 1974, then down again to £S16 in 1975.[5] Export quantities also fluctuated, for example from 1,203,000 bales in 1973 to 498,000 bales in 1974. To some extent these trends offset each other, higher quantities attracting lower prices, but this was not always the case for Sudan, as much depended on the size of the competing crops in Egypt and elsewhere.

Nevertheless, increased irrigation in the north seemed the only available course for the Sudan Government so long as trouble in the south inhibited development there. The two largest undertakings have been the Manaqil extension of the Gezira Scheme, which brought the irrigated area there to 1.8 million acres,[6] and the Rusayris project, designed to irrigate 300,000 acres in Stage I (1978–9) and a further 500,000 acres in Stage II. Plans were also laid to use the Atbara River, a tributary of the main Nile, to irrigate 600,000 acres at Setait.

It was naturally hoped that the lull in the civil war following the 1972 Addis Ababa Agreement would become a basis for a permanent settlement of the southern problem, and this revived plans for economic development there. Much the most ambitious of these was the Jonglei Canal scheme, long dreamt of in the days of British administration but first made feasible in 1974, when a cooperation agreement to bring it about for the benefit of both was reached between Sudan and Egypt. This 175-mile canal to straighten the course of the White Nile, cutting out a huge bend between Jonglei and Malakal, would not only improve river communications but also partially drain the vast southern marshes. It was calculated that this would save 4000 million cubic metres of Nile water from the 32,000 million believed to be lost on average annually as a result of evaporation and seepage. Land reclaimed for agriculture would be no less than 4 million acres.

Work on this huge project got under way in June 1978, but was unfortunately halted in 1984 by new insurrections in the south. These were stirred up by a Government decision taken in September 1983 to apply Islamic law to the whole of the country (though this was not in fact implemented) and by an unpopular reorganisation of the south into smaller administrative units.

Another tragic setback from the same cause has been to oil production. After much wishful thinking by the Sudan Government, oil was at last struck by the American oil company, Chevron Overseas Petroleum, in May 1978. Rumours quickly turned the strike into a vast oil lake which would solve all Sudan's economic problems. The reality is less miraculous. The find has been made at Bentiu in Upper Nile Province, a remote area which presents considerable production difficulties. The viability of the field will depend on the price of oil, but also on the state of security in the area. At present that cannot be guaranteed and work to develop the field was halted in 1984; there have been efforts since to resume work but the civil war has frustrated them.

There has however been one advance on the oil front which has eased the infrastructure problem in Sudan. A pipeline was opened late in 1977 to transport oil products from the country's only refinery at Port Sudan (processing imported oil) to Khartoum. This has released considerable capacity on the railway between the two, where previously about 40 per cent of traffic consisted of oil tank-wagons.

One other major scheme has gone badly wrong, the Kenana sugar project, which like the Gezira Cotton Scheme lies between the Blue and White Niles. This mammoth project was designed to produce initially 350,000 tons of sugar a year, turning Sudan from a sugar importer into an exporter, and was eventually to reach 1,000,000 tons p.a., the largest sugar scheme in the world. The project was financed largely by private Arab backers, with an investment from the British firm Lonrho, which was to manage the project. Although Lonrho had a great deal of experience in Africa, it seems that it tried to move ahead too quickly, with the result that plant and equipment imported for the project piled up in congested Port Sudan, incurring high demurrage charges and itself deteriorating. The inevitable consequence was that the project fell behind its ambitious schedule and costs soared, from an initial estimate of $150 million in 1973 to over $475 million in 1976. In 1977, Lonrho was dismissed from its management role, but by then, even though the project has since come on stream, there was no longer any way of securing an economic return on the capital invested.

This setback did much to sour Sudan in the minds of Arab financiers as a place for investment as distinct from aid. One of the problems of Sudan appears to be that it is such a large country and has such huge possibilities that it tempts developers into embarking on grandiose projects, instead of beginning on a modest scale and expanding later as happened in the 1920s with the successful Gezira Cotton Scheme.

In manufacturing, Sudan has made some modest advance since independence. The Approved Enterprises (Concessions) Act was passed in 1956 to encourage this process. Logically enough, effort has been devoted to the textile industry; it appeared paradoxical that one of the world's leading cotton producers should import all its cotton piece-goods, as was the case in 1956. Here too, however, things have not always been as simple as they at first appeared. There have been times when it would have paid Sudan not to process its own cotton, but to export it raw or ginned and import shorter-staple cotton for turning into cloth. A little short and medium-staple cotton has traditionally been grown in Sudan, mainly in the rain-belt areas, and in recent years it has been found economic to switch partially from long-staple to medium-staple even in the irrigated areas.

Other industrial enterprises in Sudan include a railway workshop area (dating from before independence but expanded since) and a cement factory (originally a British investment), both at Atbara. In the Khartoum area lie the Sudan Cotton Textiles Company, employing over 8000 people, and the Blue Nile Brewery. There is also a complex of various small factories in an industrial zone in Khartoum North. These were encouraged by an Industrial Development Act of 1968, but following a military coup on 25 May 1969 they were for the most part nationalised in 1970; then a reversal of policy led to the Development and Promotion of Industrial Investment Act of 1972, offering tax concessions and other incentives to private foreign investors.

This new Act has had some success; Bata Shoe Company took back a 51 per cent interest in a factory of theirs which had been nationalised, and Canadian and South Korean firms agreed to build a urea plant and a tyre factory respectively. The public sector now confines itself mainly to textiles, leather and sugar processing. But foreign firms are wary of investing in Sudan and manufacturing remains a minor part of the Sudanese economy.

No attempt has been made in this Chapter to trace the complicated political history of Sudan since independence, although this certainly added to the country's economic problems by causing uncertainties in the minds of both aid donors and investors. In particular, relations with the Soviet Union have fluctuated considerably, with inevitable repercussions on Western attitudes. In the post-independence period the USSR began to buy Sudanese cotton and in the aftermath of the 1967 Arab-Israel War it was able to conclude a major arms deal with Sudan. For a brief period around 1970 (following a 1969 coup which brought President Numeiry to power) the Soviet Union became Sudan's largest trading partner, taking about 20 per cent of Sudanese exports, although Britain continued to hold its long-established place as the major source of the country's imports.

The relationship with the Soviet Union then soured. The Sudanese found that their cotton exported to the USSR under special semi-barter arrangements was turning up in Lancashire at prices which undercut Sudan's direct exports. The 1972 Act mentioned in the last paragraph marked a swing back towards more orthodox trading with the West, so that by 1977 the Soviet Union was taking less than 4 per cent of Sudanese exports.

Another factor which has contributed to unsettling the Sudanese economy has been recurrent influxes of refugees across its borders. These have come from the Congo, especially during the troubled times linked with its independence, from Uganda under both Amin and Obote, and from Ethiopia as a result of both civil war and drought. The frontiers between all these countries are in practice impossible to close and there has of course been heavy movement of Sudanese in the opposite directions at times, due to Government attempts to quell southern insurrections by force. The numbers involved cannot be assessed precisely, but certainly run into hundreds of thousands in each direction; the effects on economies already under strain have been very serious, with Sudan probably the chief sufferer.

The intensification of the Sudanese civil war in recent years has also created an enormous internal refugee problem. Southerners, desperate to escape the brutality of that war and the accompanying famine caused by disruption of agriculture and severing of communications, have trekked huge distances to Khartoum in the hope of finding food and perhaps work. Such hopes have been largely disappointed, with the result that appalling shanty-towns inhabited by largely destitute Southerners have grown up around the outskirts of the capital. Given the poverty of the country, little can be done to resettle them.

More than one mention has been made of Sudan's receipt of foreign aid. As a developing country with real economic potential (however difficult it always proved to realise that potential), Sudan attracted a good deal of help from Western sources after independence, from the IBRD, from the United States and from its old administrator the UK. In later years, its membership of the League of Arab States qualified it for considerable inflows of Arab aid from oil-rich countries, especially that most generous of all donors Kuwait but also Saudi Arabia which was interested in the possibilities of developing food supplies from across the Red Sea.

Rodney Wilson has compiled an interesting table of Arab Fund projects in Sudan, divided into commercially viable projects, non-commercial projects and infrastructure projects.[7] The last two categories have been almost entirely grant-aided, but the sad fact remains that Sudan has nevertheless piled up large foreign debts which, as in so much of Africa, now impose great strains on its resources. Its economic future must be regarded as problem-ridden, with great potential which never seems to come to realisation.[8]

Although the Chapters of this book follow a generally chronological sequence, an exception has been made in this Chapter in following the economic history of Sudan from independence through to the 1980s. This seemed desirable since there will be little other opportunity to focus on this country, despite Britain's historical connection with it and continuing success in marketing a respectable quantity of exports there. Sudan has also deserved attention as a case-study of development efforts frustrated by political and sociological obstacles, culminating in the horrors of a long-lasting civil war.

10 Decline to Suez

After the events described in Chapter 7, ending differences between Egypt and Britain over the Sudan and the Canal Zone Base, it might have been thought that relations between them would be set fair. That was certainly the hope in 1954 of many people in Britain and of some in Egypt. Unfortunately for such hopes, President Nasser's opposition to a British presence extended beyond the bounds of his own country. In a book which he subsequently published[1] he set out his doctrine of the three circles within which Egypt should play a role, the Arab World, Africa and the Islamic World. Having removed British forces from Egypt, he made it his next objective to remove them from all Arab countries. He similarly wished to see French forces expelled from North Africa.

For this purpose he had available a weapon which he had been carefully forging, a powerful propaganda machine. Although spoken Arabic differs somewhat from country to country, the written language has, through the influence of the Quran, remained virtually identical in all Arab lands. The same is true of the spoken language when it is used for public purposes as distinct from conversation, for instance in sermons, in public speeches, and on most broadcasts.

Radio was widespread by this period; even if an Arab did not own a set himself, he could listen to programmes blaring from the coffee-shops in which many Arab men spent much of their leisure time. Egypt had a central place in the Middle East entertainment industry, its singers in particular being household names throughout the Arab lands, and many people beyond its own boundaries listened to its broadcasts. Nasser developed Cairo Radio, boosting the power of its transmitters and the range of its frequencies to give regional and not merely national coverage, in order to bring home his political messages to the captive audience already won by Egypt's entertainment leadership. (When transistors took over from valves and caused the price and size of personal radios to fall rapidly, the medium gained even greater influence.)

The political messages broadcast from Cairo were regularly directed against Britain and France. They called for the expulsion of 'imperialist' influence from all Arab lands. This theme was plugged even harder after Nasser had attended the Bandung Conference of Non-Aligned States in April 1955; this, his first exposure to prominence in a world forum, had an enormous effect upon him and greatly widened his political horizons. It so happened that a special target for his hostility had just emerged.

Britain had treaty relationships with Iraq and Jordan, and Arab friends in both of them. None was more Anglophile than the strong man of Iraq, Nuri Pasha Said. At a time when both Britain and the USA were worried about the 'containment' of the Soviet Union and saw a dangerous gap to the east of the area protected by the formation of NATO, Nuri, whose thoughts ran on similar lines, entered into an agreement with Turkey (the easternmost member of NATO) to resist any Soviet ambitions for expansion to the south. Having taken this initiative, Nuri called on his old friend, Anthony Eden, to add Britain's signature to the Turco-Iraqi pact.[2] In London, the Cabinet saw merit in the proposal and Eden committed Britain to the agreement on 4 April 1955, the same month in which Nasser travelled to Bandung. A small central secretariat was established in the Iraqi capital, with the result that the agreement became known as the Baghdad Pact.

Cairo Radio programmes responded by increasing the stridency of their anti-imperialist slogans. The Baghdad Pact was nicknamed the 'Big Prison'. Nuri was denounced as a colonialist 'tail', a particularly insulting word in Arabic. The people of Iraq were urged to demonstrate their hostility to the policy which, according to Cairo Radio, had been forced upon them against their will. Other Arab countries were warned not to join the Pact.

Nuri, who had a contempt for all things Egyptian, was in no way disturbed. He felt confident that his hold on his own country was secure and that his fellow-Iraqis would be properly cynical about Cairo's propaganda. In the light of subsequent events, it is clear that he seriously underestimated the power of the weapon Nasser was deploying against him. As for Eden, who had become Prime Minister the day after he added Britain to the Baghdad Pact, his reaction to the outpourings from Cairo, set before him regularly in the series of translations provided by the Radio Monitoring Service, was to equate Nasser more and more firmly in his mind with the dictators he had confronted in the past, Mussolini and Hitler.

It has been explained in Chapter 6 that arms exports from Britain, France and the USA to the Middle East were at this time governed by the Tripartite Agreement. Both Israel and Egypt were eager to buy British warships and British Centurion tanks, while Britain, for the reasons set out in Chapter 6, needed to find overseas customers for its arms production. Following the policy of 'balance', the relevant Cabinet Committee decided that Egypt and Israel should each receive two destroyers and thirty-two tanks (enough for one squadron). Both countries were pleased with the decision and pressed for further allocations of tanks. But a strange chance intervened.

With use of the Suez Canal denied to it, Israel had set about developing the port of Eilat in the Gulf of Aqaba as an outlet to and inlet from the Orient. Egypt had countered by mounting artillery at Sharm al Shaikh on the south-western tip of the Sinai Peninsula to control shipping passing through the mouth of the Gulf. The annual pilgrimage to Mecca was in prospect and the *An Shun*, a ship owned by China Navigation Co. Ltd of Hongkong, was heading for the Jordanian port of Aqaba to embark pilgrims for transportation to Jedda. There was no reason for the Egyptians to object to its passage, but its captain was not familiar with the procedures for ships to identify themselves to the command post at Sharm al Shaikh and declare their destination. Through what appears to have been a chapter of accidents and inefficiencies,[3] an Egyptian shore battery fired a shell which hit the *An Shun* between-decks above the waterline, fortunately causing no casualties.

The outcry in London was tremendous. The Red Ensign had been fired on and all Britain's maritime instincts were aroused. The Egyptians made matters worse by refusing to apologise or admit liability, even denying, in the face of the visual evidence to the contrary, that the ship had been hit at all. There could be no question of delivering further British tanks to a country which had committed such an outrage, at least until anger died down. For its part, the Egyptian Army had been keenly looking forward to getting enough modern tanks to form an armoured brigade and was equally furious at being denied them. Nasser determined to take up a hint he had already had from the Soviet Ambassador in Egypt and to look elsewhere for his arms. The outcome was the Czech arms deal, which came as a complete surprise to the Western powers. Its effect was to outflank the Tripartite Agreement and open up serious risks of a Middle Eastern arms race. It also introduced a dangerous Cold War element into the situation.

As part of his economic development programme, Nasser had opened negotiations for the building of a High Dam to replace the existing Nile dam at Aswan. This huge project, outlined in Chapter 7 above, had won support in Washington (against some objections) and in December 1955 a generous financial package was arranged for its first phase, with grant aid funds of $56 million from the USA and $14 million from Britain supplementing a $200 million loan from the IBRD. The British consulting engineers, Sir Alexander Gibb & Partners, who had designed the existing Aswan dam, had been engaged the prevous October to design and supervise the construction of the new one, an important and profitable contract. The arms deal with Czechoslovakia had the indirect effect of putting this project into doubt. In addition to the substantial foreign aid arranged for it, the Egyptian Government would also have to meet very considerable costs (estimated for the entire project at the equivalent of $900 million out of $1300 million over a period of 12–16 years) and its ability to do so had been seriously reduced by the payments now due to the Czechs (much greater than the price of further Centurion tanks, as Nasser had taken the opportunity to order large quantities of a wide range of Soviet-bloc weapons). The fact that these payments were to be made in cotton did not alter this situation fundamentally, since there would be less Egyptian cotton for export elsewhere.

While the President's advisers in Washington were mulling over these new factors, Nasser took another step which swayed the balance decisively. He had met Chou En Lai at the Bandung Conference and had discussed with him the possibility of sales of Egyptian cotton to China. He now decided to withdraw recognition from Taiwan, which still held the China seat in the United Nations thanks to American support, and to recognise the Government in Peking.[4] His doing so was the last straw for Washington. It was decided to cancel the offer of US aid for the High Dam, blaming this change of policy upon a reassessment of Egypt's ability to meet its share of the costs. The financial package thus fell apart; Britain and the IBRD followed the American lead and withdrew their own offers. Nasser seemed to have brought upon himself a serious economic calamity.

Again he proved his ability to surprise the world. The American withdrawal of aid for the High Dam had been announced on 19 July 1956, not long after the last British troops had left the Canal Zone Base. On 26 July, Nasser was due to make a major speech commemorating the fourth anniversary of Egypt's 1952 Revolution. He used the occasion to announce the nationalisation of the Suez Canal Company, declaring that the revenues from the Canal (which he estimated at $100 million p.a.) would enable Egypt to finance the High Dam without need for foreign aid. The step had evidently been well prepared (without any hint of it reaching the French or other Western intelligence services). An Egyptian team moved immediately into the Canal Company's Head Office and took over control. A legally-drafted decree for the nationalisation was at once promulgated; it must have been made ready, perhaps long before, for use at a time of Nasser's choice.

There was horror in the Western capitals, especially in Paris, since the Canal Company was in essence French,[5] and in London, where the British Government owned 44 per cent of its shares.

Apart from these considerations, there was an argument (more convincing perhaps to politicians than to legal experts) that Nasser had broken international law because the operation of the Canal was subject to the 1888 Convention. Eden became more convinced than before that Nasser was 'going communist'. Moreover, there was a strong belief, amounting to certainty in Paris and among the senior Canal Company staff in Ismailia, that the Egyptians would be incapable of running the Canal, so that world shipping would be seriously disrupted.[6] This was a cause of some concern even to those nations, such as the non-aligned, who might on other grounds have applauded Nasser's bold stroke against the 'imperialists'.

There is no need to follow in detail the course of events from the nationalisation of the Suez Canal to the Franco-British attack on Egypt in October/November 1956 in collusion with Israel. The story is well known and has been retold recently in connection with the opening of the papers in the British PRO under the 30-year rule. On the economic side, suffice it to say that Egypt proved perfectly capable of running the Suez Canal; that the American-sponsored setting up of an international Suez Canal Users Association (SCUA) led nowhere;[7] that a heavy run on sterling[8] was one of the main factors forcing Eden to yield to American, UN and some Commonwealth pressure to withdraw British forces from Egypt; and that during the fighting the Egyptians had deliberately blocked the Suez Canal by sinking ships in it.

United Nations forces took over from British and French troops in the Port Said area and the UN also took charge of organising the clearance of the Canal. British demands to help in that operation were refused with unsurprising sharpness (although Britain did in fact clear Port Said harbour). The Canal was fully reopened to shipping on 8 April 1957[9]. So short a closure had not seriously disrupted world trade, but it had been long enough to bring home some commercial lessons.

First, lessons for shipping. During the closure oil tankers loaded in Iran and at the Arab terminals in the Gulf had had to take the long route round South Africa to Europe and the USA.

For the larger tankers the extra cost, after deducting the Suez Canal dues that were saved, proved less than had been expected. A stimulus was thus given to the construction of supertankers, too large to pass through the Canal, to ply this route regularly, even when the Canal was reopened. This meant eventually some permanent loss to Egypt's earnings from the Canal. Secondly, it was brought home to the Red Sea ports, Jedda, Port Sudan and Aden, and their hinterlands, how dependent they were on the use of the Canal route. And thirdly, Beirut had a brief boost to its entrepôt trade as goods passed through it bound for overland transport to the Arabian Peninsula.

Israel came out of the conflict with some positive gains. It had demonstrated its military competence by an efficiently fought campaign in Sinai where, with approximately equal forces in terms of numbers and equipment (but with complete air command) it had captured the Gaza Strip with a relatively tiny number of casualties. In the process it had seized huge quantities of military material stockpiled there (undoubtedly intended for some future attack on Israel).

Israel had also occupied Sharm al Shaikh at the mouth of the Gulf of Aqaba, so opening the way for access to the Indian Ocean via the Red Sea from its new port of Eilat. This was a long-term gain. When Israel withdrew its forces from Sinai, as it did fairly soon under considerable American pressure, it did so only on condition that a UN force, the United Nations Emergency Force (UNEF), policed the Gaza Strip and Sharm al Shaikh. Trade was free for the next decade to flow to and from Eilat. (The first ship to use this route was in fact an American merchantman, a demonstration of the strength of the Jewish lobby in USA which quickly dissipated any gratitude the Egyptians and other Arabs had felt for American pressure on Britain and France to end the Canal invasion.) Eilat was of particular importance as a means of solving Israel's oil problems. It made it possible to import crude from Iran for processing in the Haifa refinery and in due course a pipeline was built to link Eilat and Haifa. With access to both the Mediterranean and the Red Sea, Israel was independent of the Suez Canal, so that element in the Arab boycott largely ceased to be effective.

Within Egypt, the Suez episode not surprisingly led to the seizure of British and French property; it also stimulated more widespread 'Egyptianisation' of foreign holdings in Egypt which (like the nationalisation of the Canal) had probably been intended for some time, but kept waiting for a favourable opportunity. The remaining British installations in the Canal Base were taken over and the British civilians running them were first interned and then expelled; so ended prematurely what might have been an important experiment. British and French assets, including seven banks, five insurance companies and other commercial property, were nationalised. Some assets belonging to Egyptian Jews were also seized. Laws 22–24 of 1957 required all other foreign-owned banks, insurance companies and commercial enterprises to be turned into Egyptian-registered companies with majority Egyptian shareholding and Egyptian management. An Economic Organisation was established to control the Government's holdings in the financial and industrial sectors.

On the debit side, Egypt faced heavy costs in replacing its aircraft destroyed by British bombing and its military material lost to the Israelis; the Soviet Union was ready to supply new hardware on credit but the debt would have to be repaid over the years. And revenues were at least temporarily reduced by the blocking of the Canal. The economic position of Egypt will be discussed more fully in Chapter 13.

Egypt of course broke off diplomatic relations with the UK and France; their Embassy staffs in Cairo were exchanged against safe passage for the Egyptian staffs in London and Paris. Remarkably, only two other Arab countries followed suit in breaking relations with Britain, Saudi Arabia for reasons partly connected with the Buraimi dispute (see Chapter 8 above) and Syria. Protecting powers were of course appointed in all cases and some trade continued (see Chapter 12 below). Except in the case of Saudi Arabia (because of Buraimi), the breaches with Britain were not long-lasting. In Egypt there were quite rapid moves to open negotiations on the claims and counter-claims arising from the hostilities and the seizure of property in Egypt; these began as early as 24 May 1957 and for all their complications progressed smoothly towards a settlement in 1958.[10] Diplomatic relations between the UK and the United Arab Republic were reopened in 1959 (Egypt and Syria had formed the United Arab Republic that year, so the links with both were restored together). It is surprising how quickly these particular wounds healed.[11]

But Nasser of course remained deeply hostile to Britain and France, and ever ready to use his propaganda machine[12] against their interests in the Arab countries. His chief targets were now the French position in Algeria and Britain's influence in the Arabian Peninsula, including the Colony of Aden.

11 The Iraqi Revolution

It is time to look more closely at Iraq, the most populous of the Arab countries in Asia and in 1945 the Arab land in which Britain had her largest economic investment. Measuring some 175,000 square miles and with a population in 1947 (the first official census) of just under 4.8 million people, Iraq is well described by its older name Mesopotamia, although it does in fact extend west of the Euphrates and east of the Tigris. The alluvial plain between the two rivers is its real area of habitation, containing the main agricultural resource of the country.

Iraq has rainfall which in the uplands of the north (the ancient Assyria, now inhabited by Iraqi Kurds) suffices to yield a crop without irrigation, especially as it is provided with additional water from a system of linked wells. In the plain, the winter rainfall is of variable duration and averages only some six inches annually, so that irrigation is vital for reliable agriculture. The rivers provide ample water for this purpose, the problem being to control it. The plain is nowhere higher than 150 feet above sea-level and in many places below the level of the river-banks, so that flooding is a perpetual danger during the high-water period after the snows melt in the mountains to the north. The Tigris rises around the end of March, by as much as twenty-three feet measured at Baghdad, the capital; the Euphrates rises in the second half of April by rather less, up to about 14 feet at Falluja. The two rivers unite just north of Basra, the second city of Iraq, forming an estuary known as the Shatt al-Arab, which is flanked on the east by Iran; sovereignty over the waters of the Shatt is a long-standing bone of contention between the two countries.

In ancient days Mesopotamia was of enormous strategic and economic importance. Trade routes ran through it from Europe to the Persian Gulf and from India to Europe. Great civilisations, Assyria and Babylon, rose within it. Alexander the Great marched across it in his triumphal progress to India. More recently, this importance has declined with the opening of other routes for trade, but this has been offset by the finding of substantial oil resources in Iraq, particularly in the lower reaches of the northern uplands.

When the Ottoman Empire was liquidated, a mandate for Iraq was assigned to Britain in 1920; in March 1921 Winston Churchill, as Secretary of State for the Colonies, persuaded his Cabinet colleagues to repay part of the British wartime debt to the Hashemites by installing Faisal ibn Husain (dislodged from his expected throne in Damascus by the granting of a mandate over Syria to the French) as King of Iraq. The British mandate continued for another decade, but on 3 June 1930 a treaty between the UK and Iraq paved the way for the admission of Iraq to the League of Nations in 1932 as an independent state. The 1930 treaty established a military alliance between the two countries, with Britain retaining two air bases on Iraqi soil, the more important of which was Habbaniya near the Euphrates.

Following the death of King Faisal in 1933 a period of instability ensued, culminating in an attempt in 1941 by Rashid Ali al-Qailani to establish a pro-Hitler government, with the support of some elements of the Iraqi army. The situation was for a time critical but promised German troops failed to materialise and the rapid movement of a small British force, centred around a Brigade Group from Palestine, brought about Rashid Ali's overthrow. The Regent, who, with the boy king Faisal II,[1] had fled the country, was able to return on 1 June 1941 and reassert a policy of collaboration with Britain.

Oil was discovered in Iraq in 1927 by the Iraq Petroleum Company, which had been given a 75-year concession on 14 March 1925, covering the former Vilayets of Mosul and Baghdad (this was varied in 1931 to apply to all lands east of the Tigris other than a strip of land along the Iraq-Iran frontier). The multi-company ownership of IPC was explained in Chapter 2; Britain had the largest share, approximately one-third, in ownership, and the company had its headquarters in London. The oil strike at Kirkuk proved to be of an immense field, sixty miles long and one to two miles wide. Two 12-inch pipelines were built from Kirkuk, one through Jordan to Haifa in Palestine and the other through Syria to Tripoli in Lebanon; these were being supplemented by a new 16-inch pipeline along each route when the emergence of Israel and the Arab Boycott policy led to the closure of the line to Haifa (see Chapter 3).

Two other concessions in Iraq were held by companies with ownership identical with that of IPC, the Mosul Petroleum Company with rights over areas of the Mosul and Baghdad Vilayets west of the Tigris and north of the 33°N parallel, and the Basrah Petroleum Company covering all lands not previously allocated. Although the 75-year concessions of these two companies ran from later dates than that of IPC, this proved to be an irrelevant issue, so that it will be convenient for the purposes of this book to speak of all three companies as simply the IPC.

The only non-IPC concession in Iraq was that which had been granted in 1925 to the Khanaqin Oil Company, a subsidiary of APOC, covering the strip of land along the Iraq-Iran frontier already mentioned as excluded from the concession area of IPC proper. Another company subsidiary to APOC, the Rafidain Oil Company, had the sole rights to market petroleum products in Iraq; it drew its supplies from a refinery of the Khanaqin Oil Company at Alwand and from APOC's refineries in Iran. This had the consequence that all IPC oil was exported from Iraq as crude, for refining elsewhere.[2]

As already explained in Chapter 5, one effect of the Iranian oil crisis was to increase export of oil from Iraq. This added greatly to the Iraqi Government's revenues; the royalty payment by IPC was at the rate of £0.20 gold per ton, plus a tax commutation payment of £60,000 gold on the first 4 million tons and £20,000 gold on each subsequent million tons. By a wise provision of Iraqi law, some 70 per cent of these oil revenues were reserved for projects planned by a Development Board established in 1950. Since Iraq had both land suitable for increased agriculture and the population to work it, the way was thus open for spreading the oil riches throughout the nation and turning Iraq into a very prosperous country. These prospects expanded even further when a new agreement was reached on 3 February 1952, effective from 1 January 1951, replacing the royalty system by a newly fashionable 50/50 profit-sharing arrangement. Combined with the increased crude offtake, this led to an escalation of Iraq's oil revenues from £13.9 million in 1951 to £32.6 million in 1952 and £73.7 million in 1955.[3]

The investment resources of the Development Board rose correspondingly, from about $20 million in 1951 to almost $280 million in 1958.[4] Projects chosen for investment were of two main kinds, directed towards agriculture or transport. In the first category came dam construction, combined with flood control measures. The largest project was a Tigris dam at Samarra, linked by a 40-mile canal to the Wadi al-Tharthar, a depression capable of holding 63 million cubic metres of water; this put an end to the flooding of Baghdad, provided large supplies of water for irrigation and also generated electricity. It was completed in 1956. On the Euphrates, a dam built at Ramadi allowed water similarly to be led off to basins at Habbaniya and Hawr Abu Dibs. On the transport side investments were made in railways, roads, ports and airline facilities. Social improvements were also financed; school places were doubled between 1951 and 1956 and low-cost housing was built.

It may be noticed that no mention has been made of land reform. There was some resettlement of peasants on reclaimed land at Diwaniya and Dujaila, but the Government, comprised mainly of members of the land-owning class, decided not to interfere with the rights of landlords. When land-reform was in progress in other Middle Eastern countries, notably Egypt, this policy naturally evoked opposition. Nuri paid little heed to popular unrest, believing that he could hold it in check by autocratic methods while the country moved forward towards prosperity through the development programme based on its oil revenues. It was a gamble which he might have won, had not discontent been fanned also by opposition to his foreign policy.

For Nuri, the threat to Iraq lay in the Soviet Union. He was rootedly hostile to communism and wary of Soviet expansionism. As already explained in Chapter 10, these sentiments drove him into an alliance with Turkey which developed into the Baghdad Pact when Britain joined them at Nuri's request in April 1955. This aroused Nasser's hostility and brought into play against Nuri the powerful voice of Cairo Radio. The Pact nevertheless seemed to prosper; the Turks persuaded Pakistan and Iran to adhere to it in the autumn of 1955. The USA held back from joining, but Secretary of State Dulles was known to be an advocate of a 'northern tier' policy and saw the Pact as a way of securing the support of Congress for aid, both military and economic, for its members, as part of a strategy for containing the Soviet Union. The Pact thus grew into a five-member alliance with visible American support.

In the charter of the Baghdad Pact, provision had been made for membership to be extended to any state of the Arab League which might wish to join. It was this to which Nasser most violently objected. In practice, the only other Arab country likely to adhere seemed to be Jordan, linked to Iraq by Hashemite family ties between the monarchs and like Iraq bound to Britain by a treaty with defence commitments. Jordan was also a recipient of British aid[5] to bolster its unviable economy; however, it was in need of additional funding. King Hussain made tentative enquiries about Jordanian membership, hoping no doubt to use it as a lever for obtaining American aid, and at a Pact meeting in Baghdad in November 1955 the Turks pressed upon the British Foreign Secretary, Harold Macmillan, the idea that a little more encouragement from Britain would bring Jordan in.

Convinced that this was a probability, Macmillan on his return home arranged to send the Chief of the Imperial General Staff, General Templer, to Amman the following month to discuss the subject with King Hussain and his Government. The mission was a disaster. Cairo Radio raged against it and there were riots in the streets of Amman. Hussain had to use swift footwork to put a new Prime Minister into office and have him announce that no pacts with foreigners were contemplated. The riots were quelled but Templer had to make an ignominious return to London.

In March 1956, when by ill-chance the British Foreign

Secretary, now Selwyn Lloyd, was in Cairo dining with Nasser to discuss among other things the completion of British withdrawal from the Canal Zone Base and Britain's aid for the Aswan High Dam,[6] King Hussain abruptly announced the dismissal of Glubb Pasha, the British Commander of the Jordan Army, a man who had spent twenty-six years in the service of Hussain and his predecessors. In his memoirs[7] the King makes it clear that this decision was necessary to save his throne and there is no reason to think that it was not a wise move for the interests of Jordan, but it was inevitably, especially from the manner of its doing, one more blow to British prestige in the Middle East and another encouragement to Arab opponents of the Baghdad Pact. Cairo Radio was triumphant and renewed its appeals to the people of Iraq to liberate themselves from the 'Big Prison'.

These incidents in Jordan, which played their part in deepening Eden's aversion to Nasser, were soon eclipsed by the Suez affair which followed, as recounted in Chapter 10. Iraq suffered from one of its by-products, the blowing-up by Syrian troops of the pumping-stations on the IPC pipelines from Kirkuk to Tripoli, temporarily cutting off Iraq's main source of revenues (as well as Syria's own transit dues). The Soviet Union now had considerable influence in Syria, which had followed Egypt's lead in seeking Soviet-bloc arms unfettered by the constraints of the Tripartite Declaration. Nuri feared that Syria might be about to become a Soviet satellite.

Events turned out otherwise when in February 1958 Cairo and Damascus announced that Egypt and Syria were to unite into a single state, the United Arab Republic. This was hardly more welcome to Nuri. It brought his enemy Nasser into immediate proximity, with the possibility of Egyptian forces moving to the Syrian-Iraqi frontier. He countered by negotiating the linking of Iraq and Jordan into a Hashemite federation known as the Arab Union. Nuri became Prime Minister of the Union and elections were held to a federal Parliament.

It was fear of Egyptian troops moving into Syria that triggered Nuri's downfall. He ordered reinforcement of the Iraqi side of the frontier. On 14 July 1958 an Iraqi regiment moving through Baghdad as part of the reinforcement plan carried out a well-prepared mutiny. In the massacre which followed, the young

King, the unpopular ex-Regent and Nuri himself were killed and a few days later Iraq was proclaimed a Republic. The British Government, realistically but some thought with indecent speed, decided to recognise the regicides as the Government of Iraq and maintain diplomatic relations. No doubt the position of the IPC was in their minds. If so, the tactic worked; there was no immediate threat to the company.

Iraq withdrew from the Baghdad Pact, which was renamed the Central Treaty Organisation (CENTO). The Arab Union of course came to an end, with King Hussain horrified by the murder of his cousin. Under its new ruler, Brigadier Abdul Karim Qasim, Iraq quickly established relations with the Soviet Union, China and other Communist countries. But he showed no wish to adhere to the United Arab Republic and this proved unpopular with the pro-Nasser elements among his supporters. Iraq plunged into a period of considerable political disorder.

Both Jordan and Lebanon felt vulnerable as they watched the growth of Nasserite and Soviet influence in their neighbours, Syria and Iraq. They were sufficiently alarmed to appeal for urgent military help to the United States, where President Eisenhower had in 1957 obtained Congressional sanction for such help to Middle Eastern countries if they sought American aid 'to combat international communism', the so-called 'Eisenhower doctrine'. Jordan also appealed to Britain, despite the fact that in the immediate aftermath of the Suez affair Hussain had thought it prudent to denounce the Anglo-Jordanian Treaty. After quick consultation the two Western powers decided to share the task; American marines made an unopposed landing in Beirut, to the amazement of the bathers on the landing beaches, and British paratroopers from Cyprus dropped to defend Amman.

It soon turned out that neither force had any threat to face and they were equally rapidly withdrawn. It was all a slightly ludicrous episode, but not without some local stabilising influence. It also strengthened Britain's position in the whole area by demonstrating that the UK and the USA, after their bitter quarrel over the Suez affair, had returned to a policy of cooperation. Not only in Jordan and Lebanon but also among the oil states fringing the Arabian Peninsula, that came as welcome news.

12 Trade Between Britain and the Middle East 1950–60

The British Economy

In October 1951 the Conservative Party won a general election and the now nearly 77-year-old Winston Churchill succeeded Attlee as Prime Minister. Despite the change of party in office, the 'mixed economy' brought into being by the postwar Labour Government continued. Steel was denationalised in 1955 but remained under a measure of public control, with an Iron and Steel Board empowered to regulate capital investment and fix domestic prices. Other nationalised enterprises continued in public ownership. What did change was the climate for commerce, with the remaining import controls being fairly quickly swept away.

The outcome was that during the 1950s imports expanded more rapidly than exports, with imports of manufactured and semi-finished goods particularly buoyant. The share of manufactures in British exports remained steady at about 80 per cent, although the makeup of that figure altered. Exports of certain textiles declined sharply, but there were offsetting increases in aircraft and vehicles, and in machinery generally. Britain's global balance of visible trade was never in surplus during the decade, but invisibles did well, so that the balance of payments on current account was in deficit only in 1951 and 1955. Overall, it was therefore a reasonably prosperous decade for the United Kingdom, although there was an underlying decline in the relative strength of Britain's manufacturing industry.

One change in the international oil trade during this decade deserves attention. Up to the Iranian oil crisis in 1951–3, Britain had imported Middle East oil mainly from Iran, in the form of petroleum products from the Abadan Refinery. During the crisis, these imports ceased and were replaced, as illustrated in the figures below, by oil from other Middle Eastern countries. But this oil was crude, not products, and AIOC had to make emergency arrangements for its refining elsewhere. This speeded a change in refinery policy.

As mentioned in Chapter 2, Western Governments, for balance of payments and employment reasons, were pressing for refineries to be built in their countries. The companies, and especially AIOC, were the more inclined to yield to this pressure when they had seen the difficulties caused, not by the loss of Iranian oil (which were small) but by the loss of the Abadan Refinery. The outcome was that considerable investment went into refineries in Britain (and elsewhere in Europe) and that imports henceforward were increasingly of crude oil as their feedstock, rather than of products. So even when the oil crisis was over, and Abadan was back on stream, imports to Britain were largely of crude from Iraq, Qatar and especially Kuwait, while the products from Iran were shipped to other markets. This had its impact on the visible trade statistics below.

In passing, it is worth mentioning that AIOC directed its refineries investment not only to Britain and other European countries but also to Aden, where its Little Aden refinery was built in 1953. This was in fact another case of a refinery close to its markets. Aden was then probably the greatest bunkering port in the world and the refinery produced the marine fuel oil it needed.

Visible Trade

For convenience of layout and to provide a more manageable set of figures for analysis, the statistics for trade with the Middle East during the decade will be presented as two quinquennia, with an overlap year in each case. The remarks in the opening section of Chapter 4 again apply.

Table 3: Visible Trade (£ million)[1] with:

	1950	1951	1952	1953	1954	1955
ADEN						
Exports to	3.5	4.6	11.9	19.6	14.3	7.3
Imports from	1.0	2.3	1.3	1.3	2.4	4.8
Balance	+2.5	+2.3	+10.6	+18.3	+11.9	+2.5
ALGERIA						
Exports to	2.3	2.4	3.2	3.5	3.1	2.3
Imports from	10.4	18.2	21.6	16.4	16.4	18.6
Balance	-8.1	-15.8	–18.4	-12.9	-13.3	-16.3
BAHRAIN + QATAR + TRUCIAL STATES						
Exports to			8.4	9.9	10.9	12.8
Imports from			11.2	17.8	16.3	20.9
Balance			-2.8	-7.9	-5.4	-8.1
EGYPT						
Exports to	43.0	39.0	33.0	21.4	21.5	29.1
Imports from	40.2	47.4	12.9	15.3	16.7	9.7
Balance	+2.8	-8.4	+20.1	+6.1	+4.8	+19.4
IRAN						
Exports to	30.3	19.3	5.6	4.7	8.3	18.1
Imports from	47.7	32.8	3.0	2.6	3.3	16.8
Balance	-17.4	-13.5	+2.6	+2.1	+5.0	+1.3
IRAQ						
Exports to	14.6	15.9	22.4	29.4	23.6	26.7
Imports from	8.7	13.8	51.9	64.5	44.5	32.6
Balance	+5.9	+2.1	-29.5	-35.1	-20.9	-5.9
ISRAEL						
Exports to	10.0	11.7	9.1	9.0	7.0	9.9
Imports from	5.2	5.9	5.9	6.3	9.1	7.7
Balance	+4.8	+5.8	+3.2	+2.7	-2.1	+2.2
JORDAN						
Exports to	3.1	3.6	6.8	6.7	5.8	6.2
Imports from	—	—	—	—	0.1	—
Balance	+3.1	+3.6	+6.8	+6.7	+5.7	+6.2

KUWAIT (incl. Bahrain, Qatar and Trucial States for 1950–1951)						
Exports to	7.0	7.5	10.1	16.5	10.2	8.1
Imports from	34.8	79.3	136.0	129.5	134.5	125.4
Balance	-27.8	-71.8	-125.9	-113.0	-124.3	-117.3
LEBANON						
Exports to	8.1	7.1	7.6	5.3	5.5	10.0
Imports from	0.3	0.9	0.4	0.6	0.6	1.9
Balance	+7.8	+6.2	+7.2	+4.7	+4.9	+8.1
LIBYA						
Exports to	3.0	4.2	5.8	4.9	4.9	5.6
Imports from	1.1	0.4	1.7	1.2	1.7	1.4
Balance	+1.9	+3.8	+4.1	+3.7	+3.2	+4.2
MOROCCO (incl. Tangier)						
Exports to	3.5	4.2	6.7	6.8	6.7	7.3
Imports from	13.6	15.3	10.0	13.1	11.4	10.3
Balance	-10.1	-11.1	-3.3	-6.3	-4.7	-3.0
OMAN						
Exports to	0.1	0.1	0.2	0.1	0.2	0.3
Imports from	—	—	—	—	—	—
Balance	+0.1	+0.1	+0.2	+0.1	+0.2	+0.3
SAUDI ARABIA						
Exports to	2.9	3.3	7.4	6.0	5.7	7.9
Imports from	8.2	30.2	35.6	2.2	1.8	3.2
Balance	-5.3	-26.9	-28.2	+3.8	+3.9	+4.7
SUDAN						
Exports to	9.3	12.7	21.0	17.0	13.6	13.6
Imports from	21.8	61.4	33.8	19.4	18.0	14.9
Balance	-12.5	-48.7	-12.8	-2.4	-4.4	-1.3
SYRIA						
Exports to	3.0	4.6	5.6	5.1	6.9	7.6
Imports from	2.0	3.6	10.8	6.5	3.2	4.9
Balance	+1.0	+1.0	-5.2	-1.4	+3.7	+2.7
TUNISIA						
Exports to	1.0	0.8	1.4	1.1	1.1	1.0
Imports from	6.0	10.6	10.3	6.2	5.5	6.5
Balance	-5.0	-9.8	-8.9	-5.1	-4.4	-5.5

TOTAL – MIDDLE EAST COUNTRIES						
Exports to	144.7	141.0	166.2	167.0	149.3	173.8
Imports from	201.0	322.1	346.4	302.9	285.5	279.6
Balance	-56.3	-181.1	-180.2	-135.9	-136.2	-105.8
TOTAL – ALL COUNTRIES						
Exports to	2455.0	2495.5	2728.1	2687.6	2775.0	3024.3
Imports from	2602.9	3602.7	3477.0	3343.4	3373.9	3880.9
Balance	-147.9	-1107.2	-748.9	-655.8	-598.9	-856.6
M.E. TRADE AS per cent OF TOTAL TRADE						
Exports to	5.89	5.65	6.09	6.21	5.38	5.75
Imports from	7.72	8.94	9.96	9.06	8.46	7.20

(Note: Apparent minor arithmetical errors result from rounding)

The first point to emerge from these statistics is that the importance of the Middle East in Britain's global trade for the quinquennium had not changed significantly from its status in the previous five years' figures (Chapter 4). Both for exports and imports, it accounted for over 5 per cent and under 10 per cent of visible trade between 1950 and 1955. Nevertheless, there were some large rises and falls in the figures for individual countries.

The most striking of these stemmed directly from the Iranian oil crisis. British imports from Iran declined sharply, from £47.7 million in 1950 and £32.8 million in 1951 to a mere £3 million in 1952; they remained depressed until 1955, when they partially recovered to £16.8 million following settlement of the dispute. The corollary was that Britain's exports to Iran went through a similar trough, though the decline was not quite so sharp; for the four years from 1952 to 1955 inclusive, Britain even ran a small balance of trade surplus with Iran instead of the usual sizeable deficit.

As Britain's oil imports from Iran fell, those from Iraq and Kuwait rose rapidly, with some increase also from Qatar, as AIOC switched its purchasing programme. From 1951 onwards, Kuwait became the UK's largest supplier of oil, regularly outdoing the combined supplies from Iraq and Iran. (Kuwait's figures are separately listed in the Trade and Navigation Accounts from 1952 onwards, a belated change which should have been made at least as early as 1949.)

It should be noted that there was also a large increase in Britain's imports from Saudi Arabia in 1951 and 1952, from under £10 million to over £30 million a year, and that from 1953 onwards that figure fell right back to under £4 million p.a. for the next three years. The precise reasons for this peak and trough are hidden in the secrets of the oil majors, but they certainly do not represent changes in the retail market share in Britain of the US oil companies which were the parents of ARAMCO, so they must reflect inter-company trading. They were also independent of the Buraimi dispute; at this period the oil companies and not the Saudi Government determined the direction of Saudi oil sales.

On the British export front, there was a less than corresponding increase in sales to these four beneficiaries from the Iran imbroglio. Iraq was already a considerable importer from Britain and less than doubled its purchases during the period in which its sales nearly quintupled, whilst Kuwait and Qatar, and even Saudi Arabia, had far too small populations to be able to spend much of the wealth that poured into their treasuries, at least in the short term. Britain secured a modest increase in exports to the Saudi market during the years 1952–5, but this was smaller than might have been hoped for in such a promising market; here Buraimi did play some part.

The other major fluctuations in figures are found in British imports from the cotton growers, Egypt and Sudan. Here the main influence was the Korean War, which caused a temporary boom in prices of basic commodities, including cotton. Their earnings in 1951, £47.4 million in the case of Egypt and no less than £61.4 million for Sudan, were exceptionally high, and the decline, to under £20 million a year each for the second half of the quinquennium, represented a return to a more normal level; indeed, there was a long-term tendency for UK imports of cotton to fall as man-made fibres exended their share of the textile market. The trend in British exports to these two countries was similar in direction, reflecting their fluctuating purchasing power, although the changes were more gradual.

Exports to Aden were high in the three years 1952 to 1954 inclusive and then fell back again; this was probably due to the construction of the Little Aden refinery.

Table 4: Visible Trade (£ million) with:

	1955	1956	1957	1958	1959	1960
ADEN						
Exports to	7.3	8.0	8.1	7.7	7.8	9.5
Imports from	4.8	6.8	13.5	7.1	7.5	7.3
Balance	+2.5	+1.2	-5.4	+0.6	+0.3	+2.2
ALGERIA						
Exports to	2.3	3.7	2.7	4.0	2.4	3.3
Imports from	18.6	13.8	12.3	11.4	11.0	12.1
Balance	-16.3	-10.1	-9.6	-7.4	-8.6	-8.8
BAHRAIN (incl. Qatar and Trucial States for 1955 only)						
Exports to	12.8	7.6	8.4	7.3	7.4	7.7
Imports from	20.9	9.3	6.1	10.4	12.2	14.2
Balance	-8.1	-1.7	+2.3	-3.1	-4.8	-6.5
EGYPT						
Exports to	29.1	22.8	2.3	13.0	13.9	19.6
Imports from	9.7	7.3	0.7	2.0	4.3	6.7
Balance	+19.4	+15.5	+1.6	+11.0	+9.6	+12.9
IRAN						
Exports to	18.1	26.7	35.9	38.9	38.5	36.6
Imports from	16.8	34.1	35.5	56.2	56.9	48.6
Balance	+1.3	-7.4	+0.4	-17.3	-18.4	-12.0
IRAQ						
Exports to	26.7	32.7	34.5	31.3	32.0	29.2
Imports from	32.6	24.2	12.2	50.5	53.1	54.2
Balance	-5.9	+8.5	+22.3	-19.2	-21.1	-25.0
ISRAEL						
Exports to	9.9	10.6	14.4	14.3	16.5	16.6
Imports from	7.7	9.0	11.2	12.8	15.2	14.7
Balance	+2.2	+1.6	+3.2	+1.5	+1.3	+1.9
JORDAN						
Exports to	6.2	6.3	4.9	6.6	5.8	6.0
Imports from	—	—	—	—	0.1	0.2
Balance	+6.2	+6.3	+4.9	+6.6	+5.7	+5.8

KUWAIT						
Exports to	8.1	13.3	28.2	20.5	18.3	15.2
Imports from	125.4	118.1	134.2	131.3	125.4	158.8
Balance	-117.3	-104.8	-106.0	-110.8	-107.1	-143.6
LEBANON						
Exports to	10.0	9.6	12.2	10.3	9.7	11.1
Imports from	1.9	2.5	2.2	2.2	2.4	1.9
Balance	+8.1	+7.1	+10.0	+8.1	+7.3	+9.2
LIBYA						
Exports to	5.6	5.6	6.1	13.0	8.4	12.7
Imports from	1.4	1.1	1.3	2.0	0.7	0.7
Balance	+4.2	+4.5	+4.8	+11.0	+7.7	+12.0
MOROCCO (incl. Tangier)						
Exports to	7.3	7.7	6.6	6.7	5.3	5.3
Imports from	10.3	12.5	12.9	10.5	10.7	14.0
Balance	-3.0	-4.8	-6.3	-3.8	-5.4	-8.7
OMAN						
Exports to	0.3	0.5	0.5	0.7	1.5	0.7
Imports from	—	—	—	—	—	—
Balance	+0.3	+0.5	+0.5	+0.7	+1.5	+0.7
QATAR						
Exports to		4.3	4.5	5.3	5.4	5.0
Imports from		18.9	12.4	6.7	13.0	5.2
Balance		-14.6	-7.9	-1.4	-7.6	-0.2
SAUDI ARABIA						
Exports to	7.9	9.1	7.6	8.0	7.0	6.3
Imports from	3.2	5.0	5.5	7.5	5.3	9.8
Balance	+4.7	+4.1	+2.1	+0.5	+1.7	-3.5
SUDAN						
Exports to	13.6	11.4	18.8	14.8	13.0	16.7
Imports from	14.9	23.5	13.2	13.3	18.6	16.7
Balance	–1.3	-12.1	+5.6	+1.5	-5.6	0.0
SYRIA						
Exports to	7.6	8.0	4.9	8.0	6.7	7.2
Imports from	4.9	2.0	1.8	1.4	1.7	1.7
Balance	+2.7	+6.0	+3.1	+6.6	+5.0	+5.5

TRUCIAL STATES						
Exports to		0.8	0.8	1.0	1.3	2.4
Imports from		0.1	0.1	0.1	—	—
Balance		+0.7	+0.7	+0.9	+1.3	+2.4
TUNISIA						
Exports to	1.0	0.9	0.8	2.2	2.5	2.6
Imports from	6.5	6.9	6.7	4.8	4.3	5.2
Balance	-5.5	-6.0	-5.9	-2.6	-1.8	-2.6
YEMEN						
Exports to	—	—	—	—	0.1	—
Imports from	—	—	—	0.1	—	—
Balance	—	—	—	-0.1	+0.1	—
TOTAL – MIDDLE EAST COUNTRIES						
Exports to	173.8	189.6	202.2	213.6	203.5	213.7
Imports from	279.6	295.1	281.8	330.3	342.4	372.0
Balance	-105.8	-105.5	-79.6	-116.7	-138.9	-158.3
TOTAL – ALL COUNTRIES						
Exports to	3024.3	3318.0	3420.2	3312.9	3461.0	3695.9
Imports from	3880.9	3886.1	4042.2	3745.8	3983.4	4540.7
Balance	-856.6	-568.1	-622.0	-432.9	-522.4	-844.8
M.E. TRADE AS per cent OF TOTAL TRADE						
Exports to	5.75	5.71	5.91	6.45	5.88	5.78
Imports from	7.20	7.59	6.97	8.82	8.60	8.19

(Note: Apparent minor arithmetical errors result from rounding)

Once again, the importance of Middle East trade to Britain remained relatively stable. As in the first quinquennium of the decade, it accounted for over 5 per cent of British exports and under 10 per cent of British imports, with the balance of visible trade regularly, and fairly heavily, adverse to the UK. This was, as usual, the result of huge oil imports from the Middle East oil producers, with Kuwait now by far the largest supplier, outstripping the combined sales to Britain of Iran and Iraq.

The Buraimi dispute probably played some part in keeping exports from Britain to Saudi Arabia at a low level. The Suez affair was rather more disruptive, with Britain's exports to Egypt drastically reduced in 1957 but thereafter rising again fairly quickly. British imports from Egypt fell right away in 1957 and recovered only gradually over the next three years. The closure of the Suez Canal did not last long enough to change the overall picture, but it sounded a warning for the future.

Elsewhere, there were some trends which merit a brief comment. Trade with Bahrain and Qatar in both directions became significant enough to be worth being recorded separately in the Trade and Navigation Accounts from 1956 onwards, but the Trucial States were still grouped together. After 1956, both exports to and imports from Israel grew, but there is no evidence that this was a result of the Suez collusion: it reflects rather a general growth in the Israeli economy.[2] There was a high point in imports from Aden in 1957, which may have been due to a backlog being cleared after the Suez Canal reopened. Exports to Libya in the last three years of the decade were higher than earlier.

Invisible Trade

The remarks under this heading in Chapter 4 remain relevant. During the decade, revenues earned by British oil companies operating in the Middle East increased enormously, almost, as has been seen, unaffected overall by the Iranian oil crisis. Not all of these earnings were remitted to the UK since there was a great deal of new capital investment by the oil companies in the Middle East. But there were substantial remittances, for dividends and to meet tax payments to the British Treasury, which increased, not indeed *pro rata*, but by very large sums. Banking, shipping and insurance continued to be valuable contributors to the income of the City of London. With UK austerity relaxed as the decade progressed, tourism to Britain began to grow. Remittances by British workers overseas, especially in the oil-producing countries, and fees earned abroad by British consultants and other experts were also on a rising trend.

On the other side of the account, British ships, notably tankers, paid increased sums for Suez Canal dues and other local charges as the volume of imports from the Middle East and hence of shipping movements increased. Even greater growth was seen in civil aviation expenditure as aeroplanes began to displace ships as the normal means of passenger transport to and more importantly through the Middle East, to and from India, South East Asia and Australasia. Beirut followed Cairo in becoming a major international airport. Outward tourism from Britain grew somewhat, chiefly to Israel, but also to Morocco in addition to the prewar destinations of Egypt and Lebanon.

Arms sales from Britain to Middle East countries were certainly important, economically as well as politically, however difficult they are to quantify. The success of the Soviet Bloc in penetrating this market after 1954 was confined mainly to Egypt and Syria at this stage, plus Iraq after the revolution there; additional markets which were opening up in the newly oil-rich countries looked primarily to Britain (and in the case of Saudi Arabia the USA) for their purchases.

A further major factor to be noted is an inflow of Middle East investment funds to London, particularly from Kuwait. While Saudi Arabia put such of its oil earnings as it did not spend chiefly into US Government bonds, the Kuwait Government, with a higher proportion of unspendable funds, took international advice and was ready to pursue a more sophisticated investment policy, with a portfolio of equity holdings and property as well as bonds. Having good links with the Bank of England as a member of the Sterling Area, and benefiting from tax exemption under the UK interpretation of royal immunity, it chose to establish a Kuwait Investment Office in London. Unostentatiously but ineluctably, it became a major, and much respected, operator in the London markets, as it remains to this day (its purchase of a sizeable shareholding in BP has recently given it publicity that it normally avoids).

Overall Assessment

Despite the distortions caused by the Iranian oil crisis and the Suez fiasco, this was in general another decade of very satisfactory relationships for Britain with the Middle East in the economic and commercial fields. Those distortions were smaller than might have been expected, and in each case proved temporary. Rapidly increasing imports of oil gave Britain a substantial deficit with the Middle East in visible trade throughout the decade, but this was offset to a considerable extent by invisible earnings on current account. When capital inflows are allowed for, it can be said with confidence that the overall balance of payments with the Middle East was favourable to Britain.

ECGD

During the 50s, ECGD continued quietly to expand its business and the range of its services. One of its innovations was its introduction in 1954 of an unconditional bank guarantee. This enabled the banks to charge a lower interest rate than would otherwise have been requisite on loans they made to their customers to finance export business. Exporters found this highly beneficial when competing in markets where credit facilities were becoming more and more important in winning export orders. Considerable extra business accrued to ECGD in consequence. By the end of the decade its proportion of UK exports covered had risen to 19 per cent and Parliament in 1959 had raised its maximum liability for cover to £1400 million.

Overseas Banking

During this decade Barclays (DCO), which had already been weakened in the Middle East by the British withdrawal from Palestine, lost its major investment in Egypt when its property was sequestrated in 1956 as a result of the Suez affair. It retained branches elsewhere, especially in Libya, but ceased to be a leading British bank in most of the area.

For the Imperial Bank of Iran (which had already been renamed British Bank of Iran and the Middle East in 1949), the decade included the ending of a long and at times very profitable association with the country from which it had taken its name. On 30 July 1952 its last branch in Iran was closed. This was a consequence of the Anglo-Iranian oil crisis but it was also the conclusion of a long process of decline in its Iranian business in the face of competition from the Bank Melli Iran.

The counterpart was that the Bank, which changed its name again, this time to the British Bank of the Middle East (BBME), further expanded its activities in the Arab countries. In 1952, branches were opened in Aden and Tripoli (Libya). The next two years saw new branches in Sharjah and Qatar. In 1955, a branch was opened in the Jordanian-administered sector of Jerusalem. Towards the end of the decade, a further flurry of openings took place, in Benghazi (Libya), Tunis, Mosul (Iraq) and Abu Dhabi. Not all these new ventures were profitable, either immediately or in some cases ever, but the Bank had decided to justify its new title by having the widest possible representation in the Middle East, with the added hope of benefiting from future oil discoveries. Its gains from this policy outweighed its losses.[3]

The Eastern Bank was less enterprising than the BBME, but it too opened some new branches in Arab countries. In particular, it succeeded in getting a footing in Qatar in 1950, ahead of the BBME. The Chartered Bank, which absorbed Eastern Bank in 1957, set a new pattern for British banking in the area by establishing a joint-venture bank with local interests in Iran, the Irano-British Bank, early in 1959. Only a few months later the BBME followed suit, joining with the Kettaneh family in opening the Bank of Iran and the Middle East, so reentering the country in which it had originated.

It is worth drawing attention to the fact that the countries in which British banks were operating were not all in the Sterling Area. The Arab States of the Gulf, Iraq (until 1959), Jordan and Libya were members, but Iran, Lebanon, Saudi Arabia, Syria and Tunisia were not. Any inconvenience which might have been caused by the need to seek permission from the Bank of England for investment of capital or granting of overdraft facilities to branches outside the Area was usually avoided by inter-branch transfers needing no Bank of England permission.

The decade, while it saw the spread of British banking in the Middle East, was also marked by the coming into being of indigenous banks, stimulated by the upsurge of nationalism and in some cases by political events. Iran had of course long led the way in this respect (see Chapter 4). The Rafidain Bank in Iraq had come into being in 1941. In 1952, the BBME, despite its monopoly agreement with the Ruler, wisely decided not to oppose the opening of the National Bank of Kuwait. Following the Suez attack, not only British and French but all foreign banks in Egypt were nationalised. In 1957 the National Bank of Bahrain was established (with BBME and Eastern Bank taking minority shareholdings.) This was a process which was sure to spread.

13 Egypt's Arab Socialism

The Suez affair had been a political triumph for Nasser but it left him with economic problems, at least in the short term. Egyptian bank holdings in Britain and France had been frozen since 27 July 1956, with consequential disruption to trade. The Canal dues which Nasser had claimed would enable Egypt to build the High Dam without foreign help had not yet proved to be a pot of gold. British and French and some other ship-owners, who had been in the habit of paying their dues in London or Paris, had been instructed by their Governments to continue to do so. Prior to the attack on Port Said only about 40 per cent of dues were being paid in Egypt, yet Egypt was bearing the costs of passing all ships through the Canal, since Nasser decided he could not afford the political price of denying passage to ships not paying dues locally. The blocking of the Canal had now cut off all its revenues while leaving much of its overheads unchanged. For both financial and supply reasons, emergency measures on the economic front were unavoidable in the first half of 1957.

In January, kerosene (much used for cooking) was rationed and all Government Departments were ordered to reduce their spending by 10 per cent. In February, prison terms were decreed for profiteers and the Ministry of Health published a list of substitutes for 15,000 now unavailable pharmaceutical products. To ease currency difficulties, 136 firms were reluctantly freed from sequestration. In March, imports were severely cut to conserve foreign exchange and Government Departments were told to cancel credits which had been opened for any goods not absolutely vital. In April, there were further import cuts and holidays abroad were forbidden. There were queues everywhere for such goods as were available and the cost of living rose sharply. It was no doubt pressures of this kind which induced the Egyptian Government to open talks for financial settlements in London and Paris as early as May 1957. They were bound to take time to complete.

However, the reopening of the Canal in March/April 1957 eased certain problems and some aid was forthcoming from the Soviet Union (in addition to the replacement of military hardware). In November 1957 the USSR made a loan equivalent to some £62 million to Egypt, with interest at 2.5 per cent, repayable over twelve years with a 4-year grace period. There were strings attached; the loan was only drawable for projects agreed with the Soviet Union, which would be carried out with the help of Soviet technicians and with use of Soviet materials and equipment. But it was useful none the less and Nasser embarked on what must be called a borrowing spree.

Even excluding huge Soviet credits for arms, it has been estimated that Egypt borrowed £1321 million from abroad between 1957 and 1965[1]. Some of this was for the Aswan High Dam. The boast that Egypt would finance this project herself from the Canal revenues had to be quietly forgotten and Nasser set about building it in partnership with the Soviet Union. A loan of £E35 million from the USSR in 1958 for this purpose was supplemented by another of £E78 million in 1960. There was also aid from the West, not indeed from Britain and France but from the IBRD for agreed projects, especially the improvement of the Suez Canal, and from the USA mainly in the form of wheat supplies under the Agricultural Assistance Act (Public Law 480) enacted in 1954, which enabled Nasser to hold down the price of bread, crucial to the prevention of unrest, especially in the rapidly growing population of Cairo.

Dependence on the Soviet Union in the military and other fields was accompanied by a steady movement towards a centrally-planned and public-sector-dominated domestic economy. Not that Egypt ever became communist; the Egyptian Communist Party was never allowed to gain strength and was outlawed much of the time. But Nasser evolved what, with his gift for phrases, he chose to call 'Arab Socialism'. A landmark was the nationalisation of the Bank Misr in February 1960, the first occasion on which a purely Egyptian firm had been seized, all previous measures of this kind having been directed against foreign-owned companies. Before long all banks and insurance companies were nationalised and some 300 industrial and commercial enterprises were also taken over by the state, either wholly or in part. In June and July 1961 the entire import trade was transferred to the public sector, together with much of the export trade, including in particular Egypt's main export, cotton.[2] Moves against foreign firms also continued; in 1961 all Belgian economic interests in Egypt were sequestrated, the peg on which this action was hung being a protest against Belgian policy in the Congo.

It may have been this wave of nationalisation measures which triggered the secession of Syria on 28 September 1961 from the United Arab Republic, the union of Egypt and Syria formed with so much acclaim on 2 February 1958. There were of course other causes; Nasser never had much understanding of the tact needed in handling relations with smaller Arab countries with their own pride and historical backgrounds. Syria's secession prompted the sequestration in Egypt on 22 October 1961 of the properties of 167 wealthy families of Levantine ancestry, a measure extended to some 600 families the following month. Only a few of these properties were later desequestrated.

The Five-Year Plan which had been aborted by the Suez crisis finally came into being in 1960; its declared objective was to increase the national income by 40 per cent over the period to 1965, as the first step towards its doubling by 1970. This represented an average growth rate of 7 per cent p.a. compound, an ambitious target dependent (though this was not admitted) on heavy foreign borrowing.

The Plan was followed in May 1962 by the National Charter, the fullest ever formulation of the economic strategy towards which Nasser had been feeling his way over the previous decade. The Charter prescribed public ownership of the entire economic infrastructure of the country, together with all banks and insurance companies and the great majority of heavy, medium and extraction industries. All import trade and most export trade had to be handled by public sector corporations. A good deal of this programme had already been achieved; the remainder was implemented in the course of 1962–4, so that by the end of 1964 most of the country's assets and means of production outside the agricultural sector were in Government hands.

Land reform had meanwhile made further strides. A Second Agrarian Reform Law of 1961 had reduced the ceiling on individual ownership from 200 to 100 feddans and in 1962 the substantial land-holdings of registered charities were made subject to requisition. Compensation for land taken over under the 1961 law was in bonds bearing 4 per cent interest, redeemable after fifteen years, but this proved a paper promise since in 1964 all interest payments on land bonds were discontinued and the bonds became irredeemable. The ceiling for individual land holdings was reduced again in 1969 to 50 feddans (still enough to produce a comfortable income). For their part, the beneficiaries from redistribution were generously treated. In 1961 their liability was fixed at half the compensation price and in 1964 this was reduced to a quarter, their debt being interest-free.

The rapid build-up of the public sector was accompanied by an even more than proportionate increase in public employment.[3] From 1960 to 1965 the number of civil servants rose by no less than 250 per cent. Egypt had long had a swollen bureaucracy, partly because of its reliance on stamp taxes for revenue with its corollary of an army of clerks to issue and account for the stamps. Under Nasser, it became the practice to find Government jobs if need be for all university and most high school graduates so as to avoid social discontent. The Egyptian equivalent of Parkinson's Law ensured that these idle hands occupied themselves in passing files backwards and forwards interminably, with a resultant slowdown in the pace of all Government paper-work. This in turn produced a need for 'fixers' to find their way through the labyrinth, a process naturally requiring the greasing of palms. Corruption and inefficiency thus grew together, each feeding on the other.

This was perhaps an almost inevitable consequence of the

pressure of population resulting from Egypt's high birth-rate. Census figures show that, for the whole country, population density in 1966 was more than double that in 1927, and for Cairo itself the growth was threefold. Egypt's agricultural and industrial base could not provide employment to match population growth. This caused a drift from the countryside to the towns and especially to the capital. Given his policy of Government control of the economy, it became a choice for Nasser between accepting unemployment and tolerating overmanning. For both human and political reasons he chose the latter.

The unfortunate consequence was that the economy was more and more infected with the inefficiency and low-level corruption which already afflicted the public administration. Attempts were made to deal with overmanning by reducing working hours. A decree of 1961 fixed the normal working week at 42 hours, as against the average 48 hours then worked in enterprises employing ten or more workers. This decree seems never to have been strictly enforced, but it had some effect; by 1964 the average was down to 44 hours.[4] The problem nevertheless remained.

Foreign trade was by this time very largely on a bilateral basis, governed by annual agreements not only with the Soviet Union and communist bloc countries but also with such third world countries as India. This system is convenient for planners when the economy is dominated by the public sector, but it has its drawbacks. It has little flexibility if plans go astray and it removes choice of suppliers, with the consequence that sub-standard imported goods often cannot be rejected. Bilateralism was not only an ideological decision; it was largely forced on Egypt by its lack of freely available foreign exchange. Much of the cotton crop was mortgaged to Czechoslovakia and the Soviet Union in payment for arms deals and there was no adequate substitute for foreign trade purposes. The economic aid given by the Soviet Union and the USA was to a large extent in kind rather than in cash.

It is therefore not really surprising that the attempt to achieve and maintain a 7 per cent p.a. growth rate ran into a foreign exchange crisis. For the first half of the Five-Year Plan period the ambitious target was more or less achieved overall, though not in accordance with the Plan's objectives sector by sector. A considerable growth in shipping using the Suez Canal, a largely adventitious occurrence so far as Egypt was concerned, caused transport earnings to be well above forecasts, offsetting shortfalls elsewhere.

Industry received pretty well the planned level of investment (over 25 per cent of total investment), thanks to Soviet aid, but achieved only an 8.5 per cent average annual growth rate during the 1960–5 period as against the 14.7 per cent rate planned. The actual rate sounds impressive none the less, but is not really so when considered against the overriding priority given to industry in the Plan (as compared, for instance, with agriculture). Despite the heavy investment it swallowed up, productivity in industry grew by only 3 per cent p.a.[5]

In 1963 the inevitable foreign exchange crash came and programmes had to be cut back from the planned levels. The balance of payments deficit jumped to £E 135.6 million, no less than 7.3 per cent of GDP. Most of the cuts came in investment programmes, although work on the High Dam continued under Soviet guidance (this however was still at the earth-moving stage and was many years away from making any contribution to earnings). The outcome of the Five-Year Plan was thus a growth of some 30 per cent rather than 40 per cent over the quinquennium. A 30 per cent growth in five years is no small boast, but it was achieved in a sectorally unbalanced manner and at the cost of an overall foreign exchange deficit of £E 413 million, which would hold down future investment for several years to come. It is perhaps not surprising that the intended second Five-Year Plan for 1965–70 was sent back to the planners for reconsideration and was never introduced as such.

The term 'Arab Socialism' is itself of interest. Nasser no doubt intended by it to differentiate his economic policy from Eastern Bloc Socialism, given his political hostility to the Egyptian Communist Party. (In reality, there was by 1964 not all that much difference visible: it is true that Egyptian agriculture remained in the private sector,[6] but then that is also largely true of Poland.) However, he probably had a second idea in mind, that what Egypt achieved in developing its economy along socialist lines should become a model for other Arab countries.

The federation with Syria in the United Arab Republic gave him an opportunity to begin to put this idea into practice. Socialist measures were introduced in Syria and were not popular; as was remarked above, they became one of the main causes of Syrian secession from the UAR. The Syrians, along with the Lebanese, are among the great traders of the Arab world and have all the typical distaste of the merchant for Government interference. The socialist innovations of the unity years were almost entirely cancelled when Syria returned to independence. 'Arab Socialism' reverted in 1961 to being socialism in one country, Egypt.

14 The Arabian Peninsula and North-West Africa

Mention was made in Chapter 8 of the relationship between Britain and the Shaikhs of the Arab shore of the Persian Gulf, who were autonomous in internal affairs but entrusted their defence and foreign policy to the British Indian and later to the UK Government. The British representatives in these protected states bore the title of Political Agents, reporting to a Political Resident Persian Gulf who had his headquarters in Bahrain. No other Governments had diplomatic or consular representation in the Shaikhdoms. The Political Resident, who in status was something between a proconsul and an ambassador, came under the aegis of the Foreign Office in London, not the Colonial Office. He had available to him for his defence function a small naval force based in Bahrain; the British-officered Trucial Oman Levies, renamed by the 1960s the Trucial Oman Scouts, as a locally – recruited land force; and a small R.A.F. contingent based in Sharjah, one of the Trucial States.

The Political Agents had administrative and judicial functions in respect of non-Muslim foreigners living in the Shaikhdoms, analogous to the 'capitulations' which had once prevailed in China. There was a British judge attached to the staff of the Political Resident to supervise the judicial work of the Political Agents and to act as an appellate judge in serious criminal cases; over him was a Chief Judge based in London who spent only part of the year in Bahrain. One of the administrative tasks which the Shaikhs happily left to the Political Agents was the responsibility for supervising imports of alcoholic drinks for the non-Muslims.

British control over the foreign affairs of the Shaikhdoms extended to approving the letting of oil concessions, although by the 1960s this had become something of a formality and there was no question of a Political Agent vetoing the grant of a concession to an oil company from any friendly state.

It might be thought that this system was thoroughly anomalous by the second half of the twentieth century, but the Shaikhs had watched with approval the expulsion of Saudi forces from the Buraimi oasis and most of them had no desire to see it change. The exception was the Shaikh of Kuwait, who, with vast oil revenues enabling him to govern his city-state in a modern style, wished to assume the full trappings of independence. He was a well-regarded and experienced ruler and the British Government saw no reason to stand in his way. On 19 June 1961 the Anglo-Kuwaiti Treaty of 1899 was terminated by mutual consent and a new Treaty of Friendship between Kuwait and the UK was signed to replace it. This provided for the relations between them to continue to be governed by a spirit of close friendship and for consultations to take place when appropriate on matters of mutual concern. It also stated that 'nothing in these conclusions shall affect the readiness of Her Majesty's Government to assist the Government of Kuwait if the latter request such assistance'.

There was pleasure in Kuwait at the achievement of a fully independent status. It was decreed that the term Shaikhdom should no longer be used in what was now to be known as 'the State of Kuwait', whose Ruler was to be designated His Highness the Emir. The Political Agent became Her Majesty's Ambassador, reporting directly to the Foreign Office instead of to the Political Resident in Bahrain (although naturally keeping in close touch with the latter). Kuwait applied for membership of the League of Arab States, rapidly granted, and of the United Nations Organization, delayed by Soviet veto until 1963. The Arab Governments hastened to congratulate the Emir of this tiny but enormously wealthy State.

All that is except one. Iraq since its revolution in 1958 had been ruled by Abdul Karim Qasim. On 25 June 1961 he declared to a press conference in Baghdad that, since Kuwait had been part of the Vilayet of Basrah in Ottoman days, it was now rightfully part of Iraq. Britain's 1899 Treaty with Kuwait was, he declared, 'forged' and the new Treaty they had signed was illegal; in his eyes the Shaikh of Kuwait had been Governor of the Kuwait district of Iraq and was now a 'mutineer'. Denouncing British imperialism, he proclaimed that the era of Shaikhdoms was over.

This was not a new claim but the reassertion of an old one. The Ottoman Empire had certainly had suzerainty over Kuwait from 1776 onwards and Kuwait had perhaps at one time been part of the Vilayet of Basrah. But that suzerainty had weakened even before the collapse of the Ottoman Empire and Kuwait had in practice become autonomous by the time when, in 1899, it had entered into its Treaty with Britain to become a British 'protected state'. Then in 1922, at a famous conference in Uqair, Sir Percy Cox, as High Commissioner to Iraq in the days of the British Mandate, had negotiated between Sabih Beg of Iraq, Abdul Aziz (Ibn Saud) of Nejd and Major More, the Political Agent in Kuwait, a set of frontiers between Iraq, Kuwait and what was to become Saudi Arabia. The frontiers were rather favourable to Iraq and Nejd and unfavourable to Kuwait, since Major More was distinctly overawed by Cox. They included two ingenious devices to allow for movement of the nomadic tribes, an Iraqi-Saudi and a Saudi-Kuwaiti Neutral Zone.

The latter proved of considerable economic importance when oil was found in it by that legendary figure, John Paul Getty. The onshore concession in the Zone was held jointly, by the Getty Oil Company with the Saudi half-share, and by Aminoil with the Kuwaiti half-share. For political reasons which made little commercial sense they were obliged to separate their production half-shares at the wellheads and to pump them through two pipelines to two new oil terminals, Mina Saud and Mina Abdullah. Offshore the concession (again half-Saudi and half-Kuwaiti) was won by the Japanese Arabian Oil Company, who proved equally successful in finding prolific fields. Japan is extremely dependent on imported oil; it was therefore logical that the Japanese should look for a source of oil in the Gulf in which it could make a direct investment.

King Saud had no wish to see the Kuwaiti share in the Neutral

Zone fall into the hands of an Iraqi dictator. Not surprisingly, he declared Saudi Arabia's support for Kuwait against Qasim's claim. The other nearby monarchs, the Shah and King Hussain, similarly offered Iranian and Jordanian backing. For reasons which it is still difficult to understand, Qasim took no military steps to enforce his claim; had he moved quickly, Kuwait could have put up no more than token resistance. It is also odd that Emir Abdullah delayed for six days until 30 June 1961 before asking for British military assistance under the provisions of the recently-concluded Treaty of Friendship.[1]

The request was not unexpected but the forces which could respond to it had to be brought from widely-scattered points. Bahrain and Aden could not supply a balanced force; elements were needed from Cyprus, Kenya, Singapore and the UK itself.[2] The first foreign troops to arrive were in fact 100 Saudi paratroopers who got to Kuwait on 1 July. The next day 3000 British troops were landed and the aircraft-carrier HMS *Bulwark* anchored offshore with 600 helicopter-borne Royal Marine Commandos aboard. In another three days the British force was increased to a strong brigade group including an armoured element, and additional warships were on their way, two destroyers and a second aircraft carrier from the Mediterranean. Nasser made no difficulty about their transit through the Suez Canal. There was a low-key meeting of the UN Security Council to debate the issue, at which Kuwait made its first appearance as a member of the United Nations; the Council adjourned inconclusively.

With still no military move from the Iraqis, British forces began to withdraw on 7 July, to be replaced by a mixed Arab League force drawn from Saudi Arabia and Jordan with a few Egyptians and Sudanese. On 8 July, Qasim summoned another press conference to make the point that he had merely been recording Iraq's claim to Kuwait, which, he argued, history would painlessly bring about. The crisis was over but the claim remained.

One effect of this rather bizarre episode was to bring home to the Emir of Kuwait the need to strengthen his domestic base by some moves towards democratisation and his support in the Arab world by instituting an international aid programme which would give others a vested interest in Kuwait's continued independence. Another effect was on the other Arab rulers in the Gulf Shaikhdoms; they drew the conclusion that it was really rather convenient to remain under British protection. They were not liable to have their territories coveted by Iraq, but Bahrain had long been claimed by Iran, which kept empty seats for the Bahraini deputies in its Parliament, while the mainland Shaikhdoms had a powerful neighbour in Saudi Arabia. Britain did not interfere with their internal autonomy nor impede their aspirations to oil wealth. Some day, God willing, they would follow Kuwait along the road of full independence, but meanwhile, as the Arabic saying has it, 'haste is from Satan'.

One Shaikhdom in particular could afford to wait. Oil had been struck in Abu Dhabi, both onshore and offshore, at the end of the 1950s. Production was just getting under way by 1962 and no great wealth had yet come in, but the future was extremely promising. Abu Dhabi was the largest of the Trucial States, but had hitherto been poor, as it was almost entirely desert. Now that desert seemed to cover great prospective riches. The tribesmen looked forward avidly to being as wealthy as the Kuwaitis, or at least as their neighbours the Qataris. There was just one impediment. Their Ruler, Shaikh Shakhbut, had a miserly streak. He did not, as some alleged, keep his oil money under the bed, but he kept it on deposit in the local branch of the Ottoman Bank, a procedure unsatisfactory to his people and even to the bank, which could not invest it as he was liable from time to time to insist on its being taken out and counted.[3] That situation could obviously not continue for long, as vast sums would accumulate. But Shakhbut had a forbidding mien and neither his tribesmen nor the other members of his family had yet found the courage to outface him.

On 18 September 1962, Imam Ahmad, the Ruler of Yemen, died. Yemen is a mountainous country in the south-west of the Arabian Peninsula, very different in many respects from its neighbours. Its mountains give it an agreeable climate and enough rainfall to support agriculture. In Biblical days it became rich from the incense trade and was famous for that legendary figure, the

Queen of Sheba. To the Romans it was known as Arabia Felix, 'Happy Arabia', by contrast with the deserts by which it was surrounded. It was converted to Islam in the time of the first caliph, Abu Bakr, but never came fully under the political control of succeeding caliphs for more than short periods. Its economy had depended in ancient days on a sophisticated system of water storage, based on a great dam at Marib, but this had fallen into decay by Islamic times. Nevertheless, the highlands still made good use of the rains by careful terracing, and the country supported a substantial population, about 3.5 millions. Its chief export was coffee, named after the port through which it passed, Mocha.

The Imam was the religious and secular leader of the Zaydi sect of Muslims, who inhabited the mountain area. In principle the Imamate was elective, but since 1891 it had in practice become hereditary. Ahmad was succeeded by his son, Muhammad al-Badr, who appointed a trusted aide, Abdullah al-Sallal, as his chief of staff. The trust was misplaced; on 27 September 1962 Sallal led a coup in which Badr was reported to have been killed. A Yemen Arab Republic was proclaimed, with Sallal as President. It soon appeared that the coup had had Egyptian inspiration; an Egyptian mission rapidly put in an appearance. It also soon became undeniable that Badr had not after all been killed in the shelling of his palace but had escaped and was gathering support in the mountains.

Some of that support came across the border from Saudi Arabia. In the 50s King Saud had been for the most part an ally of Nasser; Saudi gold had combined with the seduction of Cairo Radio to make life difficult for Nasser's enemies in the Arab world, particularly those old Saudi antagonists the Hashemites in Iraq and Jordan. But Nasser could never prove a comfortable ally for a monarch and Saud had begun to distrust him. The idea of an Egyptian-controlled Republic on Saudi Arabia's south-western border was distinctly unpalatable to the Saudi ruling family (Saud was by now in poor health and power was largely in the hands of his brother Faisal, who felt a personal interest in Yemen, where he had once fought a successful campaign). Badr was supplied with Saudi money and rifles to help him to rally the Zaydi tribesmen.

An Egyptian-controlled Yemen was also objectionable to Britain, since the Aden Protectorates were neighbours of that country and historically had once been part of it. There was a clear danger that the Yemen Arab Republic, if successfully consolidated, would raise irredentist claims to the Protectorates and even to the Colony of Aden. Nasser, given his avowed aim to see British power eliminated from Arab lands, would encourage and back such claims. There was therefore satisfaction, and some relief, in Aden and in London when Badr raised his standard in the mountains. If he could regain his throne, the Egyptians would be driven out of Yemen. That was uncertain, but it was at least clear that for some time to come Sallal would be preoccupied with a struggle against Badr in Yemen and would have no time to dream about extension of his country's boundaries.

Not only Arabs, but certainly Arabs among others are firm believers in the principle that the enemy of my enemy is my friend. Faisal, who became Regent of Saudi Arabia (being already Prime Minister and Foreign Minister) when King Saud withdrew to Austria and Switzerland for medical treatment, was now sure that Nasser was his enemy, and looking across Yemen towards Aden he saw that Britain, as another enemy of Nasser, might prove to be a useful friend. He concluded that it was time to put the Buraimi quarrel aside, however strongly he still felt about it, and to restore diplomatic relations with Britain. Contact was made with the British Foreign Secretary at the United Nations and the restoration was rapidly agreed. Not only was the British Embassy in Jedda reopened but it was treated as a favoured mission, with easy access to Faisal himself and to his Ministers.

This removal of the diplomatic rupture was of commercial as well as political advantage to Britain. Saudi Arabia under Faisal was likely to use its oil wealth for productive purposes instead of frittering it away as Saud had done on political intrigue and royal extravagance. British firms, which were virtually unrepresented in the Kingdom,[4] could now be encouraged to open offices there and look for contracts.

It quickly became apparent that one of the areas in which Faisal was looking for British collaboration was in military training. He already had American help for his regular forces, particularly his still embryonic Air Force, but in addition to the Army there was a force of tribal levies known officially as the National Guard and unofficially as the White Army. This was in fact a powerful counterbalance to the Saudi Army proper and was deployed in posts chosen for the task of keeping an eye on the Army's movements. The Saudi Royal Family had seen military coups in too many Arab countries to be prepared to risk one against themselves. The White Army, in whose loyalty they felt great confidence since it was drawn from tribes closely linked, by tradition and marriage, with the Royal Family, was their insurance against an Army coup. Faisal had considerable respect for British ability to train Arab tribesmen, from his knowledge of the qualities of the Arab Legion in Jordan and (shades of Buraimi) the Trucial Oman Levies. Within days of the resumption of diplomatic relations a request was on its way to London for the unobtrusive secondment of two British officers with Arab experience to advise on the training of the National Guard. The British Government was happy to supply them. It was not long before their presence led to useful orders being placed in the UK for weapons and equipment for the Guard.

The civil war in Yemen dragged on for several years. Egypt was compelled to support its protégé Republic there by sending Egyptian troops to prop it up. This was a considerable drain on Egypt's always strained economy and was deeply unpopular with the Egyptian Army on which Nasser's power was ultimately dependent. He of course turned his propaganda machine of press and radio to the task of bringing down the Saudi monarchy, but for once it made little headway. Faisal, who had succeeded Saud as King, was an austere and hard-working monarch, very different from his predecessor and by no means an easy target.

For their part, the Saudis saw a need to strengthen the air defence of the Kingdom against possible Egyptian bombing raids. With American advice, they decided to order interceptor fighter aircraft and anti-aircraft missiles and to hire foreign advisers to help them set up a coordinated air defence network. Perhaps to assist the haggling process for a lower price for the package, they opened the bidding to British as well as American suppliers, but it was all along probable that American firms would be preferred.

That was in fact the Saudi decision at the end of a long bargaining process, but Washington politics intervened. The total package was a huge one and it was unlikely that it would be approved by Congress, where it was bound to be opposed by the powerful Jewish lobby which automatically objected to all arms supplies to Arab countries. The Saudis were advised that it would be in their interest to reconsider their decision and to split the package. Bargaining resumed and in the end the order for ground-to-air missiles went to the United States, while Lightning aircraft and the services of an air support contracting firm were ordered from the UK. It was by far the most valuable arms contract that Britain had yet won from a Middle East country.[5]

Political relations between France and Arab countries are outside the scope of this book, but brief mention must be made of the progress to independence of the Maghreb countries, so as to trace the economic implications. Independence movements had entered the political lives of all of them even before the Second World War and events during that war gave them new impetus. After the war France attempted to hold on to its control of all of them, but soon recognised that it was no longer strong enough to do so and allowed Morocco and Tunisia (both French Protectorates) to become independent in March 1956. (Morocco had been partly Spanish, but Spain followed France's lead in recognising the country's independence, though it retained two enclaves at Ceuta and Melilla.) The comparatively amicable way in which this was brought about enabled France to retain considerable influence in both countries. Their currencies remained aligned with the French franc and their commercial links were primarily with France. French continued to be their main language for most international purposes, with Arabic making only very gradual progress against it (Spanish fairly rapidly lost ground in Morocco).

In Algeria, however, events took a very different course. France had conquered Algeria in the first half of the nineteenth century and had declared the country to be French territory in 1848. The country was organised into three departments on the analogy of French departments. Algerian deputies sat in the French

Parliament. On 20 September 1947, that Parliament passed a Statute of Algeria, which created an Algerian assembly but made few other concessions towards Algerian autonomy. In 1954, a nationalist uprising broke out which the French took strenuous action to put down.

The reasons for this French attitude were partly economic. There had been much more settlement by French citizens in Algeria than in Tunisia or Morocco and a great deal of the fertile agricultural land on the coastal plain was in French ownership. Moreover, oil prospects were considered to be bright in the Sahara; rich fields of oil and gas were in fact brought into production there in 1958. France consequently had a major economic as well as political stake in Algeria and was ready to deploy massive forces there to maintain its claim to sovereignty. By the early 1960s Algeria was being held by some 500,000 French troops, but the revolt still continued. Eventually, it was de Gaulle, returned to power in 1958, who had the political strength and determination to bring the struggle to an end by a ceasefire signed on 18 March 1962, accompanied by the release of Algerian leaders from imprisonment in France. A referendum held in Algeria on 1 July 1962 voted overwhelmingly for independence, and de Gaulle conceded this two days later.

It was a measure of de Gaulle's statesmanship that, despite the bitterness of over eight years of bloody struggle, he managed to rescue a continuing relationship from the wreck of France's Algerian policy. The referendum had been so worded that the voters had opted for independence 'in cooperation with France'. Although there was a large exodus of French settlers from Algeria after the ceasefire, many remained, at least for a time. Those departing abandoned over 100,000 hectares of land, some of which was distributed to landless peasants and some retained as state farms. (In theory there was a possibility of compensation for the former owners.) The Algerian dinar was aligned with the French franc. A Franco-Algerian petroleum agreement was signed on 29 July 1965. France remained Algeria's principal trading partner and French continued to be widely used in Algeria.

Nevertheless, there were strains between France and Algeria. The large Algerian minority working in France complained of ill-treatment. The remaining European, mainly French, landholdings in Algeria were eventually expropriated. Algeria became wealthy from its oil and gas, but complained that the French were manipulating their prices to Algerian disadvantage. Arabic began to oust French for many administrative purposes, though only slowly. There was even some demand for the teaching of English as an alternative to French in the Algerian educational system. There were calls for diversification of trade away from France. Undoubtedly, this should have given openings for British exporters, but very few took the trouble to seek them out, as the statistics in Chapter 18 will demonstrate.

15 The Six-Day War and its Aftermath

By the end of 1966 it was a decade since the 1956 Israeli defeat of the Egyptian Army in the Sinai Peninsula. During that decade Egyptian and Syrian forces had been reequipped with Soviet bloc weapons and trained in their use by Soviet instructors. The Jordanian forces were still largely British-equipped and partly British-trained but were no longer British-officered. The Israelis had developed an indigenous armament industry and also held a mix of American, French and British weapons, on which they had spent a high proportion of their national income. They had trained their own forces to what was believed to be a high level of efficiency, with particular attention to reserve training and to rapid-call-up exercises. There were rumours that they might have built some nuclear weapons from plutonium produced in their nuclear research reactor at Dimona, but any such weapons seemed not to have been tested and it was thought that they would not be likely to be used except *in extremis*.

The United Nations Emergency Force (UNEF), which had taken over from British and French forces at Port Said, was still in position in the Sinai desert, separating Israeli and Egyptian ground forces. As Israel had never been willing to accept it, it was deployed entirely on Egyptian territory under an agreement between the UN and Egypt. Among the positions it held was Sharm al-Shaikh at the mouth of the Gulf of Aqaba; its presence there ensured freedom of passage through the Strait of Tiran for shipping[1] bound to or from Eilat, which by now was a well-developed Israeli port, crucial in particular for oil supplies. UNEF did not operate on Israel's other frontiers; there the United Nations Truce Supervisory Organization (UNTSO) had been in place since the conclusion of the first Arab-Israeli armistices, but its role was purely a liaison function, plus a duty to observe and report. Given the hostility between the countries involved, this was a frustrating task and one which had little real influence on the course of events in the area.[2]

In January 1964, an Arab 'summit' meeting was held in Cairo, to discuss the Palestine problem. It was the first meeting of this kind and was stimulated into existence by reports that Israel was intending to divert water from the River Jordan for irrigation purposes. Its outcome was a decision to create a Palestinian 'entity', not amounting to a Government, which would replace the moribund Palestine Arab Higher Committee. In May 1964, a Palestine National Congress, meeting in Jerusalem, founded a Palestine Liberation Organisation (PLO), which in turn decided to create a Palestine Liberation Army. The Organisation and Army were financed by a tax levied on Palestinians everywhere (in practice outside Israel) and by contributions from Arab countries. The PLO before long gave birth to subsidiary bodies, some of them critical of the Organisation for moving too slowly towards the destruction of Israel. The most important of them was al-Fatah, which set up a commando organisation called al-Asifa (the storm). Fatah found its ally and base in Syria and set about organising small-scale attacks on Israel from there (and occasionally from Jordan, contrary to the policy of the Jordan Government).

Syria was by now ruled by the Baath Party, whose leaders were Alawis[3] and whose ideology was socialist amd secular. It adopted a bellicose attitude towards Israel, particularly after February 1966 when an internal struggle in the Party brought to power an extremist faction. The new Government, under Dr Nureddin Atassi, formed still closer links with the USSR and in particular preferred that country to Federal Germany as its partner in the construction of a Euphrates dam. In retaliation for the Israeli project to use water from the River Jordan for irrigation, the Syrians decided to divert the River Banias, a Jordan tributary, but abandoned this plan following a bombing raid by Israel on the diversion works in July 1966. This attack, and a declaration by the Israeli Government on 18 September 1966 that Syria would in future be held responsible for all acts of sabotage committed by Palestinian infiltrators, led to the conclusion on 4 November 1966 of a defence pact between Syria and Egypt.

Perhaps because of that pact, Israel did not in fact live up to its declaration when three of its soldiers were killed by a mine which exploded on an Israeli road near Hebron; instead, reprisals were taken against the nearest Jordanian village, Samu', where 125 houses were destroyed. Jordanian troops who attempted to intervene were roughly handled by tanks and aircraft (Mystères bought from France); they suffered casualties of 18 dead and 134 wounded. Palestinian demonstrations followed against King Hussain for not allowing troops of the so-called Unified Arab Command on to Jordanian territory. To deflect this criticism Hussain blamed Egypt and accused Nasser of using UNEF as an excuse for inactivity against Israel.

On 7 April 1967, a more serious incident occurred on the Syrian border. The Israelis provocatively set about cultivating land in the Demilitarised Zone. When an armoured tractor ploughing it came under rifle fire from Syria, Israeli aircraft were launched towards Damascus and shot down six Syrian Mig planes scrambled to defend it. There can be no doubt that this incident had been deliberately staged by the Israelis. Its purpose was presumably to relieve frustration over Palestinian raids and to teach Syria a lesson. Once again, despite the defence pact with Syria, Egypt took no action and was criticised for its passivity.

It was against this troubled background that a fateful and still unexplained development took place. In May 1967 the Soviet Government informed Nasser of an intelligence report that the Israelis were massing troops in Northern Israel for an attack on Syria. This was not in itself incredible, given previous incidents and recent warning speeches by Israeli ministers of the danger to Syria of permitting raids into Israel by the PLO, and Nasser was convinced.

Whether the report in question was fabricated by Soviet Army Intelligence or sold to them by some forger is obscure (there were certainly such forgers around). The report was not in fact true but it had its effect. Nasser, stung by previous criticisms of his sheltering behind blue berets, ordered the UNEF Commander to allow Egyptian troops to move up to the Israeli frontier in central Sinai, apparently intending to warn the Israelis off any plans they might have to attack Syria. The UNEF Commander said he could take orders only from the UN and referred back to the Secretary-General, U Thant. To universal astonishment,[4] he, on 19 May 1967, in response to an official request from the Egyptian Ambassador to the UN, ordered the whole of UNEF to suspend operations and withdraw, pointing out to objectors that, as a matter of law, the Force could only operate on Egyptian territory with the consent of the host Government.

This legalistic attitude has been much debated. It had the consequence that Egypt reoccupied not only the frontier posts but also the crucial position at Sharm al-Shaikh, which Nasser had originally perhaps not had in mind.[5] Alarm bells at once began to ring in the world's capitals, since it was clear that Israel would not submit to reimposition of a blockade on shipping bound to or from Eilat. On 22 May, Nasser announced just such an embargo on Israeli shipping and on war material bound for Israel. It was obvious to all that this was a *casus belli*. The British Government, in a desperate last-minute attempt to avoid war, tried to organise an international effort to compel Egypt to grant free passage through the Strait of Tiran to Eilat.[6] There was support, but not sufficiently decisive support, from the USA and practically none from elsewhere.

Nasser by now realised that he had gone further than he had intended, but could see no way back. On 24/25 May he moved his Armoured Division into Sinai. Arab League Governments, however hostile they had previously been to Nasser, had no alternative but to declare their solidarity with him. Hussain was perforce numbered among them; on 30 May 1967 he dramatically flew to Cairo in his personal plane for Jordan and Egypt to sign a defence pact. On 3 June, fairly token forces from Iraq and Kuwait lined up with the Egyptian Army in Sinai and a few Saudi troops moved into Jordan.

It seems likely that Nasser believed that with their new Soviet equipment the Egyptian forces could defeat the Israelis. If so, he was soon disillusioned. Despite some hasty American diplomacy by Charles Yost as an envoy of President Johnson,[7] the Israeli Air Force attacked Egyptian and Syrian military airfields at dawn on 5 June 1967 and destroyed virtually all their aircraft on the ground. Israeli ground forces were equally quick into action and once more routed the Egyptian Army (deprived of air cover) in Sinai, advancing to the Suez Canal by 8 June but making no attempt to cross it.

The Jordan Army had none of the relative success of the Arab Legion in 1948. Hussain was misled by Nasser about the course of the Sinai campaign and his army was deployed southward to cover the flank of a non-existent Egyptian advance. Before it could regroup, the Israelis had seized the Arab sector of Jerusalem and the whole of the West Bank up to the River Jordan.

The UN Security Council had been clamouring for a cease-fire. Egypt and Jordan accepted this call on 8 June and on 9 June Syria followed suit. But the Israelis ignored the appeal until they had spent another two days switching their ground forces north to capture the Golan Heights in south-west Syria, from which the Syrians had since 1948 been able to watch (and sometimes shell) Israeli movements in Galilee. The whole operation had taken six days and had been carried out with clinical precision. Israel had proved itself the military superpower of the Middle East and its Arab neighbours had been humiliated. As a demonstration of triumph, on 11 June, an Israeli freighter sailed through the Strait of Tiran to Eilat.

Britain at this time was in fairly low standing with many of the Arab countries.[8] For a brief period it seemed that for no fault of its own it was going to be calumnied for this new Arab defeat. The Jordanians had invested in air-scanning radar, but were not yet very skilled in its use and interpretation. Probably because Nasser had falsely informed Hussain (for reasons of 'face') that Egyptian planes had wiped out most of the Israeli Air Force, the Jordanian radar-watchers decided that what were in fact Israeli planes landing back in Israel were reinforcement aircraft being flown in by Britain and the USA from aircraft carriers or from Cyprus. This damaging charge against Britain was broadcast from Cairo and was likely to be widely believed in the Arab world unless decisively refuted. Fortunately, the Permanent Under-Secretary of the Foreign Office, Sir Paul Gore-Booth, was experienced in information work and at once set up a special task force in the Foreign Office to expose the falsehood, which was given the title of 'The Big Lie' for the purpose. The task force achieved a high degree of success, helped by the fact that the Jordanians, when they realised that they had been misinformed about the outcome of Israeli air action against Egypt, confessed that their radar evidence had been mistaken.[9]

But some damage had already been done. On 6 June, Syria and Sudan broke off diplomatic relations with both UK and USA. Egypt, Algeria and Yemen, which were already out of relations with UK, broke with USA. Even Lebanon withdrew its Ambassadors from the two capitals. (Jordan, after realising its own error, significantly took no such action.)

Also on 6 June Algeria and Kuwait banned shipments of oil to UK and USA; the next day Libya, Saudi Arabia and Bahrain did likewise. Abu Dhabi followed suit a little later. The oil producers soon realised their folly and at an Arab summit meeting on 17 June argued that the ban was hurting them more than it was hurting those embargoed, but on this as on other issues the outcome of that summit was inconclusive. It was not until another summit in Khartoum on 29 August, attended by all Arab countries except Syria, that it was decided to lift the ban. By that time there had been some distortion of trade patterns; in particular, Iran had not been slow to benefit at the expense of its neighbours.

The longer-term economic consequences of the Six-Day War were many and substantial. The first of them was that the Suez Canal had again been blocked (this time by Israel), and with Iraeli troops occupying the Canal's eastern bank this closure lasted not just for months but for years. It was not reopened until June 1975. Meanwhile shipping between East and West, including oil tankers bound from the Gulf to Europe and North America, had to use the route round South Africa.[10] An enormous stimulus was thus given to the building of bigger and bigger tankers, since a large tanker needs very little more crew than a small one and can be operated much more profitably when both are taking the same route.[11] Aden's usually busy harbour fell quiet as Red Sea traffic dwindled. Jordan, Saudi Arabia and Sudan found their ports languishing up a backwater instead of on a main artery of world trade; some of their imports and exports had to be switched to overland delivery, much to the commercial profit of Beirut.

Israel benefited in several ways. Large quantities of Egyptian military equipment had again been captured in Sinai; it was either put to use in Israel or sold to other users, often after reconditioning by 'cannibalisation'. Sinai's oilfields were exploited to supply Israel. There was no longer any threat to trade via Eilat and plans were drawn up to develop that seaside area into an international tourist centre for 'sun-sea-and-sand' holidays. The Arabs of the 'occupied lands', the Gaza strip and the West Bank, were soon being driven by economic necessity to work in Israel, providing cheap labour. The barbed-wire frontier between Arab and Israeli Jerusalem was swept away and the whole city put under Israeli administration. As well as satisfying profound religious and political emotions, that opened the way to further tourism possibilities, with package holidays including Jerusalem and Bethlehem in addition to such sites as Masada; both Jewish and Christian tourists from around the world, but especially from USA and Europe, found such offers irresistible.

There were some partially offsetting economic losses for Israel. The occupied territories presented security problems which were costly to deal with. They also opened up new areas for Israeli settlers, many of them religious extremists who were determined to show that Judea and Samaria were for all time to be essential parts of 'Eretz Israel'. The Israeli Government was ambivalent in its attitude to these settlements, but whatever political view was held of them there was no denying that they added to the security problem and were very expensive to establish and maintain. There was also now some increased difficulty in keeping up the flow of financial contributions from world Jewry which was so important for Israel's perpetually strained balance of payments; when the state had been revealed as a regional superpower, it was no longer so easy to attract funds to safeguard a supposed Israeli David in the struggle with an Arab Goliath.

For Israel's Arab neighbours the economic outlook after the

war looked grim. Egypt especially was in a bad way. The income from the Suez Canal was lost, for years as it proved.[12] A major reequipment of the armed forces was an urgent necessity; even if it could be done on credit terms, that would add greatly to an already heavy debt burden (Egypt had defaulted on its debt payments to the IMF in 1966). The Sinai oilfields, which had provided half Egypt's production of about 9.5 million tons p.a., were lost, probably for a long time. The continually growing population was going to have to face serious reductions in its already poor standard of living at a time of shattered morale.

On 9 June 1967, the day after the Israeli-Egyptian cease-fire, President Nasser broadcast his decision to resign. An emotional upsurge of popular support persuaded him to remain in office, but he never again wielded the authority in the Arab world which had once been his. A sign of his new weakness was withdrawal of the last Egyptian troops from Yemen.[13] The campaign there could no longer be afforded; nor, indeed, could the dispute it entailed with the Saudis, to whom Egypt would now have to look for financial subventions.

Syria and Jordan had also suffered economically. There had been fresh inflows of Palestinian refugees into their already crowded lands and they too would have to reequip their armed forces. In both these respects Jordan had suffered more than Syria. Its refugee population was increased by some 200,000, and their belligerence against Israel was fierce. There were frequent commando raids across the Jordan River, which from time to time attracted heavy Israeli reprisals, mainly by air, against Jordanian territory. The Jordan Government found it more difficult than before 1967 to control the hotheads and the internal stability of the country looked to be in danger of collapse. A particularly critical situation arose when King Hussain on 26 July 1970 backed an American peace initiative for the Middle East known as the Rogers Plan, to which the Palestinians were hostile.

In September 1970, after a PLO splinter group had hijacked two American and a British airliner to a Jordanian airport and destroyed them, King Hussain in desperation decided to appoint a military Governor-General with sweeping powers. Fighting broke out and the Palestinians, with some Syrian support, seized several towns in northern Jordan and some parts of Amman. A truce was patched up, but was not fully effective. However, it gradually appeared that the guerrillas had been seriously weakened in the fighting and Hussain patiently strengthened his hold over them. In July 1971 their last strongholds in Jordan were eliminated.

Lebanon had played no real part in the 1967 conflict. Indeed it was an indirect beneficiary from the distortion of trade routes caused by the closure of the Suez Canal. But the expulsion of the PLO from Jordan in 1970–1 proved disastrous for it in the longer run. The PLO established a new headquarters in Lebanon and began organising commando raids from there into Israel. With Jordan closed to them and the Golan Heights in Israeli hands, there was no other Israeli border open to the raiding parties of the PLO and its splinter groups. There will be more to be said on this subject in Chapter 29.

The Arab States who had been able to do no other than watch with horror as the Israeli forces swept all before them in the Six-Day War resolved at least to bind up some of the economic wounds of the main sufferers. At the summit meeting held at Khartoum in August 1967 (which terminated the oil embargo on UK and USA) substantial aid was agreed for Egypt, Jordan and Syria, to be provided by the richest oil states, Kuwait, Saudi Arabia and Libya.[14] The amount of the aid was calculated to make up for their losses, including in the case of Egypt losses from the closure of the Suez Canal; an annual £95 million for Egypt and £40 million for Jordan were to be provided out of £55 million from Kuwait, £50 million from Saudi Arabia and £30 million from Libya. After the action taken by King Hussain to drive out the PLO in 1970–1, Libya cancelled its aid to Jordan and Kuwait suspended payments, but Hussain managed to smooth things over to a large extent, releasing Palestinian guerrillas from prison in September 1973 (while not allowing them to resume operations from Jordanian territory) and playing a skilfully minor role in the 1973 Arab-Israeli War (on which see Chapter 21), with the result that aid from Kuwait was resumed.

Once the 'Big Lie' was nailed, Britain found its relations with Arab countries improving as an indirect result of the Six-Day

War. This surprising consequence was due in large part to its Foreign Secretary, that controversial character George Brown. British foreign policy towards the Middle East at this time, as laid down by Ministers, was to keep a low profile, trying to avoid giving offence to either Arabs or Israelis. Such an attitude is all too likely to end up by displeasing both sides, and that had been the consequence up to the Six-Day War. When a Special Session of the UN General Assembly was called to debate the outcome of that war, Brown set off for New York to participate. On the plane, he read the draft speech which the Department had prepared for him to deliver and found that, in keeping with policy, it was distinctly mealy-mouthed. He insisted on a redraft with some meat in it.[15] The outcome was that he made a vigorous speech of a pro-Arab nature, stressing the inadmissibility under the UN Charter of the acquisition of territory by force of arms and particularly condemning the annexation by Israel of the Old City area of Jerusalem. The Arab delegations were delighted and the Israeli delegation furious.[16]

Brown, on his return to London, capitalised on this new-found popularity with the Arabs by persuading Nasser, whom he already knew personally from a visit he had paid to Cairo when out of office, to resume diplomatic relations with Britain (broken in 1965 over Rhodesia).[17] This gave British businessmen the help of an Embassy Commercial Department to rebuild trade links with Egypt. Success breeds success, and the UK delegation to the UN was soon able to pull off a coup in diplomatic terms by getting the Security Council on 22 November 1967 to approve unanimously the British-drafted Resolution No.242 setting out a framework for an Arab-Israeli settlement. (For reasons which are outside the scope of this book, Resolution 242 failed to produce that settlement, but it still remains a key document in attempts to do so.) Britain's standing in Arab eyes by the end of 1967 was thus unusually high, a situation which, although it is impossible to quantify them, was sure to yield economic benefits. It also helped to put out of mind the humiliation there might otherwise have been in the unhappy circumstances of Britain's withdrawal from Aden, which will be described in Chapter 17.

16 Oil Developments in the 1960s

Oil production in the Middle East spread more widely in the course of the 1960s and gas production assumed a new importance. It has already been mentioned (Chapter 14) that large fields were found in Abu Dhabi, the largest of the Trucial States, in the late 50s; the next decade saw them assume world significance, both onshore and offshore. In North Africa, oil had been struck in the Algerian Sahara in the mid-1950s; production began there in 1958, but it was not until the 1960s that the full potential of its fields became apparent. It was here too that gas began to be exploited as an internationally marketable commodity, instead of, as in most of the Middle East, a nuisance to be flared. In Libya, oil was struck in 1959, and fields were then soon found at several widely separated sites; the first oil terminal was opened on 25 October 1961.

These developments began to change the Middle East oil industry in major respects. In the first place, they widened the area of competition, both between countries and also between companies, since many of these new fields were under the control of 'independents' rather than of the previously dominant 'seven sisters'. Secondly, both Algeria and Libya are Mediterranean countries, closer than other Middle East producers to the markets of Europe and, crucially, independent of transit through the Suez Canal. Thirdly, they affected the balance between supply and demand, to produce an increasing 'oil glut'.

It will be remembered that the Iranian oil crisis (Chapter 5) had ended in the formation of a consortium to enable oil from Iran to reenter the world market without too severe cutbacks in output from other Middle Eastern producers such as Kuwait, Iraq and Qatar. Nevertheless, growth in those countries was inevitably restrained by the return of Iranian oil to the world market. There had also been oil finds elsewhere in the world, notably in Nigeria in 1959. In Canada, where oil had been struck in Alberta in the 1940s, production grew rapidly in the late 50s. And the Soviet Union had entered the export market, selling oil to Western Europe to earn foreign exchange. Thus, although oil consumption was continuing to rise in the world, with a trend approximating to doubling each decade, the addition of the output from these three new countries to Middle East production was bound to exacerbate the existing surplus.

The natural consequence was that the selling price of crude oil weakened, threatening either the revenues of the host countries or the profits of the oil companies. By the end of the 50s, these were strictly speaking not alternatives; revenues and company profits had become linked by the now standard system of 50/50 profit-sharing agreements, which had replaced, or in most cases supplemented, the old arrangement of royalties at a fixed payment per ton. But the host countries were never happy to see their revenues fall and the oil companies themselves, particularly after the Iran experience of AIOC, realised the political perils into which such a fall could plunge them, so there was considerable reluctance to alter what were known as 'posted prices'. These were originally the prices at which producing companies were willing to sell crude oil to third parties but, as demand fell, they became notional selling prices at which it was assumed that crude had been sold, for the purpose of calculating the payments due from companies to governments; any shortfall in the actual price realised was treated as a discount on the posted price, to be borne entirely by the companies.

For some time, the companies tolerated these losses uncomplainingly, since sales discounts for various purposes were a long-standing practice in the industry and for commercial reasons companies preferred to keep such information to themselves rather than disclose it to governments. But once discounts became virtually a universal feature of all oil sales, and especially when the discounts began to increase to proportions which threatened profitability, the companies found themselves under pressure to reduce posted prices, however unpopular they knew this would be with their host governments. By contrast with the years 1951 to 1957, when posted prices had been raised on four occasions, they were unilaterally reduced by the major companies by 10 per cent in February 1959 and by a further 7.5 per cent in August 1960.

It was the need which governments saw to resist such reductions in posted prices which drove them in September 1960 to combine together into an Organization of Petroleum Exporting Countries, soon better known by its acronym, OPEC. The original members of this were Iran, Iraq, Kuwait, Saudi Arabia and Venezuela. Abu Dhabi, Algeria, Ecuador, Gabon, Libya, Nigeria and Qatar joined the Organization later, as their exporting levels became significant for world trade.

OPEC in its early years was far from being a cartel and it proved unable to restore posted prices to their 1957 levels, but it did succeed in preventing any further reductions. It also managed to whittle away methods of accounting which minimised the profits shown, first eliminating marketing expenses from the calculations and then, after a considerable struggle, getting agreement that royalties should be treated as an expense instead of as part of the 50 per cent profit due to the host governments. A further OPEC success was to obtain relinquishment by the companies of areas from their concessions which they were not exploiting; this was normally a matter for negotiation, as companies could argue, in many cases quite honestly, that certain at present unexploited areas were crucial to their forward planning.

This issue of relinquishment led to a major dispute between the Iraq Government and IPC. Qasim, soon after his successful revolution, opened negotiations with the company for improvements in the concession agreement. These dragged on and reached impasse in October 1961. Qasim decided on unilateral action and on 11 December 1961 promulgated Law No.80, which withdrew some 99.5 per cent of the concession areas. The company rejected this confiscatory measure and retaliated by freezing the level of oil production.[1] Negotiations continued intermittently, with IPC gradually yielding ground and eventually pressing only to retain one particularly promising field, North Rumaila.

In February 1964, the Iraq Government[2] set up the Iraq National Oil Company (INOC) and in August 1967 assigned to INOC for exploration and exploitation most of the territory it had withdrawn from IPC. INOC was authorised to enter into joint ventures with foreign oil companies for this purpose. Most such companies either did not wish to offend IPC or were warned off by that company's threat of legal action against any intruder into what it still regarded as its own rightful preserves. But a state-owned French company, ERAP, which already had a joint venture in Iran, decided to take the risk. The terms it offered were less favourable than those available from IPC, but INOC for political reasons favoured a new partnership and accepted them. However, North Rumaila was excluded from the concession area of this joint venture with ERAP.

There, at the end of the 60s, the matter rested. Iraq had become the first Middle East country to expropriate oil concession territory after Iran's failed attempt to do so, but it had paid the price of seeing its production growth held back and its proven reserves actually decline by the end of the decade.[3] From the point of view of the oil majors who were partners in IPC, the holding down of Iraqi production had had the advantage of helping to sustain prices at a time when Libyan oil had entered the market and when they were under constant pressure from Iran to increase production in that country.

There had meanwhile been political developments in the three new Middle East oil producers. Algeria's move to independence from France in 1962 has already been described in Chapter 14. Under the independence agreement, cooperation in the exploitation of Saharan hydrocarbons was reserved to French companies and it developed successfully. During the 60s more and more fields were brought into production and by the end of the decade their combined output amounted to over 40 million tons p.a. A network of oil pipelines to the Mediterranean was constructed, some of them to outlets in neighbouring Tunisia. A gas pipeline from the Sahara to Algiers was also built, partly to satisfy local consumption but mainly for processing prior to export of the gas in liquid form. Britain, which had no indigenous natural gas at this time, was an early customer. The first commercial cargo of liquified natural gas (LNG) reached a new terminal on Canvey Island in October 1964, for distribution by a pipeline network over a large part of England.

In Abu Dhabi, as oil wealth poured into the Ruler's treasury, popular discontent with Shaikh Shakhbut's miserliness grew to overwhelming proportions. Apart from his two sons, the ruling family was equally unhappy, with the result that the Arab procedure for replacement of a Ruler (described in Chapter 8) was called into play. A majority of the members of the family signed a document calling on Shakhbut's younger brother, Shaikh Zaid, to take over. He hesitated for some time,[4] but finally acepted the responsibility and after a brief and fortunately bloodless confrontation with his brother became Ruler in August 1966. Shakhbut at first went into exile on a comfortable pension, but later returned to live seemingly quite contentedly in retirement in the Buraimi village of Al-Ain.

By the time Zaid took over, Abu Dhabi oil output was in excess of 10 million tons p.a. and growing rapidly. The onshore concession was held by Abu Dhabi Petroleum Company (ADPC), a subsidiary of IPC, and the offshore concession[5] by Abu Dhabi Marine Areas (ADMA), a joint venture between BP (66.66 per cent) and CFP (33.33 per cent). Shaikh Zaid, unlike his deposed brother, was keen to develop his country and soon set about turning it into a welfare state for its tiny population. He also determined to have his own armed forces, separate from the British-run Trucial Oman Scouts (as the Levies had been renamed). Britain was the trading partner he relied on and valuable contracts, both for civil engineering projects and for arms sales, soon transformed Abu Dhabi's importance as a UK export market, as will be seen in Chapter 18.

In 1969, it was Libya's turn to undergo a revolution. Even before that, however, there had been political changes of a less dramatic character. In March 1953, Libya joined the League of Arab States, where it tended to play a rather quiet role, and in the following month it ceased to be a federation of three provinces

(Tripolitania, Cyrenaica and Fezzan) on the promulgation of a new constitution declaring it a unitary state. In 1964, it was announced that Libya's treaties with the UK and USA would be terminated, under which they had air force facilities at El Adem and Wheelus Field respectively and the UK also held a small army encampment. Negotiations for the withdrawal of the forces concerned were conducted rather slowly (Libya got a useful income from the leasing of these installations), but on 31 March 1966 the first phase of the withdrawal of British troops was completed.

When Libya had issued its Petroleum Law in 1955, it had deliberately offered many small concessions instead of a single concession. The aim had been to attract the 'independents', small companies lacking Middle East crude, who would have an incentive to develop fields rapidly if they struck oil. That strategy had been successful; in the first round of bidding, 17 companies had been awarded 84 concession areas. They were given favourable tax treatment in a number of ways,[6] chief among them that tax would be calculated on realised rather than posted prices, thus enabling them to undercut their competitors. The result was that by 1961 ten valuable fields had been found and by 1965 Libya had become the world's sixth largest oil exporter, with about 10 per cent of global exports. The closure of the Suez Canal in 1967 gave Libya (and also Algeria and Nigeria) a further advantage as freight costs increased for supplies from the Gulf.

King Idris of Libya was an elderly man even at the beginning of the 60s. He offered to abdicate in 1964 in favour of his nephew, Crown Prince Hassan Rida,[7] but yielded to popular pressure to carry on. By 1969, when he was seventy-nine years of age, his health was breaking down and his doctors insisted on treatment in Europe. While he was away, an army coup was mounted by a young officer, Captain (later Lieutenant-Colonel) Muammar Qaddafi, of whom little was known, except that he seemed to be an admirer of Gamal Abdul Nasser. The coup was not opposed, so another Arab Kingdom had become a Republic. Qaddafi was to make his mark as an oil negotiator in the 70s; that will be one of the subjects of Chapter 20.

Another oil development took place in the 60s, the formation in 1969 of the Organization of Arab Petroleum Exporting Countries, OAPEC, not to be confused with the already existing OPEC. Its founder members were Saudi Arabia, on whose initiative it was set up, Kuwait and the Libya of King Idris, so that it was something of a 'Rulers' Club', and its motivation was in fact to preempt any dangerous initiatives by the more radical Arab oil producers, Iraq and Algeria.

The Libyan Revolution put a different complexion on that idea, and by 1972 OAPEC came to include all Arab oil producers, including some who did not join OPEC. Perhaps because its original purpose was spent, it has only rarely played a crucial role on the world's oil stage, although it has been useful as a discussion forum and in a coordinating capacity. The principal exception was the 'first oil shock', which was primarily OAPEC's rather than OPEC's achievement, as will be seen in Chapter 21. This was because it was the direct consequence of the 1973 war between the Arabs and Israel, so an all-Arab forum was needed to generate it.

The time has come to move the focus of attention from the Middle East to the North Sea, where exploration for gas and oil began in the 60s. Two events touched it off, the conclusion of the United Nations Convention on the Continental Shelf in 1958 and the discovery of a huge onshore gas-field at Groningen in the Netherlands in 1959.

The Permian Basal layer of rock in which that find was made was known to extend under the North Sea, so the priority of that sea for exploration at once rose in the eyes of all petroleum geologists. (Until that time it had been thought unpromising since only small oil-fields had been discovered on-shore in Britain, the Netherlands and Germany. If only similarly small structures were present offshore in such an adverse environment as the North Sea, where exploration and production were bound to be extremely expensive, they would have been unprofitable to develop.)

Following the Groningen find, seismic surveys of the bed of the North Sea were carried out from 1961 onwards by British and many other companies, and these were encouraging. But the oil companies also needed to be satisfied about ownership of the sea-bed before going to the expense of taking their exploration beyond the seismic stage. No drilling outside territorial waters was therefore attempted until the Continental Shelf Convention had come into force, for which ratification by twenty-two members of the United Nations was required.

The UK was in fact the twenty-second state to ratify the Convention, but not until 1964. Events then moved quickly. The British Government issued licences for nearly 500 blocks of sea-bed in September-November 1964.[8] A median line between Norway and the UK was negotiated in mid-1965.[9] After three dry holes drilled by other companies, BP struck gas on 17 September 1965 in the West Sole field in the southern North Sea, only forty-two miles from shore;[10] by December it was known that the find was likely to be 'commercial', i.e. sufficiently large to be profitable if brought into production. Then, during April and May 1966, three more commercial finds were announced, by Shell/Esso, Phillips and the Gas Council, all in the same general area as the BP field but closer to the median line. Recoverable reserves were soon estimated as sufficient to permit extraction of some 4000 million cubic feet per day, with a depletion period of around 20 years. Further finds were likely to add to that period.

These four discoveries revolutionised the outlook for gas in the UK. Until the 1960s, gas, which had preceded electricity as an important domestic fuel,[11] had been produced almost entirely from coke in ugly and malodorous gas-works supplying a relatively small area around them. The building of oil refineries in Britain had made available supplies of 'lean' gas produced as a by-product of oil distillation, which could be used for domestic supply if mixed with 'richer' gas from some other source. It was for this blending process that a fifteen-year contract with Algeria had been concluded to import LNG.

Now it was suddenly clear that the North Sea would produce enough natural gas to supply all Britain's needs for decades to come. It would take a few years to reach that stage; pipelines would be needed to bring the gas ashore and to distribute it and existing gas appliances would need to be modified to use unblended natural gas, which has twice the calorific value of the coke-derived 'town gas'.[12] The investment required was considerable, but the cost price of the natural gas would nevertheless be low enough to undercut gas from any other source.

This was bad news for the British coal industry, but would have little impact on oil imports from the Middle East, though the LNG contract with Algeria might not be renewed when it expired. The trading relationship with the Middle East would not change substantially unless oil as well as gas were found in the British North Sea, and of that there was as yet no sign.

17 Britain's Withdrawal from 'East of Suez'

After thirteen years of Conservative Governments in Britain, the Labour Party returned to power in October 1964 with a tiny majority in the House of Commons. The economic state of the country was known to be troubled. It was not long since Harold Macmillan had claimed for electoral purposes that Britain 'had never had it so good', but that had been a superficial judgment.

British exports were steadily falling as a proportion of world exports and balance of payments problems were never far away. Growth in the UK economy was sluggish. Favoured access to raw materials was no longer being assured by Imperial Preference, as more and more colonies and protectorates moved to independence. The decline of Empire had not been offset by new markets in Western Europe; the EEC countries were tightening their mutual trading links without Britain, whose entry, when belatedly sought, had been vetoed in January 1963 by France. It was no substitute to look for outlets in the European Free Trade Area (EFTA), which was economically a much weaker organisation than the EEC and one with much less potential.

Harold Wilson's new Labour Government had won the election on the basis of an election manifesto weighed down with social and economic pledges. These would in any event have been difficult to carry out speedily and in full, but the Chancellor of the Exchequer, James Callaghan, was horrified to learn on assuming office that Britain was in economic crisis, facing an £800 million balance of payments deficit. The current account had turned down in June, and this had passed largely unnoticed by politicians, partly because of the Parliamentary summer recess but more especially because they were preoccupied with electioneering. An immediate decision was needed on whether or not to devalue sterling.

The decision went against devaluation.[1] This was a courageous step, but almost certainly mistaken, and, in the slightly longer run, it was unsustainable. One of the reasons for taking it was that the Labour Party was in danger of being tainted with being 'the party of devaluation', having been in office during the 1949 devaluation of sterling. But the price of the decision was that for years the Government found itself driven from one expedient to another to prop up the exchange rate, including round after round of cuts in public expenditure and more and more foreign loans from the United States and the IMF. At the same time it was desperately trying to carry out its manifesto pledges, most of which were tending in the opposite direction, towards additional expenditure, rendering the need for cuts all the more agonising.

In this situation, it was inevitable that the thoughts of most people in the Labour Party, including in the Cabinet, should turn towards cuts in defence expenditure. Apart from debt servicing, there are only two main areas of Government expenditure, social services and defence; by comparison with these two, departmental spending elsewhere seems tiny and the savings achievable minuscule. A Labour Government is sure to give very high priority to social services and to wish to spend more on them, since ideologically it takes the view that they should be state-run. The necessary consequence is that it will search for savings on defence. From the time when the Government took office, the Defence Secretary, Denis Healey, was engaged in a series of 'defence reviews' which seemed to be never-ending; as soon as one was completed, another was being called for.[2]

Chief of the difficulties in this process was that substantial defence savings could only be made by reducing defence commitments. Britain's armed forces were widely spread around the world's potential trouble-spots. To many of them they were bound by treaties which could not lightly be abrogated. Moreover, the United States Government, at a time when it was heavily committed in Vietnam, attached great importance to the honouring by Britain of these responsibilities, and the British Government, having taken the decision not to devalue, needed US sympathy and support to negotiate its foreign loans. It is perhaps not surprising that the Cabinet had to take several bites at the tempting cherry of defence cuts.

The White Paper setting out the conclusions reached in the first major defence review was published on 22 February 1966. Its crucial decision was that defence expenditure should run at an annual rate of £2000 million p.a. (at 1966 prices) right through to 1969–70, implying a cut of £400 million p.a., some 17 per cent. It was by no means clear how this was to be achieved, since the commitments to NATO, CENTO and SEATO were to be maintained, along with defence responsibilities towards Gibraltar, Malta, Cyprus, the Gulf Emirates, Singapore and Hong Kong. In the short term, the savings would come from the cancellation of several military aircraft projects (even though this would necessitate the purchase by the R.A.F. in future years of American planes, adding to the dollar deficit), and from one important reduction in commitments, a decision to withdraw from the Aden Base on the independence of that territory, which was to be achieved not later than 31 December 1968.

Aden was in a twofold relationship with the British Crown. The city of Aden itself was a colony but its hinterland was a protectorate, or rather two of them, the Western and Eastern Aden Protectorates, each consisting of a multiplicity of small states. In the colony, there had been a nationalist movement of a Nasserist type for the best part of a decade, and it had grown recently to be a serious political force. In the protectorates, the authority of the tribal rulers had been weakened by the partial success of neighbouring tribes in Yemen in rebelling against their spiritual and temporal leader, the Imam. British interests were the port of Aden, the small but important military base set up after the evacuation of the Suez Canal Base in 1956, and a BP-owned refinery in Little Aden supplying the port with oil bunkers.

Considerable steps in the direction of eventual independence for the entire area had been taken before the Labour Government took over from their Conservative predecessors. A federation of six of the states of the Western Protectorate had been brought into being in February 1959. It had grown to ten states, covering almost the whole of that Protectorate, and then had made the major stride forward of merging with the colony of Aden in January 1963. That stage had been marked by a new treaty with the UK and by the dropping of the title 'Governor of Aden' in favour of the cumbersome nomenclature 'High Commissioner for Aden and the Protectorate of South Arabia'.[3] Further states were attracted to the new entity, which eventually, in 1965, came to number 17 states (all except 4).

This Federation was of course continually attacked by Cairo Radio and had aroused the opposition of the anti-colonialist group in the UN. It needed time to prove its worth and time was no longer available. Following the defence review decision to achieve savings there, the British Government confirmed that the Federation, including Aden, would become independent in 1968, a date already fixed at a constitutional conference in London in the summer of 1964. It also announced that, although military aid would be given to expand and modernise the South Arabian armed forces, no British defence guarantee would be offered to the new Government.

That announcement sealed the Federation's fate. It soon began to look more and more irrelevant as two extremist groups fought each other for the real power in the territory, while British troops struggled to preserve a semblance of order in Aden itself. In May 1967, a new High Commissioner, Sir Humphrey Trevelyan, called out of retirement by Foreign Secretary George Brown to deal with a deteriorating situation,[4] arrived in Aden to announce that the date for independence would be 9 January 1968. Additional military and civil aid of some £60 million over about three years was promised to the Federal authorities, but that promise soon proved useless to preserve them (and consequently lapsed).

By October, it was becoming clear that the pro-Communist extremists had got the upper hand over the pro-Nasser extremists, and the matter was put beyond doubt when the South Arabian Army declared for the former group, known as the National Liberation Front (NLF). A degree of respectability was given to the otherwise rather humiliating circumstances of Britain's final process of decolonisation by a conference held in Geneva in November 1967 between British Government representatives and a delegation from the NLF to negotiate arrangements for the handover of power. On 30 November, the NLF delegation returned triumphantly to Aden to announce the formation of the People's Republic of Southern Yemen (later retitled the People's Democratic Republic of Yemen). The final transfer arrangements had worked smoothly and the last British contingent had left Aden quietly, with their dignity preserved,[5] the previous day.

The new state announced a 'progressive' foreign policy, including support for national revolutionary movements, a threat mainly to its eastern neighbour, Oman. This flew in the face of its need for aid from the conservatively-minded rich states of the Gulf. It thereby ensured that the new Republic, with the Suez Canal closed and the port of Aden idle in consequence, would suffer severe economic difficulties.

The financial savings from the defence review which had led to the decision to withdraw from Aden had not solved the British Government's problems. Pressure on the pound mounted during 1966–7 and further foreign borrowings proved only a palliative. The blocking of the Suez Canal in the 1967 Arab-Israeli War and a domestic dock strike provided the final straws, and on 18 November 1967 it was announced that sterling would be devalued from $2.80 to $2.40 to the pound. On this occasion, by contrast with 1949, only twenty-two countries devalued along with the UK, those whose currencies were closely tied to sterling or which looked to Britain as their primary market. The exchange rate change had been agreed with the IMF, which organised a $1000 million stand-by credit, but in return insisted on a British austerity programme, including cuts in Government expenditure. Among them were certain to be further defence cuts.

Defence reviews in London had in fact soon resumed after the 1966 White Paper. Labour backbenchers were by no means satisfied with its provisions and pressed for complete British withdrawal from what was known, in Kipling's phrase, as 'East of Suez'. So far as the Middle East was concerned, this meant the commitments to the Gulf Emirates.

Given the size of Britain's oil interests in the Gulf, the cost of defending the Emirates was relatively low (some £12 million p.a.). There was a small naval flotilla in Bahrain and a tiny R.A.F. contingent on the Omani island of Masirah, plus a small Army/R.A.F. detachment in the Trucial State of Sharjah. The main problem was that the Chiefs of Staff had convinced themselves that they could not guarantee security in the Gulf without an aircraft carrier available in the Indian Ocean area, and, Ministers had decided, that Britain could no longer afford to build new aircraft carriers (a Minister, Christopher Mayhew, who was both pro-Navy and pro-Arab resigned on this point). It thus became inevitable that a decision would finally be reached that the commitments to the defence of the Gulf Emirates must be abandoned. This formed part of a major withdrawal from all responsibilities in the Pacific area and in Asia, other than for the colony of Hong Kong and, on a temporary basis, the continued protection of Brunei.

In 1968, therefore, a Minister of State in the FCO, Goronwy Roberts, went out to the Gulf to inform all the local rulers that British forces would be withdrawn from the area by 1971 and that they must then provide for their own protection.[6] The Shah of Iran was among those so informed, although in his case there was no British defence responsibility, except in the context of CENTO. He raised no objection and began immediately to plan to take over the hegemony of the Gulf area. He had already built up substantial forces with modern weaponry and set about adding to them, looking to Britain among others as his supplier.

The Shah's rival for Gulf hegemony was likely to be Iraq, where a Baath Government had seized power on 17 July 1968, but the Emir of Kuwait, when informed of HMG's decision, did not seem worried that a new attempt would be made to assert the Iraqi claim to sovereignty over Kuwait. No doubt he rightly judged that by his generosity in aid programmes he had built up adequate support in the Arab world for Kuwait's continued independence.

The Shaikhs in the Southern Gulf were considerably more worried,[7] but were told that HMG's decision was irreversible. This proved to be the case despite a change of party in office in the UK in 1970. The new Conservative Government thought hard about it but finally announced on 1 March 1971 that the withdrawal from the Gulf would take place that year, as planned by their predecessors, and that the treaties with the Gulf rulers would be terminated.

There were good grounds for some of the Shaikhs' worries and the British Government set about removing as many as possible of them before the time came for withdrawal. First, there were frontier disputes. Iran professed a claim to Bahrain and to small islands in the Gulf held, under British protection, by the Shaikhs of two of the Trucial States, Sharjah and Ras al-Khaimah. The Buraimi dispute with Saudi Arabia was still unresolved. Dozens more disputes between the Shaikhs, usually turning on the ownership of wells in the desert, were of less significance.[8]

Secondly, there was an organisational problem. The seven Shaikhdoms of the Trucial States were too small to survive as separate entities, especially if they fell to bickering about their boundaries. Despite more than one unfortunate experience in its recent past in attempts to form federations among states moving towards independence, the British Government saw no alternative but to try this ploy once again in the Gulf.

Happily, several of the more important problems were solved in the time available. Most crucially of all, the Shah was persuaded in 1969 to allow sovereignty over Bahrain to be decided by a referendum of the population, conducted under UN auspices; the people opted for independence under their current Emir and the Shah acquiesced. When the Conservatives took office in 1970, Sir William Luce, a recently retired and well-respected Political Resident Persian Gulf, was recalled to service to speed negotiation of the outstanding problems. He had considerable success.

In November 1971 a compromise was reached with Iran on the island of Abu Musa, held by Sharjah.[9] Both sides maintained their claims to sovereignty over the whole island, but the Shaikh of Sharjah accepted an Iranian presence in part of it, so that it was effectively partitioned. In return, Sharjah was to receive economic aid from Iran and the two countries were to divide equally any revenues accruing from oil finds in Abu Musa's territorial waters. Finally, a Federation was achieved between the seven Trucial Shaikhdoms, though Bahrain and Qatar decided not to join it.

The prospect of sharing Abu Dhabi's oil wealth proved sufficient incentive to the six less wealthy Trucial States, and Shaikh Zaid of Abu Dhabi became President of the Federation, which took the title of the United Arab Emirates (UAE) when it was formally inaugurated on 2 December 1971.[10]

The Buraimi dispute was not settled at the time, although Sir William Luce, on behalf of the Ruler of Abu Dhabi, put forward a compromise proposal. King Faisal declared it unacceptable but on 21 August 1974 reached an agreement with Shaikh Zaid, apparently on very similar lines.[11]

The one really annoying feature for HMG was that, on 30 November 1971, the day before the termination of Britain's protecting role, the Shah seized the two Tunb Islands (just off the Iranian mainland) as a demonstration of his power. He was allowed to get away with this tweaking of the lion's tail, and was persuaded to offer the Shaikh of Ras Al-Khaima a measure of financial compensation, which the Shaikh refused. Qaddafi was so infuriated by this episode that he nationalised BP's shareholding in an oil concession in Libya; his logic was that HMG had failed to protect Arab territory, that HMG was a shareholder in BP, and that therefore BP deserved to be punished. Iraq, as a token of its intention to be protector of the Arab states of the Gulf, broke off diplomatic relations with the UK in protest.

So ended the UK's responsibilities in the Gulf (and indeed its last power base in the Arab world). In less than a decade the Iran-Iraq war broke out, but it would be harsh to regard this as a direct consequence of Britain's withdrawal. On balance, it can be argued in retrospect that the decision to withdraw was justified,[12] not so much by the resultant financial savings which were its immediate objective, but by the settlements of disputes which it precipitated. Certainly, British economic interests (other than BP in Libya) did not much suffer from the change; as will be seen later, exports from the UK to the Gulf area increased enormously in the 70s and early 80s. Although that was basically due to rising oil prices, the continuing good relations between Britain and the Gulf States following withdrawal played a significant part in giving British exporters favourable opportunities.

18 Trade between Britain and the Middle East 1960–70

The British Economy

By the beginning of the 1960s, the apparatus of physical controls over the British economy which had so long survived the war had at last disappeared. This left fiscal and monetary measures as the instruments available to the Government for the management of the economy. Monetary policy during this decade was used mainly in times of crisis, to ward off a flight from sterling by increases in bank rate,[1] so it was being employed primarily as a balance of payments weapon. Fiscal policy was extensively used, both in the annual budgets and between them, to control the pressure of demand on the economy, by varying tax levels and by determining the level of public expenditure.

As taxes were the quicker-acting of these two devices, they were more useful as a crisis measure; for that reason, power was taken in the 1961 Finance Act to vary indirect taxes up or down by either 5 per cent or 10 per cent. by Government order. This 'regulator', as it was called, was politically unpopular, so was used less than might have been expected, but resort was had to it in July 1961, July 1966 and November 1968. The taxes most used for management purposes were those on tobacco, alcoholic drinks and petrol, together with the level of purchase tax[2] on consumer goods. Demand was also manipulated by the tightening and slackening of hire-purchase restrictions, and by instructing the commercial banks to limit their granting of credit.

Together with the fluctuations in interest rates, it was measures of this kind which earned the nickname 'stop-go'. They made it very difficult for manufacturers to pursue a rational investment policy and certainly contributed to a decline in the competitive performance of manufactured goods. This in turn produced balance of payments problems which were tackled by further stop-go measures. The opportunity to break out of this cycle by devaluation when the Labour Party took office in 1964 was not taken (see Chapter 17 above) and when devaluation could no longer be fought off in 1967 it was perhaps insufficiently radical (less than half the depreciation adopted in 1949).

All this could be expected to have had a bad effect upon the export side of the decade's trade statistics, but in fact they grew reasonably in money terms except in 1967 itself, and resumed growth after that year's devaluation. The decline in competitiveness of British manufactures showed itself rather in the home market, where imports grew steadily and if anything accelerated after 1967.

On the import side, there was again an increase in volume terms in imports of oil. However, in value terms this was partly offset by a weakening of oil prices (see Chapter 16) and most of these imports were by now of crude rather than of products, so that the added-value factor of refining was a benefit to the UK. Nevertheless, the cost in foreign exchange remained considerable and began to grow sharply in the later years of the decade. In the postwar period the coal industry had never really regained its prewar and wartime dominance in Britain's fuel planning. Coal shortages persisted well into the second half of the 50s and oil in effect came to the rescue; without it there would have been no industrial growth in the 50s. During the 60s the price of oil was so competitive that it was actually displacing coal, which ceased to be in short supply largely because it was no longer so much in demand.

Visible Trade

The statistics will again be split into two quinquennia with an overlapping year, as in Chapter 12 above. From 1965 onwards, the Trade and Navigation Accounts were replaced by the series entitled Overseas Trade Statistics of the United Kingdom, published by the Board of Trade, which were generally compatible.

Table 5: Visible Trade (£ million) with:

	1960	1961	1962	1963	1964	1965
ABU DHABI						
Exports to				2.2	2.2	1.5
Imports from				7.3	15.7	19.8
Balance				-4.5	-13.5	-18.3
ADEN						
Exports to	9.5	11.0	10.5	11.4	11.9	14.1
Imports from	7.3	7.2	10.1	10.7	10.0	13.5
Balance	+2.2	+3.8	+0.4	+0.7	+1.9	+0.6
ALGERIA						
Exports to	3.3	3.1	1.6	2.5	5.4	7.1
Imports from	12.1	9.2	10.1	6.8	7.3	18.0
Balance	-8.8	-6.1	-8.5	-4.3	-1.9	-10.9
BAHRAIN						
Exports to	7.7	8.2	7.6	7.0	7.0	9.0
Imports from	14.2	13.8	14.6	13.8	14.1	4.8
Balance	-6.5	-5.6	-7.0	-6.8	-7.1	+4.2
EGYPT						
Exports to	19.6	22.4	21.7	30.6	23.8	19.9
Imports from	6.7	4.9	10.1	8.2	8.0	7.1
Balance	+12.9	+17.5	+11.6	+22.4	+15.8	+12.8
IRAN						
Exports to	36.6	33.8	26.1	25.9	25.0	38.3
Imports from	48.6	48.9	31.6	32.2	36.9	41.0
Balance	-12.0	-15.1	-5.5	-6.3	-11.9	-2.7
IRAQ						
Exports to	29.2	28.6	18.6	16.5	18.2	21.7
Imports from	54.2	45.0	48.1	54.5	70.5	70.0
Balance	-25.0	-16.4	-29.5	-38.0	-52.3	-48.3
ISRAEL						
Exports to	16.6	20.8	20.6	21.6	26.5	54.0
Imports from	14.7	13.7	14.2	16.7	17.0	24.2
Balance	+1.9	+7.1	+6.4	+4.9	+9.5	+29.8

JORDAN						
Exports to	6.0	7.7	6.9	8.4	8.1	8.5
Imports from	0.2	0.2	0.5	0.3	1.2	0.5
Balance	+5.8	+7.5	+6.4	+8.1	+6.9	+8.0
KUWAIT						
Exports to	15.2	17.0	16.1	19.6	17.9	18.9
Imports from	158.8	163.7	152.6	142.4	118.1	88.9
Balance	-143.6	-146.7	-136.5	-122.8	-100.2	-70.0
LEBANON						
Exports to	11.1	16.3	10.9	13.3	13.9	15.5
Imports from	1.9	1.8	2.8	3.7	2.4	2.1
Balance	+9.2	+14.5	+8.1	+9.6	+11.5	+13.4
LIBYA						
Exports to	12.7	12.6	12.1	14.4	16.5	22.2
Imports from	0.7	2.9	18.4	38.3	59.2	71.6
Balance	+12.0	+9.7	-6.3	-23.9	-42.7	-49.4
MOROCCO						
Exports to	5.3	5.1	4.5	4.7	4.9	4.7
Imports from	14.0	12.8	11.0	9.3	9.7	11.4
Balance	-8.7	-7.7	-6.5	-4.6	-4.8	-6.7
OMAN						
Exports to	0.7	1.1	1.1	1.2	1.5	2.2
Imports from	—	—	0.1	—	—	—
Balance	+0.7	+1.1	+1.0	+1.2	+1.5	+2.2
QATAR						
Exports to	5.0	4.6	4.7	3.3	2.5	3.7
Imports from	5.2	5.6	6.3	5.8	5.9	4.4
Balance	-0.2	-1.0	-1.6	-2.5	-3.4	-0.7
SAUDI ARABIA						
Exports to	6.3	6.7	8.3	9.0	12.5	12.8
Imports from	9.8	13.1	19.2	12.9	10.7	26.1
Balance	-3.5	-6.4	-10.9	-3.9	+1.8	-13.3
SUDAN						
Exports to	16.7	20.0	21.2	26.4	18.7	16.7
Imports from	16.7	12.7	12.0	11.4	8.0	7.7
Balance	0.0	+7.3	+9.2	+15.0	+10.7	+9.0

SYRIA						
Exports to	7.2	6.1	7.7	7.8	5.9	6.2
Imports from	1.7	1.1	1.7	1.4	0.8	2.1
Balance	+5.5	+5.0	+6.0	+6.4	+5.1	+4.1
TRUCIAL STATES (less Abu Dhabi from 1963)						
Exports to	2.4	3.7	4.1	3.4	2.9	2.8
Imports from	—	—	—	0.1	0.3	2.5
Balance	+2.4	+3.7	+4.1	+3.3	+2.6	+0.3
TUNISIA						
Exports to	2.6	2.1	2.6	2.6	3.4	3.9
Imports from	5.2	6.2	2.8	2.3	2.7	3.5
Balance	-2.6	-4.1	-0.2	+0.3	+0.7	+0.4
YEMEN						
Exports to	—	—	—	—	—	—
Imports from	—	0.1	0.1	0.2	0.1	—
Balance	—	-0.1	-0.1	-0.2	-0.1	—
TOTAL – MIDDLE EAST COUNTRIES						
Exports to	213.7	230.9	206.9	232.4	228.7	283.7
Imports from	372.0	362.9	366.3	378.3	398.6	419.2
Balance	-158.3	-132.0	-159.4	-145.9	-169.9	-135.5
TOTAL – ALL COUNTRIES						
Exports to	3695.9	3840.1	3948.7	4235.0	4407.6	4900.8
Imports from	4540.7	4395.1	4487.2	4812.7	5513.5	5751.1
Balance	-844.8	-555.0	-538.5	-577.7	-1105.9	-850.3
M.E. TRADE AS per cent OF TOTAL TRADE						
Exports to	5.78	6.01	5.24	5.49	5.19	5.79
Imports from	8.19	8.26	8.16	7.86	7.23	7.29

(Note: Apparent minor arithmetical errors result from rounding)

The importance of the Middle East region as a trading partner with Britain changed relatively little during this quinquennium, but as usual there were shifts in the importance of individual countries within the region. This is particularly true of the oil-exporting countries, as shown overleaf:

Table 6: UK Imports from Middle East Oil Producers (£ million)

	1960	1961	1962	1963	1964	1965
Abu Dhabi				7.3	15.7	19.8
Algeria	12.1	9.2	10.1	6.8	7.3	18.0
Bahrain	14.2	13.8	14.6	13.8	14.1	4.8
Iran	48.6	48.9	31.6	32.2	36.9	41.0
Iraq	54.2	45.0	48.1	54.5	70.5	70.0
Kuwait	158.8	163.7	152.6	142.4	118.1	88.9
Libya	0.7	2.9	18.4	38.3	59.2	71.6
Qatar	5.2	5.6	6.3	5.8	5.9	4.4
Saudi Arabia	9.8	13.1	19.2	12.9	10.7	26.1
TOTALS	303.6	302.2	300.9	314.0	338.4	344.6

It will be seen that the large increases were from Abu Dhabi (after 1963), Algeria (in 1965, due to NLG imports), Iraq (from 1964), Libya (every year of the quinquennium) and Saudi Arabia (in 1965). The falls were from Bahrain (in 1965), Kuwait (in 1964–5) and marginally in Qatar. In 1960–2 the totals remained virtually static; they grew from 1963–5, when the increases and falls just noted occurred, with only partly offsetting effects. Had this growth in the total figures not taken place in 1963–5, it would have been difficult to accomodate the new output from Abu Dhabi in the British market.

It must of course be remembered that the major oil companies, which were the main suppliers to Britain, were selling internationally, so that the UK figures given above will not correlate closely with global developments arising from relations between companies and host governments as outlined in Chapter 16. However, the dispute between IPC and Iraq does seem to be reflected in the virtually level figures for imports from Iraq in 1960–3, although it is less clear why there was a sudden increase in 1964. The operations of the major oil companies have been much studied but always retain an element of mystery.

Table 7: Visible Trade (£ million) with:

	1965	1966	1967	1968	1969	1970
ABU DHABI						
Exports to	1.5	3.4	6.9	9.6	15.0	10.8
Imports from	19.8	11.1	5.9	14.5	16.6	18.7
Balance	-18.3	-7.7	+1.0	-4.9	-1.6	-7.9

ADEN (PRSA from 1968)						
Exports to	14.1	13.4	9.6	8.2	6.8	5.0
Imports from	13.5	13.8	10.6	6.8	14.6	9.6
Balance	+0.6	-0.4	-1.0	+1.4	-7.8	-4.6
ALGERIA						
Exports to	7.1	3.3	3.2	4.8	9.5	16.8
Imports from	18.0	22.7	15.6	21.2	22.1	21.2
Balance	-10.9	-19.4	-12.4	-16.4	-12.6	-4.4
BAHRAIN						
Exports to	9.0	8.1	8.6	10.9	12.8	24.3
Imports from	4.8	5.6	2.9	1.9	2.1	1.6
Balance	+4.2	+2.5	+5.7	+9.0	+10.7	+22.7
EGYPT						
Exports to	19.9	18.6	11.1	12.4	15.5	18.7
Imports from	7.1	8.7	7.3	10.3	9.3	10.9
Balance	+12.8	+9.9	+3.8	+2.1	+6.2	+7.8
IRAN						
Exports to	38.3	39.6	43.3	61.0	71.6	66.3
Imports from	41.0	38.2	136.7	90.7	73.8	76.1
Balance	-2.7	+1.4	-93.4	-29.7	-2.2	-9.8
IRAQ						
Exports to	21.7	26.3	17.3	15.9	21.9	23.8
Imports from	70.0	65.6	24.1	28.0	31.1	18.7
Balance	-48.3	-39.3	-6.8	-12.1	-9.2	+5.1
ISRAEL						
Exports to	54.0	53.2	50.2	88.1	102.8	96.2
Imports from	24.2	26.5	32.3	43.8	39.3	45.1
Balance	+29.8	+26.7	+17.9	+44.3	+63.5	+51.1
JORDAN						
Exports to	8.5	9.0	7.2	8.3	16.5	12.3
Imports from	0.5	0.4	0.1	0.1	0.2	0.2
Balance	+8.0	+8.6	+7.1	+8.2	+16.3	+12.1
KUWAIT						
Exports to	18.9	26.0	25.3	29.3	41.5	36.2
Imports from	88.9	92.7	75.6	151.4	172.0	165.4
Balance	-70.0	-66.7	-50.3	-122.1	-130.5	-129.2

LEBANON						
Exports to	15.5	16.9	13.6	21.0	21.4	23.0
Imports from	2.1	2.6	3.1	4.2	4.0	3.1
Balance	+13.4	+14.3	+10.5	+16.8	+17.4	+19.9
LIBYA						
Exports to	22.2	29.4	23.1	34.8	43.2	24.3
Imports from	71.6	60.7	66.4	156.9	151.6	166.9
Balance	-49.4	-31.3	-43.3	-122.1	-108.4	-142.6
MOROCCO						
Exports to	4.7	5.2	7.0	9.6	12.9	12.6
Imports from	11.4	11.2	12.3	13.8	15.7	16.3
Balance	-6.7	-6.0	-5.3	-4.2	-2.8	-3.7
OMAN						
Exports to	2.2	3.1	2.3	2.9	5.3	7.8
Imports from	—	—	1.1	11.1	10.4	7.8
Balance	+2.2	+3.1	+1.2	-8.2	-5.1	0.0
QATAR						
Exports to	3.7	3.3	3.7	7.2	5.8	7.4
Imports from	4.4	16.8	4.3	24.3	24.7	30.6
Balance	-0.7	-13.5	-0.6	-17.1	-18.9	-23.2
SAUDI ARABIA						
Exports to	12.8	20.9	16.2	47.0	57.0	35.2
Imports from	26.1	39.7	62.5	68.7	86.8	104.2
Balance	-13.3	-18.8	-46.3	-21.7	-29.8	-69.0
SUDAN						
Exports to	16.7	16.4	17.6	19.3	21.8	18.2
Imports from	7.7	4.9	6.6	7.5	7.3	7.6
Balance	+9.0	+11.5	+11.0	+11.8	+14.5	+10.6
SYRIA						
Exports to	6.2	7.0	5.3	5.0	7.2	6.0
Imports from	2.1	1.0	0.5	0.5	1.2	0.5
Balance	+4.1	+6.0	+4.8	+4.5	+6.0	+5.5
TRUCIAL STATES (less Abu Dhabi)						
Exports to	2.8	2.9	5.3	9.1	13.5	13.7
Imports from	2.5	3.2	6.6	36.7	13.6	13.4
Balance	+0.3	-0.3	-1.3	-27.6	-0.1	+0.3

TUNISIA						
Exports to	3.9	2.7	1.8	2.7	3.5	4.3
Imports from	3.5	4.0	2.3	3.7	2.8	2.5
Balance	+0.4	-1.3	-0.5	-1.0	+0.7	+1.8
YEMEN						
Exports to	—	—	0.1	0.3	0.7	1.9
Imports from	—	—	—	—	—	0.3
Balance	—	—	+0.1	+0.3	+0.7	+1.6
TOTAL – MIDDLE EAST COUNTRIES						
Exports to	283.7	308.7	278.7	407.4	506.2	464.8
Imports from	419.2	429.4	476.8	696.1	699.2	720.7
Balance	-135.5	-120.7	-198.1	-288.7	-193.0	-255.9
TOTAL – ALL COUNTRIES						
Exports to	4900.8	5241.3	5213.6	6402.2	7298.0	8062.8
Imports from	5751.1	5946.8	6434.1	7890.1	8315.1	9051.5
Balance	-850.3	-705.5	-1220.5	-1487.9	-1017.1	-988.7
M.E. TRADE AS per cent OF TOTAL TRADE						
Exports to	5.79	5.89	5.35	6.36	6.94	5.76
Imports from	7.29	7.22	7.41	8.82	8.41	7.96

(Note: Apparent minor arithmetical errors result from rounding)

It will be seen that once again the importance of the Middle East region as a trading partner of the UK, taken as a proportion of global UK trade, did not change in any startling way during the quinquennium. Also as usual, this steady pattern conceals some striking fluctuations in the figures for individual countries.

On the export side, there was significant growth after 1967, resulting largely from the increased purchasing power of countries which had benefited from rising oil revenues, but also partly attributable to greater competitiveness of British exports following the 1967 devaluation of sterling. Purchasing power created the opportunities while competitiveness enabled exporters to grasp them, or at least some of them. This is true of such oil exporting countries as Abu Dhabi, Algeria, Bahrain, Iran, Kuwait, Libya, Oman (a newcomer to the oil producers), Qatar, Saudi Arabia and (another addition to the oil producers) the Trucial States other than Abu Dhabi.

But it is notable that there is a similar trend in some non-oil-producers, Israel, Jordan, Lebanon, Morocco, Sudan and even such a tiny trading partner as Yemen. In these cases it is the increased competitiveness that must be the cause. Israel merits particular mention; it was moving more and more from the category of developing to developed country. British exports to Israel quadrupled between 1964 and 1969, when they passed the £100 million figure, making Israel at that time the largest single market for British exports in the Middle East. This is remarkable for a country with no oil exports to boost its purchasing power (on the contrary, it had to meet a considerable import bill for oil, much of it from Iran).

Britain's imports from the Middle East were, as always, predominantly of oil and it is worth looking again at the fluctuations between countries during the quinquennium:

Table 8: UK Imports from Middle East Oil Producers (£ million)

	1965	1966	1967	1968	1969	1970
Abu Dhabi	19.8	11.1	5.9	14.5	16.6	18.7
Algeria	18.0	22.7	15.6	21.2	22.1	21.2
Bahrain	4.8	5.6	2.9	1.9	2.1	1.6
Iran	41.0	38.2	136.7	90.7	73.8	76.1
Iraq	70.0	65.6	24.1	28.0	31.1	18.7
Kuwait	88.9	92.7	75.6	151.4	172.0	165.4
Libya	71.6	60.7	66.4	156.9	151.6	166.9
Oman	—	—	1.1	11.1	10.4	7.8
Qatar	4.4	16.8	4.3	24.3	24.7	30.6
Saudi Arabia	26.1	39.7	62.5	68.7	86.8	104.2
Trucial States*	2.5	3.2	6.6	36.7	13.6	13.4
TOTALS	347.1	356.3	401.7	605.4	604.8	624.6

*other than Abu Dhabi

It will be seen at once from the totals that Britain's oil imports, which had risen only slowly from over £300 million in 1960 to under £350 million in 1965, accelerated to over £400 million in 1967 and then shot ahead to over £600 million in 1968. This last jump may have been caused in part by a decision to hold larger stocks following the closure of the Suez Canal, but that would not account for continued imports above the £600 million level in 1969–70. There was clearly a real increase in demand in Britain for oil; this applied particularly to industry, but also to domestic use, especially for oil-fired central heating. Coal was increasingly seen as a dirty and old-fashioned fuel, and moreover as unreliable because of the danger of miners' strikes. Oil therefore, with its relatively low prices, was gaining ground rapidly.

Natural gas was discovered in the southern North Sea in 1965 (see Chapter 16) and by 1968 was to some extent replacing coal-derived town gas as a domestic fuel supply. But it was not yet a major fuel source for industry in Britain and in the domestic market was only beginning to compete with oil to meet the rapidly expanding demand for central-heating.

The other notable feature of Table 8 is the distortion of trading patterns in 1967. This was of course the year of an Arab-Israel war and in the bitterness of defeat (see Chapter 15) a number of Arab countries banned oil exports to Britain and the United States, causing temporary dislocation of supplies before better sense prevailed and the ban was lifted.

The figures show that the impact of this embargo on trade with Britain was very uneven. As might be expected, imports from Iran as a non-Arab supplier jumped, by nearly £100 million, while imports from most of the Arab suppliers in the Gulf area fell. Iraq was the biggest loser, with its supplies to Britain dropping by about 63 per cent, and most of this loss was not regained in the next few years. Kuwait's exports to Britain also fell in 1967, by about 18 per cent, but this was a temporary setback, followed by a doubling in 1968. Abu Dhabi's loss in 1967 was also more than made up from 1968 onwards. Iraq's case was thus unique and must be attributed to a worsening of relations between IPC and the Iraq Government in 1967 (see Chapter 16).

There were however some Arab countries which gained as well as Iran. Most surprising (since it took part in the embargo) is Saudi Arabia with a gain of over £20 million. Libya also sold some 10 per cent more to Britain in 1967, and that was far outdone by another rise of over 135 per cent in 1968, when Libya was the largest Middle East exporter to the UK, just outdoing Kuwait. The reasons for this are clear enough; Libyan output was growing, and above all Libya was on the Mediterranean side of the blocked Suez Canal. It should be noted that the Trucial States other than Abu Dhabi are now listed among the oil producers; Dubai Marine Areas struck oil offshore of Dubai in 1966 and again in 1967. This increased the hopes of the other five Trucial States that they too would one day grow rich from finds of oil in their territories; at the very least it encouraged the oil companies to explore there, which in itself brought in some income for the host countries.

Arms Sales

These grew in importance during the decade. The British Ministry of Defence had found it worth while to set up a Defence Sales Department in the 1960s and even to bring in a prominent businessman to head it.[3] British armoured vehicles were much in demand. No further Centurion tanks were sold to Egypt after 1954, but Israel was a major purchaser of them; by 1966, as many as 250 Centurions had been bought, of which 100 had been fitted with French 105 mm. guns, and by 1969 the figure was 400. Jordan held 160 Centurions by the end of the decade and Iraq had 55. There were also sales of British armoured cars, scout cars and armoured personnel carriers to Jordan, Libya, Sudan and even Tunisia, amounting in all to not far short of 500 vehicles.[4]

On the naval front, Israel ordered two British submarines in 1965. Middle East air forces also bought from Britain. The small Jordanian Air Force was equipped with Hunter fighters. When these were all wiped out by the Israelis in 1967, replacement orders were placed; 20 had been delivered by 1970. Iraq also bought 50 Hunters and Saudi Arabia took a few of them, mainly for use as trainers. The major Saudi purchase was the large order for Lightnings mentioned in Chapter 14; these were delivered gradually, some 35 by 1970. Jet Provost trainers were also popular; Saudi Arabia took some, Iraq bought 20 and Sudan 8.[5]

Invisible Trade

This continued to be a very favourable influence on the balance of payments between Britain and the Middle East, though as usual no precise figure can be put upon it. During the decade Britain's worldwide earnings from invisibles were second only to those of the United States, while no Middle East country figured in the list of the top twenty invisible earners. The flow of these earnings was thus very much one-way, and especially so after the Suez Canal ceased to bring in revenue for Egypt. The City of London was Britain's chief earner of invisibles, with banking and insurance prominent as usual. Tourism to Britain was also on the increase in the years of the 'swinging sixties'; the visitors from the Middle East included some heavy gamblers at London's casinos.

Capital Flow

Here too the pattern remained as in the previous decade. British investments in the Middle East were substantial, almost entirely of course in oil exploration and development. In the opposite direction Kuwait and some of the newer oil producers such as Abu Dhabi looked to London as the natural channel for the surplus funds they had available for investment; in consequence Arab banks began to establish a larger presence in London. The balance of these two tendencies was probably a net inflow to the UK. Offsetting this to some extent was aid from Britain to the poorer Middle East countries, but the sums involved were not great, as the aid offered was largely technical assistance.

ECGD

Business handled by ECGD again increased substantially during the decade. Parliament three times extended its maximum liability, in 1964 to £2800 million, in 1967 to £3900 and in 1970 to £6500 million. By 1970 it was insuring 36 per cent of global UK exports. The buyers' market which prevailed worldwide ensured that virtually all but the smallest overseas sales were now for credit rather than cash, and the credit periods were lengthening as a result of competition between sellers. More and more exporters therefore turned to ECGD for credit insurance. The Department extended its facilities to meet the demand, including increasing its number of branch offices in the UK to twenty.

One innovation of the decade was the concept of 'matching' foreign competition; if a British firm bidding for an important overseas order found that a non-British competitor was offering credit longer than ECGD's normal maximum for that type of business, the Department would extend the length of its cover to remove that particular disadvantage. More important still was the introduction of the 'buyer credit' system. The principle here was that ECGD would guarantee a UK bank loan to an overseas buyer, the loan being provided at preferential fixed rates of interest, with the result that the purchases so financed became effectively cash sales for the supplier. A further benefit to exporters was that the expansion of ECGD business made possible reductions in the Department's charges, despite some increase in claims. For the standard short (6-months) cover, average premium rates almost halved during the decade.

Middle East Association

On 15 April 1961, some 50 British industrial and commercial concerns joined together to found the Middle East Association in London. Its purpose was to provide them with a forum for discussion of developments of mutual interest in Middle East markets (subject naturally to commercial secrecy by firms about their own intentions). The small permanent staff of the Association, knowledgeable about Middle East affairs relevant to businessmen, was available, both at and between meetings of the members, to answer enquiries on a confidential basis. HMG saw in the Association a welcome self-financing institution which could be beneficial in helping British exporters and so gave it its blessing. The Association's membership has grown over the years to around 350 British companies, plus some fifty individual overseas members.

Council for Middle East Trade (COMET)

The British Government had set up in 1958 an Advisory Council on Middle East Trade (ACMET), chaired by the Minister of State, Board of Trade, and with a Secretariat provided by that

Department. Its membership had included leading businessmen. On 21 January 1963, the Board of Trade announced that ACMET would be replaced by COMET, a non-Governmental Council chaired by the Earl of Inchcape (the Inchcape Group included Gray Mackenzie, an overseas trading company with important interests in the Middle East, particularly in the Gulf area). Although the Council was independent of Government, its meetings were regularly attended by representatives at official level of the Board of Trade, the Foreign Office, the Treasury and the Bank of England, but the majority of its members were Chairmen or Directors of companies investing in or trading with the Middle East countries. Its remit was to help to promote British exports to the area. To ensure close liaison between this new Council and the Middle East Association, COMET's Secretariat was given offices in the Association's headquarters and COMET meetings were held there. The Director-General of the Association was made an ex-officio member of COMET.

Overseas Banking

In the 1940s and 50s, the BBME had built up its branch network to a size which made it much the most important British bank in the Middle East. With the large deposits accruing to it in consequence, especially in the oil-rich countries, it had begun to outgrow its capital base, even though this was doubled from £1 million to £2 million during the 50s. This made it a tempting target for a takeover bidder and the price of its shares became volatile. The problem was solved in 1960 by an agreed takeover of the BBME by the Hongkong and Shanghai Bank, another British overseas bank with a stronger capital base.[6] The BBME continued to operate in the Middle East under its own name and was given virtually complete autonomy for over a decade, so most of its customers hardly noticed the change, but it was more secure as part of a more powerful entity.

The 1960s were marked by a considerable growth in the number of indigenous banks in the Middle East, with inevitable increase in competition for the British banks operating there. Moreover, the nationalisation of banks in Egypt spread during the decade to other Arab countries. In the process the BBME lost four of its countries of operation, Syria in 1961, Iraq in 1964, Aden in 1969 and Libya in 1970. These were not its most profitable branches, in fact some of them were regular loss-makers, so the damage done was not too serious.[7] The branch at Jerusalem was also closed by order of the Israeli authorities when they captured that city in 1967. On the other hand, there was some further expansion by the BBME into new territories. Branches were opened in Morocco, at Casablanca in 1961, where the Ottoman Bank was already operating, and at Tangier in 1964. A 90 per cent share was taken in the ownership of Middle East Finance Company, based in Dubai, in 1970. In that year, BBME was required to cease business in Kuwait, but what would have been a painful loss was partly offset by the grant to it of a 5-year management contract for its successor bank, the Bank of Kuwait and the Middle East. It was altogether an eventful decade, but the BBME never ceased to be highly profitable overall.

19 British Membership of the EEC

The formation of the European Economic Community (EEC) in 1957 without British membership was followed in May 1960 by the creation of the European Free Trade Association (EFTA). Of this the UK was the leading member, with a volume of trade worldwide far surpassing that of any of the other members, Austria, Denmark, Norway, Portugal, Sweden and Switzerland. EFTA's objectives were limited to the achievement by 1970 of an industrial free trade area; there was no agricultural or fisheries component, nor was there any harmonisation of external tariffs (which caused some practical problems). Above all, there was no surrender of sovereignty by its members, beyond that involved in any entry into an international agreement. The original seven members were joined later by Finland as an associate member, and on 1 March 1970 by Iceland.

The existence side by side in Western Europe of these two disparate international bodies was an uneasy one, at least for EFTA. That organisation at first hoped to be able to extend its membership to include the EEC, so creating a wider free trade area for industrial goods, within which the EEC would be able to pursue its own aspiration towards complete economic union of its members; but it quickly became clear that this would not be acceptable to the EEC countries. The outcome was that in July 1961 the British Government announced its intention to seek direct negotiations for EEC membership. Denmark and Norway followed suit, and the other members of EFTA expressed interest in some looser form of association with the EEC. The Republic of Ireland, which was a member of neither international body but which had economically vital links with the UK, its major market, also decided to seek EEC membership.

The details of the negotiations which followed are outside the scope of this book. Suffice it to say that British entry into the EEC was twice vetoed by General de Gaulle's France, first on 14 January 1963 when the UK had a Conservative Government and again on 19 December 1967 when a Labour Government was applying. By 1967 it was clear that the other EEC members would have favoured British entry, on suitable terms, but unanimity was required for any change in the membership laid down in the Treaty of Rome which had brought the EEC into being, so a French veto was decisive.

One problem was that Britain was seeking EEC membership from a position of economic weakness and to some extent in the hope that membership would rescue it from that weakness. In the view of some, this would come about because a wider market would be open to British exports. Others, more pessimistic about British competitiveness, believed that exposure of Britain's home market to tariff-free imports from EEC countries was the only way of shocking British industrialists and trade unions into putting their house in order by ridding the country of their incompetence and restrictive practices.

Harold Wilson's first Labour Government, from 1964 to 1970, had hoped to cure these ills by winning the cooperation of the unions through a combination of economic planning and expansive social policies, together with the return of the iron and steel industry to public ownership,[1] but had failed to obtain their effective support. Labour policy, set out in a White Paper optimistically entitled 'In Place of Strife',[2] could not be carried against union and parliamentary opposition, and had to be withdrawn in return for vague promises by the unions to improve their own procedures for dealing with unofficial strikes and inter-union demarcation disputes. These promises turned out to be worth very little.

When the Conservative Party under Edward Heath gained office on 18 June 1970, a renewed effort to achieve EEC membership was one of its prescriptions for economic progress. This objective seemed the more achievable because de Gaulle was no longer President of France; he had resigned on 27 April 1969 when a referendum to give him powers to change the constitution failed to win a majority. Any personal animosity which he felt against Britain, dating from wartime slights he believed he had been made to suffer, was thus removed from the French decision-making process. Following his departure from office, the EEC agreed in December 1969 to enter into new negotiations with Britain, and also with Denmark, Norway and the Republic of Ireland. On 30 June 1970, the new Conservative Government formally revived the UK's application for membership and negotiations began in July. Considering the complicated issues involved, the talks made rapid progress and were completed in twelve months.

The issue of EEC membership had split the Labour Opposition. Although a Labour Government had applied for membership in 1967, there had always been doubters in its ranks; there were outright opponents in the Parliamentary Labour Party and its rank and file supporters, especially in trade union circles. This group found a face-saving pretext for opposing membership in 1971, claiming to have no objection to the principle of membership but to be outraged by the terms on offer; their leader from February 1971 was James Callaghan. The opposite view was held by a minority of Labour pro-marketeers, led by Roy Jenkins and George Thomson.[3] When the issue came to the vote in Parliament on 28 October 1971, sixty-nine Labour MPs voted in favour of membership, their support being crucial to giving the Government their majority of 112 (the Conservatives, unlike Labour, had been allowed a free vote). Harold Wilson, intent above all on party unity, had hedged on the subject before finally but unenthusiastically joining the anti-marketeers, losing a good deal of credibility in the process. He eventually found a formula to reconcile the two factions, namely that when Labour returned to office it would offer the British public a free choice on the issue through that very un-British procedure, a referendum.[4] (To anticipate events a little, that referendum was held on 5 June 1975, the vote proving in favour of membership.[5])

Denmark, Ireland and Norway had been conducting parallel

negotiations for membership and had all achieved terms which their Governments felt able to recommend to their legislatures. Ratification was required from all the applicants and also from the original six EEC members. 1972 was allowed for this process, with 1 January 1973 set for the formal enlargement of the Community. Referenda were required in many countries; that in France, crucial in view of past history, was carried on 23 April 1972. An Irish referendum had a positive outcome in May. In the UK, the Parliamentary procedures, without a referendum, were completed in July. Referenda in Norway and Denmark were scheduled for September, and to the surprise of many Norway decided against membership,[6] but Denmark, despite voting a week later when the Norwegian outcome was already known, opted for membership with a 2 to 1 majority.

The six thus became nine, from 1 January 1973, with a five-year transitional period for implementation of some of the more radical changes, including particularly the abolition of internal tariffs, which reduced by 20 per cent p.a. Full application of EEC regulations among the nine was thus postponed to 1 January 1978. The transitional period gave time for redirection of trade not only to the three new EEC members, but also to the non-EEC countries for which they had been important markets, and which now needed to find new outlets.

There were some exceptions to this general situation. As has been mentioned, the remaining EFTA members sought arrangements which would preserve their free trade in industrial goods with the three new members of the EEC; to achieve these they also had to be given similar arrangements with the original six EEC members. The slightly ironical result was that the wider industrial free-trade area sought years before by EFTA and at that time rejected by the EEC came into being after all. The EEC also had a privileged arrangement with certain developing countries, instituted originally to preserve France's links with former French colonies in Africa. A similar problem arose with British entry and the EEC during 1973 agreed to extend the privileges enjoyed by 18 African countries and Mauritius to a further 24 countries in Africa, the Caribbean and the Pacific.

This extension of what was called the Lomé Agreement has

worked quite well and the UK has not been unhappy with it. It does however draw attention to the fact that the EEC is a supranational body which acts as an entity for the purpose of trade negotiations. The days of bilateral trade agreements between the UK and Middle Eastern countries were over.

The EEC at this time contained only two Mediterranean members, France and Italy (not yet , of course, Greece, Spain and Portugal). It did however think it proper to have a wider Mediterranean commercial policy and this brought the possibility of favoured arrangements with certain of the Middle East countries bordering that sea. In 1973 negotiations to this end were conducted with Algeria, Israel, Morocco and Tunisia, and trade agreements were also concluded with Egypt and Lebanon. For the most part, however, Middle Eastern exports to EEC countries consisted of raw materials, first and foremost oil, and these were zero-rated under the EEC's common external tariff. The accession of the UK to the EEC thus had comparatively little effect on its imports from the Middle East.

As for British exports, the gradual opening over the 5-year transitional period of a wider European market was likely to cause some redirection of effort by exporters, but the Middle East remained a very attractive market. Indeed, as will be seen in the next Chapter, its attractions increased greatly with its enhanced purchasing power from 1973 onwards, and the statistics in Chapter 26 will show that British exports, particularly to Saudi Arabia and the United Arab Emirates, then began a period of rapid growth, for reasons unconnected with EEC membership.

There was one area of the Middle East where EEC membership actually helped British exports, albeit mainly indirectly. This was the Maghreb area, Algeria, Morocco and Tunisia, where British exporters have, ever since those countries' independence from France, achieved far less penetration than might have been expected. The French language was a factor in this to a rather ridiculous extent, when it is considered that no great obstacle seemed to be provided by the ignorance at that time of any other language than Arabic by many importers elsewhere in the Arab world.[7] However that may be, one result of growing British exports to France once tariff barriers were removed was that

French firms with good Maghreb links began to reexport some British products to that area. The reader will appreciate that in such cases the trade statistics will show the exports as being to France rather than to the country of ultimate destination, thus marginally understating Britain's trade with the Middle East.

In the second half of the 1970s, the Arab States accepted an invitation to open discussions in Brussels with the EEC members collectively. The meetings became known as the Euro-Arab Dialogue. The Arab side made it clear that they regarded trade and politics as inseparable, no doubt hoping in this way to win political concessions, especially in relation to the Arab-Israel conflict, from those European members of the EEC who were striving for closer economic ties with the Arab states. Both sides professed for some time to find the exchanges of views valuable, but in practice not much of importance materialised and the Dialogue gradually faded into the background, though no doubt it could be revived if circumstances seemed propitious.

Two disputes in recent years between the EEC and Middle East countries are worthy of mention. The first arose from the development of petrochemical industries in the Arabian Peninsula (on which see Chapter 27 below). Because these used indigenous gas supplies as feedstock their production costs were low and EEC countries became worried about competition from such petrochemicals in their home markets. The EEC therefore decided in principle in late 1984 to be ready to impose tariffs on petrochemicals from countries of the Gulf Cooperation Council (see Chapter 27). In January 1985 tariffs of 13–14 per cent were in fact placed on Saudi methanol and polyethylenes. The Arab States concerned naturally consider such barriers to trade highly unethical, but it is undoubtedly within the EEC's competence to vary the common external tariff provided that no breach is involved of obligations under the GATT. The UK as an EEC member must abide by collective EEC decisions on such matters.

The second dispute has been between the EEC and Israel. It was discovered that among the items which Israeli exporters were selling under the favoured conditions of Israel's association agreement with the EEC were goods from the Israeli-occupied Palestinian territories of the West Bank and Gaza. The EEC did not seek to prevent such goods from benefiting from the tariff concessions, but demanded that they should be adequately marked or labelled to show their real origin. The Israelis reluctantly undertook to make arrangements for this but in practice have not yet done so. In the face of this failure, the EEC ruled that Israeli exports in the categories concerned could no longer benefit from tariff reductions, since goods were being passed as Israeli which were not in fact Israeli. This dispute has only come to a head in 1987 and at the time of writing is unresolved. Here too, the UK is bound by the EEC ruling.

20 Oil Developments in the Early 1970s

The second half of the 60s had seen the discovery of gas in the British sector of the southern North Sea; in the 70s it was the finding of oil in important quantities which revolutionised the economic outlook for Norway and for Britain. It was on the Norwegian side of the median line that oil was first found in November 1969, by a consortium led by Phillips Petroleum (an American company) and including only Shell from among companies with any British ownership. The field was named Ekofisk and a tussle developed over where the oil should be landed.

As was mentioned in Note 9 to Chapter 16, the deep Norwegian Trench runs parallel to the Norwegian coast and not far offshore. To lay a pipeline across it was not necessarily impossible but would certainly be difficult. The engineers preferred to find an outlet in another direction. The main contenders were Britain and West Germany, or just possibly Denmark. In the end a kind of judgment of Solomon was made by the Norwegian Government in 1973; the more highly prized oil pipeline would run to Teesside in North-East England and a gas pipeline, for the associated gas which would be separated at sea, would run to Emden in Germany.[1]

The discovery of Ekofisk stimulated exploration in the northern part of the North Sea's British sector, away from the already known gasfields. It was rapidly successful, the first find being by BP of the Forties Field, in 1970. By mid-1974, ten oilfields had been discovered in the British sector and the race was on to bring them into production, with plenty of Government encouragement since oil imports at the prevailing high prices were having very adverse effects on the UK balance of payments (during 1974 the deficit on visible trade was running all too regularly at over £400 million a month).

But production platforms for such a hostile environment as the North Sea, in comparatively deep water and exposed to gales and huge waves, took time to build and erect (erection required a fair weather 'window' which occurred all too rarely in the meteorological forecasts). Hopes of more than token production in 1975 had to be abandoned and even in 1976 output forecasts were scaled down considerably. It became clear that Britain could not expect to be self-sufficient in oil before the 1980s. Nevertheless, the build-up towards self-sufficiency was already of great economic value in the second half of the 1970s and the prospects for the 1980s cast their glow before them to encourage investment in the UK, particularly but not only in the oil equipment industry.

There were other successes in oil exploration outside the Middle East. Most important of them for Britain was the discovery by BP (consistently lucky or skilful or both in its exploration around the world) of a large oilfield on the North Slope of Alaska. Again this was a very hostile environment for production, with ecological damage a particular danger, so there was bound to be a long delay before the oil came to market.

High oil prices encouraged experimental work on the extraction of oil from shales and tar-sands, of which there were plentiful deposits in the Western Hemisphere. Technological progress was made and the outlook was sufficiently promising for a few pilot plants to be set up, but the costs proved too high for economic production. Nevertheless this possibility remained in the background as a ceiling to oil prices.

These efforts to develop oil production elsewhere did little in the early 1970s to detract from the global importance of Middle East oil. The 1960s had seen the spread of 50/50 profit-sharing as the norm for concessionary agreements between host Governments and foreign oil companies. The chief argument as the decade wore away had been over the calculation of these profits, particularly the 'expensing of royalties'. In the 1970s, with victories on this battlefield already won, host Governments were ready to make new advances, and they were encouraged to do so by the growing value of their association with each other in OPEC.

OPEC foreshadowed the direction in which Governments intended to move by a 'Declaratory Statement of Petroleum Policy in Member Countries' adopted in June 1968.[2] This called for:

(a) The ownership by Governments of 'a reasonable participation' in the equity of companies holding concessions;
(b) The right of Governments to determine the price of oil used for calculation of payments to them by companies;
(c) Payments per barrel to Governments to rise in line with the price of the industrial products they needed to import;
(d) 'Excess' profits of companies, as determined by Governments, to be surrendered to Governments.

At the time, the oil companies, particularly the majors, paid scant attention to this Declaratory Statement. That was a serious mistake on their part. By the middle of the 1970s, most of these policy objectives had been secured.

Of course, Governments could not have made such advances had they not been in a strong bargaining position.[3] There were a number of factors converging in the 1970s to make this the case.

(1) Demand for oil in the world was running high. The USA was still a major oil-producer and gas-producer, but these indigenous fuels were beginning to decline from peak levels and, apart from the prospect of oil from the Alaskan North Slope, new fields were not being found on American territory on a scale sufficient to prevent an increasing reliance on imported oil.[4] With the exception of Norway and foreseeably Britain, such dependence was even more true of the other Western industrialised countries and notably also of Japan.[5]
(2) The major international oil companies were increasingly being confronted by newcomers, the 'independents', permitting Governments to play off one group against the other. In any dispute these newcomers, with their smaller

resources, were likely to be the first to crumble before Government pressure and so to compromise the stand of other oil companies.

(3) The power of the US and UK Governments to influence the policies of Middle East Governments had declined, as a result of British military withdrawal from the area and of the increasing Soviet presence.

(4) Several important Middle East producers with small populations had become rich enough to be able to survive a temporary interruption of their oil income for longer than the industrialised countries could tolerate an interruption of their supplies. This was true of Saudi Arabia and Kuwait especially, but also of the UAE, Qatar and significantly Libya.[6]

It was Libya, following its 1969 Revolution, which took the lead in pressing for better terms from its concessionaires. Libya was radical at a time when most others among the really large producers were under conservative regimes. It also had the great advantage of having easy access to European markets at a time when the Gulf States were distanced from them by the closure of the Suez Canal and tankers were in short supply. Moreover, for reasons already explained in Chapter 16, many Libyan concessions were held by independents.[7] There was also a technical advantage favouring Libya: its oil was of low sulphur content, avoiding the need for costly sulphur-removal when concern about pollution was growing. All in all, Libya was thus in a very powerful bargaining position. In May 1970, the Algerian, Iraqi and Libyan Governments, all from the radical wing of the Arab oil-producers, agreed to work together within OPEC and in their dealings with the oil companies. Significantly, they expressed in the agreement a joint preference for proceeding towards their goals by 'legislative or regulatory' measures rather than through 'lengthy and fruitless' negotiations with the companies.

The pattern which now developed, much to the fury of the oil companies, was for these radical Arabs, with Libya in the van, to take bold steps to enforce unwelcome changes in concession terms and for the more moderate Arab producers then to make irresistible demands for equal treatment. Negotiations between the oil companies and Libya for an increase in posted prices had been due to start on 1 September 1969, the day on which King Idris was deposed *in absentia*. The Libyan bid had been for a 10c. increase; a month after coming to power Qaddafi replaced this with a demand for a 44c. increase, a figure loosely related to the profit differential to the oil companies in selling Libyan as against Saudi crude (because mainly of the transport factor). It was no coincidence that the other Mediterranean producer, Algeria, made similar demands of its French concessionaires. An initial meeting was held with the oil companies in Libya collectively, but Qaddafi then cleverly switched tactics by announcing company-by-company negotiations.

He began with Exxon, the largest producer in Libya, and Occidental, which had the largest reserves, both American companies. To put pressure on all concessionaires, Qaddafi in May 1970 ordered general production cutbacks, which for most of them were in the range of 15 to 31 per cent. Exxon was also refused permission to export from a new LNG plant in which it had just invested $350 million. Occidental's oil exports were reduced from 800,000 to 440,000 b/d. (It is relevant that May 1970 was the month in which the 500,000 b/d TAPline from Saudi Arabia to near Sidon, Lebanon, was closed by an accident and then kept closed because of a dispute over transit tolls.)

In July, it was Algeria's turn to apply pressure; it raised its posted price unilaterally, increasing its own share of the profit from 78.6 c. to $1.21 per barrel. This was a historic move, the first example of a Government imposing a posted price on a company with no element of agreement. In Libya, Exxon now offered a 10c. increase in posted price plus 11c. 'freight premium', which was refused, with the Government breaking off the talks. Occidental, left negotiating alone, yielded by offering 30c. on the posted price, plus an increase in Libya's profit share from the usual 50 per cent to 58 per cent. This was accepted and Occidental's production quota was raised to 700,000 b/d.

The next company selected by Qadaffi for negotiations was Oasis, owned by a consortium of Royal Dutch Shell and three American independents (Amerada-Hess, Continental and Marathon). This was a disparate consortium; Shell drew only 3 per cent of its global crude supplies from Oasis, while the other three were dependent on it for more than half of their crude. The outcome was predictable. On 21 September 1970, the three independents accepted a package similar to that agreed by Occidental; Shell rejected the package and ceased to obtain Libyan oil.

Qadaffi now felt himself to be in an impregnable position. The income secured from Occidental and the Oasis independents would meet all the Libyan Government's current expenditure. He decided to force the pace with the remaining concessionaires. They were ordered to accept the package deal by 27 September, or be shut down. Some of the majors wished to resist, but they found no support from their own Governments, and the fact that Qaddafi's demands were in line with OPEC policy suggested that it might be difficult for them to find replacement oil by raising production elsewhere if they were cut off from Libyan oil. By the end of September they had all decided that they had no alternative but to yield.

The effect was that the price of Libyan crude was raised from \$1.40 to \$1.70 per barrel and that Libya would receive a 55 per cent share of profits, so breaching decisively the 50/50 sharing agreement which had prevailed world-wide for the last twenty years. To rub salt into the wound, Qaddafi made the companies sign letters admitting that Libyan oil had been underpriced since 1965. This was not merely a political gesture; it was in Qadaffi's eyes an acknowledgement by the companies that his gains were no more than the righting of past injustices. He saw it as leaving him free to press for further advances, in particular higher posted prices, freight differentials and a premium for the low-sulphur quality of his crude. The companies' difficulties in Libya were by no means over.

Iraq, Iran and Kuwait swiftly demanded parity of treatment with Libya. The oil companies decided to extend the 55 per cent tax rate to all the Gulf countries and to make some upward adjustment in posted prices. They had to do the same for Nigeria. In Venezuela the Government followed Algeria's lead in imposing increases on the companies unilaterally. In December 1970, OPEC threatened'concerted and simultaneous action by all Member countries' unless the oil companies universalised the Libyan package by giving all Governments a 55 per cent profit share, increasing posted prices and eliminating payment disparities between producing countries. At the same time, the Organization supported Libya's claim to a 'short-haul premium' and a 'Suez premium'.[8]

The companies were summoned to begin negotiations in Tehran by 12 January 1971 with the Gulf producers. This produced what a few years before would have seemed an amazing reply from the companies, that they wished to negotiate with all OPEC countries together. They now understood the dangers of 'leapfrogging' and had formed their own joint body, the 'London Policy Group' (the American authorities agreed not to regard this as a breach of anti-trust legislation). Their resistance was short-lived; on 30 January, under pressure from the Gulf States, they reluctantly agreed to hold split negotiations, in the Gulf and in Libya simultaneously. Even this was unacceptable to Libya, which refused to negotiate until the Gulf negotiations were over, signalling clearly its own intention to 'leapfrog'.

It is worth pausing here to recall the political background to these manoeuvres. The UK Government in 1968 had given notice that British forces would be withdrawn from the Gulf by 1971. The Shah at once resolved that Iran would then take over the hegemony of the Gulf. But he was deep in debt and needed higher oil revenues to buy the military hardware which he hoped would enable him to achieve that ambition. It was he at the Gulf end who was the most insistent on holding separate Gulf and Mediterranean negotiations. The US Government regarded the Shah as best fitted to take on new security responsibilities in the Gulf, so had no real objection to seeing him win higher oil prices. This weakened the stance of the American oil companies, majors and independents alike.

OPEC increased the pressure by announcing that if the companies did not complete their Gulf negotiations by 15 February Governments would impose new terms unilaterally, and that any company not accepting such imposed terms would face a total embargo. This was another novel tactic; there had been embargoes on countries, but never hitherto on companies.

With such horrors facing them, the companies capitulated on 14 February (they of course reckoned that they could pass on their increased costs to their consumers). The deal struck was a five-year agreement, involving an immediate increase of 30c. per barrel in Governments' take, plus an annual upward adjustment of 2.5 per cent and an additional 5c. The effect would be to increase Governments' revenues by an immediate $1400 million in 1971 and a total of a staggering $11,700 million over the 5-year period. It was the most costly settlement in the history of the industry. In return, the Gulf States promised no 'leapfrogging' during the five years, but the companies can hardly have placed complete confidence in the enduring value of such a pledge.

It was the turn for Mediterranean negotiations. Algeria, and also Iraq and Saudi Arabia which had Mediterranean pipeline outlets (the TAPline had reopened on 29 January 1971), agreed that Libya should act for them all. Algeria however applied new pressure by announcing on 24 February that it was taking a 51 per cent controlling interest in the equity of the French oil companies operating in its territory. The negotiations began to drag, with the companies surviving two Libyan deadlines, but on 15 March the four countries threatened to shut in all their oil production. This broke the resistance; on 17 March the companies surrendered. They were made to accept a 65c. per barrel increase in payments to Governments (as against the 30c. in the Gulf). This meant that the tax-paid cost of Libyan oil had risen from $1.40 to $2.30 over a period of a mere six months.

The impact of all this on the consumer was less than might be thought. Even with such large increased payments to host Governments, 90 per cent of the retail price arose elsewhere in the chain. The marginal extra cost to the consumer was calculated to be only some 3 to 5 per cent. Indeed, in real terms, the cost of crude landed in Europe and Japan actually fell between 1957 and the end of 1971. This was partly due to weakening of the dollar, in which oil was traditionally priced, and partly to other factors such as greatly increased tanker efficiency following the building of super-tankers. By passing on their increased tax costs to the consumer, the major oil companies achieved larger profits in 1972 than in previous years. This was not lost on the producing countries, who concluded that to increase prices did not necessarily mean reduced sales.

The US and UK Governments, for their part, were not unhappy with the situation. Most of the increased payments had gone to host Governments with which they were friendly and which they were happy to see grow stronger. Following the Tehran and Tripoli Agreements, there was a huge increase in arms expenditure by Saudi Arabia, Iran and Kuwait, almost entirely on American and British weapons systems and equipment. Saudi Arabia's arms purchases from the USA, for example, rose from $2.6 million in 1970 to $307 million in 1972. Iran spent $500 million there on arms in 1972 and placed a $2000 million order in the spring of 1973.

On the ground, other benefits began to show. Oman had been under threat from revolutionaries based in the neighbouring territory of the People's Democratic Republic of Yemen (PDRY), as South Yemen had renamed itself in November 1970. The Sultan appealed for help to Saudi Arabia and Iran. The Saudis responded with money, which was useful but not decisive. On 20 December 1973, the Iranians sent 10,000 troops, which enabled the Sultan to turn back the revolutionaries and ultimately to crush the insurrection. The increased oil payments were thus yielding some useful political dividends.

21 The Yom Kippur War[1] and the First Oil Shock

When President Nasser died suddenly on 28 September 1970, Anwar Sadat as Vice-President automatically became Acting President for a period of 60 days. His duty under the Egyptian Constitution was to hold a plebiscite to choose a successor President. Sadat's prominence was thus fortuitous; indeed, it seems that his position as Vice-President was itself somewhat fortuitous. He had been one of the 'Free Officers' who carried out the Egyptian Revolution in 1952 and was one of the original members of the Revolutionary Command Council set up following its success, but he was not one of its leading figures. He held a number of posts,[2] but not ministerial posts. It was therefore a surprise when Nasser, acting on a whim according to Mohamed Heikal[3] (the best, even though hostile, source for Sadat's Presidency), swore him in as Vice-President in December 1969.

Politically, Egypt is a country well fitted to illustrate the cliché that nothing succeeds like success. His Acting Presidency virtually assured Sadat of victory in the presidential plebiscite on 15 October 1970 and he polled over 90 per cent of the votes cast. When, after his election, he appeared before Parliament, he pledged himself to continue on the path followed by his predecessor:'My programme is Nasser's' he declared. It was natural that he should say so: Nasser's great prestige had been further enhanced by the outpouring of popular grief which his death occasioned. And Sadat was not known to hold any strong views on policy. Heikal tells us that those around him were content with his candidature for the presidency because they thought he was a weak man whom they could manage.[4] They were to be proved wrong when Sadat, as President, steered Egyptian policy in very new directions. Economic policy was one of the fields in which this became evident, but not immediately.

On 27 May 1971, Sadat, although he had earlier rid himself of his pro-Soviet Egyptian advisers such as Ali Sabri, signed a treaty of friendship and alliance with the Soviet Union. This was indeed following Nasser's path, to the extent of outdistancing his predecessor. One of Sadat's objects was to secure increased deliveries of Soviet arms. Yet at the same time he was opening contacts, both through the Saudis[5] and directly, with the United States Administration. On 8 July 1972, acting with the suddenness which became his political trademark, Sadat ordered all Soviet advisers, civil and military, out of Egypt. This was the turning-point, although it took two more years for that to become completely apparent.

Since the Six-Day War in 1967, Israel had remained in occupation not only of the West Bank and Gaza Strip areas of Palestine, but also of Egyptian territory in Sinai and of the Syrian Golan Ḥeights. Egypt and Syria had rearmed with Soviet weapons and rebuilt their shattered forces, but were believed to be militarily much inferior to Israel. Israeli politicians had become complacent about the 'no war, no peace' situation prevailing on their frontiers, even though their intelligence chiefs sounded warnings from time to time that a new war might be imminent.

There were perhaps too many such warnings, four major ones in four years, none of which seemed to be justified by the course of subsequent events. In April 1973, Israeli intelligence did cause some real alarm in political circles by reporting a major Egyptian military build-up in the Suez Canal Zone which was interpreted as the prelude to an attempt to cross the Canal. Israeli armed forces were placed on alert, but nothing happened. Mrs Meir, now Prime Minister of Israel, believed that Sadat had backed away from a suicidal course, perhaps under pressure from the Soviet Union following US representations in Moscow. Less attention was therefore paid to a new warning from Israeli intelligence in June that Sadat was determined to go to war in the autumn.

This time Israeli intelligence was right and the evaluation of it by the politicians was mistaken. The April build-up in the Canal Zone had been a bluff but also a rehearsal. At 2 p.m. on 6 October 1973, Yom Kippur (the Day of Atonement) in the Jewish religious calendar, Egyptian and Syrian forces struck. Surprise was such that the thin Israeli forces facing the onslaught were driven back. The Israeli Air Force, hitherto all-conquering, found itself facing damaging fire from Soviet-supplied SAMs (surface-to-air missiles). The Egyptians rapidly achieved an effective bridgehead on the east bank of the southern sector of the Suez Canal. But they were too slow in advancing on the Sinai passes and Israeli forces had time to rally. Mobilisation, so often practised, was completed within three days and the passes were held.

The Israelis went over to the counter-attack, driving the Syrians back to within 20 miles of Damascus by 17 October and penetrating Egyptian lines in Sinai to cross the Canal north of the Egyptian bridgehead. By 22 October, they had overrun the SAM sites, had swung south to encircle the Egyptian 3rd Army and were in a position to threaten a move on Cairo. The Arabs thankfully accepted a UN call for a cease-fire and the Israelis, under American pressure, acquiesced.

The cease-fire lines, with Egyptian troops on the east bank and Israeli troops on the west bank of the Suez Canal, were clearly unstable. Stimulated by fears that the USA and USSR were in danger of being sucked into the conflict, the United Nations sent observers to separate the combatants and organised armistice talks in Geneva. These began on 21 December 1973, with Egypt, Israel, Jordan, USA and USSR attending under UN auspices. Only Syria refused the invitation.

The talks made some early progress but then became bogged down and it took some shuttling between Aswan and Jerusalem by the US Secretary of State, now Henry Kissinger, to bring them to a conclusion. On 18 January 1974, the parties agreed that Israeli forces would make a partial withdrawal in Sinai and that limited Egyptian forces would occupy a 6-mile strip along the whole of the east bank of the Suez Canal, with another 6-mile strip to the east forming a demilitarised zone occupied by UN forces. This relocation of troops was completed on 4 March 1974.

Although the fighting had ended with the Israelis holding the upper hand and it was the Arabs who had had to hasten to accept the call for a cease-fire, Egypt had thus won the negotiations. Indeed, for the Arabs as a whole there had been encouraging features of the campaign. The Israelis had proved vulnerable to a surprise attack and their aircraft and tanks had suffered heavy casualties from anti-aircraft and anti-tank missiles. The Arabs had shown better unity and coordination of effort than in the past. Egypt and Syria had concerted the initial attack, and forces from Iraq and Jordan had moved to reinforce the Syrians. Nor had these Arab troops flinched from suffering casualties; they had fought hard against the Israeli counter-attacks and ended the war with their morale intact, for the first time in an Arab-Israeli war.

The Israelis, for their part, could congratulate themselves that, even though starting the war at a disadvantage, they had ended on top, thanks to the qualities of their forces and the superiority of their generals. But they had had to yield some ground in the final settlement, and ground of enormous economic importance to the Egyptians, since control of both banks of the Canal would enable them to clear it and reopen it to traffic, as well as to begin the redevelopment of the Canal Towns, Port Said, Ismailia and Suez. However, Israel still held the crucial Sinai passes and also the Sinai oilfield at Abu Rudeis. And the Gulf of Aqaba remained open to Eilat shipping.

Other economic consequences of the war affected the whole world. The Arab oil producers met in OAPEC in Kuwait while the fighting was still in progress and agreed to cut back production by 5 per cent per month until Israel withdrew from 'occupied territory' (the usual phrase by now for the territory occupied in 1967) and until there was a restoration of 'Palestinian rights' (not further defined). From the reduced output, supplies would be maintained at normal levels to countries with 'satisfactory' attitudes, such as France, Spain and (wonder of wonders) the UK, but exports would be embargoed to 'pro-Israeli' countries, identified as the USA and the Netherlands (Portugal, Rhodesia and South Africa were later added to this list).

This use of the 'oil weapon' was effective because oil was

already in short supply, for reasons given in the last Chapter. The Saudis had been under American pressure for some months to increase output and had refused to do so unless there was an improvement in US policy in the Middle East, i.e. over the Arab-Israeli conflict. The new export restrictions thus had a considerable impact. The embargoed countries did in practice continue to satisfy their essential oil needs, but not without real difficulty and some disruption of supplies to the consumer.

Many other countries thought it prudent to slant their Middle East policies in a direction more favourable to the Arabs. The EEC members on 6 November 1973 issued a joint statement which did little more than reinterpret UN Security Council Resolution No. 242, but did so in language more welcome to the Arabs than to the Israelis. Japan, urged by Saudi Arabia to break off diplomatic relations with Israel as the price for oil supplies, rejected that pressure but did issue a statement favourable to the Arab side. Sixteen African countries agreed to end diplomatic relations with Israel, which had even earlier been out of relations with another seven of them, leaving only five African countries (including South Africa) still in relations, and that in a continent in which Israel had made particular efforts to forge ties of goodwill and cooperation. By December 1973, the Arab oil producers felt sufficiently satisfied with their progress to abandon the monthly reduction programme, increase output by 10 per cent and step up the supply of oil to most countries, although the embargo on exports to the USA and the Netherlands was kept in force for some time longer.

In parallel with the Arab use of oil as a political weapon had gone action by OPEC (not only its Arab members) to induce further steep increases in its price, which had been rising even before the war. By the end of 1973, the cost of a barrel of Gulf crude had risen to an unheard-of $11 a barrel, an increase of no less than 470 per cent in the year. This threatened to throw the economy of the whole world into recession and to a large extent did so, though other factors played a part (some recession was already visible before the oil shock). Particularly hard hit were those developing countries which needed increased use of fuel for their development but could not afford to buy it at the higher prices.

Industrialised countries formed their own strategies for dealing with this new situation. One obvious course was to seek to reduce oil consumption. Conservation by energy-saving devices such as better insulation of buildings received a new priority. Both Governments and industries planned to move away from oil to alternative fuels, to some extent coal but much more to gas and nuclear energy, the difficulty being that there was a long lead-time to many of these measures (it can take ten years to plan and build a nuclear power station). Exploration for oil in new areas away from the Middle East was stepped up further. Fields found in the North Sea, which might have been of doubtful commercial viability at low oil prices, suddenly seemed much more attractive prospects for development.

One other thing which the industrialised Western countries and Japan did in response to the first oil shock was to set up international machinery to cope with any repetition of the crisis. Their chosen instrument was the International Energy Agency (IEA), with sixteen member nations[6]; the Agency was not part of, but was closely linked with, the OECD. It called on its members to build up emergency oil stocks to common agreed levels and to prepare programmes for cutting oil consumption by agreed common rates in an emergency. It also urged them to make plans for the smooth allocation of available oil, both domestic and imported, should new shortages arise (this had in fact been done not by inter-Governmental planning but competently by the oil companies during the Arab embargo on the USA and Netherlands). Subsequently, the Agency called on its members to reduce oil consumption through conservation, to create a $25,000 million fund to help any member which fell into serious balance of payments difficulties because of high oil prices, and to fix a common floor price for oil (to encourage development of marginal fields outside the Middle East).

These were all admirable measures for dealing with the crisis which was now over, but as that crisis receded in time Governments became less enthusiastic about implementing the IEA's recommendations. It is doubtful whether this ostensibly impressive body really caused any Government to take steps which it had not separately decided to take for its own reasons.

Major oil-producing countries, already rich particularly where populations were low, became rich beyond their dreams at the increased oil prices. In the short term, the only thing they could do with their new wealth was to invest it abroad through the banks and in Government bonds, but they began frantically to work out plans to use it on a longer term basis for the development of their own countries, together with a stepping up of aid to those poorer countries with which they felt some affinity.

Frantic was all too often the appropriate word for their development efforts. Orders for construction materials were placed abroad without regard to the ability of their ports to handle so great a flow of imports. Some of the foreign contractors engaged to work on the new projects proved under-capitalised and inexperienced in the difficulties of working in countries with untrained labour forces and inadequate infrastructure. Much money was certainly wasted. But the money was in such plentiful supply that the waste could be written off to experience, and experience was in fact gained rapidly. Despite a good deal of initial chaos, much was achieved, and some of the oil-producing countries began to alter out of all recognition. This was true most of all of Saudi Arabia, and also of Kuwait, Abu Dhabi and some of the other Gulf Shaikhdoms. In the more populous countries, such as Iran and Iraq, the contrast was less sharp, but there too there were notable steps towards industrialisation. At the same time, in all these countries, a sizeable part of the new wealth was diverted to the purchase of arms for enlarged defence forces.

Any fears which economists had of early balance of payment crises in the industrialised world were largely allayed by the short-term reflux of funds, already mentioned as the immediate outcome of the steeply increased oil prices. The Western banking system became awash with 'petrodollars', for which investment outlets had to be found.

This was largely a desirable development, but it had some unfortunate consequences, the effects of which are still being felt. One apparently attractive outlet was the 'third world' where, as already noticed, oil purchases at the new prices put great strain on developing economies and created a corresponding need for credit.

The banks were able to demand high interest rates and in all too many cases paid insufficient attention to ability to repay; most of them have since had reason to regret this folly.

In the longer term, purchases abroad by the oil producers for their own development projects, and of course for arms, had the same consequence of offsetting the balance of payments difficulties which might have been experienced by industrialised countries needing to finance their oil bills. So far as the UK is concerned, this will be very apparent in the trade statistics.

22 Lebanon and the Civil War of 1975–6

In very many ways Lebanon is exceptional among the Arab States. Chief among its differences is the fact that Christians, of many different sects but predominantly Maronite Catholics, constitute approximately half its population (the exact proportion is highly controversial). Under French patronage these Maronites came to play the leading political role in the country following the breakup of the Ottoman Empire after the First World War. Moreover France, which held the League of Nations mandates over both Lebanon and Syria and governed them to some extent as a single territory (*Les Etats du Levant*), fixed the frontier between them in such a way as to enlarge 'Christian' Lebanon into *Grand Liban* at the expense of 'Muslim' Syria.[1]

There had been considerable emigration from Lebanon during periods of economic stringency during the nineteenth century, most of the emigrants being from the Christian community.[2] This had created links, including trading links, between Lebanon and a score of countries, not only in Europe but in North and South America and in Africa, particularly West Africa. The Lebanese have a reputation as skilful merchants (inherited, they claim, from their Phoenician ancestors), so they turned happily to international trade. In this they were helped by their possession in Beirut of one of the best ports on the Eastern Mediterranean coast, well situated to serve as an entrepôt port for Syria and Iraq, and, when the creation of Israel removed the competition of Haifa, also for Jordan and the countries of the Arabian Peninsula.

Lebanon had the further commercial advantage of a high level of educational facilities. The French poured resources into French-language schools and colleges, and the United States, attracted by Lebanon's 'Christian' character, also founded educational institutions there, most famous among them the American University of Beirut (AUB), of which many leading Arabs, Muslim as well as Christian and from many countries, were and are alumni.

Lebanon became officially independent in 1943, with a complicated governmental framework based on a confessional division of political offices, among which the key post of executive President was reserved for a Maronite Christian. French political and military withdrawal was completed in 1946. Having no army of any military importance, Lebanon was not significantly involved in the Arab attack on Israel in 1948 (there was a small frontier skirmish), and played no real part in the wars between Israel and her Arab neighbours in 1967 and 1973. This peaceful posture served Lebanon well economically. Her snow-capped mountains had already won her the title of 'the Switzerland of the Middle East' and she seemed also to be acquiring something of the Swiss reputation for neutrality in time of war.

In another way too Lebanon resembled Switzerland. Between 1945 and 1966, banking in Lebanon grew phenomenally. The country had only seven banks of any size in 1945, but no less than ninety-three in 1964. A halt was called to this expansion in 1966, when the Intra Bank failed and banking regulations were tightened in consequence. Israel's crushing defeat of Egypt, Jordan and Syria in the Six-Day War in 1967 also weakened financial confidence. The outcome was a reduction in the number of banks, through a process of mergers and failures, to the still considerable total of seventy-four; at this it stabilised, since the 1966 regulations made the establishment of new banks virtually impossible. Eighteen of these banks were foreign, six of them foreign Arab and twelve non-Arab.[3] It was a profitable sector of the economy but the crash of the Intra Bank had been a shock and the whole system remained somewhat fragile.

Apart from its seaport, Beirut has an airport which until the Lebanese Civil War was the leading international air centre in the

Middle East, surpassing even Cairo in aircraft movements to and from foreign destinations. The great majority of these movements were on scheduled services, many of them provided by Lebanon's two national airlines, Middle East Airlines (MEA) and Trans-Mediterranean Airways (TMA). Of these, TMA was an all-freight operation, the first airline to provide, in 1971, a scheduled cargo service around the world. Both these airlines were privately-owned and highly successful, operating profitably without subsidies in competition with foreign airlines many of which were Government-owned and heavily subsidised. Beirut Airport, situated 11 km. south of the city centre, close to the sea and to main roads, had an excellent safety record, with good navigational and other equipment. Within it lay a Civil Aviation Safety Centre, run in conjunction with the International Civil Aviation Organization (ICAO), which was the principal training centre for pilots, crews and ground staff of all Middle Eastern airlines.

Lebanon's role as an international telecommunications centre began in the days of the French mandate, when Radio Orient, a private company, was established in 1921 to operate an international radio-telegraph service. From 1952 it also provided a radio-telephone service, with an international telex service following in 1961. After the company's concession expired at the end of 1972, Radio Orient was reconstituted as a government-owned company. Its HF radio network had even before then been found inadequate for Lebanon's growing needs; it was supplemented by a satellite tracking station (able to track either an Atlantic or an Indian Ocean satellite) in 1969, and by the opening of a submarine cable link between Beirut and Marseilles in 1970.

With these excellent infrastructural facilities, the genius of the Lebanese for commerce was able to flourish. Political events which damaged other Arab countries were also sometimes directly favourable to Lebanese trade. In particular, the closing of the Suez Canal from 1956 to 1957 and more importantly from 1967 to 1975 acted as a stimulus to Lebanon's entrepôt trade with Saudi Arabia and other parts of the Arabian Peninsula.

Lebanese industry suffers from a lack of indigenous raw materials, but none the less presents a success story: in particular, light industries based in Lebanon were able to build up a very useful level of exports, mainly to other Arab countries along the trade-routes developed for entrepôt trade. Lebanon has no oil but is the terminal for two important Arab pipelines, the older of them the line from the Northern Iraqi fields to the Lebanese port of Tripoli and the other the TAPline (Trans-Arabian Pipeline) from the ARAMCO fields in Saudi Arabia to Zahrani, near Sidon. There are Lebanese refineries at both these terminals and supplies of their feed-stock were negotiated, at favourable prices, as part of the oil transit agreements.

Invisible income accrued to Lebanon from a multiplicity of sources. In peaceful times tourism was a major contributor, the Lebanese mountains and beaches acting as a magnet to a great number of Arabs and to not a few non-Arabs. Banking has already been mentioned and insurance was also important. There were remittances from Lebanese abroad, not only the permanent émigrés but such professional men as civil engineers working temporarily in the oil-rich states. There were also the commissions earned by Lebanese commercial agents, many of them covering the whole of the Mashriq or even the whole of the Middle East for foreign companies. Investments (mainly from rich Arabs) poured into Lebanon for the construction of hotels and other real-estate, and for such less obvious ventures as the purchase of influence in the extensive range of Lebanese newspapers and magazines, read widely in the Arab countries and beyond them. Statistics for invisibles are always difficult to come by, but there is no doubt that Lebanon's total invisible income was substantial.

All this prosperity became imperilled when Lebanon's complex governmental structure began to be seriously challenged. It was suspected that the Muslim elements in the population, with a higher birthrate, had come to outnumber the Christians, but the latter had no mind to release their grip on the Presidency. Fighting, amounting to civil war, broke out in 1958, but on that occasion was fairly soon brought to an end. The country felt relief that it had drawn back from the brink of strife which would have been an economic catastrophe.

What wrecked the fragile equilibrium restored in 1958 was the establishment in Lebanon of what amounted to a state within a state by the Palestinians and particularly by the Palestine Liberation Organization (PLO). Refugees from Palestine had spilled into Lebanon in 1948 and had been either absorbed into the community or segregated in refugee camps. After the 1967 war, and especially after the expulsion of the PLO from Jordan in 1970–1, their numbers grew to around 300,000, about 100,000 of whom were housed in 15 squalid camps, 5 of which lay on the outskirts of Beirut.

Most of these refugees, including virtually all of those in the camps, were Muslims, and the Lebanese Christians, especially their right-wing militias, became very suspicious of their intentions. Those intentions were in fact little directed towards Lebanese internal politics; the refugees in the camps wanted mainly just to survive, and the PLO wanted to use Lebanon as a base for operations against Israel. But this latter intention the Lebanese Christians opposed, since they had no wish for their country to become involved in active hostilities with Israel. To do so would detract from the image of a peaceful and virtually neutral Lebanon which was so useful for attracting investments; it was also likely to bring down upon them Israeli reprisals, which had a reputation for being distinctly heavy-handed.

There was a further complication. Syria had had the Golan Heights wrested from it by the Israelis in 1967 and was eager to hit back, but preferably from someone else's territory. With the routes for infiltrators through Jordan blocked after 1971, Lebanon was the obvious choice. The Syrians therefore gave backing and supplies to the PLO in Lebanon, especially to Saiqa, a Palestinian commando group controlled by Syrian Army Intelligence. The PLO had by this time suffered a good deal of fission as extremist groups found the policies of its leader, Yassir Arafat, and his military wing Al-Fatah, too moderate for their liking, and broke away into splinter groups which looked to one or other of the extremist Arab states as patrons. As well as the Syrian-backed group, there were others backed by Libya and by Iraq. Arafat had a loose suzerainty over them, largely because he was recognised by the Arab League (and for that matter by the UN) as the spokesman for all Palestinians, but there were divergencies of policy and dangers of hostility among them. They were all however at one in being beyond the control of the Lebanese Government.

Other complicating factors were the Druze and the Shi'a. The Christians, especially the Maronites, were for the most part very right-wing; their Phalange party, with its militia the Kataeb, was organised on an Italian fascist model. By contrast, the leader of the Druze, Kamal Jumblatt, although himself a tribal chieftain and a millionaire, had taken up a very left-wing attitude and regarded himself as the natural leader of all leftist groups, whatever their religious basis. The Sunni and Shi'a leaders had their own reasons for rejecting such pretensions, besides which they regarded the Druze faith (with good reason, theologically) as non-Islamic, even though Druze were counted with Muslims for purposes of the dispute about the existence of a Muslim or Christian majority in the country.

The Shi'a had traditionally been the inhabitants of South Lebanon (and to a lesser extent of the Beqaa Valley between the Lebanon and anti-Lebanon Mountains). However, they had become more widely scattered in recent years, partly as a result of being turned into refugees by Israeli cross-border reprisal raids, aimed at Palestinian guerrillas but in the process destroying Shi'a villages. Many of these refugees had moved into shanty towns on the southern outskirts of Beirut, close to some of the Palestinian refugee camps.

Because the Shi'a were mainly low-income farmers, growing poor-quality tobacco in Southern Lebanon, they had done badly in the confessional division of powers enshrined in the Lebanese governmental system. They provided the Speaker of the Parliament, but he was much less influential than the (Maronite) President or the (Sunni) Prime Minister. Now however, just as the Muslims claimed that they had come to outnumber the Christians in the country, so among the Muslims the Shi'a believed that their higher birthrate had enabled their numbers to outstrip the Sunnis. They thus felt themselves doubly unfairly treated. And whereas in the past they had lacked leaders to push their claims in Beirut, they had now found one in the Imam Musa Sadr, an Iranian of Lebanese descent who had returned to the land of his ancestors and made his mark there by sheer force of personality.

After some preliminary skirmishing, the Lebanese Civil War broke out definitively in May 1975. Its very complex details, as fighting spread from one area to another, with alliances being formed and breaking up again, cannot be traced in this book.[4] But certain of its main consequences can be briefly outlined. One of the most damaging was that the Lebanese Army, which had held together in the brief civil war of 1958, this time became polarised, the Muslims breaking away into what called itself the Lebanese Arab Army and the Christian troops becoming regarded as an extension of the Maronite militia.

Another consequence was that the country itself began to separate into two main parts, the Christians centred on the old Mount Lebanon area which had been their heartland in Ottoman times, and the Muslims and Druze controlling the rest of the country. Within these two areas a 'purification' policy was pursued, with Christians wiping out Muslim villages and vice versa. A particularly significant atrocity for its future consequences was the massacre of most of the inhabitants of the Christian village of Damour in a fruit-growing area just south of Beirut (itself a reprisal killing). The capital similarly fell apart into a Christian East Beirut and an increasingly Muslim West Beirut, divided by a no-man's-land known as the 'Green Line', with few and on some days no crossing-points.

Syria had a natural interest in events in its neighbour Lebanon and watched the progress of the civil war with the closest attention. Indeed, it did more than watch; weapons supplies for the Muslim side came in overland through Syria, though the Palestinians also shipped some in for themselves through the southern ports of Sidon and Tyre. (The Christians used the port of Junieh, north of Beirut, as an arms import route, mainly from Israel.)

The course of the fighting might have been thought likely to please President Assad of Syria, as it was his allies, the Muslim Left and the Palestinians, who began to gain the upper hand. But in the Levant things are rarely as they seem. Assad saw the Palestinians becoming too powerful and threatening soon to become the dominant force in Lebanon. In the process, they were moving away from his influence; Saiqa had failed to establish a leading role among the Palestinians. Moreover, if the Palestinians came to control Lebanon, he had no doubt that Israel would attack it, in which case Syria would be in danger of becoming involved in war with Israel at a time not of his choosing.

The odd situation therefore arose that Assad was driven to conclude that he must intervene, with the Syrian Army if necessary, to save the Lebanese Christians from destruction. He tried to avoid military involvement, expending a great deal of effort on summoning Lebanese leaders to Damascus and arranging cease-fires, but these all too regularly broke down. On 1 June 1976, Assad (who had first assured himself through secret channels that both the USA and Israel would understand his pro-Christian intentions and not oppose him) sent his tanks into Lebanon. To his surprise, they did not sweep all before them. They quickly occupied the Beqaa Valley and began to move from there along the two roads towards the coast at Beirut and Sidon. But the Palestinians had made effective defence preparations, with anti-tank guns and field guns well sited. They drove the Syrians back from Sidon and halted their advance outside Beirut.

During the military stalemate which ensued, diplomacy had a chance to play its part. The Arab League took a hand and it was agreed that an Arab peacekeeping force should take over from the Syrians. An Egyptian General was placed in command and Libya, Saudi Arabia and Sudan offered troops. The Syrians undertook to pull back to the Beqaa. But the peacekeeping force was not in sufficient numbers to impose its will on the various Lebanese factions and fighting between them continued. The Palestinians had been weakened by their efforts against the Syrians and were humiliated when they could not prevent their refugee camp at Tel Zaatar being wiped out by the Christians, who had been rearmed through Junieh.

On 18 October 1976 an Arab summit meeting in Riyadh of the main countries concerned, attended by a subdued Arafat, produced a united front of Presidents Assad and Sadat to end the struggle. A full summit in Cairo ratified their agreement. The terms were that the Lebanese President Sarkis would select which Arab countries should supply a 30,000-strong peacekeeping force. To nobody's surprise Sarkis chose that most of them should come from Syria, with token contingents from Abu Dhabi, Libya, Saudi Arabia and Sudan. The war came to an end on 15 November 1976, with Syrian forces controlling Beirut and most of the rest of the country. Lebanon had fought off Palestinian control at the expense of accepting Syrian military occupation.

The cost of the war, in human and economic terms, had been appalling. It was estimated that 44,000 had been killed and 180,000 injured,[5] many of them very seriously. Public services had been badly damaged and agriculture disrupted. Industry had also suffered; the refinery near Sidon had been shelled and the cement factory at Checka caught in crossfire. Prospects for tourism had been wrecked and the facilities for it ruined; hotels in West Beirut had been fought over and turned into burnt-out shells. Huge sums had been squandered on armaments (even though some had been supplied free by third parties). The exceptions to the general economic chaos were that banking had somehow kept going and that the currency was still surprisingly strong. There were funds for reconstruction, but only if peace had really returned. Of that no one could feel sure. The militias, including the Shi'a Amal (Hope) which had been set up during the war, were still in existence and still heavily armed. Many of them felt cheated of victory and all nursed longings for revenge. It was not a recipe for a lasting peace.

During the war there had been a good deal of emigration, both personal and economic. Businesses had been transferred to Cyprus and elsewhere, including Paris and London. In the process, London had become a new centre for the publication of Lebanese newspapers and magazines. After the war died down, there was some counter-flow, but not a total return. House-owners and businessmen went back to examine their properties; if they found them destroyed, as many did, they often decided to cut their losses and settle abroad.

Cyprus had not only accepted displaced Lebanese, but had become the transshipment area for weapons and ammunition bound for the warring Lebanese factions. The Christians used Larnaca as their staging-port for Junieh, and the Palestinians arranged shipments from Limassol to Sidon and Tyre. Beirut Port had been one of the war's casualties; as well as suffering physical damage, it had become too public a place for the import of such politically delicate supplies as munitions.

Israel had acquired a new role in Southern Lebanon. While the war continued, the Palestinians were too preoccupied to have time to mount commando raids into Israel. The Israelis enjoyed the lull and in their turn had no need to launch reprisal attacks on the Shi'a area, with a few Christian villages, adjoining their northern border. Instead, they were able to embark on a 'hearts and minds' operation which was of genuine humanitarian value. South Lebanon was always short of health facilities; during the war it was almost denuded of doctors and nurses, who moved away or were commandeered to serve the militias. The Israelis opened two gateways through their barbed-wire border defences and offered medical treatment to those Lebanese who wished to cross, as many did. They also helped the economy of the Shi'a farmers by buying their tobacco crops. Some of the Shi'a began to look upon the Israelis, with their 'good fence' policy, as their saviours; however, as will be seen in Chapter 29, it was a feeling which did not last.

23 Egypt under Sadat

Shortly after the ceasefire in the Yom Kippur War, President Sadat on 7 September 1973 held a meeting with Kissinger in Cairo. It turned out to be a major policy discussion. Sadat told Kissinger (who, according to Heikal was 'dumbfounded') that he regarded the Soviet Union as 'the real enemy', that Egypt had fought her last war with Israel, and that in view of 'the failure of the socialist experience in Egypt' he wanted to develop the country's economy along different lines.[1]

Kissinger was evidently convinced of his sincerity, for American policy towards Egypt turned distinctly more favourable. Not only did Kissinger exert himself to obtain armistice terms which were advantageous to Egypt, as recounted in Chapter 21, but diplomatic relations between the USA and Egypt were resumed on 28 February 1974, after a rupture which had lasted seven years. From 1974 also, aid from the West to Egypt began to flow, under American influence. On 24 April 1974, President Nixon asked Congress for $250 million in aid for Egypt. Wheat supplies under US Public Law 480 began to be shipped, the currency generated from the sales of this wheat being available for expenditure by Egypt either domestically or in the USA. The way was opened for Egypt to draw heavily on loans from the IMF and the IBRD.[2]

All this was additional to aid from Arab countries. Libya no longer provided such aid (relations between Egypt and Libya had deteriorated sharply towards the end of 1973), but King Faisal on a visit to Egypt in July-August 1974 pledged Saudi aid of $300 million, and Kuwait and Abu Dhabi also promised to increase their aid to Egypt. At an Arab Summit meeting in Rabat in 1975 it was decided to give Egypt and Syria $500 million each in compensation for their losses in the 1973 war. There is difficulty in obtaining accurate figures but the evidence suggests that Arab aid to Egypt from 1971 to 1977 totalled at least $14,000 million and may have been as much as $22,000 million.[3]

Even before his November pronouncement to Kissinger, Sadat had begun to shift his economic policies away from Nasser's pattern. In the summer of 1973, currency and trade restrictions had been relaxed somewhat and tentative moves made to encourage foreign investment in Egypt. On 1 August, a 'parallel' foreign exchange market had been opened to supplement the availability of exchange at the official rate. Negotiations had been started for the construction of an oil pipeline from Suez to the Mediterranean (the SUMED line) and on 14 December these matured with the award of the contract to the American engineering firm Bechtel; finance for it was to be organised by a consortium of American banks, with Saudi Arabia and Kuwait ready to supply 50 per cent of the capital.

From the beginning of 1974, the momentum behind this policy redirection increased considerably. The change was marked by the introduction of a new word into Egypt's political vocabulary, 'infitah' (from a root meaning to open). The 'opening-up' applied to several different fields. Press censorship was ended in February 1974; a warts-and-all reassessment of the Nasser era was encouraged and there was talk of 'deNasserisation'. But infitah came to be applied chiefly to economic policy, covering both an opening-up to Egyptian private enterprise and an opening-up to the West.

On 15 May 1974 a programme for economic and social reform was put to a referendum and achieved a near-100 per cent positive vote. In June, Law 43 was passed giving foreign investors at least a 5-year tax holiday and freedom from many controls; the rule that all companies must have at least 51 per cent Egyptian ownership was abolished. Port Said, now recovering with Arab aid funds from devastation and disuse during the long Canal closure, was declared a free port, into which foreign manufacturers could import goods duty-free for assembly and re-export. Egyptians were allowed to act as agents for foreign companies. On 25 September Sadat, who had temporarily been Prime Minister as well as President, handed over the premiership to Abdul Aziz Hegazy, an ex-Finance Minister who was a committed advocate of infitah.

In certain fields only[4] there was no shortage of foreign investors willing to take advantage of these exceptionally attractive conditions. Chase Manhattan Bank was one of the leaders, setting up Chase-Ahli in partnership with the Egyptian Ahli Bank; Chase's President David Rockefeller became a close friend and adviser of Sadat. Other foreign banks followed.[5] Much of the investment went into construction projects. This applied both to Arab aid, an early target of which was the rebuilding of the Canal Cities, and to private investment, Arab and Western. Much of the private investment in construction was directed to the development of the tourist industry, particularly in the building of new hotels, and tourism grew considerably. Private investment was attracted also to the erection of modern office blocks and luxury apartments for the foreigners encouraged by infitah to work in Egypt. Their requirements for consumer goods, including luxury items, were met by imports; although intended in the first instance for resident foreigners and tourists, these were inevitably bought also by the wealthier Egyptians.

Unfortunately, the economic ferment thus produced soon turned sour. The unaccustomed liberal conditions gave openings for corruption; it was reckoned, for instance, that as much as 80 per cent of the goods imported into the Port Said free port area were not reexported but leaked instead into the Egyptian domestic economy without payment of duty. A new class of Egyptian millionaires made its appearance, the 'fat cats' as they were called by the Secretary-General of the Socialist Union. There were estimated to be 500 of them as early as 1975 and their numbers grew rapidly; by 1981 it was reported to the Egyptian Parliament that there were 17,000. Their high standard of living contrasted with the abject poverty of very many Egyptians and caused great social discontent. The trouble was that, although the economic boom created some employment, the population growth from which Egypt perennially suffers more than cancelled out the benefits so derived.[6] And the economic projects undertaken were mainly of a kind to emphasise social disparities.

There were some positive developments in the Egyptian economy, but mainly unrelated to infitah. The most important of them was the reopening of the Suez Canal on 5 June 1975. This brought welcome income from dues, amounting to over $200 million in the first twelve months, rising to some $600 million by 1979. But the pattern of the shipping transiting the Canal had changed; about 70 per cent now consisted of dry cargo vessels and only about 30 per cent of tankers, laden or in ballast. This was because of the wide use by this date of supertankers too large to pass through the Canal, even empty. There were plans to enlarge the Canal, but the estimated costs were high and could only be met by borrowing.

Oil was another success story, though on a limited scale. There were no huge fields like those in Kuwait and Abu Dhabi, much less Saudi Arabia. But several small fields came into production and in 1975 the Israelis were persuaded by American pressure to return the Sinai oilfields to Egypt as part of a second partial withdrawal of Israeli forces. By 1978, when there were no less than twenty-six foreign oil companies operating in Egypt, net revenues from oil had risen to about $700 million p.a., a striking contrast to a decade earlier when Egypt had been a net importer. There had also been some gas discoveries. Egypt became a member of OAPEC on 1 February 1973, but not of OPEC.

Remittances from Egyptians working abroad were a valuable source of invisible income. With its surplus of educated manpower Egypt had become an exporter of teachers, administrators and other professionals and skilled workers to the Gulf States and Libya. Most of them had no desire to settle permanently abroad and many left their wives and families behind in Egypt, supporting them with remittances. Their families thus became affluent by Egyptian standards, adding to the demand for imports.

The net effect of all these changes was that Egyptian indebtedness grew alarmingly. When Sadat came to power, it was already considerable. The largest element was then the debt to the Soviet

Union for military equipment, amounting to $1700 million ($500 million had been repaid and repayment of the rest was suspended). There was also $380 million of debt to the Soviet Union from loans for economic projects, principally the High Dam and related industries. $205 million was owed to the United States, mainly for wheat shipments in the period 1958–65. $130 million was due to Kuwait, $122 million to Italy, $106 million to Federal Germany, and smaller sums to East European countries and Japan. (Britain hardly figured in the list, since relations with Nasser's Egypt had so often been bad.) Altogether the debt total was of the order of $4000 million.

During Sadat's Presidency, accurate figures soon ceased to be available (Heikal is interesting on the devices used to keep Arab aid funds out of the published national accounts[7]), but they reemerged when Husni Mubarak succeeded Sadat in October 1981. By that date, the civil debt amounted to no less than $19,500 million and the military debt to $5,700 million, a crippling total of over $25,000 million. The mere servicing of this debt cost some $2000 million p.a., more than offsetting Egypt's income from the Suez Canal and oil combined.

With loan funds being pumped into the economy at this rate and the gross national product failing to rise correspondingly because of corruption and waste, inflation became a serious problem, adding to the upswell of social discontent. The IMF became alarmed at the situation, and on 16 October 1976 advised the Egyptian Minister of Economic Affairs that corrective action was required; their recommendation was devaluation plus a sharp reduction in the heavy subsidies on basic foodstuffs, fuel and clothing. Economically, this was a fairly standard IMF package and in many countries it could be effective in removing market distortions. But in Egypt, where it ignored the social factors, it was a recipe for disaster.

The Egyptian Government resisted the package but the IMF was in a position to wreck Egypt's credit rating at a time when the country needed new loans, so in the end the IMF prevailed. It was announced that price rises on staple foods would take effect on 17 January 1977. On 18 January, rioting erupted in Alexandria and Cairo and spread rapidly to other cities. Sadat, who was giving a press interview in the rest house in Aswan where he was preparing to receive a visit from Tito, had to flee ignominiously when a mob approached.[8] The next day, he was compelled to cancel the price increases and bring in the army to restore order. The IMF had to relax its pressure.

This episode had a traumatic effect on Sadat: Heikal believes that it was decisive in turning his mind to a dramatic foreign policy move of the kind which appealed to his theatrical imagination.[9] The move, when it occurred, certainly seized the attention of the whole world; in November 1977 Sadat flew to Jerusalem for public peace talks with the Israeli Government.

There had of course been preliminary contacts to prepare the way for the visit. Sadat's original plan, hinted at in April 1977 when he had his first talk with President Carter, had been for a secret meeting with Shimon Peres, whom he expected to win the Israeli elections due in the summer. Soundings were made through President Ceausescu of Romania. However, it was not Peres but the much more hawkish Begin, leader of the hard-line Likud Party, who emerged as the new Israeli Prime Minister. At first, this seemed to kill the plan, but Begin let Carter know that he would be willing to meet Sadat, and Carter passed on the message with an assurance that he would be ready to play a part himself to achieve an Egyptian-Israeli settlement. Further soundings took place through intermediaries, with Ceausescu again playing a crucial role in assuring Sadat when they met on 29 October that Begin was not only anxious for peace but confident that he could deliver his side of any bargain that was struck. Ceausescu drew the convincing parallel of de Gaulle and the settlement with Algeria.[10]

It was on the return flight from Bucharest that Sadat, worried over the risk of leaks about a secret meeting, conceived the bold idea of an open visit to Jerusalem. He cleverly brought the possibility into his speech at the opening of the Egyptian Parliament on 9 November, phrasing it in such a way that it appeared to be a piece of rhetorical hyperbole but having made sure that the leader of the PLO, Yasser Arafat, would be in the audience to hear it.[11] Within days, the hyperbole had become reality and the Egyptians, along with the rest of the world, were glued to television screens to see their President meeting the Israeli leaders whom they had been taught to regard as demons. It was a great shock, but also a great excitement, and the optimists among the Egyptian people began to hope that it might solve all their problems.

When he returned from Jerusalem, among plaudits from the leaders of the Western countries including of course President Carter, Sadat sought to convince even the doubters among his people that he had achieved great things and received binding promises. But the reality soon turned out to be rather different. All that had actually been achieved was agreement to negotiate and even negotiations proved difficult to mount. The Egyptian Foreign Minister and his Deputy both resigned and Sadat for a time had to put the Foreign Ministry in the hands of Boutros Ghali, an able man but an Egyptian Christian with an Egyptian Jewish wife.

The whole of the Arab world outside Egypt reacted to the Jerusalem 'initiative', as Sadat called it, with real or pretended horror. All Arab aid was stopped.[12] A preliminary negotiating meeting was held with the Israelis in Cairo in early December but made no progress; predictably, none of the Arab delegations invited put in an appearance. Then on Christmas Day (which was Sadat's birthday) Begin returned Sadat's visit by coming to Ismailia. By this time Egypt had at least got a Muslim Foreign Minister. Substantive talks took place, but served mainly to highlight the areas of disagreement.

Months slipped by with no progress. But Carter had meant what he said about helping to bring about a settlement. He took the political risk of inviting Begin and Sadat to a tripartite summit meeting at his Presidential retreat, Camp David, on 8 September 1978. Intensive negotiations there culminated in two agreements, one entitled 'A framework for the conclusion of a peace treaty between Egypt and Israel' and the other 'The framework of peace in the Middle East'. It was a great achievement for Carter, though as it turned out not enough to win him reelection.

The first of these agreements was elaborated into the Treaty of Washington, signed on 29 March 1979. It provided for a phased Israeli withdrawal over three years from Sinai (but not from the

Gaza Strip which had been administered but never annexed by Egypt), in return for the opening of full diplomatic and commercial relations between Egypt and Israel. The US Government and Congress regarded this treaty as an American triumph and rewarded Egypt with greatly increased aid, both economic and military. Egypt was promoted to rank second only to Israel as a recipient of American largesse.

Negotiations were opened on the elaboration of the second Camp David agreement, but tragically they made no real headway. It turned out that Sadat could not win from Begin, even with American help, any settlement which would be acceptable to the Palestinians. His failure to do so in effect signed Sadat's death warrant. Had he achieved a settlement of the Palestine problem, his prestige would have been unassailable. Without it, he was open to the accusation that he had sacrificed the wider Arab cause to a selfish national interest.

Egypt was suspended from membership of the Arab League, the headquarters of which moved from Cairo to Tunis. The Arab Boycott of Israel was extended to Egypt. Opposition to Sadat among his own population grew, from those who felt that he had betrayed the Arab cause, from those who disapproved of his pro-Western policies and from those who regarded him as a traitor to Islam. On 6 October 1981 he was shot dead by religious extremists from his Army while attending a military parade to commemorate the anniversary of the opening of the 1973 War. He was succeeded as President by his Vice-President, Husni Mubarak.

24 Price Rise Consequences for the Oil Producers

Whereas consumers had taken in their stride the oil price rises of 1970–2, which as explained in Chapter 20 had little impact at the retail level, the quadrupling of prices in late 1973 was a different matter. This time, retail prices had to rise to a noticeable extent, and consumption fell in consequence. More importantly, there was a severe worsening of the terms of trade for industrialised countries, which brought about a sharp recession. This further depressed oil consumption. Seeing these tendencies, many Western economists forecast that oil producers would begin to fight over market shares, that prices would weaken, and that OPEC would soon drift into disarray.[1]

These forecasts proved largely inaccurate. What the economists had not allowed for was that several major producers would be willing to lower their output, indeed might insist on lowering it. For this, there were two main reasons. With the exception of Saudi Arabia and perhaps Abu Dhabi, which were confident that they had large reserves relative to their output, most producers were becoming increasingly conscious that oil was a finite resource which would one day run out. Worldwide attention had been drawn to this prospect by the famous report by the 'Club of Rome', entitled *The Limits to Growth*, which was criticised by academics but produced scare headlines in the world's press. Moreover, the Gulf States had actually seen this happen to one of their number. Bahrain, an early producer with small reserves, had virtually come to the end of its indigenous resources of oil and was now dependent for the crude processed in its refinery on Saudi oil delivered by submarine pipeline. Depletion policy therefore assumed a new importance. Kuwait cut its output in 1972 as a deliberate act of conservation and by doing so brought about singlehanded a shortage of heating oil in the USA the following winter.[2]

The other relevant factor was the demand of the producers for what had by now become their new slogan, 'participation'. It may be remembered that Bevin in his farsighted way (see Note 5 to Chapter 5) had proposed to AIOC in 1946 that the Company should make the Iranian Government the co-holder of their equity on a 50/50 basis. Over 20 years later, OPEC had included equity participation in the objectives set out in their Declaratory Statement of 1968 (see Chapter 20). This was by the 1970s an idea whose time had come.

There had of course been some steps towards it at earlier dates. Following Iran's lead, virtually all oil-producing countries had gradually set up national oil companies (NOCs), one of whose functions was to take over acreage relinquished by concessionaires or removed from them. Being initially unable to explore and exploit such territory themselves the NOCs had looked for foreign expertise to do so for them, and many of them had chosen to proceed through the mechanism of joint ventures. Iran, Saudi Arabia and Egypt were examples. Nearly all the new concessions granted in the 1950s and 1960s had in fact been in this form. The oil producers were now determined to go a logical step further by converting existing concessions into joint ventures. By 1971, OPEC was talking of 'enforcing' effective participation.[3]

It was mentioned in Chapter 20 that Algeria had already acted unilaterally to this end by legislating in February 1971 to nationalise 51 per cent of the French concessions in that country. The concessionaires had protested, but more over the inadequacy of the compensation offered than over the principle involved. By improving the compensation terms, the Algerian Government had won their acquiescence by the end of the year. Saudi Arabia had proposed participation to ARAMCO as early as 1968, but the company had then been resistant. By the end of 1971, the pressure on them had been greatly increased[4] and in March 1972 they yielded to the extent of granting 20 per cent participation to the

Saudis' NOC, Petromin. It should be noted that the moderate Arab States were only demanding 20 per cent participation at this stage, whilst the radicals wanted 51 per cent or else outright nationalisation; Iraq had of course already confiscated IPC acreage in 1961 and Libya had recently nationalised the BP shareholding in a Libyan concession (see Chapters 16 and 17).

In October 1972, OPEC succeeded in negotiating a participation deal with the companies jointly. The plan was that there should be a gradual process; on 1 January 1973, 1979, 1980, 1981, 1982 and 1983, Governments would acquire equity in their concessionaires to the extent of 25 per cent, 30 per cent, 35 per cent, 40 per cent, 45 per cent and 51 per cent respectively. The terms were to include adequate compensation plus 'buy-back' arrangements under which companies would be allowed to purchase from Governments the oil they would have lifted had they still owned the concessions outright. However, it rapidly became clear that OPEC had not had the full backing of its members in striking this deal. Libya had just acquired by agreement 50 per cent of the equity in a concession operated by the Italian State Oil Company ENI and was determined to accept no less from its other concessionaires. And the Kuwait Government, although itself satisfied, found its National Assembly unwilling to ratify so slow a pace of movement into participation.

The deal, instead of bringing stability as the oil companies had hoped, fell apart, and in doing so accelerated the process of their surrender. Between January and September 1973, Libya extracted 51 per cent Government participation from nearly all the independents and even some of the majors. Iraq meanwhile in March 1973 reached a settlement to its long-standing quarrel with the IPC Group, under which it paid compensation for the fields it had nationalised and IPC withdrew its objections to Law 80; IPC also undertook to expand production from its Basrah fields. In July 1973, Iran legislated to take full control of all oil production, reducing the role of the Consortium to that of a contractor for NIOC in the running of the fields and of a purchaser of crude and products for its members' downstream activities. Following the demonstration of the Arab producers' power in the 'first oil shock', Abu Dhabi, Kuwait, Qatar and

Saudi Arabia all achieved 60 per cent participation in the course of 1974 and Kuwait went on to a complete takeover of KOC in December 1975. Qatar did the same with QPC and with Shell's concession in 1976–7. Iraq's 1973 settlement was not of long duration; it proceeded to full nationalisation in 1975. Libya took over those companies which had resisted its 1973 demand for 51 per cent participation. Algeria also nationalised all its concessions except CFP, where it contented itself with keeping its 51 per cent holding. In 1977, Saudi Arabia negotiated 100 per cent takeover of ARAMCO, but complications arose and the transaction had still not been completed by the end of the decade.

Thus by the end of the 70s the general picture was of achievement by Middle East Governments, with a few exceptions, of their aspiration to sovereign ownership of their oil and gas resources. The companies were to a large extent still running the fields, but as agents of Government operating on some kind of fee arrangement. They were also for the most part continuing to draw oil from their old acreage, under various buy-back systems giving them priority access and in some cases fixed prices as part of the settlements. However, there had been a few failures to reach agreement, notably in Libya, and one of the consequences had been lower output than might otherwise have been achieved. This withdrawal of oil from the market, coupled with deliberate reductions by some Governments in the interests of new depletion policies, helped to keep OPEC together and to prevent any sharp fall in oil prices (at least in monetary terms) as consumption fell away during the years of recession induced by the massive price rises of 1973–4.

One effect of this movement to participation and nationalisation was a marked falling away in exploration by the previous holders of Middle East concessions. The new roles assigned to them gave them no real incentive in this direction, which was perhaps short-sighted on the part of the host Governments. This cut-back in exploration in the Middle East had begun in the second half of the 60s, particularly where relations between Governments and concessionaires were strained. From 1974 onwards, exploration by these companies virtually ceased. As they were the holders of both geological knowledge and drilling expertise in the area, it was not easy for the NOCs to replace them; they lacked expertise themselves and it would take them many years to develop it.[5] The consequence was a fall during the 70s in the reserves/production ratio (R/P) of these countries even though their production expanded much less rapidly than in the 60s.[6] By 1979, the Kuwaiti Minister of Oil was publicly advocating an R/P of 100, much higher than that then (or now) experienced in most Middle East oil-producers.[7]

The attainment by Middle East Governments of complete or at least majority ownership of their oil production should logically have meant that their national oil companies marketed the whole or the larger portion of their crude. In practice, this was by no means the case, even at the end of the decade. Yusuf Sayigh, writing in 1982, estimated that something between 75 per cent and 90 per cent of crude was lifted directly by the oil companies, and mainly by the majors who had been the concessionaires.[8] This was because of the arrangements for preferential purchase made with the companies stripped of all or part of their concessions, supplemented by straight sales by NOCs to the companies they knew best, often under long-term contracts. The international oil companies, in adjusting themselves to their new situations, had come to realise that what really mattered to them was not so much ownership of production (now often gone) but assured access to crude at fair (or where possible favourable) prices.

Governments, seeing the oil companies still making large profits after losing ownership of the concessions producing much of their crude, were bound to give renewed thought to the idea of moving into downstream activities. They had long had suspicions that the vertically-integrated majors had manipulated the posted price of crude in such a way as to enable them to make their main profits somewhere else in the chain of operations between crude shipment and retail sales. These suspicions had in fact been false or at least greatly exaggerated, but they persisted.

With surplus funds to invest, it was natural that the Middle East Governments should aim at industrialising their countries (some of course were already doing so), and the obvious opportunity for them seemed to be in oil-related industries.

OAPEC played a useful part in crystallising their thinking by producing well-researched papers on such possibilities. The three main directions which seemed worth exploring were oil refining, gas utilisation and petrochemicals. For the 70s, exploring of possibilities was in fact their main activity; even this planning process did not really begin seriously until 1974 and it takes time to build industries. But there were some results to show by the end of the decade.

Refining was of course not new in the Middle East. Abadan had once been the largest refinery in the world. But, as was seen in Chapter 12, the received wisdom had shifted in the 50s from location close to the source of crude to a preference for proximity to markets. Hence, most Middle East refineries were by the 70s supplying local markets rather than providing products for export. This was true both of the oil-producers such as Iran, Iraq, Saudi Arabia and Kuwait, and of non-producing countries, some of whose refineries had been built at the end of pipelines (Haifa in Israel, Sidon and Tripoli in Lebanon, Banias in Syria) or on trade-routes (Aden in PDRY). Such refineries, even if originally intended to produce products for export, had not been much enlarged and were now supplying mainly local distribution. The oil-rich Arab countries, particularly those with small populations and few agricultural possibilities, set out to change this situation. But they proceeded cautiously, since they were not too sure where they would find markets for their oil products and since there was, if anything, a surplus of refining capacity elsewhere in the world. By 1980, Middle East refineries, including Abadan, could only process under 3 million b/d, not much more than 3 per cent of world refining capacity. But additional refineries under construction or planned were likely to raise this figure to some 5 million b/d within a few years. Saudi Arabia was moving fastest in this direction, with 765,000 b/d capacity in 1980 and another 1.185 million b/d under construction.[9]

With the exception of Algeria, where gas fields had been found and gas was being exported both in LNG form (see Chapter 16) and by pipeline to Italy, the Middle East producers had had to deal mainly with 'associated gas', i.e. gas produced in solution in crude oil and needing to be separated from it. For the most part, they had had a short (and wasteful) way of dealing with such gas; they simply flared it. Travellers could see Middle East oilfields miles away from the flames and smoke of the gas flares. For technical reasons, gas sometimes needs to be reinjected into oilwells to maintain pressure, but the geology of the Middle East fields was such that this had rarely been necessary. Only a small proportion of the associated gas had been used for fuel, either by the oil companies for their plant on the fields or by Governments for desalination plants and electricity production.

In the 70s, use by Governments increased and the range of uses widened; feedstock for the production of fertilisers was one example. Abu Dhabi followed Algeria's lead by building a liquefaction plant, for supplies to the Japanese market. But at the end of the decade, the amount put to use in the Middle East had increased only to about 50 per cent; the other half was still being flared. This contrasted with worldwide practice, where the average proportion flared was around 10 per cent and would have been even lower if the Middle East had not pushed up the figure. The countries still most given to flaring were Iraq, with only just over 15 per cent and Saudi Arabia with around 30 per cent utilised; at the other end of the scale were Algeria and Libya putting nearly 80 per cent to use, with Kuwait not far behind them.[10] There were however firm plans to bring the Middle East profligacy to an end during the 1980s; this applied particularly to Saudi Arabia. One factor encouraging movement in this direction was a steady rise in the selling price of gas, bringing it nearer to the price of its oil equivalent. Algeria had long been pressing for equivalence and had had partial success.

Petrochemicals is a term which covers a wide range of products, particularly if it is extended to include fertilisers. The Western oil majors, who had their own petrochemical plants as part of their vertically-integrated structures, had considerable worries about the entry of Middle East producers into this industry. They feared undercutting of their prices, since the feedstock of the Middle East plants would be virtually free, to the extent that it would consist of gases previously flared. They also feared that pressure might be put on them to find markets for any products which might not sell well, with Governments insisting on their help in this respect in return for renewal, for instance, of their oil supply contracts.

In retrospect, it can now be said that these fears proved almost entirely groundless. Some Western petrochemical companies may have lost sales or had to sell at reduced profit margins. But that was more the consequence of a general overcapacity in the industry (to which admittedly the construction of new plants in the Middle East contributed) than to competition of a type which the Western companies could consider 'unfair'.

Caution again marked the entry of Middle East Governments into this field of activity during the 70s, as it had in the case of refining. The technology involved was both complex and massive, since this is very much an industry in which economies of scale apply. The skills and knowhow required were lacking among the Governments' own nationals, so that they would be likely to depend for a considerable time on expatriate staff until they could train their own replacements. The competitors they would have to face were powerful multinationals with great experience and vast financial resources. However, towards the end of the 70s, as they became rich enough themselves to face possible losses in bringing new industries on stream, one after another of the Middle East Governments decided to take the plunge into what seemed a supremely logical type of industrial activity for them to enter.

By the end of the decade, the investment they had made or were in process of making in petrochemical plants was of the order of $25,000 million, with Saudi Arabia well in the lead with around $14,000 million.[11] The range of products covered was quite wide and on the whole well balanced. Basic products such as ethylene and methanol were naturally the largest part of the output at this early stage, especially as they acted as feedstock for the intermediates. The latter consisted mainly of ethylene dichloride, ethylene glycol, monovinyl chloride and styrene. Final products, amounting to over a quarter of a million tons, were chiefly synthetic fibres, synthetic rubber, detergents and carbon black, with others planned. Fertilisers produced were entirely nitrogenous, derived from the ammonia separable from natural gas. It was an impressive beginning and clearly in the 80s this would be very much a growth area for Middle East industry, especially in Saudi Arabia.

25 The Iranian Revolution and the Second Oil Shock

The Iranian Revolution should really be called a counter-revolution. It was the Shah who was the revolutionary. He was determined, following his father's lead, to turn Iran from a rather backward example of a traditional Middle East state into a modern, industrialised, Westernised, strongly-armed country, and to do it in his own lifetime. In making the attempt, he was bound to create domestic enemies. First among them were the clerics, powerful figures in their influence on Iran's Shi'a people; what they opposed was any secularising tendency, since they held firmly to the Islamic view that there was no division between Church and State and that the whole community should be guided only by the Quran and the Sharia (religious law), applied of course by themselves. The other inevitable opponents were the traders of the bazaar, relatively well-off families who feared that modernisation of the economy would give rise to competitors able to undersell them.

Following the downfall of Musaddiq (see Chapter 5), who had for a time allied his own nationalist fervour with these entrenched antipathies to change, the Shah had been able to make some real progress towards his goal, though much less than he had hoped and intended. By a series of Seven-Year and Five-Year Plans, he had set about the carrying through of his 'white revolution'.[1] The First (7-year) Plan from 1949 to 1956 was frustrated by Musaddiq's nationalisation of the Iranian oil industry and the consequent disappearance of the oil revenues on which the Plan depended. The Second (7-year) Plan from 1956 to 1962 got under way under better auspices, with the oil crisis resolved and the Shah's authority strengthened. It planned to invest $1160 million and did in fact invest $979 million.[2] Some 40 per cent of this went on infrastructure, roads, railways and port facilities and another 20 per cent on starting large hydroelectric projects which would benefit *inter alia* agriculture.

The Third (5-year) Plan from 1962 to 1967 had an investment target of $3067 million and achieved $2728 million. It was of particular significance because of its priority of land reform, to which the Shah rightly attached great importance and for which he set an excellent example by making available for it a large part of the imperial estates. Theoretically, this reform had begun in 1960, with legislation which restricted land ownership to 800 hectares of unirrigated or 400 hectares of irrigated land. This proved unenforceable for the simple reason that land records were totally inadequate; Iran had no cadastral survey. In 1962 the law was amended to provide that no single owner might hold more than one village. At a time when over 70 per cent of cultivable land was made up of large estates, most of them owned by absentee landlords, this simple criterion, coupled with reasonable compensation provisions,[3] proved effective and before the end of the Third Plan about a quarter of the rural population, over half a million families, had benefited from the redistribution of over 14,000 villages.

This process continued in subsequent years. In addition, Iran's first large agro-industrial project, which had been embarked on in 1961 at Haft Taffieh for the growing of sugar-cane, was carried through during the Third Plan and proved successful, producing sugar at the high average rate of 12 tons a hectare.

The Fourth (5-year) Plan ran from 1968 to 1973. This was before the 'first oil shock', but nevertheless covered a period of rising oil revenues, which allowed the original plan to be enlarged by some 20 per cent. The planned investment thus became $10,854 million, but achievement fell considerable short at only $6757 million; even so, this was well over double the investment during the Third Plan. This was the first Plan in which the allocation to industry, which had been under 10 per cent in the Second and Third Plans, grew substantially, to over 22 per cent, while agriculture fell back from some 23 per cent in the Third Plan to not much more than 8 per cent in this Fourth Plan, marking substantially the end of the land reform programme.

One institution which played a considerable part in helping private sector industrialisation was the Industrial, Mining and Development Bank of Iran (IMDBI), with a capitalisation of over $2000 million, which not only provided funds for projects but also helped to identify suitable projects by carrying out feasibility studies. Manufacturers whom it supported made Iran virtually independent of imports in supplying the domestic markets for consumer goods such as radios, television sets (built under licence) and 'white goods', notably refrigerators.

The Second, Third and Fourth Plans, covering a total period of 17 years, had thus been on the whole successful. There had of course been some waste and some corruption, but not on a scale to discredit the planning process. There had also been recurrent bouts of inflation as the sums provided under the Plans followed a continuously upward course, but these had been checked from time to time by measures of restraint, usually pressed upon Iran by experts from the IMF (and consequently blameable on foreigners). Much money had been spent on armaments, especially after the British withdrawal of forces from the Gulf, and that was economically unproductive. Iran had a small armaments industry of its own, but it produced only the simpler weapons.

One particularly disappointing outcome from the Plans was agriculture. The land reform had served a valuable social purpose but it had not led to any sizeable growth of production. Official figures showed increases of the order of 7 per cent p.a. but they were false. Iran had become an importer of foodstuffs. Moreover, with farm incomes lagging behind the wages being paid in industry and in other areas such as tourism, there had been a movement of population from the country to the towns, which had soon proved to be in excess of the jobs available. Slum areas had grown up, especially in South Tehran, making a painful and indeed disgraceful contrast with the affluence visible elsewhere in the city. This might have been only a temporary phenomenon, which could have been corrected by housing measures and other social advances under the Fifth Plan, had that been used for consolidation.

The tragedy was that it was the Fifth (5-year) Plan from 1973 to 1978 which went disastrously wrong. The huge increase in oil prices at the end of 1973 caused the Shah to double the size of the Plan to a massive $37,214 million and this proved to be beyond the country's capacity to handle. There was an enormous boom during 1974, accompanied by roaring inflation. When in 1975 demand for oil began to fall away, the boom suddenly petered out but the inflation remained, especially as the prices of imports from the West had risen sharply to reflect the extra costs imposed by higher energy charges.[4] Grandiose projects, which had been begun in the boom year when funds seemed unlimited, ran out of money and were left unfinished. Not only did the investment already committed to them remain unproductive but the plants actually deteriorated, with costly machinery rusting in the congested ports or on the abandoned sites.

This was true of agriculture as well as industry. Large-scale agrobusinesses, which the Shah had hoped would restore his country to self-sufficiency in food, proved to have been based on inaccurate data and the foreign firms which had been encouraged to take part in them pulled out one after another. Among them were the British participants in Iran Shellcott, a 15,000 hectare scheme for which only one-third of the promised irrigation water actually materialised. Shell International and Mitchell Cotts, disappointed by this failure and by yields even on the irrigated land well below the forecasts of a local research station, reluctantly found themselves forced to withdraw, leaving the state-financed Agricultural Development Bank of Iran with a hopeless project.

Apart from these economic failures, there was an even more deep-seated political problem. The Shah had totally failed to make the people feel that his goal was their own goal. He was an autocrat, relying unhealthily upon the support and loyalty of his armed forces, who lived lives of great privilege, and of SAVAK, his very powerful secret police. He from time to time tried to organise political support through a party system, the latest of which was the Rastakhiz (Resurgence) Party set up in 1975, but he was never prepared to devolve any real power, with the result that any political party was soon exposed as ineffective and became a laughing-stock. He had few confidants and even fewer real advisers bold enough to tell him truths which he did not want to hear.[5] His own family was no asset to him, most of his relatives being surrounded with an atmosphere of corruption.

It came as a surprise to the ruling circles in Tehran, and to well-qualified observers such as the British Ambassador, Sir Anthony Parsons,[6] when the Shah in late 1976 decided to relax his political control. Given the economic unrest caused by the expiry of the boom, there could have been no less appropriate moment. No doubt the Shah calculated that if matters went otherwise than he intended, he could always reimpose control, using SAVAK and if necessary the armed forces to repress unrest. This proved to be a fatal miscalculation.

It is beyond the scope of this book to follow developments in any detail.[7] Suffice it to say that a crucial part in fanning unrest was played by Ayatollah Ruhollah Khomeini, long exiled, first in Iraq and later in Paris, who used the medium of cassette-recordings of his inflammatory messages smuggled into Iran; and that when the military were finally called in to restore order, with General Azhari as Prime Minister, they were unable to halt the progress of events, proving in particular helpless in the face of widespread strikes. On 16 January 1979, the Shah flew to exile in Egypt, and ten days later Khomeini returned to Tehran in triumph. The outcome was an Islamic Republic, established by a referendum held at the end of March 1979.

Inside Iran, the economic effects were serious. There was a good deal of political unrest in several parts of the country, which impeded production. Major projects begun under the Shah were cancelled; this was undoubtedly necessary but caused much unemployment. Entrepreneurs escaped abroad or were liquidated. There was a flight of capital. In June 1979, all private banks and insurance companies were nationalised, as, in July, were the firms run by the country's major industrialists. Many foreign contracts were cancelled and others scaled down.

Oil production fell away, partly as a result of trouble among the Arabic-speaking inhabitants of the oil province, Khuzistan. In September, this fall was rationalised by a declared policy of conserving Iran's oil reserves. Throughout the country, production of all commodities was by now down to around 50 per cent of normal. Large food imports became unavoidable despite an attempt to encourage surplus town population to return to the country, in the hope, among other things, of boosting agricultural output.

Financially, however, Iran's position was better than might be thought from this tale of woe. Budgetary expenditure had been much reduced, because of cancelled projects and cuts in defence spending, and income had risen as a result of higher oil prices which more than offset the lower volume of exports. Iran's foreign exchange holdings actually rose in 1979.

The higher oil prices just mentioned were a direct result of the alarm caused in the international market by the downfall of the Shah. Governments and oil companies desperately sought to build up stocks and drove prices up in the process; having risen five-fold in 1973–4, but then held almost steady (which meant that they were declining in real terms), they now doubled in the course of a few months. This was the 'second oil shock'. Coming so soon after the previous rises, it had a very serious impact on the world economy. Doubling sounds less drastic than quintupling but it was of course from a higher base; a rise from 1 to 5 is in fact smaller than a rise from 5 to 10. In retrospect, it is clear that this was to a large extent a self-inflicted wound, caused by panic buying for which there was no real need. Iranian exports of oil, after the first disruption, levelled off at about two-thirds of the 1978–9 rate, a volume reduction with which the oil companies could easily have coped at the old price levels. It was an over-swing of the pendulum.

There were several reasons for the panic buying, which it will be worth while to disentangle. By ill chance, oil stocks at the time of the crisis were unusually low, to the extent of some 80 million barrels.[8] More important was the fact that the major oil companies were affected to different extents by loss of supplies from Iran. BP, as 40 per cent participant in the Consortium, was the worst hit. From its normal position of being crude-long, it suddenly became crude-short, and had to invoke the *force majeure* clauses in its supply contracts. This cut off its sales to third parties, particularly to Exxon and to refiners in Japan. Other Consortium members were similarly reducing third-party sales, so a tight market quickly developed. The refiners who needed to find new supplies had usually had long-term links with one or other of the majors and were short of experience at meeting their needs on the spot market. They were competing there with those of the majors who now had refining capacity in excess of their crude availability. In this tussle the independent refiners, with their comparatively small orders, were at a disadvantage and, being inexperienced bargainers faced with fears of bankruptcy, tended to end up paying excessive prices.

The IEA's emergency allocation scheme was not relevant to this situation, since it was geared to making up shortfalls to countries rather than to individual companies. Seeing the spot prices rising, some oil producers, including a few members of OPEC among whom were Libya and Algeria, began to default on deliveries to contract customers in order to have more crude to sell on the spot market.[9] This spread the problem and with it the panic. It is easy to see now that it was overdone, but that is with the advantage of hindsight.

26 Trade between Britain and the Middle East 1970–80

The British Economy
The 70s were, for the most part, a disappointing decade for the British economy, despite the boon of North Sea oil in its second half. Politically, Conservatives and Labour alternated in office during the period, so both must bear responsibility for its failures. The alternation itself caused damage, as economic measures adopted tended to be short-term expedients, looking to no horizon beyond the next election under Britain's Quinquennial Act. Indeed, at times the horizon shrank to a mere matter of months, as 'mini-budgets' became all too regular a feature of Government policy in the intervals between the annual budgets.[1]

Most of the problems which became acute had been present in gradually intensifying form ever since World War II (indeed, many of them can be traced even further back) and had begun to appear incurable; they were summed up, especially by foreigners, as 'the British disease'. Among them were:

(1) Bad industrial relations. It was a relic of the 30s Depression that management and labour were steeped in an attitude of 'them and us', so that all dealings between them tended to be confrontational. This bad situation was compounded by the fact that the trade unions were organised on a craft rather than an industry basis, with the consequence that there were recurrent demarcation disputes between unions, often leading to industrial closures quite beyond the control of management. The frequency of strikes in Britain meant that

exporters were very liable to miss delivery dates; worst of all from this point of view were dock strikes.[2]

(2) Poor management. There were some honourable exceptions, but the general standard of management was low. This too had deep roots, traceable to a nineteenth century snobbery that trade was 'ungentlemanly', with the result that in the twentieth century those who were best educated sought social status in the professions rather than applying their talents to commerce or industry. British universities still, for the most part, regarded business management as falling short of being an academic discipline worthy of their attention. At middle management level, some of the larger firms gave in-house training, but most British managers had to learn by doing. Many of them learnt little, and did what they did incompetently. Inattention to quality control was a notorious management failing.

(3) Excessive pay settlements. These, themselves a symptom of weak management, reduced profits which might have been used for investment or else pushed up prices, making products uncompetitive. They contributed heavily to wage-led inflation.

(4) Inadequate investment. This was particularly noticeable in respect of machine tools. The British machine tool industry had performed badly, partly as a result of a low level of orders, so that high-quality tools were only available as imports. Lack of capital, plus shortage of foreign exchange, as well as sheer ignorance of what was available outside Britain, led to the prevalence of outdated machinery in all too many factories. Trade unions opposed the introduction of new machinery which might be operated by a smaller workforce; any technological advance was also liable to blur craft boundaries and lead to new demarcation disputes. Profit margins might seem to benefit in the short term by prolonging the use of obsolescent machinery rather than incurring the cost of replacement. All these were reasons, but no excuse, for an ultimately fatal underinvestment.

(5) Overmanning. This was most prevalent in the nationalised industries, where the unions tended to be especially powerful

and where losses which would have caused the bankruptcy of private concerns could be accepted complacently under cover of Government subsidies. But it existed also in the private sector, usually as a result of weak management. Its natural consequence was uncompetitive products, particularly fatal to export prospects.

(6) Insufficient research. There were certainly firms which attached great importance to research and spent heavily on it, but they were in the minority. Like underinvestment in new machinery, failure to spend money on research and development could improve profits in the short term but ruin longer-term viability.

Government was not unaware of these failings, but with its own short-term preoccupations did too little to cure them. Corporate taxation was modified in an attempt to encourage investment by special allowances or accelerated depreciation; this had some effect but not enough. Some public money was spent on research, but mainly in the area of defence. The worst failure by Government was in not tackling the inefficiency of the nationalised industries. One reason for this was that the full employment which had existed in Britain for more than two decades was now being undermined by the lack of adequate growth in the economy. Ministers were particularly unwilling to permit the closure of unproductive coal mines or steel mills[3] when the result must be to swell the unemployment totals. This was most of all the case where the uneconomic plants were located in areas already suffering from low employment. Since the nationalised industries were producing for the most part basic materials, fuels and services required by the private sector, their inefficiency added to industrial costs over a very wide area of the economy.

Another problem with which successive Governments struggled ineffectively was inflation. Under the Conservative Government led by Edward Heath, elected on 18 June 1970, an attempt was made by the Chancellor of the Exchequer, Anthony Barber, to overcome unemployment and poor productivity by a 'dash for growth'. This was not a totally unreasonable venture in the period around 1971–2 when sterling was temporarily strong and oil revenues were beginning to be visible only a few years away. The experiment seemed to have some initial success but bad industrial relations wrecked it; when it failed, it left sharply increased inflation as its legacy. This was a problem which was now afflicting many industrialised countries. There had come into being a novel situation in which economic stagnation and inflation flourished together. In the past it had been taken for granted that inflation could be cured by slowing down the economy. That now seemed no longer to be the case and the new phenomenon was given the portmanteau name 'stagflation'. It was a thoroughly unpleasant experience and one which seriously afflicted the UK.

One device which successive Governments frequently resorted to in the 70s was a statutory incomes policy. This took a variety of forms, ranging from a prices/incomes/dividends freeze (for a period usually of months, though then sometimes renewed) to income norms to be used in wage settlements. Whatever the details, these manoeuvres were uniformly unsuccessful. Freezes restrained inflation for a time, at the expense of inhibiting the expansion of progressive firms, but then released a pent-up wave of inflation once the freeze was relaxed or removed. Norms which were meant as maxima for wage settlements too often became minima instead.

The Government itself was liable to set a bad example in this respect by exceeding the norm for its own employees. There was nothing that a militant trade union leader enjoyed more than outbargaining the Government, or its accolytes, the heads of the nationalised industries. When Labour was in power, attempts were made to combine wages norms with social measures likely to appeal to the trade unions and so win their acquiescence in pay restraint. Phrases such as 'social compact' came into fashion. These too failed when it proved that the trade unions lacked the will to deliver their side of the bargain. It was a failure of this kind, culminating in a rash of strikes in local government services such as garbage disposal and even the burying of the dead, which earned the title of 'the winter of discontent' and ended Mr Callaghan's Labour Government in 1979.

The poor performance of the British economy inevitably led to weakness of sterling as an international currency. After a few years of balance of payment surpluses from 1969 to 1971, at the end of which the value of the pound was (misguidedly as it soon proved) raised from $2.40 to $2.60[4], the deficits which had been all too regular a problem for decades returned. They were of course exacerbated by the oil price quintupling of 1973–4, which affected not only Britain but the whole world. Britain should have been better placed than most countries to deal with this problem in view of its North Sea gas and its huge coal resources, but industrial action by coal-miners to enforce massive wage claims frustrated this possibility and eventually brought down the Heath Government (after the country's industry had been reduced to a three-day working week) at an election on 28 February 1974.

That Government had however meanwhile introduced on 23 June 1972 a new measure to deal with sterling crises, the 'floating' of the pound to find its own level on the currency markets. This proved to be a lasting change, the direction of floating in the 70s being generally downwards.[5] In October 1972 the Bank of England's Bank Rate, which had for nearly three centuries been used as a monetary regulator determining a whole pyramid of domestic interest rates, was abolished, leaving the market rate for Treasury Bills as the main monetary influence (although Minimum Lending Rate, which replaced Bank Rate, soon came to play much of the role of its predecessor).

Visible Trade

As usual, the statistics for the decade will be presented as two quinquennia with an overlapping year. There were some changes during the decade in the layout of the Overseas Trade Statistics, partly as a result of standardisation with the remainder of the EEC, but the figures remained generally comparable with previous years. Dubai achieved a separate listing in the statistics in 1974.

Table 9: Visible Trade (£ million) with:

	1970	1971	1972	1973	1974	1975
ABU DHABI						
Exports to	10.8	12.5	15.3	24.7	42.6	91.3
Imports from	18.7	26.5	42.5	33.5	149.5	98.9
Balance	-7.9	-14.0	-27.2	-8.8	-106.9	-7.6
ALGERIA						
Exports to	16.8	27.8	33.8	37.9	54.7	78.7
Imports from	21.2	17.0	22.9	45.7	36.2	87.5
Balance	-4.4	+10.8	+10.9	-7.8	+18.5	-8.8
BAHRAIN						
Exports to	24.3	25.2	19.6	24.3	33.7	60.9
Imports from	1.6	4.0	8.6	15.8	20.3	17.8
Balance	+22.7	+21.2	+11.0	+8.5	+13.4	+43.1
DUBAI (plus 5 other Members of UAE until 1974)						
Exports to	13.7	13.8	15.8	24.7	53.8	104.8
Imports from	13.4	20.6	11.3	35.7	56.4	60.2
Balance	+0.3	-6.8	+4.5	-11.0	-2.6	+44.6
EGYPT						
Exports to	18.7	20.2	18.4	27.1	52.4	107.7
Imports from	10.9	15.8	12.6	23.7	37.3	40.9
Balance	+7.8	+4.4	+5.8	+3.4	+15.1	+66.8
IRAN						
Exports to	66.3	78.6	117.0	169.4	278.6	494.6
Imports from	76.1	109.5	123.8	237.4	513.3	700.9
Balance	-9.8	-30.9	-6.8	-68.0	-234.7	-206.3
IRAQ						
Exports to	23.8	24.8	26.8	27.1	59.8	136.5
Imports from	18.7	36.8	34.1	30.7	106.6	102.5
Balance	+5.1	-12.0	-7.3	-3.6	-46.8	+34.0
ISRAEL						
Exports to	96.2	117.0	134.6	187.2	219.2	237.2
Imports from	45.1	53.8	57.2	69.9	78.7	91.3
Balance	+51.1	+63.2	+77.4	+117.3	+140.5	+145.9

JORDAN						
Exports to	12.3	11.1	11.3	13.4	20.6	36.8
Imports from	0.2	0.3	0.7	0.5	1.6	0.7
Balance	+12.1	+10.8	+10.6	+12.9	+19.0	+36.1
KUWAIT						
Exports to	36.2	35.3	31.3	36.1	59.8	99.2
Imports from	165.4	198.8	176.5	235.3	569.5	419.3
Balance	-129.2	-163.5	-145.2	-199.2	-509.7	-320.1
LEBANON						
Exports to	23.0	26.3	35.6	42.0	60.8	69.5
Imports from	3.1	3.9	6.5	8.0	28.6	8.0
Balance	+19.9	+22.4	+29.1	+34.0	+32.2	+61.5
LIBYA						
Exports to	24.3	31.0	46.3	61.1	62.5	107.0
Imports from	166.9	191.6	144.2	164.5	390.1	127.8
Balance	-142.6	-160.6	-97.9	-103.4	-327.6	-20.8
MOROCCO						
Exports to	12.6	12.8	13.3	16.2	28.1	35.5
Imports from	16.3	15.6	16.1	23.1	52.5	51.9
Balance	-3.7	-2.8	-2.8	-6.9	-24.4	-16.4
OMAN						
Exports to	7.8	13.1	17.2	22.2	42.9	98.0
Imports from	7.8	4.0	2.9	15.9	32.8	114.0
Balance	0.0	+9.1	+14.3	+6.3	+10.1	-16.0
QATAR						
Exports to	7.4	15.7	12.8	19.4	22.1	55.7
Imports from	30.6	41.3	39.3	47.3	166.0	156.7
Balance	-23.2	-25.6	-26.5	-27.9	-143.9	-101.0
SAUDI ARABIA						
Exports to	35.2	38.9	45.2	58.5	119.7	199.8
Imports from	104.2	172.8	183.7	322.2	1178.1	856.6
Balance	-69.0	-133.9	-138.5	-263.7	-1058.4	-656.8
SUDAN						
Exports to	18.2	17.7	23.1	26.9	36.0	63.9
Imports from	7.6	6.5	5.3	8.4	8.4	8.6
Balance	+10.6	+11.2	+17.8	+18.5	+27.6	+55.3
SYRIA						
Exports to	6.0	7.4	10.0	11.6	20.9	35.1
Imports from	0.5	0.8	0.4	1.2	20.6	4.9
Balance	+5.5	+6.6	+9.6	+10.4	+0.3	+30.2

TUNISIA						
Exports to	4.3	4.8	6.2	7.6	11.5	26.7
Imports from	2.5	2.0	2.3	3.6	6.2	3.0
Balance	+1.8	+2.8	+3.9	+4.0	+5.3	+23.7
UAE (less ABU DHABI and DUBAI)						
Exports to					0.5	2.5
Imports from					—	—
Balance					+0.5	+2.5
YEMEN AR						
Exports to	1.9	2.4	3.0	3.2	6.0	9.0
Imports from	0.3	—	0.1	0.4	1.4	0.2
Balance	+1.6	+2.4	+2.9	+2.8	+4.6	+8.8
YEMEN, PRSA (PDR YEMEN after 1973)						
Exports to	5.0	5.3	4.3	4.5	6.0	8.4
Imports from	9.6	5.9	1.8	3.4	8.1	3.6
Balance	-4.6	-0.6	+2.5	+1.1	-2.1	+4.8
TOTAL – MIDDLE EAST COUNTRIES						
Exports to	464.8	541.7	640.9	845.1	1292.2	2158.8
Imports from	720.7	927.5	892.8	1326.2	3462.2	2955.3
Balance	-255.9	–385.8	–251.9	–481.1	-2170.0	-796.5
TOTAL – ALL COUNTRIES						
Exports to	8063	9176	9746	12455	16494	19762
Imports from	9052	9834	11155	15854	23117	24028
Balance	–989	-658	-1401	-3399	-6623	-4266
M.E. TRADE AS PERCENTAGE OF TOTAL TRADE						
Exports to	5.76	5.90	6.58	6.79	7.83	10.92
Imports from	7.96	9.43	8.00	8.37	14.98	12.30

(Note: Apparent minor arithmetical errors result from rounding)

It will be seen at once that the importance to Britain of trade with the Middle East grew significantly during the quinquennium both in absolute terms and as a proportion of total trade. This was mainly due to the oil price rises of 1973–4, which greatly increased the cost of imports from the Middle East and at the same time provided the oil-rich states with the wherewithal to spend huge sums on the purchase of British exports (including arms). They could of course have shopped elsewhere and did indeed do so. But this was the time when the UK's long association with the Gulf States paid off particularly well in commercial dealings. The 80 per cent increase in the cost of imports from the Middle East in 1974 was followed by a 40 per cent increase in the value of exports to the Middle East in 1975. It was not enough to close the gap but it most usefully narrowed it.

The striking effect of oil price increases on Britain's import bill can best be seen from a table presenting these separately:

Table 10: UK Imports from Middle East Oil Producers (£ million)

	1970	1971	1972	1973	1974	1975
Abu Dhabi	18.7	26.5	42.5	33.5	149.5	98.9
Algeria	21.2	17.0	22.9	45.7	36.2	87.5
Bahrain	1.6	4.0	8.6	15.8	20.3	17.8
Dubai	13.4	20.6	11.3	35.7	56.4	60.2
Iran	76.1	109.5	123.8	237.4	513.3	700.9
Iraq	18.7	36.8	34.1	30.7	106.6	102.5
Kuwait	165.4	198.8	176.5	235.3	569.5	419.3
Libya	166.9	191.6	144.2	164.5	390.1	127.8
Oman	7.8	4.0	2.9	15.9	32.8	114.0
Qatar	30.6	41.3	39.3	47.3	166.0	156.7
Saudi Arabia	104.2	172.8	183.7	322.2	1178.1	856.6
TOTALS	624.6	822.9	789.8	1184.0	3218.8	2742.2

Looking first at the totals, it will be seen that the cost of UK imports did not quite quintuple in 1973–4 along with the price of oil. If the 1972 and 1974 totals are compared, there is an approximate quadrupling and then around a 15 per cent reduction from 1974 to 1975. This suggests that there was some switching from oil to coal and North Sea gas as soon as the price of oil shot up, and that this for a time continued. Britain thus did get some temporary benefit from her indigenous fuel resources, even though North Sea oil from the British sector was not yet on stream to any important extent. Unfortunately, from this point of view, the prices of coal and gas soon began to move up towards the equivalent oil price level; if the price of coal in particular had been held down, there could have been the beginning of a new golden age for the British coal industry, but this was ruled out by the militancy of coal-miners seizing the opportunity to press successfully for higher wages.

Although all the Middle East oil producers naturally gained bigger incomes from sales to Britain after 1973, there are some interesting fluctuations in their relative successes. First, it should be noted that the greatest beneficiary of all was Saudi Arabia, which had established itself over the quinquennium as by far Britain's biggest supplier, considerably outdoing the next two, Iran and Kuwait. This may seem surprising when it is taken into account that no British oil company had any participation in ARAMCO, whereas there was a large British interest in the Iran Consortium and in the Kuwait Oil Company. There are always mysteries in the doings of the oil majors, but it can be said in partial explanation that the American partners in ARAMCO had built up their retailing operations in the UK and had also won the approval of the UK Government by investing heavily in oil exploration in the northern North Sea.

It is also noticeable that purchases from Iran rose sharply from 1974 to 1975, while those from Kuwait fell; this is probably due to the Kuwait Government's own wish to restrain the rate at which its reserves of oil were depleted. In percentage terms, the greatest gainer during the quinquennium was Oman; here oil price rises coincided with rapidly rising output from a low base.

So far as British exports are concerned, the large gains in 1975 have already been mentioned. Countries where this was most evident were Abu Dhabi, Egypt, Iraq, Oman, Qatar and Tunisia, to all of which exports more than doubled during the year, as indeed they had already done to Saudi Arabia a year earlier. In other countries, Dubai, Iran, Kuwait, Libya and Sudan, there was a near-doubling. Tunisia and Sudan show that good export performance was not confined to the oil-producers, although the latter were far and away the most important markets in absolute terms. Exports to Israel, a valuable market not blessed with oil wealth, rose very healthily over the quinquennium, with a balance of trade much in the UK's favour. Taking nearly 11 per cent of total UK exports by 1975, the Middle East as a whole had grown greatly in stature as a British export market.

The visible trade figures for the next quinquennium, with the usual overlapping year, are as follows:

Table 11: Visible Trade (£ million) with:

	1975	1976	1977	1978	1979	1980
ABU DHABI						
Exports to	91.3	125.7	138.9	126.5	159.4	214.6
Imports from	98.9	77.8	138.6	123.3	94.0	246.3
Balance	-7.6	+47.9	+0.3	+3.2	+65.4	-31.7
ALGERIA						
Exports to	78.7	101.8	98.7	121.4	115.0	140.4
Imports from	87.5	80.2	50.1	37.9	87.5	113.8
Balance	-8.8	+21.6	+48.6	+83.5	+27.5	+26.6
BAHRAIN						
Exports to	60.9	89.6	118.9	119.9	123.5	100.5
Imports from	17.8	30.1	20.7	34.6	22.8	13.1
Balance	+43.1	+59.5	+98.2	+85.3	+100.7	+87.4
DUBAI						
Exports to	104.8	188.7	269.5	273.0	305.3	268.5
Imports from	60.2	121.9	130.6	148.7	141.9	235.2
Balance	+44.6	+66.8	+138.9	+124.3	+163.4	+33.3
EGYPT						
Exports to	107.7	171.9	191.9	205.1	264.5	324.0
Imports from	40.9	65.3	89.4	99.9	252.7	333.9
Balance	+66.8	+106.6	+102.5	+105.2	+11.8	-9.9
IRAN						
Exports to	494.6	510.9	659.0	752.0	231.8	392.7
Imports from	700.9	1049.3	789.0	527.8	243.6	107.2
Balance	-206.3	-538.4	-130.0	+224.2	-11.8	+285.5
IRAQ						
Exports to	136.5	149.9	167.4	216.7	201.2	322.1
Imports from	102.5	279.5	332.1	496.7	393.7	532.3
Balance	+34.0	-129.6	-164.7	-280.0	-192.5	-210.2
ISRAEL						
Exports to	237.2	249.4	276.1	243.4	270.7	230.6
Imports from	91.3	127.8	162.3	187.3	227.6	232.7
Balance	+145.9	+121.6	+113.8	+56.1	+43.1	-2.1

JORDAN						
Exports to	36.8	55.7	48.9	67.4	86.9	94.6
Imports from	0.7	0.9	2.0	6.1	7.9	6.2
Balance	+36.1	+54.8	+46.9	+61.3	+79.0	+88.4
KUWAIT						
Exports to	99.2	144.3	253.8	331.9	233.4	250.8
Imports from	419.3	587.1	554.9	606.0	743.1	646.8
Balance	-320.1	-442.8	-301.1	-274.1	-509.7	-396.0
LEBANON						
Exports to	69.5	10.1	48.8	58.9	65.8	70.7
Imports from	8.0	6.1	8.4	8.1	9.9	9.1
Balance	+61.5	+4.0	+40.4	+50.8	+55.9	+61.6
LIBYA						
Exports to	107.0	134.6	173.9	214.3	253.2	288.4
Imports from	127.8	166.6	141.7	98.0	62.2	46.2
Balance	-20.8	-32.0	+32.2	+116.3	+191.0	+242.2
MOROCCO						
Exports to	35.5	60.5	69.6	76.5	67.6	64.7
Imports from	51.9	56.8	46.2	44.2	50.4	60.5
Balance	-16.4	+3.7	+23.4	+32.3	+17.2	+4.2
OMAN						
Exports to	98.0	102.3	191.9	125.7	129.7	121.0
Imports from	114.0	73.2	34.2	41.7	31.8	19.2
Balance	-16.0	+29.1	+157.7	+84.0	+97.9	+101.8
QATAR						
Exports to	55.7	86.7	117.5	91.8	101.5	102.0
Imports from	156.7	248.8	102.5	30.4	40.5	44.7
Balance	-101.0	-162.1	+15.0	+61.4	+61.0	+57.3
SAUDI ARABIA						
Exports to	199.8	400.4	601.1	785.7	893.6	945.2
Imports from	856.6	978.5	1132.4	870.5	1108.6	1874.3
Balance	-656.8	-578.1	-531.3	-84.8	-215.0	-929.1
SUDAN						
Exports to	63.9	92.0	87.6	114.1	106.4	121.3
Imports from	8.6	14.2	14.9	19.4	19.7	13.3
Balance	+55.3	+77.8	+72.7	+94.7	+86.7	+108.0

SYRIA						
Exports to	35.1	64.4	57.2	57.7	66.7	81.6
Imports from	4.9	7.7	5.3	4.3	7.0	12.2
Balance	+30.2	+56.7	+51.9	+53.4	+59.7	+69.4
TUNISIA						
Exports to	26.7	23.0	28.4	21.4	24.7	29.8
Imports from	3.0	3.1	12.6	12.0	9.1	17.2
Balance	+23.7	+19.9	+15.8	+9.4	+15.6	+12.6
UAE (less ABU DHABI and DUBAI)						
Exports to	2.5	9.0	56.4	37.1	23.5	17.5
Imports from	—	0.2	1.7	0.8	1.1	0.8
Balance	+2.5	+8.8	+54.7	+36.3	+22.4	+16.7
YEMEN AR						
Exports to	9.0	19.7	41.5	48.7	49.2	36.5
Imports from	0.2	1.5	15.6	7.3	2.3	0.5
Balance	+8.8	+18.2	+25.9	+41.4	+46.9	+36.0
PDR YEMEN						
Exports to	8.4	12.3	22.6	28.9	18.9	25.4
Imports from	3.6	0.8	0.2	0.2	2.7	5.7
Balance	+4.8	+11.5	+22.4	+28.7	+16.2	+19.7
TOTAL – MIDDLE EAST COUNTRIES						
Exports to	2158.8	2802.9	3719.6	4118.1	3792.5	4242.9
Imports from	2955.3	3977.4	3785.4	3405.2	3560.1	4571.2
Balance	-796.5	-1174.5	-65.8	+712.9	+232.4	-328.3
TOTAL – ALL COUNTRIES						
Exports to	19762	25778	33331	37382	42804	47364
Imports from	24028	31213	36978	40930	48467	49773
Balance	-4266	-5435	-3647	-3548	-5663	-2409
M.E. TRADE AS PERCENTAGE OF TOTAL TRADE						
Exports to	10.92	10.87	11.16	11.02	8.86	8.96
Imports from	12.30	12.74	10.24	8.32	7.35	9.18

(Note: Apparent minor arithmetical errors result from rounding)

It will be seen that the Middle East continued to take around 11 per cent of total UK exports over the four years 1975–8 and that they then fell back to under 9 per cent. This fall was due to some decline in purchasing power of the oil producers as the real price of oil declined prior to the 'second oil shock'. As for imports, they were on a downward trend from 1976 to 1979 as North Sea oil began to supply more and more of Britain's requirements; the increase in 1980 is due to the doubling of prices more than offsetting a further reduction in volume. There were of course some exceptions to this downward trend in imports from Middle East countries. Most notable is Israel, which much increased its exports to Britain during the quinquennium; this can be attributed to its success in developing and diversifying its industries and to the high quality of its citrus exports.

Looking at the imports from particular oil producers gives the following picture:

Table 12: UK Imports from Middle East Oil Producers (£ million)

	1975	1976	1977	1978	1979	1980
Abu Dhabi	98.9	77.8	138.6	123.3	94.0	246.3
Algeria	87.5	80.2	50.1	37.9	87.5	113.8
Bahrain	17.8	30.1	20.7	34.6	22.8	13.0
Dubai	60.2	121.9	130.6	148.7	141.9	235.2
Iran	700.9	1049.3	789.0	527.8	243.6	107.2
Iraq	102.5	279.5	332.1	496.7	393.7	532.3
Kuwait	419.3	597.1	554.9	606.0	743.1	646.8
Libya	127.8	166.6	141.7	98.0	62.2	46.2
Oman	114.0	73.2	34.2	41.7	31.8	19.2
Qatar	156.7	248.8	102.5	30.4	40.5	44.7
Saudi Arabia	856.6	978.5	1132.4	870.5	1108.6	1874.2
TOTALS	2742.2	3703.0	3426.8	3015.6	2969.7	3878.9

The downward trend in the totals is evident from 1976 to 1979, but some countries lost exports to the UK faster than others. One of the factors relevant here is that the North Sea produces mainly light crude oil. To provide the right mix of products for sale in Britain, a good deal of heavy crude therefore still needs to be imported for refining, however high North Sea output rises. When that output is enough to more than meet the domestic market's needs, the excess is exported, but not of course to the Middle East which has its own supplies of both light and heavy crude (though it may import certain products). So Britain becomes simultaneously an exporter and an importer. It follows that the Middle East oil displaced will be chiefly light crude similar to that from the North Sea, and the principal Middle East producer of such crude is Libya. The value of British imports from Libya dropped even in 1980.

Because of the overall fall in imports up to 1979, combined with rising British exports over the same period, there was actually a surplus on the UK's balance of visible trade with the Middle East in both 1978 and 1979. This was an almost unprecedented event; certainly there had been no favourable balance since the abnormal postwar years of 1946 and 1947. Oil price rises reversed the position in 1980, but the years of heavy deficit in Britain's visible trade with the Middle East were over, at least so long as North Sea output remains high. When it is remembered that as recently as 1974 that deficit had been £2170 million, the turn-round in four years is startling.

Arms Exports[6]

In the 70s, British exports of armoured vehicles to the Middle East continued to be important. The market for Centurion tanks declined as they became oldfashioned, except in Israel which had its own capacity for upgunning them (Israel's holdings grew from 450 in 1971 to 1000 in 1978) and in Jordan which found their low prices attractive (Jordan's holdings rose from 150 in 1971 to 250 in 1975). But a new and more expensive British tank, the Chieftain, at once won sales in Iran, even to the extent of delaying the reequipment of the British Army. Iran ordered 800 of them; the first 60 arrived in 1973 and delivery was completed in 1977, by which time additional numbers had been ordered. By 1979, Iran had 875 of them, after which sales were suspended as a result of the outbreak of the Iran-Iraq war, leading to a British Government embargo on sales to both countries. Kuwait also bought Chieftains, the first 12 being delivered in 1977 and the holding rising to 160 by 1980. A number of Arab countries equipped themselves with British armoured cars, scout cars and armoured personnel vehicles, the list even extending to Lebanon and Tunisia, which rarely bought British armaments.

Naval sales were not impressive during the decade. Libya was the only Middle East country to buy large British vessels, a frigate and a corvette. A few patrol craft were bought by Libya, Oman, Qatar and the U.A.E. British hovercraft found some buyers, being used as coastguard vessels and as minelayers; Egypt, Iran and Saudi Arabia took them, but in small numbers.

Aircraft sales were also low during the decade. The Lightning was now oldfashioned. Small numbers of counter-insurgency aircraft and trainers were sold and there was some demand for British helicopters. The Skyvan freighter, able to operate from desert strips, won a few orders. There was a reasonable market for spare parts, including replacement engines, for aircraft bought in earlier years. Hunters in particular seemed to have been so well built that they could remain in service almost indefinitely, although by now their use was mainly as trainers.

Invisible Trade

The British Invisible Exports Council (previously known as the Committee on Invisible Exports from 1968 to 1983) has published a valuable worldwide study of invisible trade covering the period 1972 to 1986. It reveals how far the developed countries outpaced the rest of the world in invisible earnings.[7] The surprise lies not in this outpacing in itself, but in the magnitude of the difference. Of 113 countries for which statistics were gathered, only 36 had a surplus on invisibles and no less than 77 per cent of their total surplus accrued to the leading 5. The UK was consistently second in this earnings league, outstripped only by the USA. The figures show also that in almost all countries invisible trade grew faster than GNP, especially during the 70s; in the case of the UK, invisible receipts rose from 11.1 per cent of GNP in 1972 to 16.3 per cent in 1980.[8] Britain's ratio of invisible earnings to visible export earnings was extraordinarily high; in the 70s it was consistently between 70 per cent and 80 per cent on a worldwide calculation.

As always, there are no regional figures available for these transactions with the Middle East, but it would be a very safe guess that the invisible surplus with the Middle East countries was at least average. It follows that in the case of the Middle East the UK's net gain from invisibles can be taken to be some 75 per cent or more of its income from visible exports. This has a significant impact on the combined balance for visibles and invisibles together. In 1974, for instance, when Britain had a record deficit of £2170 million on visible trade, the combined balance would be reduced to a deficit of £1200 million or less; and in 1978 the record visible surplus of £713 million would soar to a combined surplus of £3560 million or more. Neither of those combined figures can be regarded as other than very approximate, but they give an idea of the orders of magnitude involved. In the 70s, as in earlier decades, there can be near-certainty that the UK's balance of payments with the Middle East was throughout in valuable surplus.

ECGD

ECGD continued to expand during the 70s. Its maximum permitted liabilities were increased to £6500 million in 1970, to £12,200 million in 1972 and to £25,000 million in 1977. A number of new facilities came into being. Particularly important for trade with the Middle East were guarantees for bonds, since the stipulation of performance bonds for capital goods contracts became widespread during the 70s in the rapidly developing oil-rich countries; cover against the unfair calling of bonds was made available by ECGD in 1976. Looking at the range of the products and services it insured, in its history published in 1979, it is notable that of the eight examples given at random, no less than five were to Middle East destinations.[9]

Overseas Banking

The 1970s marked some decline of British banking in the Middle East and a flowering of Middle East banking in London, both changes due to the growth of nationalism in the Arab countries and to the escalating wealth of a number of them.

The BBME managed to open a branch in one more Arab country, at Taiz in the Yemen Arab Republic in 1971. It also expanded its chain of branches and sub-branches in a number of countries in which it was already operating. In addition, it took over a Lebanese bank, Trust Bank SAL, in 1971, renaming it the British Bank of Lebanon. But in the middle 70s it was forced by pressure against foreign banking to close its branches in Morocco and Tunisia and in 1979 the Bank of Iran and the Middle East was seized following the Iranian Revolution. In 1978 the BBME branches in Saudi Arabia were transferred to the Saudi-British Bank in which it had only a 40 per cent shareholding, the other 60 per cent being owned by the Saudi public. And even in Jordan it was restricted in the same year to four branches only. However, this shrinkage in BBME's network in Arab lands was offset by a considerable growth in deposits as oil prices rocketed, so that the Bank became more profitable than ever before.[10]

In London there had been a modest representation of Middle East banks before 1970. The Bank Leumi (Israeli) is the oldest of them all, dating back to the Anglo-Palestine Company founded in 1902 with various changes of name since, becoming an Israeli Bank technically in 1957. The Rafidain Bank (Iraqi) opened in London in 1952, followed by the Bank Saderat Iran in 1963, the United Bank of Kuwait in 1966 and the Bank Melli Iran in 1967. During the decade to 1980 another eleven Arab, three Israeli and two Iranian banks set themselves up in London; of the Arab-owned banks the most important were the Arab Bank (Palestinian-Jordanian), the Bank of Credit and Commerce International (Pakistani-managed but UAE-financed), the Saudi International Bank, the Qatar National Bank and the National Bank of Abu Dhabi. By 1980 their presence justified the formation in London of the Arab Bankers Association.

It should be noted that the British banks in the Middle East and the Middle East banks in the UK served for the most part rather different purposes. The principal objective of the former was to attract local deposits, to lend them at a profit to local merchants (mainly short-term to finance imports), and to invest any surplus funds in London (or Bombay when the rupee was the Gulf currency). On the other hand, most Middle East banks in the UK only attracted British deposits to a very minor extent; their primary function was to act as a channel for funds from their home countries and to deploy them profitably for trade or investment in Britain (and sometimes elsewhere in Europe). The main flow of funds was therefore in both cases from the Middle East to the UK, which is why the net effect of this overseas banking, by British and Middle East banks alike, was favourable to Britain from the points of view of invisible income and also of capital flow. (It was naturally also beneficial to Middle Eastern investors in other ways or it would not have occurred.)

Joint Arab-British Chamber of Commerce[11]

Chambers of Commerce play an important role in most Middle Eastern countries. Membership of them is usually compulsory for traders, especially for those active in the international market. This is probably what persuaded the Arab League to resolve to seek the establishment of Joint Arab-Foreign Chambers in the capitals or principal commercial cities of the industrialised world. In Europe, the first such body was set up in Paris. London lagged a little behind, partly because the British Government was not at first convinced that a Joint Chamber would serve a useful purpose. However, a licence was eventually granted and the Joint Arab-British Chamber began operations on 6 October 1976. It was a genuinely joint body, with Arab and British directors, Arab and British staff and Arab and British members.

Although it provides many other services, such as business information, technical translation and bilingual printing, its main service to British exporters (and indirectly to Arab importers) has from the beginning been the efficient processing of export documents, most of which require legalisation by the Arab Embassies in London. The Chamber, with its Arabic-speaking staff and close links with the Embassies, streamlines the accurate completion of these formalities, with the result that exporters can be sure that their shipments will not fall foul of the Customs authorities in any Arab country of destination.[12]

27 Industrial Development in the Arabian Peninsula

Oil wealth, particularly after the spectacular price rises of 1973–4 and 1979–80, provided the richer countries of the Arabian Peninsula with the financial means to carry through important programmes of industrialisation. The industries established were largely, but not entirely, hydrocarbon-based. It is time to look at these programmes in more detail and to examine to what extent British firms took advantage of the enormous opportunities they presented.

The richest of the states concerned was Saudi Arabia. It was also by far the largest in area and (although it is sparsely inhabited) in population.[1] From 1970 onwards, its development programme has proceeded on the basis of 5-year plans. The first of these, that for 1970–5, concentrated on social improvements and infrastructure, particularly in the field of transportation – roads, ports, airports etc. It was in the second plan, for 1975–80, that the country's major industrial project got under way. This, originally conceived by King Faisal but begun by his successor, King Khalid, and mainly carried through under the present ruler, King Fahd,[2] is the bringing into being of two entirely new industrial cities, Jubail and Yanbu, on seaside sites on the east and west coasts respectively.[3]

On 21 September 1975, King Khalid issued a decree setting up a Royal Commission for Jubail and Yanbu. Its importance was marked by his later nomination of the Crown Prince, Fahd bin Abdul Aziz, as Chairman of its Board of Directors, a position he significantly chose to continue to hold after succeeding to the throne. The Board, assisted by a Secretariat-General in Riyadh currently headed by one of the younger Princes with engineering qualifications, is responsible for policy and oversight, but devolves all planning, construction and operations to two Directorates-General at Jubail and Yanbu. These are assisted by the Arabian Bechtel Company Limited at Jubail and by Saudi Arabian Parsons Limited at Yanbu.

The first construction teams arrived on site at what were to be the new cities in 1977. They found there nothing but empty spaces (of which there is no shortage in Saudi Arabia). They were of course not 'green-field' but 'desert' sites, though not in the sense of continuous stretches of sand dunes. Jubail consisted mainly of marsh-lands with a little scrub and Yanbu of fairly level hard sand with some clay content. Both sites were close to good natural harbours with existing small towns (from which the industrial cities have taken their names); of these Yanbu al-Bahr was the more important, as its port was used by pilgrims visiting Madinah.

Detailed plans for the zoning of both cities and for the locations of the principal industrial plants had been prepared before work began. Jubail is the bigger city, with a planned area of 920 km^2, the industrial zone being to the south and the residential zone to the north (upwind). Its ultimate population is calculated at 280,000. Yanbu is smaller, 180 km^2, with the industrial zone south-east of the residential zone; its population is planned to be 130,000.

The first task of the construction teams was to provide temporary housing for their own use, together with wells and diesel generators to supply water and electricity. What then followed was a massive earth-moving phase to level the sites; in the course of this, dredging of the adjacent seabottoms produced fill for the land and at the same time carved out deep-water channels for shipping. At Jubail, most of the development area had to be raised 2.5 metres to set it above the marine flood level. Yanbu did not have this problem, but even so levelling required the movement of nearly 60 million m^3 of earth. Soil stabilisation was needed at both sites, but especially at Jubail, to prevent wind erosion.

It was during the period of the third 5-year plan, 1980 – 5, that industrial plants began to be completed, and this process is speeding up in the fourth plan, 1985 – 90. The primary industries include a steel mill at Jubail, but otherwise are all based on hydrocarbons, especially the associated gas that would otherwise have been flared. Most of the technology needed had to be imported, so two existing enterprises, the General Petroleum and Minerals Organization (Petromin) and the Saudi Basic Industries Corporation (SABIC), formed joint ventures with foreign firms. From the beginning, it was intended that a large proportion of the production of some of these primary industries should ultimately be exported, as much as 85 per cent – 90 per cent in certain cases.

By the end of the third 5-year plan period in 1985, 16 primary industries were in operation at Jubail and Yanbu, producing steel, petroleum products, industrial gases, sulphur and petrochemicals. In addition, Yanbu, which had been linked to the Eastern Province by pipelines, had a crude oil storage and shipment terminal, giving the oilfields an export outlet to the Red Sea. Both cities have impressive ports and airports, and are connected by roads to the Kingdom's extensive main road network. They are also well provided now with telecommunications (this was a problem in the early days).

Secondary industries at Jubail and Yanbu were mainly intended for the domestic market as import-savers, though it was envisaged that there could be exports of surplus production. They cover such items as automotive and electrical parts, plumbing and hardware, furnishings, clothes, photographic film, magnetic tapes, office stationery, packaging and dozens of small products. Both primary and secondary industries are mainly publicly owned, but there is a third tier of support industries, which give scope for private ventures. These include suppliers of building materials and industrial equipment, maintenance services, printing works and bakeries. Also in private ownership are light industries for the manufacture of paints, plastic products, furniture and household appliances. And of course there are privately-owned shops to supply the residents. Initially, virtually all the labour force and most of the technical and supervisory staff were expatriates, but this has recently been changing quite rapidly. The Royal Commission set up at an early stage a Human Resources Development Institute (HRDI) to take charge of training. The Institute's Jubail Training Centre was opened in 1984, with a capacity for 1000 boarders and 500 day students. It runs a Vocational Training System to produce skilled and semi-skilled workers and a Career Development Program (CDP) to turn college and high-school graduates into applied engineers, administrators and commercial managers; CDP courses include English-language training. Saudis will soon be in a majority in all the non-manual occupations; indeed, that stage has probably already been reached at Jubail. Manual workers, whose numbers fell considerably with the completion of the initial construction period, are still mainly foreign, as Saudiisation is unlikely to progress very far in manual employment, and in all menial jobs Yemenis and other foreigners will no doubt continue to be employed, as elsewhere in the country. Saudis are just too rich to take such work.

British multinationals have played a very minor part in the development of these two huge industrial complexes. At one time, it appeared that Burmah Oil Company might be a favoured partner; the Saudis had turned to them at an early stage, partly because they were not already involved in oil production in the Peninsula. But unfortunately they were at that time running into financial problems (which led to their having to sell their holding in BP) and were in no position to take on major new commitments. Their place was taken by Bechtel, an American multinational already well established in the Kingdom. Shell were partners of Petromin in building a 250,000 b/d refinery at Jubail, but Shell are only partly British-owned. British consulting engineers, who have a high reputation throughout the Middle East, have won valuable contracts, and Britain has done well generally in the field of services.

Among British civil engineering contractors Laing won favour by entering into a consortium with powerful local interests, and British firms have come in for a useful amount of subcontracting work (though this is increasingly being directed now towards Saudi firms). The trade figures (Chapters 26 and 31) show that British exports to Saudi Arabia, especially of machinery, grew enormously from 1976 onwards; but certain other countries' exports grew still more rapidly. The British professionals and technical experts who have found lucrative employment in Saudi Arabia have in many cases been working for foreign employers. It has overall been a rather sad story from a UK view-point.

Why was this? There is no single answer. One respectable reason for the apparent lack of enterprise by British contractors was that some of the best of them were already heavily committed elsewhere in the Peninsula, with the result that it was genuinely beyond their capability to compete also for the huge contracts on offer in Saudi Arabia. Another reason was the very size of those contracts. Most British firms were too small to compete with the mammoths such as Bechtel and Parsons. The risks (which were very real) were incompatible with their financial bases.

Nor were they willing to enter into British consortia to overcome this problem; the rivalries between them were too great and they were not sufficiently flexible. And in the 1970s it was no part of the UK Government's philosophy to put pressure on rival firms to cooperate. Indeed, it was generally unwilling even to back a single British firm openly in bidding for a contract abroad, for fear of complaints by other British firms of partiality or of damage to Government prestige if the contractor ran into problems in the execution of the project. There has been a considerable change in these British Government attitudes during the 80s.

Low-cost labour from, for example, Korea, men willing to work hard in the adverse climate and unfamiliar surroundings of Saudi Arabia, allowed Far Eastern bidders for contracts to underprice UK competitors. And Britain's reputation for quality did not stand high before the management reforms of the 1980s. One British company which did have the financial base required ruled itself out of consideration. BP, when asked to participate in the development of Jubail, decided, for its own commercial reasons, that it was not interested in a Saudi offer of 'incentive crude', i.e. permission to buy a tonnage of Saudi crude oil related to the level of its investment. It was no doubt right so to decide, but it made insufficient effort to explain its reasons to the Saudis or to put up alternative proposals, with the result that it earned

Saudi ill-will. BP's attention was by then set rather on its growing interests in North America.

In addition to the construction of these two new industrial cities, extensive industrial estates have been built outside Jeddah, Riyadh and Dammam, and others are under construction near several large towns. In these most of the firms are from the private sector and their products are aimed chiefly at the domestic market. Many of them are joint enterprises with foreign firms (the Saudis supplying the finance and the foreigners the technology and some of the top management) but here too in the early years it was hard to find a UK company participating.[4] Most British firms seem to have known too little about the capabilities of Saudi firms to risk partnership with them and they were unhappy at the idea of any dispute with their partners being settled under Saudi law, while the Saudis for their part were chary about accepting international arbitration.

A consolation was that from the start quite a lot of the machinery installed was British. In more recent years, as fears were shown by experience to have been unfounded or certainly exaggerated, the interest of British companies in Saudi joint ventures has increased sharply. Figures issued by the Saudi Industrial Development Fund for 1985 even showed the UK leading the list of EEC members as foreign partners in twenty-eight projects, representing 8.3 per cent of all joint ventures in the Kingdom; this was quite a remarkable turn-around. In the business field, for reasons which will be discussed in Chapter 31, the Britain of the 1980s is showing more enterprise than it did in the 1970s.

Because of the recession in oil trading, the fourth 5-year plan, 1985–90, has got off to a slower start, but Saudi Arabia has considerable foreign exchange reserves and can afford to keep its development programme moving ahead, even if at a more sedate pace. SABIC alone (now partly privatised) plans to invest $4500 million during the plan period. Half of this is expected to be in petrochemicals, despite reduced profitability of the existing Saudi plants. These suffered from a reduction in feedstock cost advantage when naphtha prices halved between the last quarter of 1985 and the first quarter of 1986, cutting sharply the price differential between European naphtha-based and Gulf gas-based petrochemical products. The addition of shipping costs and tariffs (this latter being a sore point between Saudi Arabia and the EEC – see Chapter 19) meant that the Saudi plants could only retain their distant markets by price-cutting on a scale which eroded profit margins. Methanol, for instance, of which Saudi Arabia produces large quantities, had to be priced down from $140 to $100 a tonne. Nevertheless, SABIC's new investment will add output of another 3.7 million tonnes of petrochemicals during the fourth plan and by 1990 Saudi Arabia will have invested altogether the massive sum of $14,500 million in this field (including fertilisers).

There has also been a considerable Saudi investment in modern agriculture, which because of the natural disadvantages it faces has to be planned very much as an industrial-type operation. Although so much of the country is arid desert, hydrological surveys showed that there was a large aquifer under the Central and Eastern Provinces which could be tapped for irrigation. The drawback is that it is fossil water accumulated some 30,000 years ago and non-renewable. Nevertheless, it is estimated to be large enough to last at least 30, and perhaps up to 100 years. Saudi Arabia has become self-supporting in wheat,[5] and is on the way to meeting its needs for meat, poultry and egg production, a situation which a generation ago would have seemed utterly incredible. Attention has now been turned to crops such as tomatoes and avocados which need heat, and flowers are also being cultivated. Admittedly, all this has been done at a price. Wheat production costs, for instance, run at something like five times world levels. For that reason, there are commercially-minded Saudis who think their agricultural policy a great mistake.

It should be noted that the plans for agriculture provide for extensive resettlement of the remaining nomadic tribes. It seems that Saudi Arabia is becoming the land of the vanishing beduin.

Industrialisation has also made considerable strides in the smaller Gulf states. Here the situation differs from that in Saudi Arabia, since they have only tiny populations (even counting in foreigners), so the domestic markets are too small to support the output from large enterprises unless the entire Arab shore of the Gulf is regarded as a single outlet. The trouble has been that until quite recently there was no planning machinery to coordinate economic requirements for the whole Gulf (to its credit, OAPEC tried to fill this gap, but it was not really organised to do so and it had no authority devolved to it from its members). The result has been uneconomic duplication, arising from local jealousies and a desire to outdo neighbours.

Bahrain was one of the first on the industrialisation trail. Its oil was found early but in limited quantities, so it soon had to think about what would happen when the oil ran out. It had certain assets, among them a relatively highly-educated population and a tradition of friendship with its larger (and soon much richer) neighbour, Saudi Arabia. One of its early good decisions was to build a major oil refinery at a time when there were no refineries on the Arab shore of the Gulf; the capacity of the Bahrain refinery is 260,000 b/d. Bahraini crude now provides only a small fraction of this throughput; the rest comes from Saudi oil delivered by submarine pipeline (Bahrain is an island, or rather a small archipelago). Luckily, there are no fears that this supply will cease, despite the refineries being built inside Saudi Arabia. Indeed, Bahrain and Saudi Arabia have been brought into closer cooperation by the recent completion of the 15-mile King Fahd Causeway linking the two countries, and are continuing to seek opportunities for joint enterprises.

Two other industrial plants in Bahrain are the ALBA aluminium smelter (cheap energy is vital to the economics of aluminium production), recently complemented by a rolling mill, and a dry-dock for vessels of up to 500,000 tons. The latter, which cost $300 million, was built between 1974 and 1977 with financial backing from OAPEC. An aluminium foil plant with a capacity of 6000 tons p.a. is due to be completed in 1988.

As well as industrialising, Bahrain saw itself as a provider of services for the Gulf and made particularly strong efforts to become a financial centre, offering international banks licences to set up 'offshore banking units' (OBUs) there, which were not allowed to compete for the local business in Bahrain itself. This seemed very attractive to the banks when the oil boom was at its height, but more recently enthusiasm has waned somewhat and the number of OBUs operating has been falling.

Kuwait has gone in for import-saving plants, such as flour milling and manufacture of soft drinks (alcohol is forbidden there), and has also specialised in building materials. There is a cement factory and production of concrete, asbestos, tiles, bricks, and even prefabricated buildings. Paint is another local product. As Kuwait City has been nearly totally rebuilt, not once but several times,[6] there is a heavier domestic demand for these products than might be expected from the size of its population (only a little over 1 million, including many foreigners, a good number of them permanent residents).

Kuwait has constructed extensive dock areas in its ports and these have handled a great deal of freight for Iraq during the Gulf War (though shipping bound for Kuwait faced increased dangers during 1987 from Iranian attacks, not only in transit but occasionally even in port). It also has a sizeable oil refinery (135,000 b/d) and a large petroleum gas liquefaction plant producing butane, propane and natural gasoline (designed for 5 million tonnes a year, but running below capacity, since it uses associated gas and crude oil production is now lower than was forecast when the plant was planned). There is a petrochemical plant for the production of ethylene, and there is fertiliser manufacture.

Boat-building used to be an important Kuwaiti industry, but has declined in importance since oil took over from pearling. Fishing, especially for shrimps, is still important, and about half of the annual catch of around 10,000 tons is exported, mainly to Japan. There is a little farming, supplying eggs, poultry, vegetables and milk to the population, but not on a scale of self-sufficiency.

Qatar has also built a large cement works and when the cautious Kuwaitis decided against building a steel mill to supply their construction industry, the Qataris took the risk of building a 400,000-ton plant, which came into operation in 1978, importing sponge iron from India for processing. At the time, they hoped that this would be the only steel mill on the Arab shore, but in this hope they have been disappointed by Dubai.

Qatar has a small oil refinery, purely to supply local consumption. It also has a gas liquefaction plant and an ethylene plant, both smaller than Kuwait's.

As in Saudi Arabia, there is some large-scale farming in Qatar. Low-cost ground water has been found there and it has been carefully exploited to avoid the danger of salinity. The chief crops are cereals and vegetables (of which there is an export surplus, easily sold to its neighbours), and there is some dairy farming. Fishing is sufficient to meet local needs. A fertiliser plant supplies the farmers and has a surplus for export.

The UAE counts as a single state politically, but it is a loose federation, with much rivalry between the individual emirates. This has certainly shown itself in development plans. One of the early pieces of duplication was the building of international airports by both Abu Dhabi and Dubai, a third being built more recently in Sharjah. Luckily, UAE lies abreast of many major civil aviation routes, so the three have so far all been able to attract traffic. But it is clear that a single airport would have been more profitable and this will soon become still clearer, since long-range aircaft are beginning to be able to overfly the Gulf between Europe and the Far East.

Abu Dhabi has industrialised by building two large oil refineries and also has a big gas liquefaction plant. It has cement factories, both at Abu Dhabi itself and in the Buraimi Oasis at Al Ain.

However, it is Dubai which has been the most ambitious (even reckless) in the industrialisation stakes. As a late entrant, for it was behind its northern neighbours in finding oil, it has decided to catch up at the expense of duplicating facilities existing elsewhere in the Gulf, particularly in Bahrain. It has therefore constructed another aluminium smelter and a huge dry-dock facility, capable of taking a million-ton tanker, one of 500,000 tons and one of 350,000 tons simultaneously. There was much international headshaking over these (British-built) dry-docks, which were universally expected to be uncommercial, and they remained inoperative for four years after completion, before a contract for their management was awarded to the British company A & P Appledore. But the Gulf War at least temporarily brought them very much into their own with ships damaged by Iranian and Iraqi attacks limping in for repair there. Qatar as well as Bahrain has suffered duplication of its facilities by Dubai, since it has also built a steel mill.

Offering safe anchorage in its creek, Dubai was an important trading post long before oil was found and has a strong merchant tradition. With extensive new port facilities, it carries on considerable entrepôt trade, supplying those Emirates which are still not oil-rich, and even Oman which now is. It had a big reputation for gold trading before the Gulf War, importing gold in large quantities, perfectly legally, and shipping it in small boats to India and Pakistan, where the importation by the inhabitants of those countries was by no means legal. There are rumours that this experience in what was at least at one end smuggling has been put to profitable use in semi-licit trade with Iran in the disturbed conditions of the Gulf War, but on that there are naturally no statistics available. This extensive entrepôt trade by Dubai has to be borne in mind when interpreting the import figures from the UK for the Gulf States.

Oman lies mainly outside the Gulf (it has however frontage on to the Straits of Hormuz, which has made it of great strategic importance in the Gulf War). Its ruler at the time when oil was found, the charming but ultra-conservative Sultan Said bin Taimur, was unwilling to develop his state, for a mixture of psychological and religious reasons,[7] but his son Qabus, who took over in a palace coup in 1970, is much more modern in outlook[8] and development has gone ahead since his accession.

However, this has so far involved not very much industrialisation. Infrastructure expenditure had to take priority in what was an extremely backward country, so there has been much work on building ports, roads and airports, plus social requirements, particularly schools and hospitals. Agriculture has long been important in Oman since, unlike the Gulf States proper, it gets some rainfall from the monsoon, and money has rightly been spent on its improvement and expansion. Oman produces dates, limes, bananas and vegetables, and is suited to the rearing of livestock. Light industries are now beginning to come into existence. Joint ventures with foreigners are permitted if the local ownership is at least 65 per cent, and some have been established. A 5-year tax holiday is given to companies satisfying the Government that they are engaged in a 'development' project.

A more encouraging account can be given of British participation in the development of the smaller Gulf States than was the case in Saudi Arabia. Most of these countries had of course close links with the UK from the days when they were under British protection, and they had little knowledge of other Western countries. In this respect they were quite unlike Saudi Arabia which, because ARAMCO was American-owned, naturally looked towards the United States. British firms therefore had a head start in the Gulf States and performed well enough there to keep this advantage, even when British protection had gone and the now independent states had much wider contacts.

Particularly striking was the virtual monopoly, despite international tenders, of Sir William Halcrow and Partners as consulting engineers and of Costain as contractors in winning work in Dubai when its ambitious industrialisation programme got under way. Costain had brought in one of the early projects ahead of time and below budget, and the Ruler, Shaikh Rashid, liked to employ those he already knew and trusted rather than look for new friends. British machinery was familiar in the Gulf States and much of it was imported as soon as it could be afforded. Some ground was lost here by late deliveries, all too often with no forewarning and no convincing explanation, but the better British firms kept their customers happy and their own exports flowing, as the trade statistics reveal (see Chapters 26 and 31).

The Gulf Cooperation Council (GCC)

It was said above that the Gulf States originally had no institution, other than to a small extent OAPEC, for coordinating their industrialisation programmes and avoiding duplication. This gap has now been filled, in principle and to some extent in practice, by the establishment of the GCC. Saudi Arabia is very much its leading member, the others being Bahrain, Kuwait, Oman, Qatar and the UAE. The Gulf War forced upon it a preoccupation with defence coordination and internal security, but it was always envisaged as very much an economic and political body, and is in no sense a military alliance.

The Council came into existence in February 1981 and a flurry of meetings followed during that year, including three at ministerial level. This pace in holding conferences has been kept up subsequently but it is less clear that the activity has produced much in the way of practical results. Economic cooperation (except in keeping Iraq, a non-member, financially afloat) has become less urgent, since most major investments have been inhibited by the Gulf War and by the fall in revenues which has resulted from the oil slump of the 1980s (see Chapter 29). However, looking to the future, the machinery does now exist for coordinating economic investment programmes when the Gulf War is over and when oil prices rise again, as they are forecast to do in the 1990s.

The GCC has adopted a Unified Economic Agreement; this was signed in 1981 and was intended to come into force in March 1983. It partially did so, but implementation is still incomplete. Some steps have been made towards a common market by the abolition of customs duties between members (not always observed in practice) and a phased movement towards a common external tariff. A Gulf Investment Corporation (GIC) has been established and there are plans (which have run into difficulties and seem likely to take time) for alignment of currencies. But none of the member states has surrendered any sovereignty to the GCC and its pleas for coordination and harmonisation seem often to be ignored. As a prime example, yet another Emirate in the UAE, Umm al-Qaiwain, is planning to set up yet another aluminium smelter, and there are rumours that a fourth and even a fifth such smelter may come into being in the 1990s.

The GIC has an authorised capital of $2,100 million, to be subscribed equally by the six GCC members; of this only $540 million has so far been called. It is not an aid-giving body and its investments are expected to generate profits. It began work in 1984 and has had to build up staff and establish procedures. It is therefore understandable that it has not yet achieved much except to identify possible projects,[9] and those mainly in a reactive way in response to approaches for help in financing other people's ideas. Of 90 projects examined by the end of 1987, 11 had been approved, with a total GIC commitment of only around $60 million. However, its own project research was then beginning to come through and it seems likely to start using its available investment funds rather more actively from 1988 onwards. It has probably been wise to hasten slowly, especially in an atmosphere of relative recession for oil producers.

Another institution which deserves a mention is the Gulf Organization for Industrial Consulting (GOIC). This was set up in Qatar in 1976, so it predates the GCC. It also differs from it in including Iraq as well as the six GCC members. Its remit is to prepare economic and industrial studies for the region. Naturally, it has now established close links as an adviser and consultant with the GCC, and especially with the GIC. It is ready to advise both public and private clients and is tending to concentrate on medium-scale ventures. Its most important project so far has been the Gulf Aluminium Rolling Mill Company (GARMCO) set up in Bahrain to process the output of the smelter there. One of its favoured plans has been held up by the war, the development of float glass production in Iraq with cooperation from the British company of Pilkington Brothers; its capacity was to have been 100,000 tons p.a. This seems a desirable project when peace returns, although no doubt a large reconstruction programme will have to take priority.

28 Post-Revolutionary Iran and the Gulf War

The fall of the Shah had come as a shock, especially to the USA which had regarded him as one of the two bulwarks, along with Saudi Arabia, of Western policy in the region. Yet his reputation had been sullied internationally by his autocratic rule and the excesses of his secret police SAVAK, so there was no obvious reason why his revolutionary successors should not have gained support in the UN and in the world generally. There was no ill-feeling about their decision in 1979 to withdraw from CENTO. But from the first they seemed to care nothing for international opinion and to be almost determined to isolate themselves. This was partly the result of their rigid Shi'ism. They regarded the theocratic state they rapidly established in Iran as a model for export to other Islamic countries, whether Shi'i or Sunni, and the non-Islamic world was for them a matter of unconcern, or even for contempt.

The USA, as a former strong supporter of the Shah, was viewed with particular hatred and suspicion, and this quickly resulted in the Embassy hostage crisis, when young extremists were allowed to occupy the American Embassy in Tehran and seize its staff. Such a blatant breach of diplomatic immunities could not fail to unite international opinion against the revolution. Iranian funds in US banks were blocked and American exports to Iran, including a large arms shipment which had already been paid for, were suspended. Other countries scaled down the size of their diplomatic representation in Tehran or closed down their Embassies entirely. Although a negotiated end to the hostage situation was eventually reached, through the mediation of Algeria, and the American Embassy staff were allowed to leave, the Iranian regime took a delight in humiliating President Carter (who had authorised a commando operation to free the hostages which turned into a fiasco) by holding up their release until just after a new President had taken over from him. The settlement involved the release by the Americans of some Iranian funds, a complex banking operation in which the Bank of England played a key part.

Opposition to the USA implied no love for the USSR. Ayatollah Khomeini regarded Soviet atheism as anathema, and the Iranian Tudeh (Communist) Party as a subversive movement to be watched quite as suspiciously as it had been by the Shah. In Afghanistan, where Soviet troops were propping up a puppet regime, Iranian sympathies were with the rebel mujahidin as Islamic believers and it seemed likely that Iran would give them material help. There was also sympathy for the Muslims demanding religious freedom inside the Soviet Union, some of whom were Shi'a, and Moscow certainly feared the effect that the Iranian revolution might have in encouraging an Islamic revival which was already under way in Soviet Asia.

The supply of Iranian natural gas to the Soviet Union soon proved a bone of contention. Deliveries through the pipeline had fallen off in the period of the revolution, as a result of the general disruption of oil production, and Moscow found itself faced by a demand from Tehran for quintupling of the price for Iranian gas, to bring it up to world market levels regardless of the existing contract. When the Soviet side rejected this demand, the Iranians cut off gas exports entirely in March 1980. They also insisted on a reduction in the size of the Soviet diplomatic staff in Tehran, closed the Soviet Consulate in Rasht, banned Soviet reporters, shut down the Iran-Soviet Bank and suspended the Soviet-Iranian Cultural Relations Society. The Kremlin could certainly feel outraged by such treatment in view of the kind words that Brezhnev had originally spoken about the Iranian revolution.[1]

Iran's immediate neighbours, whatever they had thought about the Shah, viewed the Ayatollah's regime with a distinct lack of enthusiasm. Those with large Shi'a elements in their population were particularly alarmed at the prospect of unrest among them. Bahrain has a Shi'a majority, which admittedly had made clear at the time of the UN referendum that it did not wish to be under Iranian rule. Saudi Arabia has a Shi'a minority in its eastern region, where its oilfields lie. Most concerned of all was Iraq. Not only is the southern part of Iraq inhabited by a Shi'a population which outnumbers the northern Sunnis, but the Shi'a holy places of Karbala and Najaf are in Iraq. And the Iraq Government knew all about Khomeini, who had lived among them in exile for years before moving on to Paris; they regarded him as a fanatic and a trouble-maker.

Antipathy between Iran and Iraq is historically very deeply rooted. Quite apart from the early quarrels about the Imamate which had led to the original split between Sunnis and Shi'is, there were two causes of more recent disputes. These were the Kurds and the Shatt al-Arab. The Kurds are a linguistically distinct group of tribes living in the Zagros mountains and in the eastern extension of the Taurus range. They have never been a nation state, though they nearly became one under the Treaty of Sèvres in 1920. Having failed in that, they have ever since given trouble to Iran, Iraq, Syria and Turkey,[2] within whose borders most of them live. They are a warlike people, helped in their trouble-making by the mountainous terrain they inhabit. Iraq finds them particularly dangerous, since they live close to the main Iraqi oilfields in the Kirkuk/Mosul region. It might be thought that Iran and Iraq would have a common interest in keeping order in their adjoining Kurdish areas, but it has rarely worked out that way. Rather, each country has from time to time used the Kurds to stir up unrest in the territory of its neighbour.

The Shatt al-Arab is the sheet of water produced by the confluence of the Tigris and the Euphrates, and is of great importance to both Iran and Iraq for navigation to their ports, Basrah in the case of Iraq, and Khorramshahr and Abadan in the case of Iran. A border dispute in this region had existed for centuries between the Ottoman Empire and Persia,[3] and had if anything been exacerbated during the period of the British mandate over Iraq after the First World War. In 1937, a Treaty was signed in Tehran between Iran and Iraq, declaring the Shatt open to the merchant shipping of all nations and to the warships of the two contracting parties. Jurisdiction over the whole waterway, with the exception of anchorage zones off Khorramshahr and Abadan, was assigned to Iraq, without prejudice to the user rights of both nations. This meant, however, that Iranian ships had to take on board Iraqi pilots and to pay tolls to Iraq. When, following the announcement of Britain's decision to withdraw its forces from the Gulf, the Shah was set upon taking over the hegemony of the area, one of his early moves was to denounce the 1937 Treaty. This he did on 19 April 1969 and five days later the Iranian navy, escorted by fighter aircraft, convoyed an Iranian merchant ship through the Shatt without payment of Iraqi tolls.

Iraq was then unprepared to enforce its 1937 rights. To strengthen its position, it concluded a Treaty of Friendship with the Soviet Union on 9 April 1972. The Shah's response was to give the Iraqi Kurds sufficient support to stir them into rebellion in August 1972, bringing to an end sensible plans for Kurdish autonomy by 1974 to which the Iraqi Government had agreed in 1970. The rebellion proved difficult for the Iraqis to suppress; finally they decided to cut their losses by signing the Algiers Agreement of 6 March 1975, under which Iran undertook to end its support for the Kurds, and Iraq, in return, accepted the *thalweg* (a mid-channel line) in the Shatt al-Arab as the international boundary. This Agreement seemed to work; Iranian support for the Kurds ceased and the Iraqis were able to put down their rebellion, while peace reigned temporarily in the Shatt.

Although the Iraqi Government made some initial attempts to win Khomeini's friendship after he came to power in Iran,[4] these soon ceased when in June 1979 an anti-Baath propaganda campaign was mounted from Tehran, with broadcasts calling on Iraqis to rise against their rulers. The Iraqi response was the expulsion of Iranian citizens and the suppression of Shi'ite political movements, particularly the Da'awa Party. Relations deteriorated towards outright hostilities, with incidents such as an unsuccessful attempt by Iranian agents to assassinate the Iraqi Deputy Prime Minister on 1 April 1980 and reports from both sides of border skirmishes.

In September 1980, fighting reached the scale of actual war. On 10 September Iraqi troops occupied two strips of border territory which the Iranians had failed to return to Iraq as they should have done under the 1975 Agreement.[5] Artillery exchanges across the Shatt followed between 11 and 15 September and on 17 September the Iraqi President formally denounced the 1975 Agreement and reiterated Iraq's ancient claim to full sovereignty over the Shatt al-Arab. On 28 September, he put forward a set of war aims, concentrating mainly on the Shatt and on non-interference by Iran in its neighbours' affairs, but also interestingly demanding the restoration to the Shaikhs of Sharjah and Ras al-Khaimah of the three islands seized by Iran in 1971 (see Chapter 17). This suggested that Iraq was aspiring not only to taking complete control of the Shatt but also to becoming the protector of Arab rights in the Gulf as a whole.

It is not for this book to trace in detail the course of the Gulf War.[6] Suffice it to say that it has moved through three main phases. The first was an Iraqi advance into Iranian territory, including the capture of Khorramshahr but not of Abadan, though the refinery there was heavily damaged. The second was a series of Iranian offensives to drive Iraqi troops out of Iran and advance across the border, particularly in the south where attempts were made to capture Basrah or cut the Basrah-Baghdad road, without success. The third has been a land stalemate, coupled with an Iraqi effort to wreck Iran's economy by air-raids on shipping designed to stop or at least reduce Iranian oil exports through the Gulf, these in turn leading to Iranian attacks on shipping on the Arab side of the Gulf.

This third phase continues at the time of writing and has had international repercussions on which more must be said. Many attempts to bring about a settlement of the war, or even a cease-fire, have failed, with even a unanimous Security Council resolution (rare event) so far proving ineffective, but these attempts will certainly be continued and must surely eventually succeed; both sides have suffered heavy casualties and great damage, so that there is a growing mutual feeling of war-weariness, which must ultimately prevail.

The economic consequences of the Gulf War have naturally

been considerable, both for the participants and for the world which still depends so heavily on Middle East oil (for its global impact see Chapter 30).

In the early years of the war, Iraq adopted a policy of carrying on its development programme as though peace still reigned.[7] Its navy was no match for the Iranians, so exports from its southern ports ceased, including oil exports from its main terminal at Fao. A number of merchant ships of other nations were trapped in the Shatt al-Arab; efforts to negotiate their release failed and they became war casualties. Alternative port facilities were therefore required by Iraq. Kuwait supplied these to a large extent, but the Iraqi Government also financed the enlargement of the Jordanian port of Aqaba as a further supply channel. Overland freight through Turkey assumed increased importance.

The annual Baghdad Trade Fair was kept going and attracted plenty of foreign exhibitors, including many from Britain. The Iraqis at this stage clearly expected the war to be a short one, relying on the fact that the Iranian army had been weakened by desertions and purges after the fall of the Shah, but in that they miscalculated. After 1982, their foreign exchange reserves became depleted and development programmes had to be postponed for the duration of the war, so that Iraq has settled down to what amounts to a siege economy.

Having lost its opportunities for oil exports through the Gulf, Iraq became dependent on its pipeline outlets to the Mediterranean. In the first nine months of 1980, Iraq had been exporting an average of 3.4 million b/d; in October 1980, this fell sharply to 500,000 b/d. It recovered gradually, to 1 million b/d by September 1981 and 1.2 million b/d by March 1982. That was not in theory the maximum capacity of the pipelines; the line through Turkey could carry 700,000 b/d and that through Syria was rated at 1.4 million b/d. But the second of these lines had long been unreliable. Its outlet to Tripoli in Lebanon had since 1975–6 been closed as a result originally of the Lebanese civil war, leaving only the Syrian terminal at Banias. This too had been closed intermittently over the years, mainly as a result of bad relations between Iraq and Syria, where the two Baathi regimes had no love for each other. It had therefore been neglected, building up arrears of maintenance, and could only operate well below its theoretical capacity. Worse still for Iraq, the war found Syria tending to side with Iran against it, and after the signature of a 10-year trade agreement between Syria and Iran in March 1982 the Banias line was closed, bringing Iraqi exports down again to a maximum of 700,000 b/d.

This would have been a crippling blow had it not been for financial aid to Iraq on a massive scale from Saudi Arabia and Kuwait, and to a lesser extent from Qatar and UAE. The size of this aid has been regarded as a war secret, but there is no doubt that it amounts to many billions of dollars. It was for some time given the cloak of an oil 'loan' to Iraq, to be repaid in kind at some unspecified future date, and the output from the Saudi/Kuwaiti Neutral Zone was hypothecated for this purpose. But the length of the war has made any such cloak extremely threadbare. Iraq has taken steps to develop new pipeline outlets, both through Turkey to the Mediterranean and through Saudi Arabia to a Red Sea terminal north of Yanbu. In recent OPEC negotiations it has refused to accept any firm ceiling for its oil exports (see Chapter 30).

Iran saw the Abadan Refinery crippled in the first phase of the war, so ceased to be an exporter of oil products, but Iraq was not initially able to reduce Iranian crude exports to any major extent. The main crude terminal had already been moved from Abadan to Kharg Island in the northern Gulf, a purpose-built terminal for supertankers, supplied by pipelines from the mainland. Although Iraq had air superiority and Kharg was well within range of its planes, it had originally no suitable air-to-ground missiles to reduce the terminal's throughput. This changed with Iraq's purchase from France of a plentiful supply of Exocet missiles (whose power had been demonstrated by Argentina in the Falklands War). In the third stage of the Gulf war, the Iraqis had therefore been able to attack Kharg heavily.

Iran is almost totally dependent on its oil exports to provide the foreign exchange needed to carry on the war, so has had to improvise means of keeping its exports flowing. It has developed new terminals further south in the Gulf, most recently at Larak close to the Straits of Hormuz, and has chartered a fleet of tankers to run the gauntlet between Kharg, which has never been put completely out of action, and Larak. These tankers have suffered severely from Iraqi air attacks, but have usually been capable of being patched up again (often in Dubai's dry-docks) and sent back to their dangerous task. It is a very expensive way of exporting oil, but Iran has no option save to continue it or to make peace, which it has so far refused to do except on terms which it knows to be unacceptable to Iraq.

As a reprisal for these Iraqi air attacks on its oil exports, Iran has adopted a policy of delivering matching attacks on shipping trading to ports on the Arab shore of the Gulf. Its logic for this has been that the Arab states are co-belligerents with Iraq through their financing of the Iraqi war effort. The first to be singled out for this treatment was Kuwait, which was doubly guilty in Iranian eyes since it was passing freight through to Iraq as well as supplying money. Kuwait decided to look for safety for its shipping by using the flags of more powerful nations; it opened negotiations to this end with both the Soviet Union and USA and met with success in both these directions. The Kremlin agreed to charter Soviet-registered ships to Kuwait. Washington accepted the transfer of Kuwaiti ships to its flag and Britain, a little later, did likewise.

In consequence, each of these three powers has found itself under an increased obligation to protect shipping flying its flag from Iranian attacks. This has led to the concentration of warships which has now developed in the Gulf. British warships had in fact been operating quietly in the area since the beginning of the Gulf War, and since 1986 three frigates (the Armilla patrol) have been taking turns to accompany British merchant ships, not indeed to Kuwait but as far north as Jebel Ali (the main port of Dubai).[8] They have kept a low profile and the Iranians seem to have accepted their presence to the extent of avoiding action against either them or shipping under their charge. Two Soviet destroyers have equally quietly escorted the three tankers the USSR has chartered to Kuwait.

The American presence has been very different in nature, and massive, including aircraft carriers, and has had a distinctly high profile. They escort convoys of American-flag shipping the full length of the Gulf, to and from Kuwait. Particularly in their early days in the Gulf they gave an impression of coat-trailing, as though hoping that some Iranian indiscretion would give them a pretext to use their massive power against Iranian targets both at sea and on land, but this policy has moderated more recently.

Iranian mining of Gulf waters, particularly of the channels leading to the Arab ports, produced a still wider build-up of European naval units. As well as from Britain, minesweepers have come from Belgium, France, Italy and the Netherlands. They have worked in collaboration but not as a NATO force.

The Iranians (despite having spent an estimated $1000 million on Chinese 'Silkworm' missiles which could attack shipping transiting the Straits of Hormuz) have for the most part been sufficiently disciplined to avoid bringing down major reprisals upon themselves. Merchant ships, including Kuwaiti-owned vessels, under American, British and Soviet flags have therefore passed through the Gulf virtually unscathed, but ships of other nations have suffered quite heavily from Iranian attacks; many of them have been holed and not a few have been destroyed.[9] There has been some loss of life, though less perhaps than might have been expected (tanker crews are small these days).[10] There have also been large repair bills, with the inevitable corollary of high insurance premiums on all shipping bound for the Gulf.[11]

29 Israel and the Invasion of Lebanon

The state of Israel has never been fully at peace. Surrounded by enemies from the day of its birth, it has had to spend vast sums on defence. The counterpart was that, partly because of its apparent vulnerability, it also received vast sums, in grants and loans from the US Government, in donations and investments from international Jewry, and in reparations from West Germany. Apart from defence, it spent enormous amounts on the absorption of Jewish immigrants, especially poor immigrants from the Arab lands who no longer felt safe in their birthplaces. There too there was some counterpart, in the properties taken over from Palestinian Arabs who had fled as refugees, but it was more than offset in the expenditure required.

In foreign trade, the Arab Boycott shut Israel off from what might have been its natural markets and also from regional producers of such vital commodities as grain and oil (though for oil Iran was a regular supplier). Israel was therefore forced to trade at longer distance, adding to its costs and compelling it to achieve high quality standards for its exports, so that they could compete in the markets of the developed world.

That need, together with its determination to give its population a 'European' rather than a 'Middle Eastern' standard of living (in the days before oil riches in the Middle East), inspired Israel to progress from the status of a developing to that of a developed country. Beset always by balance of payments problems, it could not have done so without generous overseas aid. Nevertheless, the achievement, over a short space of time, was a remarkable one and does great credit to the skills and dedication of its population.

In the process, Israel achieves a high standard of published statistics, so it is not difficult to chart its progress. Between 1949 and 1973, its GNP grew at the staggering average rate of nearly 10 per cent p.a. It then went through a bad patch for four years (caused mainly by heavy defence expenditure after the 1973 war), being 5 per cent in 1974, zero in 1975 and only 1 per cent in 1976 and much of 1977, before shooting up again to nearly 12 per cent in the last quarter of 1977. The breakdown of its GNP shows a pattern typical of a developed country, nearly 7 per cent from agriculture, more than 28 per cent from industry, and a little over 20 per cent from the public services. More than half of the working population is engaged in services of all kinds. Growth at so high a rate is the more meritorious as Israel lacks most raw materials, especially oil, and its agriculture is heavily dependent on irrigation from by no means plentiful water resources, which are very skilfully managed.

For its first twenty-nine years Israel, ruled by coalitions in which the Labour Party was the dominant factor, followed socialist policies. Particularly notable was the very important part played in the economy by the Trade Union Federation, the Histadrut, which engaged as a principal in a wide range of development projects, investing its own funds in them for the benefit of its members.

In 1977, after the slowdown of growth already mentioned, a right-wing coalition led by the Likud Party took power and introduced its New Economic Programme, based on monetarist policies combined with a strong movement towards liberalisation from controls. The Israeli currency was freed to float, most foreign exchange regulations were abolished, VAT was raised to 12 per cent, and there was a sweeping away of import levies, export subsidies and the travel tax. This revolution in the economy had its effect, with growth resuming at a high level. But the price that had to be paid was a surge in inflation. Faced with rising unemployment, the trade unions at first agreed to fight inflation by holding down wages, but as prices continued to rise this policy could not be sustained and Histadrut returned to wage demands designed to match or run ahead of inflation. By 1980, average annual price increases had soared to around 100 per cent. The floating Israeli shekel plunged on the currency markets.

The Camp David Agreements brought Israel peace on its Egyptian front, but the resulting economic benefits were much smaller than Israel had hoped and in the short term were more than offset by extra costs. The Israeli army had to be redeployed from Sinai. New or upgraded military airfields were needed in the Negev. Civilian settlers removed from Sinai (protesting bitterly) had to be rehoused. Part of these costs were met by American aid grants for the purpose, totalling $3000 million, but this covered by no means all of them. The return to Egypt of the Sinai oilfields was a great loss; although it was agreed that the oil from them should still come to Israel, it now had to be paid for. With no boycott barriers between Egypt and Israel, some trade began to flow, and Israeli ships were at last allowed to transit the Suez Canal, but a series of political disputes kept relations between the two countries well below cordiality, and one small patch of territory near Eilat was (and is) still disputed.

So the positive benefits to Israel, even allowing for services such as tourism, were disappointing.[1] There had been dreams that Egypt would supply Israeli needs of water, oil and gas, along with cheap labour, and that Israeli industry would expand to supply the Egyptian market, but very little of this materialised. The Egyptian economy had its own serious troubles under Sadat (see Chapter 23) and when Mubarak succeeded him a policy of gradual rapprochement with the moderate Arab countries ruled out the forging of anything approaching economic integration with Israel.

One industrial field in which Israel made particularly rapid progress was that of armaments manufacture. Unwilling to depend to more than the minimum extent which was unavoidable on other countries, the Israeli Government gave this a very high priority and achieved spectacular results, even in such sophisticated arms as aircraft and missiles, which might have been thought beyond the economic capabilities of so small a country. Israel was able to enter the select group of countries which are arms exporters. Even where Israel imported weapons assemblies, improvements in them were often effected. Thus Centurion tanks, purchased from Britain at low prices as they were replaced in the British Army of the Rhine by Chieftains, were 'upgunned' with much more powerful guns to make them a match for the Soviet tanks used by Syria and Egypt. The Israelis also developed their own tanks known as Merkavas.

One weapon which the Israelis manufactured very secretly was a nuclear bomb. As early as the 1960s, it was suspected that plutonium was being diverted from the nuclear research reactor at Dimona for weapons manufacture. The Israelis denied this but a major leak to a British newspaper by an Israeli technician employed at the plant appears to have confirmed that some scores of bombs have been produced over the years and are stockpiled for an ultimate emergency.[2] Despite strenuous efforts, particularly by Libya, to encourage the production of an 'Arab' nuclear weapon, or its purchase, it seems that this is an area in which Israel is far ahead of its neighbours. More recently, it has been reported[3] that a nuclear-capable Jericho-2 ballistic missile has been successfully tested with a range of over 500 miles.

Following the end of the Lebanese Civil War of 1975–6 (see Chapter 22), Israel continued and developed the links with South Lebanon which had been opened up through its 'good fence' policy. The Syrians, warned by Israel on 14 April 1976 to keep north of a 'Red Line' approximating to the Nabatiyah – Hasbaya line fixed in the 1949 General Armistice Agreement between Israel and Lebanon as the northern boundary of a limited-forces area,[4] had tacitly complied with the instruction, leaving a power vacuum in South Lebanon. The Palestinian guerrillas who had moved north during the civil war began to move south again when that war was over. They found facing them, as a surrogate of the Israeli Army, a splinter force from the Lebanese Army commanded by a Christian, Major Haddad. This force, consisting mainly of Christians but with some Shi'a recruits (the Shi'a of South Lebanon had no wish to see the Palestinians return to their area), had been taken under Israel's wing for both supplies and training, although it still professed its loyalty to the (Christian) Lebanese Commander-in-Chief and to the (Christian) Lebanese President.

During 1977, there were several clashes between Haddad's men and Palestinian guerrillas; an attempted cease-fire (reached with American support) soon broke down[5] and the guerrillas began to launch sporadic rocket attacks into Israeli border villages, which they could do from beyond the very limited areas controlled by Haddad. On 11 March 1978, Palestinian infiltrators from Lebanon seized an Israeli bus near Tel Aviv; thirty-seven people were killed and an Israeli reprisal was inevitable. It came on 15 March with a large-scale invasion of South Lebanon, which was occupied up to the River Litani, except for an enclave around the port of Tyre.

This invasion did not succeed in its ostensible purpose of wiping out the Palestinian guerrillas; they simply headed north out of the battle area, leaving the Shi'a villagers to bear the brunt of the destruction. It did however have two consequences. The first was the establishment by the United Nations of yet another peacekeeping force, UNIFIL (United Nations Force in Lebanon), set up by Security Council Resolution No.425 to assist the Government of Lebanon to restore its authority in South Lebanon and allowed by the Israelis to play a buffer role south of the Litani, though not right up to the border. The second was the enlargement of the area entrusted by the Israelis to Major Haddad as a 'peace zone'; this now ran the full length of the border, with a depth of 5 to 8 kilometres most of the way but a larger bulge in the east to include the main local town of Marjayoun.

The Israelis thus secured a double buffer to protect their border. However, despite the presence of UNIFIL, the Lebanese Government was not able to regain control of South Lebanon. A force from the partly rebuilt Lebanese Army was ordered south by President Sarkis on 31 July 1978 but came under artillery fire from Major Haddad and withdrew. This at least demonstrated where Haddad's real loyalties lay; on 18 April 1979 he went further by declaring the 'independence' of his little fiefdom under the grand title of 'Free Lebanon'.

UNIFIL, despite being of considerable size by UN standards with about 6000 troops of high quality, was never able to act as a wholly effective buffer between the Palestinian guerrillas and Haddad's forces, which grew in numbers by taking in more Shi'a recruits. In July 1981, the Israeli Air Force carried out attacks on Palestinian positions between Sidon and Nabatiyah and the Palestinians retaliated with rocket barrages on North Israel. A ceasefire was arranged by Ambassador Philip Habib, an American of Lebanese descent who had become President Reagan's special representative for the Middle East; it proved much more lasting than most ceasefires in that troubled area, to the fury of Palestinian extremists, who turned their attention to attacking Jewish targets in Europe.

There were several of these terrorist attacks, on a Vienna synagogue, a bus full of Jewish children in Antwerp, and on 3 June 1982 the shooting (not fatal, although nearly so) of the Israeli Ambassador in London. The Israelis, who had been growing increasingly restive, decided that the time had come to teach the PLO a decisive lesson[6] and beyond that to achieve wider political objectives.[7] They launched a full-scale invasion of Lebanon on 6 June.

The operation was codenamed Operation Peace for Galilee (despite the fact that Galilee had in fact had peace since the Habib ceasefire of the previous July). This gave the impression, which was apparently shared by several members of the Israeli cabinet, that it would be another limited invasion, probably again to the Litani River, and official statements suggested that the aim was to extend the 'peace zone' in South Lebanon to a depth of twenty-five miles, the range of the rockets then in use by the Palestinians. UNIFIL, which was certainly not capable of fighting the Israeli Army, stood aside, and the Israeli forces swept past them. Within a very few days it became clear that the Litani was not the objective, as the Israelis pushed up the Beqaa Valley and through the Shouf Mountains towards the main Beirut-Damascus road.

It is outside the scope of this book to give details of this operation.[8] It is, in any case, recent enough to be remembered by many readers. In brief it can be said that the Syrian forces in the Beqaa were completely outclassed by the Israelis, their Soviet-built ground-to-air missiles proving totally ineffective against the electronic and other counter-measures of the Israeli air force; that the PLO in Beirut fought off Israeli attacks for over two months but finally had to surrender, with the indefatigable Philip Habib negotiating yet another ceasefire on 12 August 1982; and that between 21 August and 6 September some 9000 Palestinian fighters and 3500 Syrian troops were evacuated from Lebanon by sea and road, under the supervision of a multinational force consisting of American, French and Italian contingents. Arafat himself moved eventually to Tunisia to establish there a new headquarters of the PLO, an arrangement which the Tunisians could hardly avoid as Tunis was already the Arab League headquarters following its transfer from Cairo after the suspension of Egypt from the League in the wake of the Camp David agreements.

The Israelis had thus achieved one of their main objectives, the elimination of the Palestinian 'state within a state' in Lebanon. In the process they had shocked the world by the ruthlessness of their offensive, particularly their bombing of Beirut. They did not however succeed in their hidden further objective of establishing in Lebanon a friendly and effective Christian Government with which they could conclude a peace treaty and a virtual alliance. It was an open secret that most of the arms imported by the Phalange from Cyprus during the Civil War had come from Israel, and that such support had continued after that war was over. Beshir Gemayel, the leader of the Phalangist militia, was the only candidate for the Presidential election which was now due (no Maronite was prepared to stand against him). He was likely to prove a 'strong' President and one who could force through a pro-Israeli policy, or so at least the Israeli Government believed. With some difficulty, a quorum of the Parliament was convened to elect him on 23 August 1982. On 10 September the multinational force left Beirut. But on 14 September the building in which Beshir Gemayel was addressing his party supporters was blown up and he himself was killed.

The Israeli reaction was to move their troops into the mainly Muslim area of West Beirut. Their excuse was a claim that 2000 Palestinian terrorists had not evacuated the city but were still in hiding (an unlikely story), and that they were acting to avoid bloodshed in the chaotic conditions occasioned by Gemayel's murder. So far from avoiding bloodshed, what they in fact did was to connive at a search of the Palestinian refugee camps of Sabra and Shatila by Christian Lebanese militiamen, many of them the survivors of the Civil War massacre of Christians at Damour (see Chapter 22). While the Israelis guarded the camp perimeters in south-west Beirut, the militia for two days and nights were given a free hand to take their revenge on the women, children and old men left behind by the evacuated Palestinian fighters. The number massacred will never be known, but it was certainly well over 1000. It was a shameful episode which horrified the world, including very many in Israel itself.

The multinational force which had so recently left Beirut hastily returned and the Israelis pulled out of West Beirut. On 23 September, Amin Gemayel, brother of the murdered Beshir, was sworn in as President. He was a less forceful character than Beshir, but the Israeli Government still hoped that they might be able to negotiate a peace treaty with him. Their military presence was a bargaining card in this process; talks on the terms of an Israeli evacuation of Lebanon began on 28 December 1982, with the Americans acting as a third party in the discussions.

On 17 May 1983 an agreement was signed, which was technically not a Peace Treaty but was a considerable step towards one. Its main provision was the termination of the state of war between the two parties and the recognition of the armistice line between Lebanon and Israel as an international boundary. Each side, but in practice Lebanon, undertook to prevent its territory being used as a base for incursions into the territory of the other. South Lebanon was declared a 'security region', divided into Zones A and B. The southern Zone B, running from the mouth of the Zahrani River to the Israeli ceasefire line on the Golan Heights, was to be garrisoned by a Lebanese brigade which would incorporate (and in practice consist of) Major Haddad's force. Zone A, following the Awali River from just north of Sidon and crossing the Beqaa to a point on the Syrian frontier north of Rashaya, would also be garrisoned by one brigade, this time of Lebanese regular troops. There would be a Joint Liaison Committee, charged to reach agreements on the movement of goods, products and persons (so ending the trade boycott). The military commanders on both sides of the border would be linked by direct radio and telephone circuits. The Americans' role as mediators was written into the agreement.

It was a Peace Treaty in all but name and the Israelis began their withdrawal from Lebanon by falling back from Beirut to the Awali River on 4 September 1983 (a fortified position there had already been prepared at a reputed cost of £25 million). But, unfortunately for Israeli plans, President Gemayel was not able to make the settlement stick in the face of Syrian opposition. After talks in Damascus between him and President Assad, the Lebanese Cabinet decided on 5 March 1984 to abrogate the agreement.

It was not long before Lebanon was plunged again into civil war. As soon as the Israelis withdrew to the Awali River, fighting broke out in the Shouf between the Christian militia and the Druze, with the latter getting the upper hand, although their advance was halted at Suq al-Gharb by a supreme effort on the part of the Christians (with some American naval fire in support). The Muslim militias in West Beirut resumed their struggle for local supremacy and a practice of hostage-taking was extended from the holding of Lebanese opponents to the capture of foreigners working in Beirut, some of them long-term residents. On 4 July 1986, some 500 Syrian troops were sent into West Beirut for the first time since 1982. The (Shi'a) Amal and (Druze) PSP militias (both dependent upon supplies from Syria) announced the closure of their offices there. By mid-July the Syrians appeared to have restored calm to West Beirut, although it was notable that they had not cleared the pro-Iranian Shi'a Hezbollah militia from the South Beirut slums (where the foreign hostages were thought to be held).

Meanwhile, some of the Palestinian fighters had been returning surreptitiously to Lebanon. This was not surprising, since many of them had perforce left their wives and children behind them when they were evacuated and were worried for their safety. They went into hiding in the Palestinian refugee camps. What ensued was a siege of these camps by Shi'a forces, with the refugees within them soon reduced to a state of utter misery and starvation by the blockade which the Shi'a were able to impose. On 22 February 1987 President Assad grasped the nettle by ordering no less than 7000 Syrian troops, backed by tanks and artillery, into Beirut. This force was too strong for the militias and the seige of the camps was lifted. There, at the time of writing, matters remain. The Syrians have once again restored an uneasy peace to West Beirut; East Beirut lives a parody of the life of happier days, with nightclubs open for trade again; and South Beirut, with its wretched hostages, remains in Shi'a hands.

This renewed civil war delivered a final blow to the already battered economy. This time not even the Lebanese currency could withstand the pressures; by 1987 it had suffered complete collapse. At the beginning of 1986 the Lebanese pound stood at just over 18 to the $US (inflation in 1986 averaged over 100 per cent and by the end of that year 80 per cent of staple foodstuffs had to be imported). By March 1987 the ratio was £L106 and by June £L125 to the dollar. On 11 July 1987, when the £L fell to 184 to the dollar, the official interbank foreign exchange market was closed. Life has gone on, largely because so many Lebanese have relatives abroad to finance them. Foreign currencies, particularly the US dollar, now provide the only useful medium of exchange. It is a sad fate for what was once the banking centre of the Arab world.

The economic impact on Israel of the invasion of Lebanon was also considerable. Although its losses in terms of matériel were slight, the callup of reservists which the operation required detracted severely from Israeli production. It was also a matter for serious economic concern that the ruthless way in which hostilities had been conducted, and particularly the Sabra/Shatila massacre, had outraged the US Government and had badly shaken world Jewry. At least a temporary falloff in funds from aid and donations had to be expected. Even military aid from the USA might be affected, since awkward questions had been raised about Israeli use in combat of such American weapons as cluster bombs, which Congress had approved solely for Israel's defence. In the event, Israel went through a very bad patch economically but pulled through with its usual resilience.

Inflation rose to 'Latin American' levels of 445 per cent for 1984. To counter it, steps had to be taken which brought serious unemployment. But the Israelis were sophisticated enough to know that austerity was a price they must now pay. And, as they expected, American memories proved short, so that aid and donations picked up again.[9] The first requirement was clearly to reduce defence expenditure. On 4 January 1985, the Israeli Cabinet ordered a three-phase withdrawal from Lebanon. The first two phases proceeded continuously and were completed by mid-April; the third phase followed, ending on 6 June 1985, the third anniversary of the original invasion. It is difficult to see what of value had been achieved in the second half of this period; indeed, its main consequence had been that the Shi'a villagers of South Lebanon, who three years earlier had welcomed the expulsion of the Palestinians from their home area, had been turned into implacable enemies of the Israeli Defence Force. Not quite all the Israeli troops withdrew; a small number stayed as liaison officers with the Christian militia, now called the South Lebanon Army, in its buffer zone adjacent to the frontier (enlarged again to stretch north to Jezzin on the Awali River and east along the Syrian frontier to enclose a UNIFIL area).

Shaken by the soaring inflation, which in October 1984 had reached the equivalent of an annual rate of 1260 per cent, the Israeli Government introduced a whole series of corrective measures, cuts in subsidies, wage and price freezes, devaluations of the shekel (including on 4 September 1985 the introduction of a new shekel equal to 1000 old shekels). The population suffered but the measures had their effect. For 1985 as a whole inflation was down to 183 per cent. And in July 1986 the miracle was achieved; there was no price rise during the month, the first time this had happened since the mid-70s. Painful cuts were still needed, among them the abandonment on 3 March 1987 of the development of the Lavi fighter aircraft, on which $1200 million had been spent. But the Israeli economy was under control again (a striking contrast to the sad situation in neighbouring Lebanon).

30 Oil Gluts in the 1980s

For the oil-producing countries, the 1980s were the decade in which the bubble of ever-increasing incomes burst. As was seen at the end of Chapter 25, panic buying following the fall of the Shah and the temporary suspension of Iranian exports caused a doubling of oil prices in 1979. More precisely, the price of Saudi light, which was the 'marker' crude for Gulf exports,[1] rose from $12.70 a barrel in December 1978 to $24 in December 1979. In real terms, this was not a totally unreasonable increase. Allowing for inflation and falls in the value of the dollar, $12.70 was worth considerably less in purchasing power for the oil exporters in 1978 than they had been receiving in 1974 after the first oil shock. About a third of the 1979 increase represented a catching-up process. The other two-thirds might have been sustainable if the OPEC countries had not succumbed to greed in 1980 and pushed the price even higher.

There were of course reasons for their misguided decisions. The first was that in early 1980 their official oil price was lagging far behind the prices being realised on the Rotterdam spot market (for small tonnages only, but that was a reservation they tended to ignore). The second was that some, but not all, of them badly needed the extra income; the 'hawks' among Middle East nations were Iran and Iraq, Algeria and Libya. The third reason was that there had been a new political bombshell, the invasion of Afghanistan by Soviet forces in December 1979. Although this did not in itself affect the oil supply/demand ratio which should have determined prices, it was seen as a serous threat to the security of Gulf supplies. Even the normally unhawkish President Carter was moved to warn the Kremlin in ringing tones:'The Soviet Union is now attempting to consolidate a strategic position that poses a grave threat to the free movement of Middle East oil. Any attempt by any outside force to gain control of the Persian Gulf region will be regarded as an assault on the vital interests of the United States. It will be repelled by use of any means necessary, including military force.'

OPEC has regularly been portrayed by its critics as a cartel, with the adjective 'wicked' implied if not actually inserted before that noun. In fact, as the Saudi writer Johany has pointed out,[2] it has never operated as a true cartel. It might indeed have liked to do so but, because of its large and disparate membership, could not for any length of time achieve the necessary unity of objectives and policies.

This disunity was evident throughout the 1979–80 price rises. The most powerful member of OPEC, then as now, was Saudi Arabia, and the Saudi oil minister, Shaikh Yamani, was regularly a voice calling for moderation, indeed warning the other members that if they pushed prices too high they would be sowing the seeds of future trouble for themselves.[3] But, powerful as it was, Saudi Arabia could be outvoted, as happened again and again. Since its production in 1980, at around 9.5 million b/d, already stood near its sustainable maximum, it could not at that time credibly press home its views by threatening to flood the market with extra oil if its warnings were not heeded.

Moreover, Saudi Arabia attached great political importance to a unified OPEC price (allowing of course for the differentials always attaching to the various types of 'premium' crude, amounting at this time to some $4 a barrel, for example, for Libya's low-sulphur crude at a Mediterranean terminal). Yamani therefore several times during 1980 reluctantly raised the price of the Saudi marker crude in efforts to reach unanimity on a compromise with the hawks[4]; the efforts as often failed. In September 1980, it seemed that general agreement on a price of $32 a barrel might at last be in sight, but in that month the Iraq-Iran war erupted (see Chapter 28), giving another upward impetus to spot oil prices. The result was that at the December 1980 OPEC meeting, while

Saudi Arabia refused to go above $32, the other members chose to calculate the marker as $36 a barrel (with up to a further $5 for premium crudes).

This proved to be the decisive error. By that time the oil consumers (although the IEA was still ineffective except as a statistics-gatherer) were taking a wide range of counter-measures. American controls on domestic production had been removed. Production from non-OPEC sources generally had been pushed as high as it could immediately go. The raised prices were inhibiting retail demand to a now significant extent. Switching from oil to other fuels was widespread wherever it was technically feasible. Stocks, which had reached very high levels in 1980, were being drawn down. And the renewed recession in world trade, caused by the adverse movement in terms of trade as a result mainly of high oil prices, was driving down demand for all fuels. There was also a mild winter. By the spring of 1981 there was a glut of oil on world markets amounting to 2 or 3 million b/d and prices on the spot markets were falling as rapidly as they had risen earlier. A contributary factor in the glut was that, to replace the oil which Iraq could no longer export because of the Iranian blockade of its oil port of Fao, Saudi Arabia had raised its output above 10 million b/d.

There was great reluctance in OPEC to reduce official prices but many OPEC members resorted to secret discounts (secrets which were soon penetrated). In October 1981, they finally agreed on a uniform price of $34 a barrel (with up to $4 premiums) which would remain in effect to the end of 1982. This was not much of a reduction, since for most countries it merely eliminated the discounts they were already giving, but it was of historical significance as being the first time that OPEC had ever cut the official price of oil. It did not, however, solve the problem. The glut continued and discounting soon reappeared. Moreover, the non-OPEC countries were also cutting their prices. British oil, for instance, which had been selling at as much as $39.25 a barrel in 1981, came down to $36.50 in February and to $31 in March 1982. On the spot market, Saudi marker crude fell to $29 a barrel by March 1982, despite reductions in Saudi output.

Cuts in production were the course chosen by OPEC in March

1982 to avoid a reduction in the official price below $34. A ceiling of 17.5 million b/d was agreed, with Saudi Arabia and the UAE among the members promising reductions, in the Saudi case to 7 million b/d (and the Saudis in fact cut output to 6.5 million in a unilateral attempt to save the situation). But agreement on the ceiling had not been unanimous. The Iranians, faced with the need for war expenditure, had not agreed; by June they were again discounting and they doubled their sales in consequence. Libya and Nigeria were also exceeding their quotas and, despite underproduction by Saudi Arabia, total OPEC output was 18.2 million b/d. There were bitter recriminations at OPEC meetings in July and December, but no new firm quotas could be agreed. The official price of $34 was maintained, but any respectability it conferred was dependent on Saudi Arabia continuing to produce well below capacity and on Iraq being physically unable, because of the war, to meet its allotted quota. All in all, OPEC entered 1983 in considerable disarray.

Output by the OPEC countries had fallen from 31 million b/d in 1979 to under 20 million b/d in 1982 and was still falling.[5] OPEC's secretariat calculated that 3.5 million b/d of this reduction was due to reduced demand for fuel, 3 million to stocks being run down, another 3 million to switching from oil to other fuels and 2 million to loss of markets to non-OPEC oil.[6] The last at least could be fought against, and at their March 1983 meeting OPEC reluctantly decided to make another price cut, from $34 to $29 a barrel for the marker crude. In addition, output quotas adding up to 17.5 million b/d were reaffirmed.

This cut brought some stability back to the market, at least for a time. Spot crude prices remained firm for most of 1983 and, after weakening in the last quarter of that year, recovered during a cold winter to remain strong well into the second quarter of 1984, before experiencing the cyclical downturn normal in a second quarter. There were several reasons for this relative strength. Fears about the Gulf War caused continuing uncertainty which encouraged stockbuilding; there had been some decline in oil exports from the Soviet Union; certain North Sea oilfields had temporarily run into technical problems; and Britain had increased its fuel oil consumption to face what looked like being a long coal strike.

But by June 1984 OPEC members were again exceeding their ceiling of 17.5 million b/d. Their combined output had gone up to 18.1 million b/d, largely because the 'swing' producer, Saudi Arabia, had grown tired of underproducing its quota and had raised production from 4.6 million b/d in March to 5.4 million b/d in June. Moreover, in July 1984, Saudi Arabia made a barter deal under which it would pay in oil to the extent of 34.4 million barrels for the purchase of Boeing aircraft. This vast quantity of oil, nearly two years output for the whole of OPEC and worth some $1000 million at official prices, would be sold on by Boeing and Rolls Royce (the engine suppliers), and this was almost certain to be at cut prices.

In October 1984, when heavy crude (because of the British coal strike) was trading on the spot market above its official price, the Saudis announced that they would be changing the mix of their exported crude, so that 35 per cent instead of 20 per cent would be heavy and only 45 per cent as against a previous 60 per cent would be light; the other 20 per cent would be medium as before. This was interpreted on the markets as a tacit acknowledgement that the $29 price for the marker (light) crude was too high. Still striving to resist another official price cut, the OPEC members agreed in October 1984 to reduce their ceiling from 17.5 million to 16 million b/d. This should have restored the situation, but the markets had little faith in the effectiveness of the new ceiling, especially as it had been declared to be 'temporary'.

In January 1985 the price problem had to be faced once more. By a majority decision (a thing they had always tried hard to avoid) OPEC decided to cut the price of Saudi light crude from $29 to $28 a barrel; Algeria and Libya opposed the change. The 'marker' status of Saudi light was declared to be at an end in order to ease the way for a more realistic structure of differentials, with the 'spread' for premium crudes being reduced from $4 to $2.40 a barrel. But the spot price continued to fall; in July 1985, OPEC made some rather symbolic cuts of a few cents in crude prices, but this was only tinkering with the problem as spot prices were now up to $2 below official levels.

One of the features of 1985 was a growing anger within OPEC at the uncooperative attitude taken up by some non-OPEC members, particularly the UK. OPEC argued that it was in the interests of all producers to sustain prices and that all should be ready to reduce production to correct the supply/demand ratio; a few non-OPEC producers tended to agree, but even the silver-tongued Shaikh Yamani could not persuade the British Government to do other than leave matters to the free operation of the market. By following the spot price down, the UK held on to market share or even increased it while the OPEC share was falling. Yamani threatened that there was a price at which Gulf oil would still be highly profitable measured in terms of production costs while British oil from the expensive North Sea would be driven out of production. Theoretically, this was certainly true; the question was whether those OPEC members who were more populous and less rich than Saudi Arabia would themselves be willing to see prices driven so low. And strains within OPEC were not eased by the news in September 1985 that Saudi Arabia had concluded another 'oil-for-aircraft' barter deal, and with the British of all people – see Chapter 31.

At the December 1985 OPEC meeting it appeared that Yamani's threat was to be put to the test; members decided to increase output to secure their 'fair share' of world markets. Saudi Arabia led the way with an increase of 1 million b/d by the middle of 1986 and OPEC output as a whole was then up by nearly 16 per cent. The effect on spot prices was certainly spectacular; some called it the 'reverse oil shock'. The spot price of Britain's Brent crude, which prior to February 1986 had remained above $20 a barrel, actually fell below $10 a barrel on 1 April 1986 (which implied under $8 for Gulf crude because of the transport differential). This turned out to be a temporary level from which there was some strengthening, but prices generally remained low.

In April 1986, OPEC turned the screw further by raising their production ceiling to 16.3 million b/d for the third quarter, despite opposition again from Algeria and Libya, this time joined by Iran, who argued unsuccessfully for a ceiling of 14.5 million b/d. The argument was in practice irrelevant since the second quarter OPEC output turned out to be the very high figure of 18.675 million b/d. The UK once more refused to cooperate with

OPEC to reverse this situation. In July 1986 the Brent crude price averaged only $9.63 a barrel.

At this point it was OPEC's and not Britain's nerve that broke. In August OPEC agreed a 'temporary' cut in production to 16 million b/d for September/October. Spot prices firmed at once, with Brent crude above $14 a barrel after mid-August. On 30 October 1986 came the final proof that Yamani's policy had failed; he was dismissed by King Fahd from the post of Minister of Petroleum and Mineral Resources which he had held since 1962. It was a tremendous shock to the oil world. Not only had he directed his own country's policy but he had been very much the dominant figure within OPEC for over a decade, chairing most of its important committees and making effective use of the enormous influence which he drew from the fact that Saudi Arabia could act as a 'swing' producer. His successor was the Saudi Minister of Planning, Hisham Nazir, who at once called on OPEC to aim for a price of $18 a barrel.

This of course meant a reduction in output. In December 1986 OPEC agreed a ceiling of 15.8 million b/d for the first half of 1987 (Iraq was not given a quota but was 'deemed' to produce 1.466 million b/d). This ceiling was accompanied by a declared 'average central reference price' of $18 a barrel. (It is worth noting that this price is not the same as a 'marker' price of $18 would have been under the old system; the assumed spread was of $2.65, from $16.27 to $18.92, whereas a marker price of $18 would have implied around $21 for Libyan crude.) In January 1987, the spot price for Brent crude was $18.44, so the post-Yamani policy seemed to be working.

Unfortunately for the cohesion of OPEC, the old troubles then began to return. There was cheating here and there on production levels, and when spot prices weakened in consequence discounting by some OPEC members reappeared. At the December 1987 meeting of OPEC it was agreed to fix output at 16.66 million b/d (including a deemed 1.6 million for Iraq), with the central price still at $18. Kuwait and Abu Dhabi pledged themselves to abandon their confessed over-production. At the end of the month a meeting of the GCC called for an end to oil price discounting. It remains to be seen whether these pledges and exhortations will prove effective.

31 Trade between Britain and the Middle East 1980–87

The British Economy

The Conservative Party, led by Mrs Thatcher since 1975, won office at an election in the spring of 1979. The 1980s have seen this Government effect a revolution in Britain's economic policy, overturning the system established by the Attlee Government after World War II, which had endured in essentials for three and a half decades. With eight years of the revolution now completed (at the time of writing), it is possible to see clearly its main components. These are:

(a) A substantial reduction in direct taxation, counterbalanced in part by an increase in indirect taxation.

(b) A strong and very determined campaign to reduce public spending, and thereby the Public Sector Borrowing Requirement (PSBR), even at the expense of unpopularity when some item of expenditure dear to the public has been rejected. In 1987, this brought about that rare postwar event, a budget surplus, which seems likely to be repeated.

(c) A reduction in the size of the public sector, both by a slimming down of the Government bureaucracy and by a continuing programme of return of nationalised industries to private ownership.[1] Those industries which had to remain (temporarily) in public ownership because they were loss-making were set tighter and tighter financial targets, so as to increase their efficiency to the stage when they could become profitable and in their turn be 'privatised'. The reduction of subsidies to them was an important component of the reduction of the PSBR.

(d) Legislation to curb the power of the trade unions. The process was carried forward gradually, requiring several Acts of Parliament,[2] so as to minimise the risk of a General Strike and to test out the effect of one batch of measures before embarking on the next batch. To make their policy effective, it was inevitable that the Government would sooner or later have to face a major strike and this came in the most likely place, the coal-mining industry, where a year-long stoppage from March 1984 to March 1985 ended with the miners returning to work empty-handed.[3] In the private sector, the equivalent decisive action by management was the outfacing of the once all-powerful printing unions, whose skills had been made obsolete by new technology.

(e) Tighter controls on the money supply, mainly by the use of the interest rate mechanism. Various measures of the amount of money in circulation have been monitored and action taken if they seemed to be expanding too rapidly. To provide flexibility, a range of permissible percentages rather than a specific target has recently been used.

(f) Inflation has been greatly reduced from the very high peak (over 20 per cent) of 1979–80. However, it still remains at levels (currently 3 to 6 per cent) which, if low by comparison with the 1970s, are higher than those prevailing in Britain's main industrial competitors. A reduction to zero inflation has been spoken of as a Government objective, but has not as yet been given a top priority.

(g) As well as their own central expenditure, the Government decided that the budgets of local government authorities had to be held down. Since many local authorities are in the political control of the Labour Party and are out of sympathy with the Government's objective of reining in public expenditure, this has roused intense political controversy.

(h) Legislation has been passed for the rating system (property tax) on private dwellings to be replaced by a community charge on all adults, with some relief for those less able to pay but with very few total exemptions. Rates on shops and other businesses will be charged on a uniform national basis, instead of varying from one locality to another. This controversial new system of financing local government has not yet come into effect at the time of writing.

(i) Compulsion on local authorities to sell council-owned houses and flats to their tenants, at favourable prices. This was a step both to the widening of the 'property-owning democracy' which had long been a Conservative ideal and also to the slimming down of bureaucracy, this time in local councils.

(j) The privatisation of nationalised industries was effected mainly by public offers for sale. This had an effect which was not part of the original intention but was quickly recognised as desirable in itself from the Conservative point of view, the creation of a 'share-owning' (as well as 'property-owning') democracy. At the end of 1987, a survey showed that 9 million people owned shares, three times the number doing so in 1979.

(k) With controls on foreign exchange transactions swept away, it became possible for the more successful British businesses to expand by taking over companies outside the United Kingdom. With the dollar weakening in the 1980s, the favourite area for such takeovers has been the USA and an amazing number of such overseas investments have been made in a very few years.[4]

(l) There has also been encouragement of investment by foreign companies, particularly Japanese, in manufacturing in the UK. This was considered desirable for Britain for many reasons, including transfer of technology and even more an introduction of Japanese management standards and techniques.[5] The Japanese usually insisted on single-union and virtual 'no-strike' agreements with their labour forces and have been able to negotiate them with several unions.

(m) Because British investments overseas have exceeded foreign investments of this type in Britain, the effect has been to rebuild the asset portfolio owned abroad before it had to be liquidated to pay for Britain's efforts in the two World Wars. The dividends earned from this portfolio have added substantially to the UK's invisible income.

These measures have attained many of their objectives. The British economy has grown at rates which would have been the envy of most postwar Governments. Productivity has improved beyond recognition, not only in the private sector but also in the still nationalised industries, such as steel. Relations between management and labour have generally improved. The budget has been balanced and even brought into surplus. Foreign exchange reserves have been built up to record levels. Standards of living have increased for the majority.

At the same time the Government has had to pay certain drastic prices. Much the most serious of these has been a very high level of unemployment, as labour was squeezed out of overmanned enterprises both in the public and in the private sector. The method of calculation of the numbers unemployed has been altered almost annually,[6] so statistical comparisons are difficult, but there is no argument over the fact that unemployment has exceeded 3 million and there are methods of calculating which put it at well over 4 million at its peak. This is a startling figure when it is remembered that as recently as the time of Mr Heath's Conservative Government in the 1970s an unemployment level of 1 million was considered intolerable. However, the regeneration of industry and the successful expansion of the service sector have progressed in 1987 to a stage where the level of unemployment has been falling regularly, and now seems to be headed for 2.5 million. It should fall further if present trends continue, probably to less than 2 million, but a return to below the 1 million mark seems unlikely.

Another price which has had to be paid, particularly in the early part of the decade, was a very high level of bankruptcies and forced takeovers of unsuccessful businesses. In less tight conditions of money supply and with lower interest rates, some of these firms would have been saved. The rate of closures was especially high in manufacturing industry.

Readers of this book will be particularly interested in the effects of this economic revolution on Britain's overseas trade. As might be expected, it has been both bad and good. The slimming down of manufacturing industry has proceeded to the extent that the UK now has an adverse balance of visible trade in manufactured goods, a far cry from the nineteenth century position when Britain was 'the workshop of the world'. On the other hand, those firms which remain in business are much more efficient than they were a decade ago. It can be argued that without the revolution many would have had no hope of surviving except behind a barrier of protectionist measures.

One factor which has stimulated the growth of imports of manufactured goods has been a recurrent tendency for sterling to strengthen to a point at which exchange rates rather than the relative efficiency of firms tended to make British goods uncompetitive. This is in one sense a problem of success, since it is the improvement of the UK economy which has impressed foreigners and made sterling strong, but the impact of the exchange rate on exports now needs vigilance.

Visible Trade

The course of visible trade will be examined as usual in two quinquennia, though the second will be incomplete.

Table 13: Visible Trade (£ million) with:

	1980	1981	1982	1983	1984	1985
ABU DHABI						
Exports to	214.6	246.7	272.9	219.3	215.9	246.7
Imports from	246.3	272.7	184.3	59.0	21.9	25.2
Balance	-31.7	-26.0	+88.6	+160.3	+194.0	+221.5
ALGERIA						
Exports to	140.4	173.0	199.2	233.9	272.4	176.6
Imports from	113.8	159.5	175.3	157.7	274.1	262.1
Balance	+26.6	+13.5	+23.9	+76.2	-1.7	-85.5
BAHRAIN						
Exports to	100.5	102.3	152.0	150.3	138.7	161.5
Imports from	13.1	16.7	35.5	36.8	28.2	45.1
Balance	+87.4	+85.6	+116.5	+113.5	+110.5	+116.4
DUBAI						
Exports to	268.5	230.4	253.9	313.3	298.8	345.3
Imports from	235.2	116.0	57.5	211.6	60.6	44.4
Balance	+33.3	+114.4	+196.4	+101.7	+238.2	+300.9

EGYPT						
Exports to	324.0	325.1	338.8	370.9	427.7	470.5
Imports from	333.9	414.6	412.8	79.8	179.9	162.0
Balance	-9.9	-89.5	-74.0	+291.1	+247.8	+308.5
IRAN						
Exports to	392.7	402.8	333.6	630.7	703.4	525.6
Imports from	107.2	154.4	225.9	100.6	368.6	63.3
Balance	+285.5	+248.4	+107.7	+530.1	+334.8	+462.3
IRAQ (incl. Turkish exports of Iraqi oil)						
Exports to	322.1	623.9	873.7	399.9	343.1	444.7
Imports from	532.3	130.3	203.6	96.6	144.0	423.6
Balance	-210.2	+493.6	+670.1	+303.3	+199.1	+21.1
ISRAEL						
Exports to	230.6	212.0	264.1	354.6	393.0	434.5
Imports from	232.7	255.9	276.1	313.7	392.7	404.0
Balance	-2.1	-43.9	-12.0	+40.9	+0.3	+30.5
JORDAN						
Exports to	94.6	203.7	295.2	262.7	192.4	154.3
Imports from	6.2	10.3	17.3	28.0	18.1	84.5
Balance	+88.4	+193.4	+277.9	+234.7	+174.3	+69.8
KUWAIT						
Exports to	250.8	281.2	333.1	333.5	301.5	347.9
Imports from	646.8	477.3	104.7	67.3	141.5	161.5
Balance	-396.0	-196.1	+228.4	+266.2	+160.0	+186.4
LEBANON						
Exports to	70.7	61.9	67.6	81.4	76.2	52.8
Imports from	9.1	7.5	24.2	11.5	6.9	7.9
Balance	+61.6	+54.4	+43.4	+69.9	+69.3	+44.9
LIBYA						
Exports to	288.4	530.4	261.0	274.1	246.5	237.2
Imports from	46.2	74.8	342.5	223.6	164.8	311.8
Balance	+242.2	+455.6	-81.5	+50.5	+81.7	-74.6
MOROCCO						
Exports to	64.7	55.9	95.5	99.4	79.8	92.7
Imports from	60.5	62.7	60.2	75.1	79.7	74.8
Balance	+4.2	-6.8	+35.3	+24.3	+0.1	+17.9

OMAN						
Exports to	121.0	170.8	265.2	449.1	390.4	489.9
Imports from	19.2	40.4	46.4	90.6	80.9	68.4
Balance	+101.8	+130.4	+218.8	+358.5	+309.5	+421.5
QATAR						
Exports to	102.0	135.7	245.4	216.5	133.8	142.1
Imports from	44.7	10.7	34.0	10.1	28.2	32.6
Balance	+57.3	+125.0	+211.4	+206.4	+105.6	+109.5
SAUDI ARABIA						
Exports to	945.2	1133.9	1361.5	1480.2	1386.7	1249.0
Imports from	1874.3	1892.6	1447.8	897.7	545.6	496.3
Balance	-929.1	-758.7	-86.3	+582.5	+841.1	+752.7
SUDAN						
Exports to	121.3	118.6	136.0	133.5	95.8	103.6
Imports from	13.3	10.9	9.9	18.7	16.9	21.3
Balance	+108.0	+107.7	+126.1	+114.8	+78.9	+82.3
SYRIA						
Exports to	81.6	85.2	88.7	72.3	91.9	80.8
Imports from	12.2	4.6	25.6	18.9	59.1	78.6
Balance	+69.4	+80.6	+63.1	+53.4	+32.8	+2.2
TUNISIA						
Exports to	29.8	35.1	38.6	44.7	47.1	43.2
Imports from	17.2	22.1	12.6	18.1	18.1	39.5
Balance	+12.6	+13.0	+26.0	+26.6	+29.0	+3.7
UAE (less Abu Dhabi and Dubai)						
Exports to	17.5	15.0	32.1	35.5	27.0	29.3
Imports from	0.8	2.7	25.2	48.6	4.7	27.3
Balance	+16.7	+12.3	+6.9	-13.1	+22.3	+2.0
YEMEN AR						
Exports to	36.5	31.6	52.6	56.3	58.8	94.4
Imports from	0.5	1.0	1.3	1.9	2.5	2.3
Balance	+36.0	+30.6	+51.3	+54.4	+56.3	+92.1
PDR YEMEN						
Exports to	25.4	31.5	35.6	36.7	45.2	34.8
Imports from	5.7	7.3	26.6	10.6	18.2	7.9
Balance	+19.7	+24.2	+9.0	+26.1	+27.0	+26.9

TOTAL – MIDDLE EAST COUNTRIES						
Exports to	4242.9	5206.7	5996.3	6248.8	5966.1	5957.4
Imports from	4571.2	4145.0	3749.3	2576.5	2655.2	2844.4
Balance	-328.3	+1061.7	+2247.0	+3672.3	+3310.9	+3113.0
TOTAL – ALL COUNTRIES						
Exports to	47364	50998	55558	60684	70488	78392
Imports from	49773	51169	56978	66101	78967	85027
Balance	-2409	-171	-1420	-5417	-8479	-6635
M.E. TRADE AS PERCENTAGE OF TOTAL TRADE						
Exports to	8.96	10.21	10.79	10.30	8.46	7.60
Imports from	9.18	8.10	6.58	3.90	3.36	3.35

These figures are quite exceptional. From 1981 onwards, there was a substantial surplus in the UK's balance of visible trade with the Middle East. This was of course due to sharply reduced imports of oil, as Britain's North Sea output neared its peak, coinciding with greatly reduced prices for such oil as was still imported. For the final three years of the quinquennium, total imports from the Middle East were less than 4 per cent of Britain's world-wide imports, a sharp contrast with earlier figures.

On the other side of the account, exports to the Middle East for the first time rose above 10 per cent of the UK's global exports in the three years 1981 to 1983, before dropping back into a more normal range around 8 per cent. The rise was due to continuation of many Middle East investment programmes for a few years despite the fall in oil incomes, with reserves of surplus funds being drawn down, followed by a reining-in when it was seen that low oil prices were likely to persist. This was a natural course for Middle East expenditure to take. As was seen in Chapter 27, much of it was being directed to large scale industrialisation projects which took several years to complete and bring on stream; it would have been uneconomic to cut them back overnight, when adequate reserve funds were available.

As for individual Middle East countries, the oil producers' trade with Britain reflected this general pattern. In addition, the trade figures for Iran and Iraq were affected by the war between them. Iran's exports to the UK fluctuated rather wildly, with a high figure of £368.6 million in 1984 sandwiched between two low figures of £100.6 million in 1983 and £63.3 million in 1985. Iraq, as was mentioned in Chapter 28, tried to keep going its peacetime development programme, so had very high imports from Britain in 1981 and particularly 1982, but was driven to abandon the effort thereafter, with the 1983 figure less than half that of 1982. Iraq's oil exports to Britain were sharply reduced from the outbreak of the war, even counting in those passing through the pipeline to Turkey (which are listed in the Government statistics as Turkish exports to Britain, though here reallocated to Iraq), but 1985 showed a recovery as pipeline facilities and hence volume improved.

Outside the Gulf area, UK trade with the Maghreb countries in both directions grew strongly between 1980 and 1985, showing that these largely francophone countries were not a French preserve. There was an unusually high level of British exports to Libya in the single year 1981, after which the normal pattern was resumed (breach of diplomatic relations in 1984 seems not to have affected it). Exports to Egypt were important and rose steadily during the quinquennium, although imports from Egypt fell very sharply from 1982 to 1983 and then remained at a rather low level (oil again being the explanation). Trade in both directions with Israel grew regularly during the quinquennium and was in approximate balance.

The level of imports from individual oil producers is of interest; the figures cited, being in value terms, of course exaggerate the volume changes, as the price of oil, which stood so high in 1980, began to fall sharply as the glut developed:

Table 14: UK Imports from Middle East Oil Producers (£ million)

	1980	1981	1982	1983	1984	1985
Abu Dhabi	246.3	272.7	184.3	59.0	21.9	25.2
Algeria	113.8	159.5	175.3	157.7	274.1	262.1
Bahrain	13.1	16.7	35.5	36.8	28.2	45.1
Dubai	235.2	116.0	57.5	211.6	60.6	44.4
Egypt	333.9	414.6	412.8	79.8	179.9	162.0
Iran	107.2	154.4	225.9	100.6	368.6	63.3
Iraq	532.3	130.4	203.6	96.6	144.0	423.6
Kuwait	646.8	477.3	104.7	67.3	141.5	161.5
Libya	46.2	74.8	342.5	223.6	164.8	311.8

Oman	19.2	40.5	46.4	90.6	80.9	68.4
Qatar	44.7	10.7	34.0	10.1	28.2	32.6
Saudi Arabia	1874.3	1892.6	1447.8	897.7	545.6	496.3
U.A.E. (rest)	0.8	2.7	25.2	48.6	4.7	27.3
TOTALS	4213.8	3762.9	3295.5	2080.0	2043.0	2123.6

Although there are always apparent anomalies in oil figures, the general trend is clear. Saudi Arabia remained Britain's chief supplier throughout, but suffered a heavy fall, as did all the Gulf exporters except some small suppliers. The two Mediterranean countries, Algeria and Libya (two 'hawks' who tended to flout OPEC agreements) produced much better results; discounts probably played a part in this, as did their distance from the Gulf War, with its high tanker insurance rates.

The visible trade figures for the two years remaining, with the usual overlap year, are as follows:

Table 15: Visible Trade (£ million) with:

	1985	1986	1987
ABU DHABI			
Exports to	246.7	168.1	150.0
Imports from	25.2	14.6	13.8
Balance	+221.5	+153.5	+136.2
ALGERIA			
Exports to	176.6	129.6	73.1
Imports from	262.1	140.9	172.9
Balance	-85.5	-11.3	-99.8
BAHRAIN			
Exports to	161.5	131.0	125.2
Imports from	45.1	19.7	60.7
Balance	+116.4	+111.3	+64.5
DUBAI			
Exports to	345.3	379.5	306.8
Imports from	44.4	56.2	77.3
Balance	+300.9	+323.3	+229.5

EGYPT			
Exports to	470.5	371.0	342.2
Imports from	162.0	328.1	127.3
Balance	+308.5	+42.9	+214.9
IRAN			
Exports to	525.6	399.4	307.9
Imports from	63.3	100.3	187.6
Balance	+462.3	+299.1	+120.3
IRAQ			
Exports to	444.7	443.9	271.7
Imports from	423.6	282.3	362.3
Balance	+21.1	+161.6	-90.6
ISRAEL			
Exports to	434.5	462.4	523.6
Imports from	404.0	385.2	437.0
Balance	+30.5	+77.2	+86.6
JORDAN			
Exports to	154.3	130.4	189.0
Imports from	84.5	49.8	29.3
Balance	+69.8	+80.6	+159.7
KUWAIT			
Exports to	347.9	300.6	225.2
Imports from	161.5	58.5	81.5
Balance	+186.4	+242.1	+143.7
LEBANON			
Exports to	52.8	55.9	40.7
Imports from	7.9	9.8	9.5
Balance	+44.9	+46.1	+31.2
LIBYA			
Exports to	237.2	260.5	220.6
Imports from	311.8	136.4	133.6
Balance	-74.6	+124.1	+87.0
MOROCCO			
Exports to	92.7	84.5	86.2
Imports from	74.8	65.4	61.1
Balance	+17.9	+19.1	+25.1

OMAN			
Exports to	489.9	399.6	249.9
Imports from	68.4	87.2	49.5
Balance	+421.5	+312.4	+200.4
QATAR			
Exports to	142.1	112.1	105.1
Imports from	32.6	29.6	13.8
Balance	+109.5	+82.5	+91.3
SAUDI ARABIA			
Exports to	1249.0	1507.1	1978.4
Imports from	496.3	435.9	383.1
Balance	+752.7	+1071.2	+1595.3
SUDAN			
Exports to	103.6	83.3	75.3
Imports from	21.3	12.8	18.9
Balance	+82.3	+70.5	+56.4
SYRIA			
Exports to	80.8	55.5	34.1
Imports from	78.6	31.3	24.9
Balance	+2.2	+24.2	+9.2
TUNISIA			
Exports to	43.2	39.8	24.9
Imports from	39.5	17.3	14.7
Balance	+3.7	+22.5	+10.2
UAE (less ABU DHABI and DUBAI)			
Exports to	29.3	34.2	22.2
Imports from	27.3	3.3	4.0
Balance	+2.0	+30.9	+18.2
YEMEN AR			
Exports to	94.4	58.1	55.3
Imports from	2.3	2.1	2.3
Balance	+92.1	+56.0	+53.0
PDR YEMEN			
Exports to	34.8	23.9	28.3
Imports from	7.9	4.8	1.1
Balance	+26.9	+19.1	+27.2

TOTAL – MIDDLE EAST COUNTRIES			
Exports to	5957.4	5630.4	5435.7
Imports from	2844.4	2271.5	2266.2
Balance	+3113.0	+3358.9	+3169.5
TOTAL – ALL COUNTRIES			
Exports to	78392	73009	79851
Imports from	85027	86067	94016
Balance	-6635	-13058	-14165
M.E. TRADE AS PERCENTAGE OF TOTAL TRADE			
Exports to	7.60	7.71	6.81
Imports from	3.35	2.64	2.41

(Note: Apparent minor arithmetical errors result from rounding.)

The figures for 1986 and 1987 continue the trend shown at the end of the previous quinquennium. In each of them the UK had a visible trade surplus with the Middle East of over £3,000 million. It is striking that in 1986 there was a surplus with every country listed except Algeria. The proportion of Britain's global exports provided by sales to the Middle East remained below 8 per cent in 1986 and sank to below 7 per cent in 1987, while the import ratio went on falling, to below 2.5 per cent in 1987.

Of the individual countries, much the most important market was Saudi Arabia, taking nearly £2000 million of exports from Britain in 1987 despite its small population. For comparison, this figure is comfortably in excess of the UK's exports to the whole of Latin America. This high level of sales is likely to continue, particularly as deliveries take place under two important aircraft contracts. In July 1984 it was announced that Saudi Arabia would buy ten Boeing 747 airliners powered by British Rolls Royce RB-211 engines, of which fifty would be supplied. And on 26 September 1985 an even larger British sale to Saudi Arabia was announced, of no less than 132 British military aircraft, including seventy-two Tornados.[7]

One interesting feature of these two contracts was that in the first case all and in the second case half of the purchase price was to be paid in crude oil, nearly $1000 million for the Boeings and nearly $3000 million for the military aircraft. In addition the latter contract provided for a considerable 'offset' investment by Britain in Saudi Arabia, involving transfer of technology on a large scale. This provision was of the nature of a 'best endeavours' undertaking by the UK Government, but the Saudis have shown[8] that they attach great importance to the promises made and it must be assumed that some substantial results will materialise. To the extent that they do, they will very much strengthen industrial links between the two countries.

The pattern of Britain's oil purchases from Middle East producers continued to be affected by the Gulf War:

Table 16: UK Imports from Middle East Oil Producers (£ million)

	1985	1986	1987
Abu Dhabi	25.2	14.6	13.8
Algeria	262.1	140.9	172.9
Bahrain	45.1	19.7	60.7
Dubai	44.4	56.2	77.3
Egypt	162.0	328.1	127.3
Iran	63.3	100.3	187.6
Iraq	423.6	282.3	362.3
Kuwait	161.5	58.5	81.5
Libya	311.8	136.4	133.6
Oman	68.4	87.2	49.5
Qatar	32.6	29.6	13.8
Saudi Arabia	496.3	435.9	383.1
U.A.E. (rest)	27.3	3.3	4.0
TOTALS	2123.6	1693.0	1667.4

It must be remembered that these are figures for total imports from these countries, not just of oil. Egypt, for instance, had other exports to Britain. Nevertheless, for the most part these import figures represent oil and the trends certainly do. It is striking how low were the imports from Gulf States other than Saudi Arabia – from Abu Dhabi, Kuwait and Qatar in particular. The position has been reached that Britain's exports to Saudi

Arabia alone far exceed imports of oil from the Middle East as a whole. It is a remarkable change from the pattern of the three preceding decades.

Arms Exports

British arms sales to the Middle East were small in the 80s until the huge deal was done with Saudi Arabia for Tornado and other military aircraft (see above); delivery of the first 10 Tornados began in 1987. Jordan and Oman have also expressed their intention to buy Tornado aircraft, despite their very high unit price, which Jordan could hardly afford without the financial aid it receives from other Arab countries.

Part of the reason for there being so few sales, for instance of armoured vehicles, was that the Chieftain was growing oldfashioned and its replacement in the British Army, the Challenger, lacked appeal to overseas buyers. There was also of course the fact that two large markets, Iran and Iraq, were subject to a British embargo on all arms sales during the Gulf War. Some sales elsewhere of spare parts and replacements continued, but even these were declining as old equipment, such as Hunters, Centurions, Lightnings, and even Saladins and Saracens went out of service.

Invisible Trade

To the UK's substantial surplus in visible trade with the Middle East from 1981 onwards must be added another considerable, even though unquantifiable, surplus on invisible account. There are no important new factors in this decade on the invisible front, except the effect of the Gulf War on the London market for insurance and reinsurance. Since Lloyds' accounts are made up three years in arrears, it is not clear what the balance of losses against premium income will be, but it must be assumed that the very experienced insurers in London will have fixed premiums at levels properly reflecting the perils. Indeed, there has been some restiveness in the Gulf at the high level of premiums, with efforts made to carry part of the risk locally. In 1987, although the total of attacks on shipping reached a new peak, it is striking that the number of ships damaged beyond repair was at its lowest level since the Gulf War started.[9] Lloyds reduced war risk premiums slightly in consequence. On the outward side of the invisibles balance, there was a high level of tourist visits to Morocco and particularly Tunisia, and also to Egypt and Israel, but not of course to wartorn Lebanon.

Investments

There was some drawing down during the decade of the heavy investments made by the major oil producers in the boom years, but this affected the USA more than the UK, since Britain under the Thatcher Government was seen as the stronger economy. A development which was not new but began to be significant in financial terms during the 1980s was investment by Middle East owners in British thoroughbred horses for racing in England; the sons of the Ruler of Dubai were prominent here.

More significant, at the end of the period covered by this book, was the purchase by the Kuwait Investment Office in London of an interest of over 20 per cent in BP when the sale by the British Government of its last holdings in that company coincided with a Stock Exchange crash in October 1987, leaving some 30 per cent of the shares with the underwriters, who as they sold provided buying opportunities for the KIO. Kuwait had earlier taken investment shareholdings in other oil companies, for example' Atlantic Richfield and Philips in the USA, and has said that it has no intention of launching a full bid for BP or of interfering in its management. On the other hand, it had also taken over one foreign oil company entirely, Santa Fe, so some doubt must remain in BP's mind about ultimate Kuwaiti intentions. There is no doubt some quiet satisfaction in Kuwait that instead of BP owning half of KOC, Kuwait now owns nearly a quarter of BP.

On the other side of the investment account, few British oil companies now had any significant ownership participation in Middle East oilfields, so investment by them was for the most part no longer applicable. There were occasional exceptions. For instance, in July 1984 BP took a 7.5 per cent interest in Qatargas (Qatar Liquefied Gas Company) when it was agreed that BP and CFP would participate in the development of the North Field gasfield in Qatar. But new investments of this kind were rare.

Whether the 'offset' element in the Tornado deal with Saudi Arabia will lead to extensive British non-oil investment in that country has yet to be seen. On balance, even with some drawing down of earlier investments, the net flow of investment funds in the 1980s has almost certainly been favourable to Britain.

Overseas Banking

By the 80s, the British banking presence in the Middle East was clearly contracting. Following the establishment of a central bank in the UAE, foreign banks there were ordered in 1981 to reduce their numbers of branches to no more than eight, and the BBME effected the reduction by 1983. In Oman, the BBME sold fourteen branches in 1984 to a local bank, retaining only its four main branches, and it closed its operations in the Yemen in 1985. However, this slimming process was naturally directed towards the less successful or even loss-making branches, so profitability was not affected proportionately. In many countries, BBME still ranked in size only just behind the leading local banks.

The build-up of Middle Eastern banks in London which had begun in the 70s continued and even accelerated during the 80s. Another Israeli bank and no fewer than twenty-three further Arab banks were opened there. The latter included branches of the National Banks of Dubai, Egypt and Kuwait, and of the Gulf, Jordan and Tunis International Banks; there were also four Saudi and three Lebanese banks. In addition there was considerable activity in the opening of Arab financial institutions other than banks. By the end of 1987 there were thirty-six Arab banks operating in the UK, many of them with multiple branches, and there were another twenty nine Arab-owned bodies with titles such as investment companies and finance companies. The increase in this latter category of institutions was due to burgeoning Arab wealth available for investment and also to the growing importance of London as the main European finance centre, ranking alongside New York and Tokyo in world importance. Their presence in London made an important contribution to Britain's invisible income since, as explained in Chapter 26, they were bringing funds into the U.K rather than taking them out of it.

32 Retrospect 1973 – 1987 and Prospect

Retrospect

Politically, there were watershed years for the UK in its dealings with the Middle East in 1971, when British protection of Arab countries came to an end, and for the Middle East itself in 1973, when Israel for the first time in its short history briefly faced defeat from an Arab army, even though it rallied from the shock. But economically, it is 1973 alone which is the watershed, when soaring oil prices revolutionised the terms of trade between the oil producers and the rest of the world, and opened the way to rapid industrialisation for the countries of the Arabian Peninsula.

The fourteen years which have since elapsed have seen great changes in the Peninsula, as Chapter 27 has shown; not all the development has been viable without subsidy, but it has been both extensive and rapid, and has profoundly changed the way of life of the majority of the Peninsula's inhabitants. On the whole, it has been well managed after some understandable initial errors.

But it must not be forgotten that the inhabitants of the oil-rich states of the Peninsula make up quite a small minority of the population of the Middle East. The majority have made much less impressive progress. Despite generous aid from their richer neighbours, most of them are no better off than they were before 1973. Some have brought problems upon themselves. Iran and Iraq, by the war which has raged between them since 1980, have squandered the oil wealth which should have brought them great advances. Sudan and Lebanon have been torn by civil war. Libya has wasted part of its resources on war with Chad and on supporting international terrorism. Algeria and Morocco have squabbled over the Western Sahara. The two Yemens have failed to unite and have made only minor economic advances. Israel has embarked on a costly and misconceived invasion of Lebanon and has failed to solve the serious problems inherent in its continued occupation of the West Bank and the Gaza Strip; it has, partly in consequence, been racked by intermittent high inflation. Egypt has made peace and recovered its Sinai territories but the relative failure of its *infitah* policy has left it still unable to solve its demographic problem; nor has it yet fully recovered its standing in the Arab world, of which its population size and central position should make it the natural leader.

Meanwhile, the weakening of oil prices in the 80s has posed problems which OPEC has failed to tackle effectively. Neither cutbacks in crude production to raise prices nor floodings of the market to recapture market share have been pursued consistently, with the consequence that oil reserves have been drawn down less profitably than had been anticipated. Even super-wealthy Saudi Arabia has experienced budget deficits and been forced to rein in its industrial progress. Some producers with smaller reserves will look back ruefully on lost opportunities in the 80s.

Despite some interruptions in diplomatic relations, the atmosphere between Britain and the Middle East has been generally calm following the withdrawal by the UK from direct political involvement in the area. Economic relations between them have been very satisfactory for Britain, with the balance of payments on current account and even the balance of visible trade swinging heavily in its favour as a result of its bonanza of North Sea oil. Many export opportunities for Britain have been missed, but others have been grasped, and new opportunities for joint ventures have been opened up in Saudi Arabia. When the Gulf War ends, as it must surely do in the almost foreseeable future, there should be good opportunities for British firms to win contracts for the rebuilding of Iraq, and perhaps even to some extent of Iran. Meanwhile, invisible trade with the whole area continues to be extensive and highly profitable, while arms exports are soaring again after a quiet period.

Prospect

The large UK surplus on visible trade account with the Middle East since 1981 must be regarded as exceptional. It may continue for another decade, but thereafter it seems inevitable that, as North Sea output falls and oil prices rise again, the Middle East, and especially Saudi Arabia with its huge proven oil reserves, will once more run a substantial visible trade surplus with Britain. It is to be hoped (for the sake not just of Britain but of all concerned) that by that time the UK's economy will be in such good shape, and its earnings from invisibles so flourishing, that no problem will be found in financing Britain's oil and perhaps gas imports on whatever scale may then be required.

Several factors will play their part in deciding that outcome. Most important of all will be Britain's degree of success in maintaining the good levels of economic growth and of productivity increase currently being experienced. If these remain high, and if sterling is not allowed to strengthen to rates which would make British goods uncompetitive in world markets, exports to the Middle East should prosper, especially when oil prices rise again. It is true that UK exporters will be paying increased attention to West European markets after 1992, when the EEC is due to remove the last barriers in its internal trading. But there is no reason why this should not be combined with a high degree of attention to the Middle East, where profit margins are likely to be higher than in Europe.

There may have to be some revisions of commercial tactics. In the past, British firms have not been good at forming consortia to bid for giant contracts in the Middle East. This will need to change, and is the more likely to do so as the same need will arise in trading within the EEC. An alternative would be for British companies to grow by acquisitions to a size which would enable them to match the muscle of their foreign competitors. This would require some rethinking by the British Government of its policy on domestic mergers, which currently inhibits the emergence of monopolies against the background of the British rather than the European or the wider international market. The approach of 1992 should speed such rethinking.

British firms will also need to show increased enthusiasm for the forming of joint ventures with Middle Eastern partners, particularly in Saudi Arabia. Some of the past disincentives to this process are increasingly obsolete. The partners in question are no longer unknown entities; many of them have by now impressive track records. Both sides are becoming somewhat more willing to provide for international arbitration for the settlement of commercial disputes and new institutions for such arbitration are coming into existence.[1]

Arms sales may rank high, in money terms and especially in terms of profitability, among British exports. The recent sales of Tornado aircraft seem likely to lead on to further Arab orders. Quality of future products will be paramount here, as the wealthier countries will always seek the best that money can buy.

The fact that the UK no longer has any imperial entanglements in the Arab world has simplified its trading relationships with the Middle East, but some political hazards remain. The continuing Arab-Israel conflict is the most obvious cause of possible future trouble, and of that unfortunately there is, at the time of writing, no end even remotely in sight. Britain, in Arab eyes, can never escape a large measure of responsibility for the problem and needs to tread very warily in this particular political minefield.

The motto of the Arab-British Chamber of Commerce is 'Friendship through Trade'. It is to be hoped that that will be true for relations between Britain and all countries of the Middle East.

Notes and References

CHAPTER 1: THE UK ECONOMY AFTER WORLD WAR II

1. President Truman's instruction to discontinue all lend-lease operations was issued on 21 August 1945. In a speech to the Commons on 24 August, Attlee complained:'The sudden cessation of support . . . puts us in a very serious financial position'. But, as a speech the same day by the U.S. Director of Foreign Economic Administration explained:'Congress made very clear that it intended lend-lease expenditure to end with the end of the war . . . discontinuance is not a matter of discretion with the President or with me'. For prevalent American attitudes see Richard N. Gardner, *Sterling-Dollar Diplomacy* (Oxford, 1956), Chapter IX.
2. The official figure for foreign assets sold is £4198 million. In addition, sterling indebtedness of Britain at the end of the war totalled £3355 million (£2723 million to sterling area countries and £632 million to other countries). See *Statistical Material Presented During the Washington Negotiations* (HMSO, Cmd. 6706, 1945).
3. R.A. Butler, who briefly succeeded Bevin in this post, did not modify the demobilisation plans. See Anthony Howard, *RAB: The Life of R.A. Butler* (London, 1987), p.147.
4. The author was among these students, having been within a year of finals when he volunteered for service in 1939. His Class A release was already due, but had been deferred by the Chief Signals Officer 9th Army, who planned to go on home leave and wished the author to take over from him. When a Class B release arrived, this could not be deferred as it represented an over-riding civilian priority. The CSO never did understand how the occupation of undergraduate could be regarded as more important than that of Acting Brigadier!
5. The best account of this is in Ben Pimlott, *Hugh Dalton* (London, 1985), a well-researched book which is more reliable than Dalton's own

memoirs. It is one of the principal sources for the first half of this Chapter.

6. Chief among them were Hugh Gaitskell, Douglas Jay and Evan Durbin.
7. Pressure on the companies concerned secured the siting of a large steel strip mill at Margam, petrochemicals at Grangemouth, vehicle manufacture at Linwood, synthetic fibres at Pontypool, and notably a huge ICI chemicals plant at Wilton (an area where unemployment was threatened by the likely demise of Cleveland iron-mining after the war).
8. *Daily Herald*, 9 June 1945.
9. Examples were the industrial estate at Aycliffe in County Durham (where a New Town was built after the war) and another at West Auckland in Dalton's own constituency.
10. Even in the North-East, a notorious unemployment black-spot, the rate was down to 3 per cent by 1948–9 and to 1.5 per cent by June 1951.
11. Unemployment fell to 262,000 in September 1947 and remained below 500,000 until 1958. It crept up gradually in the 1960s, reaching 600,000 in 1963, and accelerated in the 1970s. It rose to 900,000 in 1972 and to 1,250,000 in 1976. See Sir Alec Cairncross in *The Economic History of Britain since 1700*, Vol.2, edited by Floud and McCloskey (Cambridge, 1981).
12. In October 1945, Dalton reduced the interest rate on Treasury Bills from 1 per cent to 0.5 per cent and on Treasury Deposit Receipts from 1.125 per cent to 0.625 per cent. He was able in January 1947 to issue 2.5 per cent Treasury Stock at par (rapidly nicknamed 'Daltons').
13. This was particularly generous. The UK's net debt of over $20,000 million for wartime supplies was completely written off. The $650 million was made up of $532 million charged for some $6000 million of property and Lend-Lease goods located in Britain at the end of the war, plus $118 million for supplies in transit to Britain. See Gardner, *op. cit.*,p.208.
14. There have been many accounts of these negotiations. See for example Pimlott, *op. cit.*, and Roy F. Harrod, *The Life of John Maynard Keynes* (London, 1951).
15. In his memoirs, *High Tide and After* (London, 1962), Dalton more vividly described massive aid as the only way of escape from a'financial Dunkirk' (a phrase used earlier by Keynes about the ending of Lend-Lease).
16. Fuel restrictions were removed on 12 March. The fullest reporting of the problems created by the severe weather is not surprisingly in the daily press.
17. See Colin Cooke, *The Life of Richard Stafford Cripps* (London, 1957), pp.350–5. This book is the principal source for most references to Cripps in this Chapter.

18. The net invisible balance in 1938 had been + £232 million. In 1946 it was -£168 million, an adverse swing of £400 million. See Bank for International Settlements, *The Sterling Area* (Basle, 1953), p.38.
19. Transferable Accounts were held by non-sterling-area countries with which the UK had negotiated bilateral agreements on rights of transfer. Hansard (Commons) for 5 November 1947, col.219, gives examples of large conversions by, for example, Argentina and Belgium between 1 July and 20 August.
20. Cooke, *op. cit.*, p.361.
21. The 16 nations participating were Austria, Belgium, Denmark, Eire, France, Greece, Iceland, Italy, Luxembourg, Netherlands, Norway, Portugal, Sweden, Switzerland, Turkey and the UK. The Soviet Union refused to participate and pressurised the East European countries and also Finland not to join.
22. Appropriations in fact fell short of the $17000 million ceiling. But $12500 million were provided within the 4-year period and by the end of 1953 US economic aid reached $15700 million (as well as another $7700 million in military aid). See Sidney Pollard, *European Economic Integration* (London, 1974), p.158.
23. The party's pre-1939 plans for nationalisation had envisaged a gradual takeover of all industries. Even now, some ideologists hoped to nationalise at least the commercial banks, but Labour's tiny majority in 1949 ruled out any such plan. For the rest of the postwar period the Labour Party when in power contented itself with a 'mixed economy'.
24. See Cooke, *op. cit.*, pp.395–6.
25. It was the author's task in the Foreign Office to telephone to the Treasury reports from British Embassies on the course of action taken by foreign Governments. The sterling area countries virtually all devalued to the same extent as the UK but some Western European countries felt strong enough to devalue by less, for example Belgium by 13 per cent and Italy by only 8 per cent.
26. The American oil companies with distribution in Britain had been arguing against any discrimination against their market shares for purposes of dollar saving. They pointed out that so-called 'sterling oil' had a dollar content, since sterling area oil companies bought equipment in the dollar area (often the only source). In strenuous bargaining before derationing was announced (in which the author represented the Foreign Office), they undertook to increase the 'sterling content' of their 'dollar oil' sold in Britain by increasing their purchases in the sterling area. The negotiations were complicated procedurally by the need to avoid breaches of American anti-trust laws.

27. Rationing in the postwar period had been regulated not in accordance with some overall economic plan but pragmatically on the basis of the supply/demand situation. Controls had been relaxed or abolished when it was judged that this would not lead to queues or sharp price rises. 1949–50 saw major shifts away from rationing. Clothes, shoes and textiles were freed in March 1949; potatoes soon followed and bread (not rationed during the war) in July. The petrol ration was doubled for the summer months of 1949. Restrictions on the extraction rate for flour were removed at the time of devaluation, so as to offset the unpopular rise in the cost of bread by the popular restoration of a whiter loaf. In May 1950, not only was petrol derationed but the 'points' system, regulating the sale of a range of miscellaneous groceries such as canned goods, was swept away.

CHAPTER 2: THE MIDDLE EAST ECONOMIES AFTER WORLD WAR II

1. The author supervised the building of the railway telegraph circuits alongside this railway. For a summary list of the main contributions of the British and American forces to the development of infrastructure throughout the region see Martin W. Wilmington, *The Middle East Supply Centre* (New York, 1971), p.22. The chief effort of the American forces came in Iran, in order to ease the flow of Lend-Lease supplies to the Soviet Union: see T.H.V. Motter, *The Persian Corridor and Aid to Russia* (Washington D.C., 1953), *passim*.
2. The Middle East Supply Centre was set up in 1941 in Cairo and was responsible to the British Minister of State there. It was initially purely British but from July 1942 became a British-American organisation. British historians have sadly neglected the work of the Centre and its lasting value to the region. There are only brief references to it in the Official Histories of the War. Fortunately American historians have been more interested in wartime logistics. The definitive work on the Centre is Wilmington, *op. cit.* See also E.M.H. Lloyd, *Food and Inflation in the Middle East 1940–1945* (Stanford, 1956), *passim*.
3. The membership of the Sterling Area was defined by the Defence (Finance) (Definition of Sterling Area) (No.2) Order, 1944 as being the United Kingdom and 'the following territories excluding Canada and Newfoundland, that is to say:
   (a) any Dominion,
   (b) any other part of His Majesty's dominions,
   (c) any territory in respect of which a mandate on behalf of the League

of Nations has been accepted by His Majesty and is being exercised by His Majesty's Government in the United Kingdom, or in any Dominion,
(d) any British Protectorate or Protected State,
(e) Egypt, the Anglo-Egyptian Sudan and Iraq,
(f) Iceland and the Faroe Islands.'

As applied to the territories asterisked in Table 1, Aden was covered by (b) and (d); Palestine and Transjordan by (c); the three countries named by (e); and the remainder, as Protected States, by (d). Libya was under Allied Military Government pending decision on its future; in practice this was a British administration.

4. This treaty dated from 1936. The main supply bases were in the Suez Canal Zone; in 1947 they were enlarged by the transfer to them of most of the military stores removed from India prior to independence. See Chapter 7 below.
5. French troops were compelled by Britain to evacuate Syria in 1945, when serious clashes between them and Syrians demonstrating against their continued presence, and particularly their reinforcement by Senegalese units, culminated in a French artillery bombardment of Damascus, which led to British intervention. This episode is now unknown to or ignored by Syrians (liking to claim all credit for their independence for their own leaders). It is almost forgotten in Britain, but is still remembered in France as yet another example of 'perfide Albion'. The author was the senior Signals Officer of the force, drawn from the 31st Indian Armoured Division, which surrounded Damascus to compel the French to pull back to barracks, and was interpreter between the British and French Generals in their negotiations to arrange evacuation of French forces from the country. French troop withdrawal from Lebanon was completed more peacefully in 1946.
6. See R.W. Ferrier, *History of British Petroleum*, Vol.1, (Cambridge, 1982) Chapter 5.
7. Although Shell was a Dutch-British consortium with a 60 per cent Dutch ownership, its Middle East operations were managed from London. And the American oil majors also tended to run their Middle East affairs from subsidiaries in London. As mentioned, the operating companies IPC and KOC were both London-based.
8. For a penetrating discussion of this whole subject see Edith Penrose, *The Growth of Firms, Middle East Oil and Other Essays* (London, 1971), Chapter XI.
9. One example is Sudanese camels, driven on the hoof to Egypt to supply the Egyptian meat market. A less reputable example is Lebanese hashish, smuggled at that time almost solely to Egypt.

10. See J.S.R. Duncan, *The Sudan* (Edinburgh, 1952), pp.120–5. An interesting result of the establishment of the Gezira cotton scheme was a considerable admixture of Nigerian blood into the Sudanese population. Muslim pilgrims from Northern Nigeria, after making their way to Mecca via the Sudan, often stopped off in the Gezira on their way home to earn funds by labouring and cotton-picking to continue their journey. A large number of them took Sudanese wives, by whom they had children. Many never completed their homeward journey.
11. Except in respect of the need to secure the promised withdrawal of Soviet troops from North Iran. This was accomplished in May 1946, after a flurry of excitement which caused the issue to be raised in the UN Security Council. See Alan Bullock, *Ernest Bevin Foreign Secretary 1945–1951*, (London, 1983) pp.236–7.

CHAPTER 3: THE EMERGENCE OF ISRAEL

1. After considerable hesitation, the British Government had in 1944 sanctioned the formation in Palestine of a Jewish Brigade, which had served with distinction in Italy.
2. There is a vast literature on this subject, most of it distinctly partial in its approach. W. Roger Louis, *The British Empire in the Middle East 1945–1951* (Oxford, 1984), is a recent publication drawing on a wide range of evidence. For the problem as it appeared to the UK Government in 1947, see Bullock, *op. cit.*
3. U.N.G.A., 2nd Session: *Report of the United Nations Special Committee on Palestine*, Vol.1 (New York, 1947).
4. See Bullock, *op. cit.*, Chapter 12.
5. Members of the armed forces and police evacuated numbered some 100,000.
6. See David Ben Gurion, *B'Hilachem Yisrael* [*In the Struggle for Israel*] (Tel Aviv,1949), quoted by Sacher (v.i.).
7. See Harry S. Truman, *Memoirs* (New York, 1953–55).
8. Available sources give highly discrepant figures for the 1948 Palestinian refugees and there is no really convincing way of sorting truth from fiction. UNRWA Reports should be the best source, but seem to be far too high. The author believes that the figures used here (derived from comparison of several sources but not rigidly following any one of them) give a sound general picture of the movements involved. It would be misleading to claim more.
9. Ben Gurion made this clear at an Israeli Cabinet meeting on 16 June 1948. See Howard M. Sacher, *Europe Leaves the Middle East 1936–1954* (New

York, 1972). From time to time in future years Israeli spokesmen (especially Sharett when Foreign Minister) declared their readiness to accept the return of some refugees, but there was never a majority in the country for this policy and Ben Gurion remained implacably opposed to the return of even a single refugee. See Maxime Rodinson (tr. Michael Perl), *Israel and the Arabs* (Harmondsworth,1968), pp.66–71.

10. Figure from Howard M. Sacher, *From the Ends of the Earth: The Peoples of Israel* (New York, 1964).
11. For a good brief account of the work of UNRWA and the problems it faced in its early years see Stewart Perowne, *The One Remains* (London, 1954), pp.80–85.
12. In a famous financial coup, Disraeli in 1875 bought for the British Government 176,602 shares in the Suez Canal Company from the debt-ridden Egyptian Khedive Ismail.
13. In addition to making very substantial outright gifts, Jewish communities in USA subscribed heavily to Israeli government bonds. Independence and Development Loans were floated by Israel on the U.S. market.
14. On this point see Don Peretz, *Israel and the Palestinian Arabs* (Washington D.C., 1958), pp.143–4 and 165.
15. See Rodinson, *op. cit.*, p.14.
16. Buying and selling were controlled by the London Diamond Syndicate but not all stones passed physically through the UK. In particular, rough stones very often moved direct from South Africa to Israel. Israel specialises in the processing of stones of medium size. For details of the Israeli diamond industry, see Rodney Wilson, *The Economies of the Middle East* (London, 1979), pp.63–5.
17. The British Treasury announced on 22 February 1948, in preparation for the approaching end of the Mandate, that Palestine's sterling balances had been blocked and that both Palestine and Transjordan had ceased to be members of the Sterling Area (Transjordan was affected because Palestinian currency circulated there also). The size of the balances was stated as around £100 million (after heavy drawings of some £15 million in the preceding 6 months), of which £7 million were released immediately for current needs. Palestine's successor states and Transjordan might be readmitted to the Sterling Area; this could be discussed in due course if they so wished. Transjordan had in fact already informed H.M.G. that currency and exchange controls would be set up with a view to permitting a return to the Sterling Area and this duly took place on 1 July 1950. Israel did not seek to rejoin the Sterling Area.
18. An agreement between the UK and Israel was signed in London on 30 March 1950 settling all claims and counter-claims between the two

Governments. Under it, Israel undertook to pay £11.4 million for a variety of purposes, including the payment of benefits and pensions to former officials. Against this were set credits due to Israel from Palestine funds, leaving a net sum due from Israel of £3,716,000. This was to be paid £1,118,300 in cash, with the remaining £2,598,400 funded over 15 years at 1 per cent interest. A settlement with Jordan was announced on 2 March 1951, under which Jordan paid £1 million towards the liabilities of the former Palestine Government, with an annual payment of £15,000 to be made towards the pensions of former officials.

19. See Rodinson, *op. cit.*, pp.54–5.

CHAPTER 4: TRADE BETWEEN BRITAIN AND THE MIDDLE EAST 1946–50

1. See A.J. Meyer, *Middle Eastern Capitalism* (Cambridge, Mass., 1959), Chapter VI.
2. This argument was somewhat bogus, as the Middle East Governments chose to overlook the fact that the British taxes were on the profits of the oil companies earned world-wide and included all their vertically-integrated operations, not merely oil production. Nevertheless, it had some validity, and the host Governments were in any case inclined to believe (rightly or more probably wrongly) that their concession-holders manipulated oil prices for crude so as to take greater profits at some later stage of their operations. For an interesting discussion of this whole issue see Penrose, *op. cit.* pp.105–9 and 139–150: her analysis points to the conclusion that the oil 'majors' in fact maximised their profits at the production stage.
3. The global figures published by the British Invisible Exports Council and its predecessor the Committee on Invisible Exports, established in April 1968, show that Britain had a consistently favourable balance of invisible trade throughout the period covered by this book (and undoubtedly long before that). Indeed, the UK has regularly been second only to the USA in this respect in the postwar period. On the bilateral level, there is no reason to suppose that this would not have been true of Britain's balance with each of the Middle East countries individually, at least until the time when some of the oil-rich countries of the Arabian Peninsula began to receive huge incomes from their investment portfolios abroad, including in the UK. Prior to that, the only countries in the region to have substantial invisible earnings were Egypt (Suez Canal dues, tourism and airport charges) and Lebanon (banking, insurance, entrepôt trade and airport charges). A few other countries had earnings from tourism, but it

was not until long after the war that these built up rapidly in, for example Tunisia. Saudi Arabia had invisible earnings from the annual pilgrimage of Muslims to Mecca but these were not enormous, though a useful source of foreign exchange until they were overshadowed by oil revenues.

4. See *A history of ECGD 1919–1979* (London, 1979), a valuable account of its activities produced by ECGD to mark its 60th birthday. It is to be hoped that this will be updated in 1989.
5. See Geoffrey Jones, *Banking and Empire in Iran* (London, 1986), pp.243–6.
6. See Geoffrey Jones, *Banking and Oil* (London, 1987), pp.135–143. (This book and the one mentioned in the previous note form a 2-volume official history of the British Bank of the Middle East, with use of the Bank's confidential archives, although these are deliberately not drawn on after about 1966 and some discretion is apparent in quoting them from about 1960.)

CHAPTER 5: THE IRANIAN OIL CRISIS

1. A fuller account of the events covered in this Chapter will appear in Dr Ferrier's forthcoming publication, based i.a. on his access to the Company's archives, *History of British Petroleum* Vol 2.
2. See Vol 7 of the *Cambridge History of Iran*, contributed by Dr Ferrier.
3. See J.R.L. Anderson, *East of Suez* (London, 1969), p.48.
4. Le Rougetel to Foreign Office, PRO, FO 371/61976 of 6 December 1947.
5. See Bullock, *op. cit.*, p.247. Bevin had sounded out Sir William Fraser, Chairman of AIOC. In a forward-looking paper which he put to the Cabinet in July 1946, Bevin went much further with the idea that the Company should offer the Iranian Government 50 per cent ownership of AIOC, making it in a real sense Anglo-Iranian. He did this in the context of pointing out the difficulty for a British Government embarked on a major nationalisation programme of opposing an Iranian nationalisation of AIOC, should this come about. Altogether a very far-seeing paper (FO 371/52735 in the PRO). But it is not surprising that the AIOC Board at the time, even if it had been put to them which it probably never was, would have considered it visionary and irreconcilable with their duty to their shareholders.
6. For details of the personalities involved and the contacts between them, AIOC, and at times the British Government, see Ferrier in the *Cambridge History of Iran*, Vol.7.
7. AIOC did finally bring itself to offer a 50/50 agreement, together with the establishment of an Iranian subsidiary on whose profits it would be

calculated, to Razmara, then Iranian Prime Minister, in February 1951, but by then it was too late. He kept the offer secret and was assassinated on 7 March 1951 by a religious extremist. He had also kept secret the fact that the company had paid an advance against royalties under the Supplemental Agreement of £11 million, and had promised another £25 million advance. But even had all this been known it would probably have made no difference. Musaddiq's motivation was political, not economic. He was determined that Iran should have entire control of its own oil.

8. The cruiser transported 280 of them. By the time of the evacuation the Royal Navy also had six destroyers anchored in the Shatt-al-Arab, HMS *Armada, Chequers, Chieftain, Chivalrous, Gravelines* and *Vigo*. A plan existed (codenamed BUCCANEER) to seize Abadan Island, but it was not implemented. Morrison defended the Cabinet's decision not to use force in a speech to the Labour Party Conference on 3 October 1951. But (rightly or wrongly) the psychological effect in the Middle East was damaging to Britain's prestige.
9. Anthony Eden, now Foreign Secretary as the Conservatives had returned to office, conducted these talks with the U.S. Secretary of State, Dean Acheson. They narrowed the gap between British and American attitudes to Musaddiq but did not close it. See Sir Anthony Eden, *Full Circle* (London, 1960), pp.200–203.
10. Legal action was taken by AIOC in the case of two cargoes, on the *Mary Rose* in Aden and on the *Miriella* in Italy.
11. The loss of the Abadan Refinery was rather more of a problem as refinery capacity was less easily replaceable than crude oil. AIOC did have to reduce product sales in the period 1951–1954.
12. Musaddiq was charged with high treason and on 2 December 1953 was sentenced to three years solitary confinement. After serving his sentence, he retired to his estates, where he died in 1967.
13. See Kermit Roosevelt, *Countercoup: The Struggle for the Control of Iran* (New York, 1979), and C.M. Woodhouse, *Something Ventured* (London, 1982), for their rather one-sided accounts of these intelligence activities.
14. See Eden, *op. cit.*, pp.217–19.
15. See Penrose, *op. cit.*, p.207 and note 24 on p.215.
16. At governmental level, diplomatic relations, which had been broken off by the Iranians in October 1952, were resumed on 5 December 1953.

CHAPTER 6: ARMS EXPORTS POLICY 1945–55

1. Major arms export deals tend to get media coverage, despite attempts to keep them secret. But there are endless smaller deals which escape notice.

So do the profitable follow-on sales which derive from the major deals, for replacements and spare parts.

2. See Chapter 10 below.

CHAPTER 7: THE EGYPTIAN REVOLUTION

1. The total casualties in Cairo and Alexandria together were only 10, 2 killed and 8 wounded. See Mohammed Neguib, *Egypt's Destiny* (London, 1955), p.133.
2. Neguib, *op. cit.*, (or his ghost-writer) is at pains to enlarge the role he played before the coup, but this part of his story must be regarded with the greatest suspicion. It conflicts with accounts given by others of the Free Officers.
3. At a press conference on his yacht before sailing from Alexandria into exile, taking his son with him, Farouk gave vent to his famous witticism that the world would soon have only five kings, the kings of spades, hearts, diamonds and clubs, and the King of England. Although he was wrong in that prophecy, he was right in judging that the Egyptian monarchy was at an end in all but name.
4. See Neguib, *op. cit.*, p.198.
5. Robert Mabro, *The Egyptian Economy 1952–1972* (London,1974). This excellent book deals with land reform in more detail than space here permits and should be consulted by anyone wishing to know more about the subject. It forms a principal source for this and the following paragraphs. See also Neguib, *op. cit.*, pp.263–72.
6. The author, as a First Secretary in the British Embassy in Cairo from July 1953 to July 1956, was one of a group of diplomats taken to admire the project.
7. In July 1953, the author, as senior 'desk officer' in the Political Section (Chancery) of the Embassy, inherited the 'Sudan desk' from his predecessor. Before the end of the year, that desk had been reduced in priority by a smooth progress of Sudan problems towards resolution, and he moved to the 'Canal Zone Base' desk. By July 1956, he had seen that problem also resolved and left Cairo on transfer to the Foreign Office, luckily before the events to be recounted towards the end of Chapter 10.
8. British intelligence was also active and during the period of their imprisonment the British Embassy knew that they were being well treated.
9. The ending of conscription in the UK was announced in the Defence White Paper of April 1957.
10. For a fairly full account of them see Eden, *op. cit.*, pp.243–61.

11. The author acted as British Embassy Liaison Officer with the British forces and their civilian replacements during the 20 months, paying weekly visits to the Canal Zone for the purpose.
12. The contrast between 800 technicians and nearly 80,000 troops is startling enough. Suez Contractors Management Ltd. in London (a Government-run committee despite its company title) controlled 5 'non-commercial' (i.e. commercial but non-profit-making) companies in the Canal Zone, as follows:

Suez Contractors (Ammunition)	-	ICI
Suez Contractors (Electricity)	-	Balfour Beatty
Suez Contractors (Engineers)	-	Vickers Armstrong
Suez Contractors (Maintenance)	-	George Wimpey, John Laing and Holloway Bros.
Suez Contractors (Vehicles)	-	ACV, Austin Motors and Rootes Motors.

These worked entirely separately from their parent companies, who were paid an annual fee for the services of their personnel in the Base. The arrangement was thus not exactly an example of what today would be called 'privatisation' of military installations, but it was a long and interesting step on the way towards it.

CHAPTER 8: THE BURAIMI DISPUTE

1. Strictly speaking, Buraimi is the name of one of the villages in the Omani part of the oasis (or group of oases), but it is used loosely as the name of the whole area.
2. See H.St.J.B. Philby, *Arabian Oil Ventures* (Washington D.C., 1964, published posthumously by The Middle East Institute), especially the Foreword by a former Chairman of ARAMCO, pp.ix-xiii.
3. The name is again used in its loose sense; Turki in fact occupied the Omani village of Hamasa. But his presence there was in demonstration of Saudi Arabia's assertion of a claim to the whole area.
4. See the magisterial work on this subject by J.B. Kelly, *Britain and the Persian Gulf 1795–1880* (Oxford, 1968), especially Chapters IV to IX.
5. *Ibid.*, Chapter IX.
6. J.B. Kelly, *Eastern Arabian Frontiers* (London, 1964), pp.142 ff.
7. Shaikh Zaid, brother of Shaikh Shakhbut (and subsequently his replacement as Ruler of Abu Dhabi; now President of the United Arab Emirates), was reported to have been offered Rs.400 million, a vast sum in a then poor Shaikhdom, but to have rejected the offer.

8. See Sir Evelyn Shuckburgh, *Descent to Suez* (London, 1986), entry for 7 October 1955, p.289.
9. For the attitudes of Hoover, who was totally pro-ARAMCO in the matter, and of Dulles, who was unhappy but more objective, see Shuckburgh, *op. cit.*, entry for 20 January 1956, p.323.
10. Two squadrons of the Special Air Service Regiment and a troop of the Life Guards surprised the inhabitants of the Green Mountain by storming its highest peak. See J.B. Kelly, *Sultanate and Imamate in Oman* (Oxford, 1959), p.19.
11. The author, who was Counsellor in Khartoum at the time, was transferred to Jedda as accredited Chargé d'Affaires, to reopen the British Embassy in early February 1963. Prince Faisal, who was Regent (and Prime Minister and Foreign Minister), had decided to resume relations because of Aden's importance to Saudi Arabia during the Yemen Civil War. But he still felt bitterly about Buraimi. As Shaikh Hafiz Wahba, ex-Ambassador to London, told the author in Jedda at the time: 'For Faisal it is not a matter of territory but of honour; however, honour can only be satisfied by territory.' For the eventual settlement see Chapter 17.

CHAPTER 9: THE ECONOMY OF INDEPENDENT SUDAN

1. See *The Middle East* (5th Edn.) ed. Peter Mansfield (Oxford, 1980) p.495.
2. See R.M. MacGregor, *The Nile Waters*, in *The Anglo-Egyptian Sudan from Within*, ed. J.A. de C. Hamilton (London,1935) p.282, which gives the maximum discharge from the White Nile as only six times the minimum. The corresponding ratio for the Blue Nile maximum can be as high as 400 to one and would rarely be less than 50 to one. See also F.A. Lees and H.C. Brooks, *The Economic and Political Development of the Sudan* (London, 1977), p.3.
3. The £E circulated in Sudan as well as Egypt until the introduction of a Sudanese currency (£S) after independence. The Sennar Dam had been planned in 1913, but its construction was delayed by World War I.
4. This figure represents the effect of extraction in the Sudan on the flow of the Nile at Aswan. It corresponds to 20.5 million cubic metres at Khartoum.
5. See Rodney Wilson, *The Economies of the Middle East*, Table 9.2 on p.148, drawing on statistics published by the Bank of Sudan.
6. This acreage is not all used for cotton. The Gezira Scheme has always been operated as a cooperative scheme between the Government and tenant farmers, with the latter growing their own food crops, mainly millet, as well as cotton, so allowing also for crop rotation to maintain fertility and

control pests. The division of revenues from sales is 42 per cent tenants, 42 per cent Government, 10 per cent to the Sudan Gezira Board, which administers the Scheme and markets the cash crops, with the remainder going to the local government, to social services and to a Reserve Fund (for use in bad crop years). In recent years, diversification of crops has meant a large acreage under wheat, with substantial production also of maize, rice, groundnuts and vegetables.

7. See Wilson, *op. cit.*, Table 9.1 on p.144. Writing in 1977 he totalled soft loans and grants to £S1179 million, commercial loans to £S568 million and investment in equity to £S540. This funding was spread between 100 projects, of which he reckoned 62 to be commercially viable.
8. The author is sad to have to make this judgment. He served in the British Embassy in Khartoum from 1960 to 1963, for about half the period as Chargé d'Affaires, and came to like the Sudanese as well as any people among whom he has ever served. But their good qualities seem not to include an ability to solve the admittedly difficult problem of the north-south divide, and failure in that respect bedevils their economic performance.

CHAPTER 10: DECLINE TO SUEZ

1. *Egypt's Liberation: The Philosophy of the Revolution* (Washington D.C., 1955), pp.85–6.
2. For a lucid analysis of the thinking of Nuri, Eden and Nasser at this time, see Elizabeth Monroe, *Britain's Moment in the Middle East 1914–1956* (London, 1963), pp.180–5.
3. The story which reached the author in Cairo a little later from a well-placed Egyptian source was that when the captain of the *An Shun* failed to declare himself, a signaller at Sharm al Shaikh was ordered to send a lamp message demanding the ship's name and destination. Unfortunately, the signaller either did not know Morse or perhaps did not know how to operate the lamp apparatus; either way a meaningless series of flashes was sent to the ship. Puzzled, the captain continued on his course. A gunner was then told to put a shot across the ship's bows to bring it to a halt; being badly trained, he failed to allow for the ship's forward momentum and hit it.
4. The author was also told a story on this subject. It runs that an agent of Peking drew Nasser's attention to his new dependence on spare parts for his Soviet-bloc weapons and the wisdom of having more than one source for them. As the Chinese were at this time armed with Soviet weapons, Nasser was persuaded that it would be in his interest to be in diplomatic

relations with Peking, so as to be able to buy spares from there should it prove necessary. Neither this story nor that in Note 3 above is capable of being documented, but to one who was serving in Cairo at the time they had a certain plausibility.

5. Technically, the company was Egyptian in the sense that it was registered in Egypt; for that reason it was legally a simple matter for Nasser to nationalise it. But the building of the Canal had been a French project and the Company was controlled entirely from Paris; virtually all its senior staff were French.
6. Eden, *op. cit.*, p.426, quotes the 1955 figures for shipping to bring out the Canal's importance to Western countries; of the 14,666 transits of the Canal that year, three-quarters were by ships from NATO countries including one-third from Britain. Nearly 70 million tons of oil, almost half of Middle East production, passed through the Canal, most of it bound for Western European ports; this included more than half of Britain's oil supplies. Countries 'east of Suez' were similarly dependent on dry cargo ships transiting south-bound.
7. See Eden, *op. cit.*, pp.474–486 and Selwyn Lloyd, *Suez 1956: A Personal Account* (London, 1978), pp.126–134 and 143–4. Lloyd quotes Robert Murphy (US representative in many of the Anglo-American discussions following the nationalisation of the Canal) as believing that Foster Dulles thought up SCUA purely as a delaying tactic to restrain Bitain and France from the use of force prior to the US presidential elections. In theory SCUA still exists. It was not wound up, but merely reduced to a 'no-cost' basis (the arrangements for this being made by the author). Its files were transferred to Foreign Office custody and its bank account, with a minute credit balance, was left dormant.
8. See Eden, *op. cit.*, pp.556–7 and Lloyd, *op. cit.*, pp.210–11. Britain's gold and dollar reserves fell in November by $279 million, 15 per cent of its holdings.
9. Reopening was a gradual process, on 20 March for ships of up to 2000 tons, 26 March up to 4000 tons and 29 March up to 10,000 tons; 8 April was the date from which maximum draught vessels could transit.
10. The author was appointed Assistant Head of the African Department of the Foreign Office in December 1956, with Egypt as his main responsibility. It was thus his task, along with the Claims Department, to deal with these negotiations. In the final settlement the opportunity was taken to wipe the sheet clean of claims antedating the Suez affair, particularly those of the British officials of the Egyptian Government who had been dismissed before the 1952 Revolution without compensation for loss of office.

11. It is perhaps most surprising that the collusion with Israel in the attack on the Canal did not lead to more serious and more lasting damage to Britain's position in the rest of the Arab World. This was hardly because of the British Government's efforts to deny collusion, since no Arab believed those protestations. It was perhaps due to a realisation that the attack and the collusion had been very much a personal aberration on the part of Anthony Eden rather than well-thought-out and carefully planned British policy. The resignation in protest of Anthony Nutting, Minister of State at the Foreign Office, may have helped to bring this home to some Arab opinion. The opposition to the use of force against Egypt voiced by the Labour Party also won some Arab praise. And it has to be remembered that Nasser, although a hero to the Arab man in the street, was by no means popular with Arab Governments outside Egypt, even though they all rallied to him temporarily during the Suez crisis.
12. Cairo Radio had been knocked out by British bombing as a preliminary to the invasion of Port Said, but its repair had been a priority task and it was back on the air very rapidly.

CHAPTER 11: THE IRAQI REVOLUTION

1. King Faisal I was succeeded by his son Ghazi, who was killed in a road accident in 1939. His son, King Faisal II, not yet 4 years of age, came to the throne, with his uncle Amir Abdul Illah as Regent. After leaving school at Harrow at the age of 18, Faisal was crowned King on 2 May 1953, the ex-Regent becoming Crown Prince.
2. There was provision under the concessions of the Mosul and Basrah Oil Companies for the Iraq Government to take part of its royalties in oil, but little use was made of this right.
3. See *The Middle East*, 5th Edn., ed. Peter Mansfield (Oxford, 1980), pp.348–9.
4. See A.J. Meyer, *Middle Eastern Capitalism* (Cambridge, Mass., 1959), p.97.
5. In the Treaty between UK and Transjordan of 22 March 1946 (Cmd.6916), the British grant-in-aid to Transjordan was fixed at £2 million p.a. This was later raised to £9 million and then to £12 million p.a.
6. See Selwyn Lloyd, *Suez 1956 (London, 1978)*, pp.46–8. The author was serving in Cairo at this time and well remembers the late-night discussion which succeeded the dinner party, during the course of which the news of Glubb's dismissal had reached the Embassy. Selwyn Lloyd was very much inclined to believe that the timing of the announcement had been pre-arranged by Nasser. In fact, Hussain was by no means under Nasser's

thumb, nor even well-disposed towards him, and Nasser was probably just as much surprised by the announcement as the others present. The difference was that he was delighted with it. This trip was a disastrous one for Selwyn Lloyd, the more so as it came soon after his promotion to Foreign Secretary; at his next stop, Bahrain, his motorcade was stoned by excited Arab nationalists (*ibid.*, pp.49–51).

7. See King Hussain of Jordan, *Uneasy Lies the Head* (London and New York, 1962), p.138.

CHAPTER 12: TRADE BETWEEN BRITAIN AND THE MIDDLE EAST 1950–60

1. The underlying source of the figures in Tables 3 and 4 is the *Trade and Navigation Accounts* presented to Parliament. They have been rounded up or down to the nearest £100,000, which means that figures below £50,000 appear as zero.
2. Israel was beginning to change from a developing to a developed country, both by expansion of its industrial base and by increasing the intensity of its agriculture.
3. For details of the BBME's expansion and profitability in this period, see Geoffrey Jones, *Banking and Oil*, pp.34–72.

CHAPTER 13: EGYPT'S ARAB SOCIALISM

1. See *The Middle East*, 5th Edn., (Oxford,1980), ed. Peter Mansfield, p.246.
2. *Ibid.*, p.245.
3. See Galal Amin, *The Egyptian Economy and the Revolution* in P.J. Vatikiotis (ed.) *Egypt since the Revolution* (London, 1968), pp.47–8.
4. See Bent Hansen, *Planning and Economic Growth in the UAR (Egypt), 1960–5*, in Vatikiotis, *op. cit.*, p.23.
5. *Ibid.*, pp.31–6.
6. There was some Government control even in the agricultural sector, since each cooperative contained an official who laid down such important matters as cropping policy. The cooperatives were originally set up only in the redistributed lands, but were later spread more widely when small land-holdings elsewhere were reorganised into consolidated fields to increase efficiency.

CHAPTER 14: THE ARABIAN PENINSULA AND NORTH-WEST AFRICA

1. Ralph Hewins, *A Golden Dream: The Miracle of Kuwait* (London, 1963), Chapter 46, seizes on these puzzling features to argue that Qasim never intended to invade Kuwait and that the whole crisis was dreamed up by

the British War Office as an excuse for mounting an exercise to test their new rapid deployment force. This unlikely interpretation seems inconsistent with his further contention that Britain was by no means ready to move troops to Kuwait and that the whole operation was a shambles.

2. There were in fact severe problems about the lack of automatic overflying rights for the forces to be brought from Cyprus and from the UK. Simultaneous requests were put to the Governments of Turkey and Iran for the north-about route and to the Government of Sudan for the south-about route (there were rights by treaty for the overflying of Libya). The author was at the time Chargé d'Affaires of the British Embassy in Khartoum and put the request to the Sudanese Foreign Minister. The Sudan Government rapidly agreed and troops were in fact moved by both routes.
3. Information given to the author when he visited Abu Dhabi in 1963 by the then Manager of the Ottoman Bank.
4. There were only six British businessmen resident in Jedda when the author arrived there in February 1963 to reopen the British Embassy, and none elsewhere in the Kingdom. One British firm, Gellatly Hankey, had kept an effective presence throughout the period of broken diplomatic relations, since it had had the foresight to enter into a partnership with one of the Royal Princes. But it was very much the exception.
5. The author was by this time Head of the Arabian Department of the Foreign Office and was deeply involved in these negotiations. Interestingly, the Junior Minister who took a personal hand in them was Mr John Stonehouse about whom scandal later centred when he became involved in dubious financial deals and sought a way out by a faked suicide. It is possible that it was this Saudi arms contract which first put into his head the idea that he had a gift for commercial wheeling and dealing.

CHAPTER 15: THE SIX-DAY WAR AND ITS AFTERMATH

1. Very little of this shipping in fact flew the Israeli flag, although some of it was Israeli-chartered. See M. Howard and R. Hunter, *Israel and the Arab World: The Crisis of 1967*, Adelphi Papers No.41, p.24.
2. See General Carl von Horn, *Soldiering for Peace* (London, 1966), *passim*. Most of the General's frustration was caused by Israel, partly because much of it arose from incidents in the Demilitarised Zones which Israel was determined to dominate, rather in the way that aggressive commanders in the First World War set about dominating the 'No Man's Land' between the forward trenches.

3. The Alawis are a religious sect of Shi'ite origin, centred territorially around the port of Lataqia. They form quite a small minority (10 or 11 per cent) in a country with a Sunni majority and it is remarkable that they have been able to hold the major positions of power in Syria for such a long period. The fact that many of them pursued military careers has obviously contributed to this success, but does not seem sufficient to explain it entirely. There are of course many other minorities in Syria and the Alawis seem to have been skilful in profiting from this fragmentation.
4. See, for instance, George Brown, *In My Way* (London, 1971), p.136, where it is claimed that Nasser himself was surprised by U Thant's decision.
5. Nasser probably did not plan to go beyond brinkmanship. He may have intended only to produce a crisis which would put pressure on the US Government to intervene with decisive effect on Israel, as in 1956. If so, he fatally miscalculated the 1967 relationship between Israel and USA.
6. Brown, *loc. cit.*, p.137. The author, having witnessed the failure of SCUA (see Chapter 10), was fascinated to see how similar pressures drove the Government (of a different party) towards a similar policy initiative, even though failure seemed even more likely in the case of the Gulf of Aqaba, which was far less crucial to international shipping than the Suez Canal had been. The Prime Minister, Harold Wilson, was due to pay an official visit to Canada to attend Expo '67 at Montreal. He changed his plans, with the consent of the Canadian Prime Minister, to use the journey to make final pleas for support for an international declaration on navigation to Eilat, spending only 12 hours in Ottawa, followed by 24 hours in Washington to consult President Johnson, and a final 12 hours in New York to brief U Thant. The author, at that time Under-Secretary of State for Middle East Affairs in the Foreign Office, accompanied him on this strenuous but unfortunately fruitless trip; the war broke out on the following Monday.
7. See Charles W. Yost, *The Arab-Israeli War, How it Began* in *Foreign Affairs*, Vol.46, No.2, (January, 1968), pp.304–320.
8. Several Arab countries, including Egypt, had broken off diplomatic relations with the UK in 1965 in protest at British policy over Rhodesia. There was also great suspicion in Arab circles that Harold Wilson was pro-Israeli; a syndicated press photograph of him on the steps of No.10 Downing Street giving Golda Meir a farewell kiss on the cheek had been published in virtually every newspaper in the Arab world.
9. See Paul Gore-Booth, *With Great Truth and Respect* (London, 1974), pp.366–7.
10. Goods in transit through the Suez Canal were moving at a rate of 250 million tonnes p.a. in 1967 prior to the closure.

11. The closure of the Canal forestalled plans to widen and deepen it to allow passage of tankers up to 110,000 tons fully laden and 200,000 tons in ballast. The latter figure shows how the use of supertankers was growing even before this new closure stimulated it further. It also draws attention to the point that the choice for tankers was not a straight one between the Canal route in both directions and the Cape route in both directions. There was the third option of Cape route laden combined with Canal route unladen (saving time on the unprofitable passage in ballast).
12. Egypt's income from the Canal was over £E95 million in 1966, equivalent to over £76 million sterling.
13. It had become clear some time before that Egypt could not build up the Yemeni Republican forces sufficiently to win a decisive victory over the Royalists. Equally, the Saudis had come to the conclusion that the Royalists could not put an end to the Republic, which had won a great deal of international standing, including recognition by the USA as early as December 1962, followed by a UN seat. There had therefore been negotiations both between the Republicans and Royalists and between the Egyptians and Saudis. But ceasefires and political settlements on forms of government in Yemen had a tendency to break down. After the withdrawal of all Egyptian forces, the Republicans needed emergency aid from Algeria, Syria and the Soviet Union to withstand a Royalist siege of the Yemeni capital, Sanaa. However, a quarrel between the Imam and one of his cousins then weakened the Royalists seriously and Faisal was sufficiently disgusted to cut off Saudi aid to them in 1969. Further negotiations in the first half of 1970 produced a compromise appointment of a leading Royalist to a three-man Republican Council. Saudi Arabia recognised this regime in July 1970, followed by others including the UK.
14. For Libyan oil, see Chapter 16.
15. Brown was to some extent pro-Arab, in the sense that he saw Britain's interests in Arab countries as outweighing those in Israel, a view shared by many but not all of his officials in the Foreign Office. However, it was not this which caused him to demand a redraft so much as a feeling that it would be out of keeping for him to go personally to the UN and then mouth a string of platitudes. The emphasis given in the redraft to Jerusalem was consistent with the fact that the UK had always refused to accept both Israeli sovereignty over West Jerusalem (hence the British Embassy was, and still is, in Tel Aviv) and Jordanian sovereignty over East Jerusalem, since the whole city had been apportioned to an international zone in the UN partition plan which led to the termination of the Mandate.
16. On leaving the UN auditorium, elated at the applause given to his

speech, Brown found himself and his delegation having to cross the path of the Israeli delegation, led by the redoubtable Golda Meir. With only a momentary hesitation, he made to kiss her cheek (she was an old friend of his, met often at meetings of the Socialist International, and he prided himself on his gallantry to ladies). The author was fascinated to hear her respond with the one word,'Judas': from an Israeli to a Christian it seemed the perfect riposte.

17. See Brown, *op. cit.*, pp.137–140. He was able to clinch the resumption of relations by offering to send back to Cairo as Ambassador Sir Harold Beeley, who had served there previously and was personally acceptable to Nasser.

CHAPTER 16: OIL DEVELOPMENTS IN THE 1960s

1. Oil production in Iraq in 1962 rose by only 0.5 per cent, compared with 11.5 per cent in Kuwait and 12 per cent in Iran.
2. Qasim had been executed following a Baath-inspired mutiny in the army in February 1963. Political chaos ensued, with assassinations prevalent. An attempt by the Baath parties in Iraq and Syria to establish a new Arab Union with Egypt failed. In 1964 President Aref was in power in Iraq, with the Baathist Yahya as Prime Minister heading an otherwise non-Baathist Government. The death of Aref in a helicopter crash in April 1966 led to further political confusion until the Baath returned to power in 1968. This governmental turmoil made meaningful negotiations by IPC virtually imposssible.
3. Between 1961 and 1969, production in Iraq had grown by under 27 million tons as against nearly 110 million tons in Iran. Proven reserves in Iraq had fallen during the same period from 27,000 million to 23,500 million barrels, whereas in Iran they had grown from 35,000 million to 43,800 million barrels.
4. Shakhbut and Zaid were full brothers and their mother had made them swear a very binding oath not to do violence to each other (there had been a sad history of assassinations in the Abu Dhabi ruling family). This probably caused Zaid's hesitation, but happily the transfer of power in the end took place quietly. The author, as Head of the Arabian Department of the Foreign Office, obtained from the Foreign Secretary the British Government's advance sanction for the family's new choice of Ruler.
5. The whole of the Gulf is continental shelf and potentially promising for oil exploration. The author spent several years in the mid-60s intermittently negotiating on behalf of the Arab Shaikhs with an Iranian delegation to determine the 'median line' between Arab and Iranian shelf

territory. Agreement was reached for part of the line in the Qatar region, but a dispute over the sovereignty of Abu Musa (held at that time by Sharjah but claimed by Iran) prevented a settlement further south.

6. The Libyan tax concessions also included the deduction of all exploration expenditure against profits in the first year of exporting, a 20 per cent depreciation allowance prior to production and a 25 per cent depletion allowance after production started.
7. King Idris had no sons.
8. The North Sea British Sector was divided for purposes of licensing into blocks of about 100 square miles each (one-sixth of a degree of latitude by one-fifth of a degree of longitude). Between September 1964 and November 1965, licences were issued for a total of 475 blocks there, divided among 24 operators, who undertook to spend a minimum of £110 million in exploration over a period of 6 years. One operator only, Gulf Oil, also took up licences in the less promising Irish Sea. For a map of the blocks and a list of the operators see for example *North Sea Oil - The Great Gamble* (London, 1966) by Bryan Cooper and T.F. Gaskell.
9. The median line between UK and Norway was agreed on the basis of equidistance between the coastlines of the two countries, taking the whole of the intervening sea as continental shelf. This was slightly generous to Norway as it ignored, by mutual consent, the existence of the deep Norwegian Trench running parallel to and quite close to the Norwegian coast. The Convention of 1958 provided for claims to jurisdiction for mining of the sea-bed out to the 200 metre contour, so a technical argument could have been advanced that the Norwegian continental shelf should stop at the Trench, giving everything on the other side of the Trench to the UK. But geologically it is clear that the trench, even though it is some 800 metres deep in places, is only a local fault in the shelf and is certainly not ocean floor, so such an argument would have been grossly unfair to Norway and ultimately unsustainable. The two countries, with their friendly history, rightly chose to seek a fairer and above all a quick solution.
10. The strike was made from a drilling barge, the *Sea Gem*. It began work on 5 June 1965 and the first show of gas appeared on 17 September at a depth of some 8500 feet. Drilling was continued and on 1 October it was announced that gas had been found again in a lower zone. The well was finally taken down to a depth of 10,000 feet. On 9 December testing began of the quality and quantity of the find and by mid-December BP were confident of their discovery; it was announced that the flow was at 10 million cubic feet a day and that sufficient quantities were available to justify the construction of a pipeline to bring the gas ashore.

11. Gas had been produced from coal on a laboratory scale in France as early as 1618, but industrial production did not begin until early in the nineteenth century in England. The first gas-light was illuminated in London in 1802 to celebrate the Peace of Amiens, and Pall Mall was the first major street in the world to be lit by gas, in December 1807.
12. Experience had already been gained in the Netherlands in the conversion of gas appliances designed for town gas to use natural gas.

CHAPTER 17: BRITAIN'S WITHDRAWAL FROM 'EAST OF SUEZ'

1. Richard Crossman, *The Diaries of a Cabinet Minister* (London, 1975), Vol.1, p.26 shows that the Cabinet as a whole was told virtually nothing about the extent of the crisis and nothing at all about the decision against devaluation. That key decision was made by an inner group of only three Ministers, Harold Wilson, George Brown and James Callaghan. Probably all of them came later to regret it; Brown certainly did, as it hamstrung his work at the Department of Economic Affairs to produce a growth-oriented National Plan.
2. At the time of these defence reviews, the Defence Department of the Foreign Office took the lead in the discussions at official level on the foreign policy aspects of defence cuts, but the political departments dealing with the regions of the world in which commitments would be reduced or terminated were heavily involved in briefing Defence Department. The author was Head of the Arabian Department, so his role was to point out the potential risks involved in withdrawal of British forces and defence guarantees from Aden and the Gulf Emirates. The 1961 Kuwait crisis was a telling argument, but the economic imperatives resulting from the over-valuation of sterling were so strong as to prevail eventually over any arguments for maintaining commitments.
3. For a lively account of these merger negotiations see Charles Hepburn Johnston, *The View from Steamer Point* (London, 1964), especially Chapter 15.
4. George Brown, *op. cit.*, makes only a passing reference to the Aden situation, although it was one of his major preoccupations. In particular, it was he who decided that Aden needed a High Commissioner of outstanding talent to handle the unhappy and dangerous final phase of Britain's involvement with the territory and persuaded Sir Humphrey Trevelyan (Ambassador in Cairo at the time of the Suez crisis) to return from retirement to take on the assignment. Aden was at this time a Foreign Office responsibility because at the time of the merger of the Colonial Office with the Commonwealth Relations Office to form the Commonwealth Office in 1966, the author had recommended that it

would be more logical for the Aden Department of the Colonial Office to be transferred to the Foreign Office, and this had been done despite the bureaucratic difficulties in moving the Home Civil Servants concerned into the Foreign Service. Only two years later, the Foreign Office and Commonwealth Office were merged into a single Foreign and Commonwealth Office and the two services were combined into a single Diplomatic Service. In the details of this merger too the author, by then an Under-Secretary, was able to play a part.

5. It was quite conceivable that the final withdrawal of the remaining British troops and administrators might have been marked by demonstrations organised to humiliate them, or even to endanger their lives. Contingency plans were made to deal with this situation, had it arisen, but fortunately they were not required. The author, having dealt with the Aden problem for over five years, first as Head of Arabian Department and then as Under-Secretary for Middle East Affairs, was asked by George Brown whether he would like to go to Aden as the first British Ambassador after independence, but for family reasons had to ask not to be considered for the post.
6. The author accompanied Goronwy Roberts on this tour of the Gulf. Roberts courageously insisted on undertaking this duty despite the embarrassing fact that only two months before, prior to the last of the series of defence reviews, it was he who had assured the Gulf Rulers that Britain had no intention of withdrawing from its commitments to them. True though that was at the time, it seemed a very devious promise when policy was reversed such a short time later.
7. Shaikh Zaid of Abu Dhabi, when he knew that Britain's withdrawal was necessary for financial reasons, offered to pay the defence costs involved. He was told that the decision could not be reconsidered (as Denis Healey remarked in a later television interview, British forces could not be 'allowed to become mercenaries').
8. The author, on relinquishing his appointment as Under-Secretary in 1968, handed the Head of Arabian Department a check-list of some 50 disputes which should ideally be solved before the date of British withdrawal. This was of course beyond possibility, but happily a great deal was accomplished.
9. There were two disputed islands in this area of the Gulf, Abu Musa and Sirri. Both were claimed by Iran and by Sharjah. Abu Musa was held by Sharjah (under British protection) and Sirri by Iran. The outcome of the compromise with the Shah thus was that Iran occupied one-and-a-half islands and Sharjah only half an island. However, since Iran had overwhelming military might, the Shaikh of Sharjah was no doubt prudent to accept the terms.

10. Six of the Trucial States, Abu Dhabi, Ajman, Dubai, Fujairah, Sharjah and Umm al-Qaiwain, federated on 2 December 1971 as the United Arab Emirates (UAE). This new country was admitted to membership of the Arab League and of the United Nations. The seventh Trucial State, Ras al-Khaimah, after sulking for a while over the loss of the Tunbs, joined the UAE on 10 February 1972.
11. The details of the compromise proposed by Sir William Luce were not made public and are still covered by the British 30-year embargo on disclosure. The settlement eventually reached was also not published; see, however, J.B. Kelly, *Arabia, the Gulf and the West* (London, 1980) pp.210–212 for what appears to be a well-informed conjecture, illustrated by a map. Whatever the settlement was, it clearly could not cover the Omani villages in the Buraimi Oasis. Theoretically therefore these are still subject to dispute, though in practice it now seems unlikely that the Saudi claim to them will ever be revived.
12. Kelly, *op. cit.*, does not share this view. He regards the British Government's decision to terminate its defence guarantees to the Gulf rulers as a betrayal, and one with disastrous consequences.

CHAPTER 18: TRADE BETWEEN BRITAIN AND THE MIDDLE EAST 1960–70

1. Bank rate was the interest rate at which the Bank of England, as lender of last resort, declared itself ready to lend to commercial banking institutions. At this time, the interest rates of the commercial banks in the UK bore a direct relationship to bank rate, so there was no competition on interest rates between them. Thus, the Government could directly control the interest rate structure of the whole country by adjusting bank rate up or down. The usual tactic was to raise it drastically (for example by 2 per cent) at times of crisis and then to reduce it again, once the crisis was over, in a series of smaller steps.
2. Purchase tax was a sales tax on goods sold at retail level. There was a zero band rate (i.e. items exempt from tax), a standard rate, and a higher rate (or even more than one higher rate) on what were considered to be luxury items. Goods sold for export at retail level (mainly to foreign tourists) were free of purchase tax in principle, although not all retail outlets operated this exemption scheme as it involved complicated form-filling by the shop-keeper.
3. Mr Raymond Brown, who had made a reputation in his early 30s by setting up Racal Electronics Ltd. and building it into a major company in its specialised field, which included defence electronics, was Head of

Defence Sales from 1966 to 1969, when he was knighted for his services. It was in his time that the sale of Lightning aircraft to Saudi Arabia was negotiated.

4. The author, as Chargé d'Affaires in Khartoum in 1962, handed over a small number of Saladin armoured cars and Saracen armoured personnel carriers as a gift from HMG to the military government then ruling Sudan. This gift led on to Sudanese purchases of additional numbers of both vehicles.
5. The data on arms sales in this Chapter and in Chapters 26 and 31 below are derived from comparison of the annual volumes of *The Military Balance*, an invaluable publication from the International Institute of Strategic Studies. Its coverage of Middle East armed services improved as the years went on. It should be noted that its figures are for weapon systems actually deployed, thus giving information on rates of deliveries of orders often reported years earlier in the press.
6. There had been a failed attempt to merge BBME with the Chartered Bank before the eventual merger with the Hongkong Bank was agreed. See Geoffrey Jones, *Banking and Oil*, pp.73–88.
7. Iraq had at one time been very profitable for BBME but it had become loss-making before it was nationalised. Syria had nearly always been unprofitable. Aden was profitable but on a very low scale. Libya had moved from losses into profit but there had been strong competition there from Barclays (DCO), which had been the only bank in the country until 1961 and remained the leading bank thereafter. BBME sold 51 per cent of its Libyan interests to Libyan investors in 1965 and a further 10 per cent to Morgan Guarantee, an American bank, in 1967, so it had only a minority interest at the time of nationalisation. Barclays (DCO), with 19 branches in Libya, was also taken over by the Government in the wake of the 1969 revolution. See Jones, *op. cit.*, p.215 and pp.238–9.

CHAPTER 19: BRITISH MEMBERSHIP OF THE EEC

1. The iron and steel industry was renationalised on 28 July 1967 by the Iron and Steel Act, which transferred ownership of 14 steel companies to the British Steel Corporation. The Corporation then had a turnover of more than £1000 million and employed 270,000 people. The Labour Government thus fulfilled an election manifesto pledge, but was criticised for 'playing politics' with the economy at a time when there were more urgent economic problems to be faced, with the pound threatened with devaluation.

2. This White Paper was issued, with Cabinet approval, by Barbara Castle as Secretary of State for Employment and Productivity, but was soon opposed openly by some members of the Cabinet when they saw that it was unpopular with the trade unions. See Barbara Castle, *The Castle Diaries 1974–76* (London, 1980), pp.2–3.
3. It is interesting that both these pro-marketeers later worked in the EEC Commission. George Thomson left British politics to become an EEC Commissioner in 1973. He had been Minister for Europe in the Wilson Government and damaged the case of the Labour anti-marketeers in 1971 by declaring roundly that the terms negotiated by the Heath Government were as good as any that the Wilson Government could have got at the time when it was applying for membership in 1967. Roy Jenkins later resigned from James Callaghan's Government in 1977 to become President of the European Commission.
4. The idea of a referendum seems to have originated with Tony Benn.
5. The referendum again split the Labour Party more than it did the Conservative Party. Harold Wilson was this time with Roy Jenkins in calling for a Yes vote, while Michael Foot and Tony Benn, heroes of the left wing, campaigned for a No vote. On a poll of about 65 per cent, the Yes majority was approximately two to one.
6. Norwegian rejection was due to a variety of causes, but principally to fears for the future of Norwegian agriculture and fisheries within the EEC. The author was British Ambassador to Norway while these negotiations were in progress and had no great difficulty in forecasting this outcome, even before Norway's negotiations for terms of entry were completed. But it came as more of a surprise to those further distant from the currents of opinion sweeping the country.
7. It might be thought that British exporters could have ignored the widespread use of the French language in the Maghreb countries and dealt with their importers as Arabic-speakers, just as they did with merchants in say the Arabian Peninsula. But the commercial use of written Arabic in the Maghreb was then low.

CHAPTER 20: OIL DEVELOPMENTS IN THE EARLY 1970s

1. The author was British Ambassador to Norway from 1968 to 1972 and well remembers the excitement in the country caused by the discovery of the Ekofisk oilfield. It fell to him to begin the discussions with the Norwegian Government about the piping of oil from the field to Teesside, which were completed in the time of his successor.

2. See Resolution XVI.90, pp.80–82 in *OPEC Official Resolutions and Press Releases*.
3. For an excellent analysis of this subject, see Steven A. Schneider, *The Oil Price Revolution* (Baltimore, 1983), from which much of the material in this Chapter is drawn.
4. Texas 'allowables' were raised to 100 per cent in March 1971 for the first time since the early post-war period. Spare productive capacity in the Venezuelan oilfields had been exhausted in 1970 and the same situation was reached in Alberta, Canada, in 1972. American oil import quotas were abolished in April 1973. From that time on the USA grew increasingly dependent on imports of Middle East oil.
5. Japan's dependence on imported oil as a fuel source rose from under 23 per cent in 1955 to over 80 per cent in 1973. It was therefore deeply affected by the 'first oil shock' in that year.
6. IMF figures show the following currency reserve aggregates in September 1973: Saudi Arabia $4080 million; Kuwait $3210 million; Libya $2435 million.
7. 55 per cent of Libyan production was controlled by the independents. See John M. Blair, *The Control of Oil* (London,1977 – previously published in the USA, 1976).
8. Evidence on dealings with host Governments was given by US oil companies to the Sub-Committee on Multinational Corporations of the Senate Committee on Foreign Relations. The published reports of these hearings are invaluable sources of information for oil developments in the 70s.

CHAPTER 21: THE YOM KIPPUR WAR AND THE FIRST OIL SHOCK

1. The polarisation between Arabs and Israelis expresses itself in historical nomenclature as much as in other ways. It is the Israelis who call this 1973 conflict the Yom Kippur War. Arabs prefer other and blander terms, such as the October War. The Israeli name has been preferred here, partly because it is the one in more general use with the uncommitted public but also because it is the more meaningful. It was, after all, no accident that the attack was launched on the Israeli festival of Yom Kippur. Surprise was a key factor in the Arab military plan and this timing helped to achieve it.
2. Sadat was successively Editor of the newspaper *Gomhouriyeh* (Republic), Secretary-General of the Islamic Congress, Speaker of the Joint Parliament of the United Arab Republic and Speaker of the Egyptian Parliament, before becoming Vice-President.

3. See Mohamed Heikal, *Autumn of Fury* (London, 1983), p.33.
4. *Ibid.*, p.36.
5. *Ibid.*, pp.43–50.
6. The idea of setting up an IEA was first proposed by Kissinger in an after-dinner speech in London to the influential Pilgrims on 12 December 1973 and it was he who played a crucial role in the negotiations which brought the Agency into being in November 1974. See Louis Turner, *Oil Companies in the International System* (3rd Edn., London, 1983). The original 16 members were Austria, Belgium, Canada, Denmark, Federal Republic of Germany, Ireland, Italy, Japan, Luxemburg, Netherlands, Spain, Sweden, Switzerland, Turkey, UK and USA. France refused to join but established a close relationship. New Zealand joined later and Norway became an associate member.

CHAPTER 22: LEBANON AND THE CIVIL WAR OF 1975–6

1. In 1920 the French, as Mandatory, enlarged the Ottoman Sanjak of Mount Lebanon to the present boundaries of Lebanon. They thus incorporated into it large areas which were mainly Muslim or Druze-inhabited, although at that time the Christians no doubt formed a genuine majority. As time went on, doubts about that majority grew. For example the French suppressed the figures for a partial census carried out in 1943. One complication in this numbers dispute is that the Christians sometimes claim the right to add in the Christian émigrés, even those of their descendants who were born abroad and have no Lebanese citizenship.
2. No reliable numbers appear to be available for these emigrants, but their total must have been substantial to judge from the size of the Lebanese-descent communities in the USA, West Africa, Brazil etc. George T. Murray, *Lebanon: The New Future* (Beirut, 1974) gives a round figure of 5 million emigrants including 2 million in Brazil, but he does not cite his sources for the estimate. This compares with his total of about 3.1 million for the then current population of Lebanon, including some 300,000 Palestinian refugees (deaths in the Civil War and recent migrations because of the troubles have probably reduced these figures).
3. *Ibid.*, pp.127–145.
4. A vivid account of the war, with telling detail, is in John Bulloch's book, *Death of a Country* (London, 1977). This work of 'high journalism' has clearly been carefully researched and seems generally reliable.
5. *Ibid.*, p.184.

CHAPTER 23: EGYPT UNDER SADAT

1. See Heikal, *op. cit.*, pp.67–9.
2. Before 1973 the IBRD had made only small loans to Egypt, notably $60 million for widening the Suez Canal. By contrast, it lent $227 million in 1974–5, $222 million in 1975–6 and $267 million in 1976–7.
3. The lower figure was put forward by the Egyptian Finance Minister Kaisouny for the period 1971–77, the higher by the Kuwaiti Finance Minister Al-Hamad for 1971–80. The figures are comparable despite the discrepancy in the years covered since Egypt received practically no Arab aid in 1977–80.
4. Rodney Wilson, *The Economies of the Middle East* (London, 1979), pp.26–9, cites Egyptian bureaucracy as the main deterrent preventing Western businessmen from investing to any great extent outside the areas of banking and tourism. Mansfield, *op. cit.*, p.247 rightly draws attention also to the disincentive of the near collapse of Egyptian infrastructure, particularly transport and telephone services.
5. Heikal, *op. cit.*, p.83, claims that Chase Manhattan in its first year of operation in Egypt made $4 million profit on a capital investment of under $500,000. By 1981, 56 foreign banks had a foothold of one kind or another in Egypt, whereas under Nasser the banking sector had been entirely nationalised.
6. Wilson, *op. cit.*, pp.21–6, highlights the demographic factor. Indeed he entitles his chapter on Egypt 'Egypt: the Ghost of Malthus Lingers On'. One destabilising consequence of population growth which he does not stress sufficiently is the movement of population from the countryside to the towns, and especially to Cairo; this was one of the reasons for the near collapse of infrastructure and created the conditions for civil disturbances, for example the riots of January 1977.
7. See Heikal, *op. cit.*, pp.79–80.
8. *Ibid.*, p.91.
9. *Ibid.*, p.93.
10. *Ibid.*, p.96.
11. Heikal, *op. cit.*, pp.97–8, recounts how Sadat sent his presidential plane to bring Arafat to Cairo and the fury with which Arafat reacted to the mention of a visit 'even to the Knesset' in search of peace, at a time when others were regarding the phrase as rhetoric.
12. One of the projects thus brought to an end was a plan to make Egypt an arms manufacturer for the Arab world, an attempt to match the indigenous weapons manufacturing capacity which Israel had by this time established. Egypt already possessed plant for the production of small arms, rifles, machine-guns and ammunition. In May 1975, the Arab

Military Industries Organisation, with its headquarters in Cairo, was set up by Egypt with the participation and financial backing of Qatar, Saudi Arabia and the UAE. This organisation was abandoned in 1979, leaving the Gulf States still dependent on the West for arms supplies.

CHAPTER 24: OIL PRICE RISE CONSEQUENCES FOR THE OIL PRODUCERS

1. See John Maddox, *Beyond the Energy Crisis* (London, 1975).
2. *Ibid.*, p.122.
3. OPEC Resolution XXV.139.
4. See Yusuf A. Sayigh, *Arab Oil Policies in the 1970s* (London, 1983), p.52. Sayigh's book is a valuable source for this Chapter, even though it is, not unnaturally, slightly prejudiced against the international oil companies.
5. *Ibid.*, pp.72–75.
6. Growth of consumption in the 60s was a massive 320.7 per cent at an average of 12.5 per cent p.a.; by contrast, it was only 55.97 per cent in the 70s at an average of 5 per cent p.a.
7. Shaikh Ali Khalifa Al-Sabah (a member of Kuwait's ruling family), speaking at the First Oxford Energy Seminar, 1979.
8. See Sayigh, *op. cit.*, p.97.
9. See OAPEC Secretary-General's *7th Annual Report*, p.70.
10. See Sayigh, *op. cit.*, Table 3.5 on p.148.
11. *Ibid.*, Table 3.8 on p.159.

CHAPTER 25: THE IRANIAN REVOLUTION AND THE SECOND OIL SHOCK

1. See *The Revolution of the Shah and the People*, published in English translation by Transorient (London, 1967).
2. Figures for the various Plans derive from the Reports of the Iranian Plan Organization and the Annual Reports of the Central Bank of Iran. Useful tables are contained in Rodney Wilson, *op. cit.*, Chapter 1.
3. Compensation, based on landowners' past tax returns (and so very properly penalising those who had falsified such returns), was paid over a period of 10 years. The beneficiaries from redistribution, mainly sitting tenants, were given 15 years to repay the same sum, so the scheme was in principle self-financing but not entirely so because of inflation.
4. Sir Anthony Parsons, British Ambassador to Iran from 1974 to 1979, was amazed by the suddenness of the turn-around from boom to slump. See his very readable book, *The Pride and the Fall* (London, 1984), pp.11–12.

This book, unlike most others dealing with the fall of the Shah, does not concentrate almost exclusively on the religious opposition, but gives proper weight to the economic factors.

5. One of the few advisers who could speak freely to the Shah and was well placed to do so was Assadullah Alam, the Minister of Court, whose family had served the Shahs loyally for generations. But by 1975 he was a sick man, suffering from leukaemia, and no longer had the strength to outface his difficult master. He resigned in 1977 and died the following year. It is now known of course that the Shah was also a sick man, with not long to live, but that was not apparent at the time. His disease, even undiagnosed, may have been feeding his impetuosity and driving him to attempt too much too quickly.
6. See Parsons, *op. cit.*, p.48. He is inclined to attribute the Shah's uncharacteristic decision to liberalise to a desire to prepare the way for his son to take over from him. If he was beginning to realise that his strength was ebbing from illness, this is the more credible.
7. *Ibid.*, Chapter 6, for a full account of these developments.
8. See Daniel Badger and Robert Belgrave, *Oil Supply and Price: What Went Right in 1980?* (London, 1982), p.142.
9. *Ibid.*, p.113.

CHAPTER 26: TRADE BETWEEN BRITAIN AND THE MIDDLE EAST 1970–80

1. In 1974, for example, there was a mini-budget from the outgoing Conservative Government, followed by an annual budget and two more mini-budgets from the incoming Labour Government.
2. There were dock strikes in 1970 and in 1972, caused in part by disputes arising from the introduction of containers as a new method of freight forwarding. Strikes on the railways and in the electricity and gas industries were also very damaging to industrial production generally.
3. Technological advances had rendered many of Britain's steel mills obsolete (an example of underinvestment). Japan made use of the new technology and of economies of scale to sell steel at prices which most European plants could not match and to outdo them also in quality. As an example, the British steel industry could not produce steel to the specifications required for the submarine pipelines which were needed to land North Sea oil in Britain.
4. The exchange rate for sterling was fixed at $2.60 in the Smithsonian Agreement of December 1971.

5. The initial fall when sterling was floated was of the order of 18 per cent to 20 per cent.
6. The film's subject was the presenter's difficulties in investigating the death of Princess Misha'al in 1977. She was alleged to have committed adultery and to have been put to death on the orders of her grandfather, Prince Muhammad bin Abdul Aziz, the highly respected and deeply religious oldest surviving son of the founder of the Saudi monarchy. The British Ambassador had to be temporarily withdrawn from Saudi Arabia and the Foreign Secretary, Lord Carrington, had to travel personally to Riyadh to placate the Saudi ruling family. (The film was not of course shown publicly in Saudi Arabia but it circulated widely there on video-cassettes.)
7. See *Invisible Trade in the World Economy 1972–86 (London, 1988), pp.6–7.*
8. *Ibid.*, p.21, Table 8.
9. See *A History of ECGD 1919/1979* (London, 1979), p.44.
10. For a fuller account of this phase of BBME's history, see Geoffrey Jones, *Banking and Oil*, especially pp.263–9.
11. The author, on retiring from the Diplomatic Service, was encouraged by the FCO to take up the appointment of Deputy Secretary-General and Chief Executive at the A-BCC (the Secretary-General was an Arab in accordance with the Chamber's Articles of Association, so this was another example of Arab-British collaboration). He held this post from 1976 to 1983, by which time the Chamber had a membership of around 1000, a staff of over 100 and well-sited offices in Belgrave Square.
12. This service has from the beginning been organised on a national basis covering the whole of the United Kingdom. Local British Chambers of Commerce act as the A-BCC's agents for the collection and initial scrutiny of documents. The A-BCC then arranges their overnight movement to its London offices, where within a working day they are scrutinised for any errors and if correct are certified, before being passed to the Embassies or returned overnight to the British Chambers, as required.

CHAPTER 27: INDUSTRIAL DEVELOPMENT IN THE ARABIAN PENINSULA

1. The population of Saudi Arabia is not accurately known. The Saudi Government of course supplies figures to the United Nations, but these command little confidence. There are several problems. It is not easy to carry out censuses of nomadic peoples, though these are being attracted to settle by Government inducements, so this should be a declining

difficulty. There is a very large number of foreigners in the country, who are not Saudi citizens and not necessarily long-term residents; some calculations include them and some exclude them, causing confusion. There have even been suggestions that Government figures may exaggerate the population for the sake of the country's prestige. Most people would accept a total of 5 to 7 million Saudis plus 1 to 2 million foreigners, say 7.5 million in all.

2. The three Kings were half-brothers, all sons of King Abdul Aziz, but by different mothers. As explained earlier, there is no system of primogeniture for the succession; the choice is made by the ruling family from among its male members.
3. Seaside sites were chosen not only to facilitate imports and exports but because Saudi Arabia has no rivers, so sea water had to be used for industrial cooling water (despite the potential corrosion problems that then had to be eliminated). The Royal Commission publishes material in English as well as Arabic to recount its progress. In particular, it has put out an English-language book with useful illustrations, entitled *Jubail and Yanbu Industrial Cities: Ten Years of Accomplishments* (Riyadh, 1986).
4. The author was taken on a conducted tour of the Jeddah Industrial Estate in 1982 and at that time his official guides could not show him any enterprise with British participation.
5. Saudi Arabia actually exported 170,000 tonnes of wheat to the UK in 1987.
6. The Kuwait Government used rebuilding programmes as a means of spreading oil wealth through its citizen population, at the same time advancing their standard of living directly through better dwellings.
7. It was the author's duty, as Head of the Arabian Department at the Foreign Office from 1963 to 1967, to conduct negotiations with Sultan Said during his annual visits to London. (There were no serious problems which would have warranted negotiations at ministerial level.) In the course of the discussions Said repeatedly stressed his determination to avoid over-rapid change in Oman which might weaken the devotion of his people to their Islamic way of life. But there was also a personal factor in his unwillingness to spend his oil revenues. As a young man he had succeeded to the Sultanate when his father abdicated, leaving him to grapple with the problems of a bankrupt treasury. This caused him to attach a high priority to building up financial reserves.
8. During the years mentioned in the last note, Qabus was being educated in Britain. After doing very well at Sandhurst and in an attachment to the British Army of the Rhine, he was due to return to Oman, but it became clear that Said wanted to delay his arrival in the country. The author was

asked, first to give him experience of government procedures by arranging for his attachment to a County Council, and then to give him an insight into the oil industry through an attachment to Shell (the chief concession-holder in Oman). All this was done. Finally, when the Sultan could think of no further excuse for prolonging his son's stay in England, he agreed that he should return home. The author enquired what post in Government he would be given after all this education. Said replied that that could only be considered after Qabus had relearnt by heart the Quran, which he was likely to have forgotten, and after he had grown a beard; he rather reluctantly conceded that these two processes might proceed simultaneously.

9. For an interesting list of these projects see Caroline Montagu, *Industrial Development in Saudi Arabia* (London, 1987), pp.180–182. This useful book deals not only with Saudi Arabia but with the regional organisations of which that country is a member.

CHAPTER 28: POST-REVOLUTIONARY IRAN AND THE GULF WAR

1. For Brezhnev's praise of the Iranian Revolution to the 26th Congress of the CPSU see *The Iran-Iraq War: An Historical, Economic and Political Analysis* (London, 1984) ed. M.S. El Azhary Ch.8, *The Attitudes of the Superpowers towards the Gulf War*, p.98. This Chapter had earlier appeared as an article in *International Affairs* (London, 1983) Vol.59 No.4.
2. The Turkish Government does not like admitting that it has a Kurdish minority; it prefers to call them 'mountain Turks'.
3. The Ottomans claimed what is now the Iranian province of Khuzistan because its population is Arabic-speaking and of Arab descent. Indeed, the province's Arabic name is Arabistan and its chief town Khorramshahr has the Arabic name Muhammarah. The Iraq Government expected the people of this province to rally to them during the Gulf War, but their loyalty to Iran prevailed.
4. See *International Affairs* (London, 1988) Vol.64 No.1, p.87.
5. The occupation of these two strips of territory had been preceded by diplomatic notes from Iraq on 7 and 8 September, calling attention to the Iranian failure to return the territory and warning that it would be seized by force if not evacuated. See Stephen R. Grummon, *The Iran-Iraq War: Islam Embattled* (New York, 1982) in The Washington Papers series, No.92. However, the speed with which the occupation followed these communications suggests that it was intended from the outset that force would be employed to resolve the dispute.

6. For accounts of the campaigns see Grummon, *op. cit.* and El Azhary, *op. cit.* and later publications on the subject, including Efraim Karsh, *Military power and foreign policy goals: the Iran-Iraq War revisited* in *International Affairs* (London, 1988) Vol.64 No.1. Karsh argues that Iraq made the mistake of trying to fight a limited war, instead of a general war for limited political goals (but he does not consider whether a general war would have been within Iraq's capabilities).
7. For Iraq's determination to continue its economic development despite the war, see El Azhary (ed.), *op. cit.*, Ch.6 *Development Strategy in Iraq and the War Effort: The Dynamics of Challenge* by Basil al-Bustany.
8. British merchant ships, while extremely grateful for this degree of protection, would of course like the patrol to operate as far north as at least Ras Tanura (Saudi Arabia) and preferably to Kuwait, but the British Government has so far ruled this out as requiring a larger frigate force than they are prepared to distract from NATO commitments. It must be remembered that keeping 3 frigates in the Gulf area means at any one time another 3 in transit and 3 more working up for a Gulf deployment. And the nature of the task means that they must be modern frigates.
9. Lloyd's Register shows 90 ships damaged beyond repair in the Gulf during the period 1981–87, from both Iraqi and Iranian attacks. The number of attacks reached a peak of 163 in 1987, but, at first sight surprisingly, the number damaged beyond repair that year was the lowest for the whole period at only 2. This was because the presence of warships persuaded the Iranians to change their tactics. Instead of aerial attacks on shipping or the sowing of new mines (now less effective because of minesweepers, though the danger of mines is not removed entirely since old moored mines in the Northern Gulf are always liable to break loose and drift down the Arab coast in the prevailing currents), their attacks are now mainly by rocket-propelled grenades and machine-gun fire from fast patrol-boats. These cause damage and endanger life but are less likely to destroy shipping completely.
10. Total deaths for 1981–87 numbered some 250. The peak years for deaths have been 1986 and 1987, with over 60 each year.
11. Premium rates are regularly reviewed by a Lloyd's committee in London. They do not always go up; at the beginning of 1988 there was a reduction because few ships in 1987 had been damaged beyond repair, even though the number of attacks on shipping had increased.

CHAPTER 29: ISRAEL AND THE INVASION OF LEBANON

1. See Atif Kubursi, *The Economic Consequences of the Camp David Agreements* (Beirut, 1981).

2. See *Sunday Times*, 5 October 1986. The newspaper's source, Mordechai Vanunu, was subsequently lured by Israeli Intelligence from London to Rome, kidnapped and put on trial in Jerusalem. Most of his trial was held *in camera* but the verdict of guilty on charges of stealing and disclosing secrets implies that the story he told was basically true.
3. See *International Defence Review*, 21 July 1987. The Jericho-2 is reputed to have a theoretical range of 1000 kilometres, which would bring some areas of the USSR into its field of fire. In response to a warning on Moscow's Hebrew-language programme, Israeli defence sources stressed that there was no intention to threaten targets in the Soviet Union.
4. See Frederic C. Hof, *Galilee Divided: The Israel-Lebanon Frontier, 1916–1984* (Boulder, Colorado, 1985), p.79.
5. *Ibid.*, pp.82–3.
6. The attack on Ambassador Argov was carried out not, it seems, by the main PLO militia Fatah, but by the splinter group led by Abu Nidal (who had been condemned to death *in absentia* by Fatah for mutiny). It even seems that the gunmen were under instructions, after killing the Ambassador, to kill next the PLO representative in London. But the Israeli Government were never inclined to draw distinctions between different Palestinian groups, since they regarded them one and all as terrorists. In any case, reaction to the attempted murder was in reality no more than a pretext for what must have been a long-planned operation. See Hof, *op. cit.*, p.101.
7. The ultimate political objectives are usually associated with Sharon, the Minister of Defence responsible for the operation, but they must have been more widely held by senior Ministers, though probably not known to the whole Cabinet. They certainly included the bringing to power of a friendly Lebanese President, with whom an Israeli-Lebanese Peace Treaty could be negotiated. There are rumours that they may also have extended to the removal of the Hashemite régime in Jordan, followed by the installation there of a Palestinian government, so solving the problem of giving the Palestinians their own state, entirely on the east of the River Jordan.
8. See John Bulloch, *Final Conflict: The War in Lebanon* (London, 1983) for a detailed account based in part on personal experience of events.
9. U.S. aid to Israel in 1985 amounted to $2600 million.

CHAPTER 30: OIL GLUTS IN THE 1980s

1. The system of marker crudes as reference points from which differentials could be calculated was a convenient one for OPEC, which of course included in its membership countries as distant from the Gulf as Venezuela

and Indonesia, the former supplying mainly the American and the latter mainly the Japanese market. For the non-OPEC producers there was no similar alignment of prices, though competition naturally kept them in some relationship. In the North Sea, the price of crude from the Brent field is quoted in the daily press as an indicator of the trend of price movements, and it is sometimes called a marker, but by analogy.

2. See Ali D. Johany, *The Myth of the OPEC Cartel* (Dhahran, 1980).
3. Since his replacement as Saudi Minister of Petroleum, Shaikh Yamani in public lectures in several Western capitals (for example to the Royal Institute of International Affairs, London, on 1 March 1988), has described his efforts to restrain prices in the 80s and his warnings to his colleagues, which they ignored.
4. See Schneider, *op. cit.*, pp.448–451.
5. Figures from OPEC Annual Statistical Bulletins.
6. Information on this analysis is given by Dr Abbas al-Nasrawi in *OPEC and the Changing Structure of the World Oil Market*, his contribution to *Cooperation and Development in the Energy Sector* (London, 1985), ed. Atif A. Kubursi and Thomas Naylor.

CHAPTER 31: TRADE BETWEEN BRITAIN AND THE MIDDLE EAST 1980–87

1. The main industries 'privatised' were as follows:
   May 1981 British Aerospace
   Oct 1981 Cable & Wireless
   Feb 1982 Amersham
   Nov 1982 Britoil
   Feb 1983 AB Ports
   Jun 1984 Enterprise Oil
   Jul 1984 Jaguar
   Nov 1984 British Telecom
   Mar 1986 VSEL Consortium
   Dec 1986 British Gas
   Feb 1987 British Airways
   May 1987 Rolls Royce
   Jul 1987 British Airports Authority
   In addition there were sales of shareholdings in firms not wholly owned, notably BP. About 1 million jobs have been transferred from the public to the private sector. At the time of writing, there is still a considerable privatisation programme ahead, including the steel, electricity and water industries, and perhaps British Rail and even British Coal.

2. There have been four such Acts so far since 1979.
3. The coal strike was never 100 per cent effective as some pits continued to work, with the miners employed in them eventually forming a breakaway union.
4. In 1986–87 alone, British takeovers in the USA exceeded $33,000 million, as against only $1500 million of American takeovers in the UK in the same two years. One takeover which is of particular interest for readers of this book is that by BP of Standard Oil, the relic of the original great oil company from which so many of the American major oil companies originated when Standard was broken up under the American anti-trust laws.
5. The building by Nissan of a manufacturing plant near Sunderland in N.E. England has been a particularly striking example. The project has gone so well that the plant has been extended well ahead of schedule. Japanese investment would not have been attracted to Britain without British membership of the EEC, which means that goods manufactured in the UK can be exported to other Community countries tariff-free once qualifying levels of local content are reached.
6. There have usually been good technical arguments for the changes in methods of calculation introduced by the Government, for example that it was illogical that self-employed people should be counted as unemployed. Nevertheless, it is fair to say that the changes were hardly likely to have been made if they had not also had the effect of reducing the official unemployment totals.
7. The 132 aircraft consist of the following: 48 Tornado IDS strike aircraft; 24 Tornado ADV interceptors; 30 Hawk trainer/ ground attack aircraft; 30 (Swiss-built) Pilatus PC-9 turbo-prop trainers. The value of the whole contract will be approximately $5640, of which half is to be paid in oil. Unlike the sale of Lightnings in the 1960s, strike aircraft are this time being provided, a fact which no doubt added to the Israeli outcry against the contract.
8. An 'offset committee' has been set up to monitor this aspect of the agreement. At its meeting on 9 March 1987, the Saudi side is reported to have declared that it was expecting a level of offset amounting to 35 per cent of the value of the contract, while the British side is said to have denied that there was any informal undertaking on any particular figure.
9. The figures issued by Lloyd's Register show that in 1981, the first year of the war, only 7 ships were attacked but 5 of them were damaged beyond repair. By contrast, in 1987 there were 163 ships attacked yet only 2 damaged beyond repair; see Note 9 to Chapter 28. It was against this background that the War Risk Rating Committee of senior London underwriters decided to cut insurance premiums for certain parts of the Gulf area.

CHAPTER 32: RETROSPECT 1973–1987 AND PROSPECT

1. The machinery of the Joint Arab-Foreign Chambers of Commerce has been used to draw up standard texts of arbitration agreements and to establish panels of arbitrators acceptable to both sides. The Arab-British Chamber of Commerce has so acted in Britain. It is not yet clear how many firms will use these facilities.

Selected Bibliography

This makes no claim to be a full bibliography. It gathers together for convenience the publications to which references are made in the Chapter Notes.

ABDUL NASSER, Gamal (President) *Egypt's Liberation: The Philosophy of the Revolution* (Washington D.C., 1955)

AL-BUSTANY, Basil *Development Strategy in Iraq and the War Effort: The Dynamics of Challenge*, Ch. 6 of *The Iran-Iraq War* (v.i. El-Azhary)

AL-NASRAWI, Dr Abbas *OPEC and the Changing Structure of the World Oil Market*, in *Cooperation and Development in the Energy Sector* ed. KUBURSI and NAYLOR (London, 1985)

AMIN, Galal *The Egyptian Economy and the Revolution* in *Egypt since the Revolution* (v.i. Vatikiotis)

ANDERSON, J.R.L. *East of Suez* (London, 1969)

BADGER, Daniel and BELGRAVE, Robert *Oil Supply and Price: What Went Right in 1980?* (London, 1982)

BANK FOR INTERNATIONAL SETTLEMENTS *The Sterling Area* (Basle, 1953)

BEN GURION, David *B'Hilachem Yisrael* [*In the Struggle for Israel*] (Tel Aviv, 1949)

BLAIR, John M. *The Control of Oil* (London, 1977 – previously published in the USA 1976)

BRITISH INVISIBLE EXPORTS COUNCIL *Invisible Trade in the World Economy 1972–86* (London, 1988)

BROWN, George *In My Way* (London, 1971)

BULLOCH, John *Death of a Country* (London, 1977)

—*Final Conflict: The War in Lebanon* (London, 1983)

BULLOCK, Alan *Ernest Bevin Foreign Secretary 1945–1951* (London, 1983)

CAIRNCROSS, Sir Alec in *The Economic History of Britain since 1700* Vol.2, ed. FLOUD and McCLOSKEY (Cambridge, 1981)
CASTLE, Barbara *The Castle Diaries 1974–76* (London, 1980)
COOKE, Colin *The Life of Richard Stafford Cripps* (London, 1957)
COOPER, Bryan and GASKELL T.F. *North Sea Oil – The Great Gamble* (London, 1966)
CROSSMAN, Richard *The Diaries of a Cabinet Minister* Vol.1 (London, 1975)
DALTON, Hugh *High Tide and After* (London, 1962)
DUNCAN, J.S.R. *The Sudan* (Edinburgh, 1952)
EDEN, Sir Anthony *Full Circle* (London, 1960)
EL-AZHARY, M.S. *The Iran-Iraq War: An Historical, Economic and Political Analysis* (London, 1984)
EXPORT CREDITS GUARANTEE DEPARTMENT *A history of ECGD 1919/1979* (London,1980)
FERRIER, R.W. *Cambridge History of Iran* Vol.7
—*History of British Petroleum* Vol.1 (Cambridge, 1982)
GARDNER, Richard N. *Sterling-Dollar Diplomacy* (Oxford, 1956)
GORE-BOOTH, Sir Paul *With Great Truth and Respect* (London, 1974)
GRUMMON, Stephen R. *The Iran-Iraq War: Islam Embattled* (New York, 1982), The Washington Papers No.92
HANSEN, Bent *Planning and Economic Growth in the UAR (Egypt), 1960–5* in *Egypt Since the Revolution* (v.i. VATIKIOTIS)
HARROD, Roy F. *The Life of John Maynard Keynes* (London, 1951)
HEIKAL, Mohamed *Autumn of Fury* (London, 1983)
HIS MAJESTY'S STATIONERY OFFICE *Statistical Material Presented During the Washington Negotiations* (Cmd. 6706, 1945)
HEWINS, Ralph *A Golden Dream: The Miracle of Kuwait* (London, 1963)
HOF, Frederic C. *Galilee Divided: The Israel-Lebanon Frontier, 1916–1984* (Boulder, Colorado, 1985)
HOWARD, Anthony *The Life of R.A. Butler* (London, 1987)
HOWARD, M. and HUNTER, R. *Israel and the Arab World: The Crisis of 1967*, Adelphi Papers No.4
HUSSAIN, King of Jordan *Uneasy Lies the Head* (London and New York, 1962)
JOHANY, Ali D. *The Myth of the OPEC Cartel* (Dhahran, 1980)
JOHNSTON, Charles Hepburn *The View from Steamer Point* (London, 1964)
JONES, Geoffrey *Banking and Empire in Iran* (Cambridge, 1986)
—*Banking and Oil* (Cambridge, 1987)
KARSH, Efraim *Military power and foreign policy goals: the Iran-Iraq War revisited* in *International Affairs* Vol.64 No.1 (London, 1987/8)
KELLY, J.B. *Arabia, the Gulf and the West* (London, 1980)

—*Britain and the Persian Gulf 1795–1880* (Oxford, 1968)
—*Eastern Arabian Frontiers* (London, 1964)
—*Sultanate and Imamate in Oman* (Oxford, 1959)
KUBURSI, Atif *The Economic Consequences of the Camp David Agreements* (Beirut, 1981)
LEES, F.A. and BROOKS, H.C. *The Economic and Political Development of the Sudan* (London, 1977)
LLOYD, E.M.H. *Food and Inflation in the Middle East 1940–1945* (Standford, 1956)
LLOYD, Selwyn *Suez 1956* A Personal Account (London, 1978)
LOUIS, W.R. *The British Empire in the Middle East 1945–1951* (Oxford, 1984)
MABRO, Robert *The Egyptian Economy 1952–1972* (London, 1974)
MacGREGOR, R.M. *The Nile Waters*, in *The Anglo-Egyptian Sudan from Within*, ed. J.A. de C. Hamilton
MADDOX, John *Beyond the Energy Crisis* (London, 1975)
MANSFIELD, Peter (ed.) *The Middle East* 5th Edn. (Oxford, 1980)
MEYER, A.J. *Middle East Capitalism* (Cambridge, Mass., 1959)
MONTAGU, Caroline *Industrial Development in Saudi Arabia* (London, 1987)
MURRAY, George T. *Lebanon: The New Future* (Beirut, 1974)
NEGUIB, Mohammed *Egypt's Destiny* (London, 1955)
PAHLAVI, Mohammed Reza, Shah of Iran *The Revolution of the Shah and the People* (London, 1967)
PARSONS, Sir Anthony *The Pride and the Fall* (London, 1984)
PENROSE, Edith *The Growth of Firms, Middle East Oil and Other Essays* (London, 1971)
PERETZ, Don *Israel and the Palestinian Arabs* (Washington D.C., 1958)
PEROWNE, Stewart *The One Remains* (London, 1954)
PHILBY, H.St.J.B. *Arabian Oil Ventures* (Washington D.C., 1964)
PIMLOTT, Ben *Hugh Dalton* (London, 1985)
POLLARD, Sidney *European Economic Integration* (London, 1974)
RODINSON, Maxime *Israel and the Arabs* (Harmondsworth, 1968)
ROOSEVELT, Kermit *Countercoup The Struggle for the Control of Iran* (New York, 1979)
ROYAL COMMISSION FOR JUBAIL AND YANBU *Jubail and Yanbu Industrial Cities: Ten Years of Accomplishments* (Riyadh, 1986)
SACHER, Howard M. *Europe Leaves the Middle East 1936–1954* (New York, 1972)
—*From the Ends of the Earth: The Peoples of Israel* (New York, 1964)
SAYIGH, Yusuf A. *Arab Oil Policies in the 1970s* (London, 1983)
SCHNEIDER, Steven A. *The Oil Price Revolution* (Baltimore, 1983)
SHUCKBURGH, Sir Evelyn *The Descent to Suez* (London, 1986)

TRUMAN, Harry S. (President) *Memoirs* (New York 1953–55)

TURNER, Louis *Oil Companies in the International System* 3rd Edn. (London, 1983)

VATIKIOTIS, P.J. (ed.) *Egypt since the Revolution* (London, 1968)

VON HORN, General Carl *Soldiering for Peace* (London, 1966)

WILMINGTON, Martin W. *The Middle East Supply Centre* (New York, 1971)

WILSON, Rodney *The Economies of the Middle East* (London, 1979)

WOODHOUSE, C.M. *Something Ventured* (London, 1982)

YOST, Charles W. *The Arab-Israeli War, How it Began* in *Foreign Affairs* Vol.46 No.2 (January 1968)

Index

(Note: Entries not otherwise specified apply to UK)